C. S. Lewis
An Annotated Checklist of Writings
about him and his Works

C. S. Lewis

An Annotated Checklist of Writings
about him and his Works

Compiled by
Joe R. Christopher and Joan K. Ostling

The Kent State University Press

The Serif Series: Number 30
Bibliographies and Checklists
William White, General Editor
Oakland University, Rochester, Mich.

Contents

vi

Introduction

When *Screwtape Letters* burst on the scene in 1942, England suddenly had, as C. E. M. Joad wrote, a man who "had the rare gift of making righteousness readable." About the same time the resonant voice of C. S. Lewis was becoming familiar to listeners of B.B.C. as belonging to a man who also had the gift of making righteousness intelligible. Intriguingly, the voice also belonged to a distinguished Oxford scholar whose *Allegory of Love* (1936) was considered a landmark in medieval scholarship, and whose *Preface to 'Paradise Lost'* (1941) was at the center of Miltonic controversy.

Books continued to flow from Lewis's pen at the rate of one or more a year, and in astonishing variety: novels, children's books, theology, philosophical apologetics, poetry, literary criticism. A 1947 *Time* cover story attested to his popularity; the following year there began the inevitable trickle of dissertations which attest to his academic interest.

This checklist is an attempt to assist readers and students of Lewis in finding secondary source material. We do not claim that the checklist is definitive, though it includes everything significant we found which evaluates or analyzes Lewis as scholar, religious writer and thinker, novelist, and poet. The list of reviews contains approximately half of the reviews, but the more important half. Our cutoff date for inclusion was June 1972.

The most important work which has appeared after this date and before this volume goes to press is *C. S. Lewis: Images of His World*, by Douglas Gilbert and Clyde S. Kilby (Grand Rapids, Mich.: William B. Eerdmans Publishing Company, 1973), which contains not only photographs of and biographical information on Lewis but also quotations from a large number of previously unpublished letters and other writings of Lewis.

For any student of Lewis, the primary source bibliography compiled by Walter Hooper for *Light on C. S. Lewis* (1965) is indispensable. Two letters can be added to that bibliography: "On Income Tax," *The Times*, 4 April, 1932, p. 10c; "On Cross-Channel Ships," *The Times*, 18 November, 1938, p. 12e. All of Lewis's books, including those published since Lewis's death, 22 November, 1963, and which have appeared since Hooper's bibliography, are included in this checklist in the list of reviews.

Serious scholars will want to use the resources of the Bodleian at Oxford and the Wheaton College Library in Illinois. The Wheaton Collection, gathered under the direction of Clyde S. Kilby, includes original editions of nearly all Lewis's books; all doctoral dissertations on Lewis as well as 30 master's theses and many unpublished papers; well over 900 holograph Lewis letters and copies of more than 350 others; 98 holograph poems; the holograph manuscript of *Experiment in Criticism* and the essay, "Donne and Love-Poetry"; 134 pages of friendly debate over the years between Lewis and Owen Barfield; a number of notebooks and photographs; many secondary source books and articles; and significant holdings on Lewis's close friends Charles Williams and J. R. R. Tolkien. In 1973 a bequest from Lewis's brother, W. H. Lewis, brought to the Wheaton collection 11 volumes of typed and bound Lewis family papers, one of two copies; W. H. Lewis's diaries; 45 letters from

C. S. Lewis to his brother; all of Lewis's juvenilia, holograph and the only copies; notebooks, photographs, and many miscellaneous papers.

Many friends in this country and abroad generously assisted in obtaining items, but special mention should be made of the generosity of Wheaton College's Dr. Kilby for his help, his encouragement, and his placing the Wheaton College collection at our disposal. We would also like to thank Paul G. Ruggiers, professor of English at the University of Oklahoma, and Jackson Bryer, associate professor of English and bibliographer at the University of Maryland, for their suggestions. We owe grateful acknowledgments to three British publishers for opening their review files to us: Cambridge University Press, Oxford University Press, and Collins (which owns the Lewis titles published by the now-defunct Geoffrey Bles). We wish to thank the following libraries for their resources and cooperation: the Library of Congress, New York Public Library, Catholic University, Fordham University, General Theological Seminary, Princeton Seminary, Wheaton College (Illinois), and Tarleton State University. We also thank the Research Committee of Tarleton State University for a grant which allowed one of the bibliographers to make a last-minute visit to the C. S. Lewis Collection at Wheaton College. And we owe special thanks to Lynn Christopher for undertaking our long, difficult typing chores.

JOE R. CHRISTOPHER
JOAN K. OSTLING

I. General and Unclassifiable Items, Including Special Periodicals

1. Amend, Victor E., and Leo T. Hendrick. *Ten Contemporary Thinkers*. New York: The Free Press of Glencoe (The Macmillan Company). 1964.

   The eighth of the ten thinkers is C. S. Lewis. Essays of his reprinted in this anthology are "Our English Syllabus," "On Literary Criticism" from *A Preface to Paradise Lost*, "Right and Wrong as a Clue to the Meaning of the Universe" from *Mere Christianity*, "Membership," and "Screwtape Proposes a Toast." The brief introduction (pp. 357–358) emphasizes Lewis's Christian belief, and the annotated bibliography (pp. 409–411) is highly selective: it lists only nine books and three articles.

2. Auden, W. H. *Secondary Worlds*. New York: Random House, 1968, pp. 29, 116, 142.

   The book consists of four lectures given in the memory of T. S. Eliot. The first, "The Martyr as Dramatic Hero" (pp. 13–45), considers Eliot's *Murder in the Cathedral* and Williams's *Thomas Cranmer*; Lewis is quoted (p. 29) on the Divine Right of Kings as "the first form" of the "right" of governments to interfere with individuals. The second, "The World of the Sagas" (pp. 49–84), does not refer to Lewis but is of interest to the student of the Inklings since the title of the book is drawn from Tolkien's "On Fairy-Stories" and Auden indicates (on pp. 51–52) what he believes are the reasons for the creation of fictional, secondary worlds. The third lecture, "The World of Opera" (pp. 85–116), is mainly concerned with the libretti which Auden has written in collaboration with Chester Kallman; Lewis's term of Drab and Golden for Renaissance poetry (in *English Literature in the Sixteenth Century*) is applied (on p. 116) to modern poetry and T. S. Eliot's verse-dramas (Drab) and opera libretti (High or Golden). The fourth lecture, "Words and the World" (pp. 117–144), concerns the relationship of Christianity and modern literature; Lewis is quoted on the older scientific view that reality could be known by sense-experience improved by instruments (p. 142); George Macdonald is cited on a more religious point (p. 131).

3. Barnhouse, Donald Grey. "C. S. Lewis," *Religious Digest* 20 (May 1947): 14.

This item was listed in Boss's *The Theology of C. S. Lewis*; it turns out to be a two-paragraph quotation from Barnhouse used as a filler at the end of an article. It cites *Revelation* (predecessor to the evangelical magazine *Eternity*) as its source. The two paragraphs state that Lewis is important for academic background in addition to his fundamentalism, and that his books should be circulated to university students and faculty. (The article for which this note fills out the page is a condensed version of Chad Walsh's "C. S. Lewis, Apostle to the Skeptics," reprinted from *The Atlantic Monthly*.)

4. Barrington-Ward, Simon. "The Uncontemporary Apologist," *Theology* 68 (February 1965): 103–108.

The author begins with Lewis's parable of his arrival at Oxford (in *Surprised by Joy*, the third paragraph of Chapter XII) and then proceeds to follow the pattern: A lengthy discussion of Lewis's intellectual weaknesses developing from his distaste for the modern period is followed by praise for Lewis's imagistic presentation of "the light of eternity" and of internal moral evil.

5. Bergier, Jacques. *Admirations*. Paris: Christian Bourgois, 1970. 315 pp.

Not seen. According to the review by James Mark Purcell in *CSL: The Bulletin of the New York C. S. Lewis Society* 3 (July 1972):

5, this volume (in French) has a chapter on Lewis, mainly a consideration of the Ransom Trilogy in terms of witchcraft (the influence of Yeats on Lewis) *vs.* rationalistic Christianity. Purcell also mentions some application of Lewis's theology in the chapter on Stanislaw Lem.

6. Boies, Professor Jack J. "C. S. Lewis and Charles Williams: A Study in Influences and Contrasts" (excerpts). *The Bulletin of the New York C. S. Lewis Society* 2 (May 1971): 2–3.

   The paper was read at the nineteenth meeting of the New York C. S. Lewis Society (14 May 1971). See the same issue (pp. 1–2) for a report of the meeting's discussion. The paper gives a brief sketch of Williams's life and his friendship with Lewis; it finds two main features of his last novels and his Arthurian poetry to be existentialism and the Doctrine of Exchange or Substitution. In existentialism lies the difference between Williams and Lewis: Lewis is a rationalist, whose fiction moves therefore toward allegory; Williams is a nonrationalist, an existentialist, and therefore more pessimistic, whose fiction and poetry (also *therefore*) moves toward symbolism.

7. Brandt, William J. *The Rhetoric of Argumentation.* Indianapolis: Bobbs-Merrill Company, 1970. 288 pp.

   Chapter VI, "A Textual Analysis" (pp. 172-197), contains an extended rhetorical analysis of the first ten paragraphs of the third section of *The Abolition of Man.* It contains such general observations as this: ". . . only in the last two sentences [of one of the paragraphs], when Lewis has already persuaded those whom he can persuade, does he permit himself *irony* and the two very forceful *metonymies*. A modern audience is particularly apt to take alarm at such language, and Lewis always withholds it until the point has been made" (p. 194). The ten paragraphs together constitute an enthymeme. (A brief example from Owen Barfield's *Saving the Appearances*, used to illustrate a pseudo-inductive argument, appears on pp. 213-214.)

8. *The Bulletin of the New York C. S. Lewis Society.* [See
   CSL in this section for the post-February 1972 title.]
   Editor: James Como, 72-61 113 St., Apt. 2-L, Forest Hills,
   N. Y. 11375. Corresponding Secretary and Treasurer:
   Mrs. Hope Kirkpatrick, 466 Orange St., New Haven,
   Connecticut, 06511.
   Subscription: $7.00 for twelve consecutive issues.

   The Society held its first meeting on 1 November 1969. The early
   Bulletins were simply reports of the meetings and were variously
   duplicated. Beginning with 1:11 photo-offset is used. The previous
   Bulletin had first included some material besides a meeting report
   and business notices. With 1:11 letters were gathered into the
   Bulletin (previously duplicated separately); in 2:1/13 appeared
   the first essay in the *Bulletin* (several addresses had previously been
   duplicated separately). This checklist has not tried to list
   the meeting reports, the "Question Box" and answers (even
   though some authoritative answers from Walter Hooper and others
   have appeared to various problems), the business notices, and
   the extended correspondence. Unlike the letters listed elsewhere
   in this checklist this material appears in an obvious source.

9. Carnell, Corbin S. "C. S. Lewis: an Appraisal." *Mythlore* 1
   (October 1969): 18-20.

   An appreciation of Lewis's four contributions to the literature of
   our time: (1) a sense of sanity and Order, (2) a belief that
   literature should delight a large number of readers, (3) a sense
   of the present as a historic period, and (4) an ability to make
   popular theology into art.

10. *The Chronicle of the Portland C. S. Lewis Society.*
    Address: 9439 N.E. Prescott, Portland, Oregon, 97220.
    $6.00 for 12 issues.

    The early issues (the first is dated 4 February 1972) are photo-
    offset on one side of legal-sized sheets; the first issue has five pages,
    the second, four. The contents follow the pattern of *The Bulletin
    of the New York C. S. Lewis Society*: first a summary of a meeting,
    followed by such materials as an essay read at the meeting, various

announcements, "favorite quotations" from the work discussed at the meeting, perhaps another essay, and letters.

11. *CSL: The Bulletin of the New York C. S. Lewis Society.*

The journal began simply with the current subtitle as title; from March 1971 through February 1972, the top of the first page read "CSL: Voluntas Dei diem ex die," but the previous title appeared in a box with the publication information; from March 1972, the top of the page reads, "CSL: The Bulletin of the New York C. S. Lewis Society." Most of the items annotated in this bibliography (those through February 1972) are listed under the first title (see it in this section for fuller information on the price and on the Society).

12. Daiches, David. *The Present Age in British Literature.* Bloomington: Indiana University Press, 1958, pp. 13, 139, 144, 352–353.

Three references to Lewis in the survey of the post-World War I literary scene: one is to Lewis's Christian writings (in connection with Charles Williams and Dorothy Sayers) and two to his critical works and ideas. The bibliography (pp. 352–353) is incomplete.

13. Del Zanna, Lorenzo. "La nostalgia dell'Eden in Clive Staples Lewis." *Letture* 16, pp. 83–94.

An interesting essay by a person connected to the publishing of the Ransom trilogy in Italy—which, he comments, lost money, unlike *The Screwtape Letters* (*Le lettere di Berlicche*) which was published by someone else. He discusses Lewis's psychology, following *Surprised by Joy* (his title refers to Lewis's *Sehnsucht*), and then briefly surveys all the prose fiction volumes with an excursion into *The Problem of Pain* (*Problema della sofferenza*) and, at the end of the essay, *Mere Christianity*. After a quotation (in Italian) from the latter, Del Zanna concludes: "The sincerity and passion with which Lewis 'pronounces' these ancient but somehow always new words are so intense that, against his will, he loses his *self-control* [term in English] and recovers, for a moment, the authentic mantle (*stoffa*) of a prophet (*predicatore*). But it is also so sympathetic that it causes one to happily pardon this 'upset of moderation.' "

On unnumbered pages between pp. 88 and 89 appear a drawing of
Lewis, a brief life, a list of Lewis's publications, a list of Lewis's
works which have been translated into Italian, and a bibliography of
studies of Lewis's writings, five of which are other Italian essays.
(We wish to thank Lynn Christopher for translating part of this
article for us.)

14. Futch, Ken. "The Syntax of C. S. Lewis's Style: A
    Statistical Look at Some Syntactic Features." Ph.D.
    dissertation: University of Southern California, 1969;
    University Microfilms, No. 69-19,370.

    After an elaborate analysis of Lewis's sentence structure, with
    statistical tables in the appendices, Futch has isolated such
    characteristics as Lewis's avoidance of the nominative absolute
    structure. He also suggests that much of Lewis's appeal is probably
    found in such matters as diction, which he is not considering.
    (Based on the abstract in *Dissertation Abstracts International*; see
    § VII-B for volume and page.)

15. Gibb, Jocelyn (ed.). *Light on C. S. Lewis*. London:
    Geoffrey Bles, 1965; New York: Harcourt, Brace and
    World, 1966.

    Contents: Jocelyn Gibb, "Preface"; Owen Barfield, "Introduction";
    Austin Farrer, "The Christian Apologist"; J. A. W. Bennett,
    " 'Grete Clerk' "; Nevill Coghill, "The Approach to English";
    John Lawlor, "The Tutor and the Scholar"; Stella Gibbons,
    "Imaginative Writing"; Kathleen Raine, "From a Poet"; Chad
    Walsh, "Impact on America"; and Walter Hooper, "A
    Bibliography of the Writings of C. S. Lewis."

    The essays are listed separately in this checklist: Barfield, in
    § II; Farrer, § V; Bennett, § II; Coghill, § II; Lawlor, § II;
    Gibbons, § III-A; Raine, § II; Walsh, § V-A; and Hooper, this
    section.

16. GoodKnight, Glen (ed.). *Mythcon I Proceedings*. Los
    Angeles: The Mythopoeic Society, 1971.

    Contents: C. S. Kilby, "Tolkien, Lewis, and Williams"; Randel
    Helms, "The Structure and Aesthetic of Tolkien's *The Lord of*

the Rings"; Virginia Dabney, "On the Natures and Histories of the Great Rings"; Kathryn Lindskoog, "Farewell to Shadowland: C. S. Lewis on Death"; Laura A. Ruskin, "Three Good Mothers: Galadriel, Psyche, and Sybil Coningsby"; Nancy-Lou Patterson, "Archetypes of the Mother in the Fantasies of George MacDonald"; Alexis Levitin, "The Lure of the Ring"; Ethel Wallis, "Surprising Joy: C. S. Lewis' Deep Space Trilogy"; Gracia Fay Ellwood, "A High and Lonely Destiny"; Roland Kawano, "The Impact of Charles Williams' Death on C. S. Lewis"; Lois E. Newman, "Beyond the Fields We Know: An Appreciation of Lord Dunsany"; Nan Braude, "The Two-Headed Beast: Notes toward a Definition of Allegory"; Judy Winn Bell, "The Language of J. R. R. Tolkien in *The Lord of the Rings*"; J. R. Christopher, "Considering *The Great Divorce*, Parts I and II"; Ellen Rothberg, "The 'Hnau' Creatures of C. S. Lewis"; Robert Foster, "Sindarin and Quenya Phonology"; Glen GoodKnight, "The White Tree"; Alpajpuri and Bernie Zuber, "Mythcon Report."

Those essays on Lewis or mentioning him are listed separately in this checklist: Kilby, in this section; Lindskoog, this section; Ruskin, § III-H; Patterson, this section; Wallis, § III-D; Ellwood, § III-G; Kawano, § II; Braude, § V-B; Christopher, § III-F; Rothberg, § III-A; and GoodKnight, this section.

17. ———. *Mythcon II Proceedings*. Los Angeles: The Mythopoeic Society, 1972.

Contents: Glen GoodKnight, "Transcending the Images: Archaisms and Alternatives: Opening Address." Nancy-Lou Patterson, "Anti-Babels: Images of the Divine Center in *That Hideous Strength*"; Joe R. Christopher, "Considering *The Great Divorce*, Parts, III, IV, and V"; Robert Foster, "The Heroic in Middle Earth"; Gracia Fay Ellwood, "The Return to the Past in Williams and Eliade"; Kathryn Lindskoog, "Introducing C. S. Lewis: Sincerity Personified"; Ian Myles Slaten, "Selected Materials from a Study of *The Worm Ouroboros*"; and Mary McDermott Shideler, "Are These Myths True?"

The essays on Lewis or referring to him are listed separately in this bibliography: GoodKnight, in this section; Patterson, § III-D; Christopher, § III-F; Lindskoog, § II; and Shideler, this section.

18. ————. "Transcending the Images: Archaisms and Alternatives: Opening Address." In *Mythcon II Proceedings*, ed. Glen GoodKnight, pp. 3–5, 25.

The volume is listed in this section.

The Keynote Address of the Second Mythopoeic convention. Extensive citation of Lewis—*Surprised by Joy, Perelandra, Arthurian Torso*, "De Descriptione Temporum," *Letters to Malcolm*, and *The Discarded Image*—in the process of describing a liberation from current cultural images which the Mythopoeic Society offers.

19. ————. "The White Tree." In *Mythcon I Proceedings*, ed. Glen GoodKnight, pp. 56–59.

The volume is listed above.

Lewis's comment on Williams's realm of Broceliande (the unconscious), in his Arthurian poems, is quoted (pp. 56-57) in the process of a Jungian defense of uniting the conscious, rational mind and the unconscious, mythopoeic mind.

20. Hannay, Margaret. "C. S. Lewis Collection at Wheaton College." *Mythlore* 2 (Winter 1972): 20.

A description of the Wheaton collection, not an exhaustive catalogue. Lewis's letters to Owen Barfield during their "Great War" are there, as are about 675 letters from Charles Williams to his wife—in addition to works which have been published.

21. "Hard, polemical, black-or-white, them-or-us."

Listed in § VI-A-1; nominally a review, actually a general discussion of Lewis's life and works.

22. Hooey, Sister Mary Amy, R. S. M. *An Applied Linguistic Analysis of the Prose Style of C. S. Lewis*. Ph. D. dissertation: University of Connecticut, 1966; University Microfilms, No. 67-3882.

A study of five passages in Lewis's prose—three from *English Literature in the Sixteenth Century* and one each from *The Allegory of Love* and *The Four Loves*—in order to analyze diction, metaphor, literary allusions, and especially, syntax in an attempt to achieve more precise methods for examination and description of applied English linguistics. In an analysis of Lewis's syntax, Sister Hooey finds his expansion of predicates rather than subjects especially important. Other significant syntactical elements include avoidance of excessive embedding of clauses, use of additive rather than repetitive conjuncts in structure of coordination, use of common conjunctions as sentence-openers, and placing subjects as the first element in sentences.

Sister Hooey finds several pedagogical implications: consistent expansion of predicates rather than subjects is virtually ignored in writers' handbooks; mingling of at least two functional varieties of the same level of language is seldom treated; use of coordinating conjunctions to open sentences, and the consistent placing of the subject as the first element in the sentence contradict some time-honored recommendations.

23. Hooper, Walter. "A Bibliography of the Writings of C. S. Lewis." In *Light on C. S. Lewis*, ed. Jocelyn Gibb, pp. 117–160.

Hooper's bibliography is the most valuable part of Gibb's book—and it is indispensable for studies of Lewis. After a brief introduction, Hooper divides his materials into seven sections: A. Books, B. Short Stories, C. Books edited or with Prefaces by C. S. Lewis, D. Essays and Pamphlets, E. Poems, F. Book reviews by C. S. Lewis, and G. Published Letters. "An Alphabetical Index of the Writings of C. S. Lewis" concludes the bibliography.

There are minor differences between the versions published in the British and American editions of the book: the most important is that the American edition adds the first American publication of each book in brackets. Other variants: the American edition drops the two forthcoming book titles listed in the British edition (both since published); the American edition adds a new essay, a new poem, and a new letter; the American edition also corrects the date of the first book publication of *The Great Divorce*.

24. ———. "A C. S. Lewis Mystery," *Spectator*, No. 7216 (14 October 1966), 481; No. 7218 (28 October 1966), 546; and No. 7220 (11 November 1966), 616.

Rev. Hooper writes of a difficulty of deciphering a manuscript passage in one of Lewis's addresses, and asks if any auditor of the speech could help him. The second letter sums up the replies he received. (There is also another guess by a letter writer following Rev. Hooper's second letter.) The third letter advances further reasons for the tentative answer of the second. The passage under consideration appears in "The Language of Religion" (*Christian Reflections*, p. 134, with a footnote reference to the second letter).

25. ———. "C. S. Lewis's Mss." *Times Literary Supplement*, 29 February 1968, p. 213.

A letter stating that the Bodleian Library is collecting Lewis's mss., with an expressed hope for contributions.

26. Huttar, Charles (ed.). *Imagination and the Spirit: Essays in Literature and the Christian Faith presented to Clyde S. Kilby.* Grand Rapids, Michigan: William B. Eerdmans Publishing Company, 1971, pp. v, xiii, 25n, 33n, 34–35, 41, 49, 189–227 *passim*, 248, 259–339 *passim*, 341–351, 392–393, 401n, 402, 471–475.

The third section, "Inklings and Ancestors" (pp. 187–351), is of primary interest to this bibliography. Daniel K. Kuhn's "The Joy of the Absolute: A Comparative Study of the Romantic Visions of William Wordsworth and C. S. Lewis" (pp. 189–214) is listed in § IV-A; Glenn Edward Sadler's "The Fantastic Imagination in George MacDonald" (pp. 215–228), § V-E; Marjorie Evelyn Wright's "The Vision of Cosmic Order in the Oxford Mythmakers" (pp. 259–276), § III-A; Walter Hooper's "Past Watchful Dragons: The Fairy Tales of C. S. Lewis" (pp. 277–340), § III-G; and Corbin Scott Carnell, "C. S. Lewis on Eros as a Means of Grace" (pp. 341–351), § IV-A. Of the essays in other sections, Owen Barfield's "Either : Or" (pp. 25–42) is listed in § IV-A; Robert Warburton's "Fantasy and the Fiction of Bernard Malamud" (pp. 387–416) in § V-A; and Paul M. Bechtel's "Clyde S. Kilby: A Sketch" (pp. 467–478) in § II.

27. "Index to most of the works of C. S. Lewis." Typescript of 216 pp. Available only at the C. S. Lewis Collection, Wheaton College, Wheaton, Illinois.

   Indices of thirty-five of Lewis's books, most of which were prepared either by C. S. Kilby or by Margaret Hannay. Lianne Payne has also prepared an index to the unpublished letters from Lewis to Arthur Greeves on IBM cards at Wheaton College, with plans to index all the Lewis letters. Presumably the Greeves index will be printed and available for use at Wheaton by the time this Checklist is published.

28. Kilby, Clyde S. "C. S. Lewis: Everyman's Theologian." *Christianity Today* 8 (3 January 1964), issue pp. 11–13, volume pp. 313–315.

   A memorial survey of Lewis's most popular writings and major ideas.

29. ———. *The Christian World of C. S. Lewis.* Grand Rapids, Mich.: William B. Eerdmans, 1964; Appleford, Abingdon, Berks.: Marcham Manor Press, 1965. 216 pp.

   This is a survey of Lewis's fiction and nonfiction "Christian works" (it excludes his literary scholarship). Each book is paraphrased, then evaluated and interpreted with a tracing of recurrent themes. Some readers will find the summaries of plots and arguments excessive, but the critical comments are often acute.

   An introductory chapter on Lewis's "search for joy" includes some biography, discussion of *Surprised by Joy,* and a helpful map through the intricate lands of *Pilgrim's Regress.* In a good discussion of the complex *Till We Have Faces,* Kilby emphasizes Lewis's distinction between myth and allegory and sorts out three main themes: "a rationalist versus a Christian interpretation of the universe"; "Orual's case against the gods and the gods' case against Orual"; and "the significance of the great myths of mankind." Kilby says Lewis regarded this novel as his best book, and he quotes letters from Lewis in working out the interpretation.

   In "Psalms, Miracles and Orthodoxy," Kilby is especially concerned with Lewis's views on bibliology. He thinks Lewis considered the Bible itself as having a "creative rather than abstractive quality," literature but not mere literature. He says Lewis believed the Old Testament was not the "Word of God" but "carries" that word in its overall message; he pressed the historical reliability of the New Testament. Kilby quotes a long letter from Lewis on inspiration (written in response to his query) and discusses Lewis's definition of "myth" as related to Biblical interpretation.

The final chapter ties together the strands with discussion of major Lewisian themes other than myth: the modern world, man's capacity for choice, death, God as creator-transformer-possessor, obedience, *Sehnsucht* or longing, the evil of repeating pleasures for their own sake, intrinsic moral nature of the universe. An appendix describes five Ph. D. dissertations and six books devoted wholly or in large part to Lewis.

30. ———. "The Lewis Collection at Wheaton." *Wheaton Alumni* 34 (July–August [September on cover] 1971): 3.

A general discussion of the holdings of the collection and its use. A list at the bottom of the page is of "Funds Needed for the Lewis Collection"; a photograph of Kilby accompanies the note, and a drawing of Lewis appears on the cover of the magazine.

31. Kranz, Gisbert. *Christliche Literatur der Gegenwart*. 2nd ed. Aschaffenburg, 1963. Pp. 70–78 for material on Lewis.

Not seen. Possibly only the section on Lewis is by Kranz. The title means "Contemporary Christian Writing."

32. ———. "The Reception of C. S. Lewis in Germany," trans. Henry Noel. *The Bulletin of the New York C. S. Lewis Society* 2 (April 1971): 6–7.

A survey of Lewis's books and essays which have been translated into German, their poor sales and the cause, the Roman Catholic interest, and the current prospects for a larger readership.

33. Kranz, Gisbert (ed.). *Stories by C. S. Lewis*. Verlag Diesterweg, 1971.

Not seen. An anthology for use in German schools; it may have some critical framework.

34. Kreeft, Peter. *C. S. Lewis: A Critical Essay*. Contemporary Writers in Christian Perspective, series ed. by Roderick Jellema. Grand Rapids, Mich.: William B. Eerdmans, 1969. 48-page pamphlet.

Kreeft discusses Lewis's objectivity (or rationalism), romanticism and Christianity, which he sees as corresponding roughly to the three main genres of his writing (literary criticism, imaginative fiction, apologetics). In evaluating Lewis's attack on the modern world, Kreeft lists three reasons for Lewis's rejection of "Universal Evolutionism."

Describing Lewis's orthodox beliefs, Kreeft seeks to rid Lewis of the "conservative" label. He regards Lewis's fiction as overly didactic and by conventional standards weak on characterization but rich in its combination of romanticism with rationalism; he thinks Lewis's supreme success is his portrayal of God. Evaluating Lewis's historical significance, Kreeft thinks Lewis may become popular after the age he rebelled against has passed but remain minimal in an age which demands originality above all else in religious ideas. The bibliography misses several important studies of Lewis.

35. Kuhn, Helmut. "C. S. Lewis: Der Romancier der Unerbittlichen Liebe [The Novelist of Inexorable Love]." *Wort und Wahrheit* (Freiberg), 10 January 1955, pp. 113–126.

Helmut Kuhn recognizes C. S. Lewis's contribution to criticism, particularly Lewis's interpretation of Milton from within Milton's works and not from within Milton's biography; however, Kuhn's main concern is in that realm he chooses to call Lewis's "hobby," an interest in theology, philosophy (particularly Aristotelean, Kuhn believes), allegories, and fiction. Lewis gets more than an earthly joy from this "hobby," for he writes both as an apologist and as a Christian believer who cannot self-contain his belief. Christianity fills a void created by a generation too concerned with its own emancipation from the past, but Lewis does not oversimplify the difficulties belief creates for reason. The difficulties exist, but they pale "in the victorious clarity which flows from belief." Kuhn finds Lewis's gifts most richly developed in those works which combine thought and picture, analysis and fantasy, particularly in *The Great Divorce* and *The Problem of Pain*: however, Kuhn asks (in the last paragraph) if the use of the fantastic sacrifices the great, if fantasy is a sufficiently substantial medium for dealing with the important human concerns. (We wish to thank Fr. Raleigh Dennison, Assistant Professor of Languages at Tarleton State University, for great assistance in preparing this summary.)

36. Lawlor, John. " 'Rasselas', Romanticism and the Nature of Happiness." In *Friendship's Garland: Essays Presented to Mario Praz on his Seventieth Birthday*, ed. Vittorio Gabrieli, I, 243–270 [259-268]. Storia e Letteratura: Raccolta de Studi e Testi: 106. Roma: Edizioni di Storia e Letteratura, 1966.

Basically, Lawlor surveys the answers which Johnson, Keats, and C. S. Lewis have given to the nature of happiness in *Rasselas*, four odes, and autobiographical writings respectively. For Johnson, the imagination is a danger to happiness: dutiful virtue is the goal. This is achieved in the young by their setting up their ideals and striving for their accomplishment in the self-conscious delusion that they can achieve them; in the old, by composing themselves in tranquility, by setting aside all hopes.

For Keats, as for the Romantic poets generally, happiness lies in moments of ecstatic insight into (and perhaps through) objects perceived. Thus imagination is the means. Lawlor suggests that "Ode to Psyche" and "Ode on Melancholy" show the poet's dependence on inspiration, while "Ode to a Nightingale" and "Ode on a Grecian Urn" indicate that Keats resolved the psychological problem of the momentary nature of such happiness by indicating the eternal nature of beauty (the nightingale's song, the urn) which will remain to inspire others.

For C. S. Lewis, happiness is found in a fusion of Johnson's Christianity with the Romantic imagination. Lawlor uses as his evidence Lewis's non-Christian lyrics in *Spirits in Bondage*; his first Christian work, *Pilgrim's Regress*; and his autobiography, *Surprised by Joy*. The first of these shows a contrast, not reconciliation, between "sweet desire," *Sehnsucht*, and God; but in the latter two Lewis identifies the ecstatic moment, "the visionary gleam," with perception of God, and thus reconciles Christian Belief and Romantic Imagination.

37. Lindskoog, Kathryn. "Farewell to Shadowlands: C. S. Lewis on Death." *Mythcon I Proceedings*, ed. Glen GoodKnight, pp. 10–12.

The volume is listed in this section.

Note: The material in this essay was used by Lindskoog, in a revised form, as Chapter 5, "Death," in her *C. S. Lewis: Mere Christian* (Glendale, California: Regal Books, 1973), which appeared after the terminal date for this Checklist.

A survey of Lewis's comments on death in his fiction and in his nonfiction, followed by a biographical section on death in Lewis's life (his mother's, Charles Williams's, his wife's, his own) and on Lewis's two appearances after death to J. B. Phillips. No sources given.

38. Longaker, Mark, and Edwin C. Bolles. *Contemporary English Literature*. Appleton-Century Handbooks of Literature, under the general editorship of Albert C. Baugh. New York: Appleton-Century-Crofts, 1953, pp. 451–453.

In the section "Other Prose: 1890–1950," Clive Staples Lewis is given three pages: five paragraphs, a photograph, and a bibliography. As part of a guide, the summary is satisfactory— although incomplete because of the date. The bibliography misses *Spirits in Bondage*.

39. Martell, Clare Lorinne. "C. S. Lewis: Teacher as Apologist." M. A. thesis: Boston College, 1949. 91 pp.

Author thinks Lewis's effectiveness stemmed from his understanding of the learning process. Stresses Lewis's simplicity, his clever use of analogy, and his use of such pedagogical techniques as repetition and anticipating problems.

40. *Mythlore*, edited by Glen GoodKnight for the Mythopoeic Society, P. O. Box 24150, Los Angeles, California, 90024. Subscriptions are four issues for $3.50.

The Mythopoeic Society, whose chapters meet monthly to discuss the works of C. S. Lewis, J. R. R. Tolkien, and Charles Williams, has fourteen or more chapters, centered in southern California (one chapter in Ohio and one in Illinois). The essays in *Mythlore* (which is, in intent more than practice, a quarterly) are annotated separately in this bibliography.

A note on art: in vol. 1, no. 1 (January 1969), the cover by Bernie Zuber shows Tolkien (reading a ms.), Lewis, and Williams. In 1:2 (April 1969), Tim Kirk's cover illustrates *hnakra* hunting in *Out of the Silent Planet*; on p. 31 is a full-page drawing of *Perelandra*'s Tinidril by George Barr; on the back cover is an illustration based on *That Hideous Strength* by Bonnie Bergstrom. In 1:3 (July 1969) a full-page drawing by Don Simpson, on p. 29, illustrates Ransom being carried on the back of a *sorn* in *Out of the Silent Planet*, and one by Tim Kirk on the back cover illustrates the Passion of Aslan in *The Lion, the Witch and the Wardrobe*. In 1:4 (October 1969), on p. 4, is a full-page drawing by Bernie Zuber, "The Lady, the Dwarf and the Tragedian," based on *The Great Divorce*. In 2:1/5 (Winter 1970), the back cover, by Tim Kirk, illustrates Charn in *The Magician's Nephew*. And 2:3/7 (Winter 1971) has a cover by Bonnie Bergstrom of the Fox and Orual watching Psyche's adventures in a wall-picture, from the latter part of *Till We Have Faces*. In addition to these large drawings, a number of smaller ones accompany various articles on Lewis and some of the announcements.

41. *Mythprint*: *The Monthly Bulletin of the Mythopoeic Society*. Begun January 1970; started carrying "Branch News" with 2:6 (December 1970). Twelve issues for $2.00.

The earlier issues are primarily announcements of meetings and topics; the "Branch News" are reports of discussions at the various chapters of the works studied—these works are primarily those of Lewis, Tolkien, and Williams, but include other fantasies at times. Of course, these discussions are not usually at a scholarly level, but they may be of interest to scholars as reflecting what intelligent, often young readers find in various books. (Before *Mythprint* began carrying the Branch News, such reports were gathered in a mimeographed publication, *The Mything Link*, which these bibliographers have not seen.)

42. Noel , Henry. "What Is the C. S. Lewis Society About?",
    The Bulletin of the New York C. S. Lewis Society 2 (May
    1971) : 6. Reprinted in *The Chronicles of the Portland
    C. S. Lewis Society* 1 (4 February 1972) : 2–3.

    "It is about a person. Not anything else. And not merely part of a
    person." Note also the short history of the New York C. S. Lewis
    Society, untitled but prepared by Eugene McGovern, on the bottom
    third of the same page.

43. *Orcrist: A Journal of Fantasy in the Arts.* The magazine
    began subtitled as "The Bulletin of the University of
    Wisconsin J. R. R. Tolkien Society"; with its seventh issue
    it is to become the official journal of the M.L.A. Seminar
    on "The Medieval Tradition in Modern Literature."
    All issues are available from the editor, Richard C. West,
    614 Langdon Street, Madison, Wisconsin, 53703,
    at $1.00 each.

    Of special interest to students of Lewis is the sixth issue, "Special
    C. S. Lewis Issue," set with Gothic print in the titles and a
    photograph of Lewis on the cover. The six essays are annotated
    separately in this bibliography.

44. Ostling, Joan K. "A Bibliography of Writings about C. S.
    Lewis." Unpublished bibliography: University of Maryland,
    1970. 156 pp. (with six loose pages at the end).

    The origin of half of this bibliography; the ms. is available at the
    Lewis Collection, Wheaton College, Wheaton, Illinois.

45. ————. "A Brief Bibliography on C. S. Lewis: Secondary
    Sources." A 5-page dittoed listing, dated 30 June 1970;
    see the listing of *The Bulletin of the New York C. S. Lewis
    Society* in this section for an explanation of these early
    separate publications.

    In four parts: "Complete Books and Pamphlets" (10 items with
    1 forthcoming), "Selected Books in Part on Lewis" (7 items),
    "Dissertations (Unpublished)" (13 items), and "Selected
    Articles" (34 items).

46. ———. "A Selected Bibliography of C. S. Lewis." *The Bulletin of the New York C. S. Lewis Society* 2 (March 1971): 11–13.

"Part I. Primary Sources" lists those books by Lewis which have appeared since Walter Hooper's bibliography; "Part II. Secondary Sources" is divided into four sections: "Complete Books and Pamphlets" (12 items), "Selected Books in Part on Lewis" (10 items), "Unpublished Dissertations" (12 items), and "Selected Articles" (34 items).

47. Oury, Scott. "The Value of Something Other: A Study of C. S. Lewis's Attention to 'The Object Itself.' " Unpublished M.A. thesis: Fairleigh Dickinson University (Madison, N.J.), n.d. 42 pp.

Oury suggests that one underlying assumption of Lewis, which explains some apparent paradoxes in his thought, is his attention to something outside of himself, although he is often (at least in some contexts) hesitant about assigning it a value. Biographically, this is *Sehnsucht*, which Lewis only found to be outside himself after confusing it with other things. Philosophically, this is the *Tao* (although Oury does not use the term), as Lewis defines it in *The Abolition of Man*. Experientially, this is myth. Literarily, this is the writing itself, divorced from the author's personality. Oury also makes clear Lewis's belief that any "model" of the something other, whether God or the universe, cannot be an ultimately accurate representation. 5-page bibliography. The essay, while poorly proofread, is a valuable discussion.

48. Patterson, Nancy-Lou. "Archetypes of the Mother in the Fantasies of George MacDonald." In *Mythcon I Proceedings*, ed. Glen GoodKnight, pp. 14-20.

The volume is listed in this section.

C. S. Lewis is mentioned for his comments on myths (p. 14), as a spiritual follower of MacDonald (p. 14), for his presentation of the benign *anima* as the Green Lady of *Perelandra* and the malign *anima* as the White Witch of *The Lion, the Witch and the Wardrobe* (p. 15), and for a comment on an atheist's reaction to God which parallels Curdie's reaction to a dove (p. 16).

49. Philmus, Robert M. *Into the Unknown*: *The Evolution of Science Fiction from Francis Godwin to H. G. Wells*. Berkeley and Los Angeles: University of California Press, 1970, pp. 1, 3, 22, 22n, 28n, 149.

   The references to the Ransom Trilogy are passing comparisons to works by Wells; *An Experiment in Criticism* is quoted once, and *The Discarded Image* is cited in a footnote.

50. Robson, W. W. "C. S. Lewis" or "The Romanticism of C. S. Lewis."

   Listed in § VI-C-2; a summary of Lewis's achievements, although nominally a review of *Light on C. S. Lewis*.

51. Rogers, Margaret Anne. "C. S. Lewis: A Living Library." Unpublished M. A. thesis: Fairleigh Dickinson University, 1970. 119 pp.

   A catalogue of Lewis's personal 2,710-volume library now (except about 200 volumes owned by Walter Hooper) at Wroxton College, England, owned by Fairleigh Dickinson University. The thesis opens with an essay discussing the collection and Lewis's holograph annotations.

52. "The Scholar's Tale."

   Listed in § VI-B-47; a summary of Lewis's ideas.

53. Shideler, Mary McDermott. "Are These Myths True?" In *Mythcon II Proceedings*, ed. Glen GoodKnight, pp. 37–39.

   The volume is listed in this section.

   The Guest of Honor address at Mythcon II. Mrs. Shideler distinguishes between four sources of "liberty and power" in myth (the quoted phrase is Charles Williams's, speaking of poetry): (1) social, "myths unite the people who share them"; (2) allegorical, myths give people perspective on this world; (3) psychological, myths release the unconscious parts of people's minds and allow them to find new psychic balances; and (4) metaphysical, myths reflect, *probably*, some type of supernatural otherness in the universe. Her preparation for and discussion of this thesis involves references to Lewis's *Experiment in Criticism*, Ransom Trilogy, and Chronicles of Narnia. P. 39 contains a partial recording of the question-and-answer period which followed the address.

54. ————. *A Creed for a Christian Skeptic*. Grand Rapids, Michigan: William B. Eerdmans Publishing Company, 1968, pp. 14, 117, 124–125, 142, 163–164.

The creed of the title is the Apostles' Creed, which is considered phrase by phrase (given as chapter titles). Shideler writes, "Because I am writing specifically for laymen, my language and approach are not those which are generally used by professional theologians or by ministers. I have taken them principally from lay writers like Charles Williams, C. S. Lewis, and Charles Morgan" (p. 14)—not that she writes as popularly as Lewis. Passages quoted from Lewis come from *The Discarded Image* (p. 117), *An Experiment in Criticism* (pp. 124–125), and "Williams and the Arthuriad" in *Arthurian Torso* (p. 142).

55. Wain, John. "C. S. Lewis," *Encounter* 22 (May 1964): 51, 53, 56.

A memorial essay, discussing Lewis's impersonal public personality—his persona and role as *laudator temporis acti*. Wain thinks Lewis's writing improved "as it gets further from the popular and demagogic." His novels "simply bad." Rates Oxford history volume highest, written with just the right mixture of idiosyncracy and zest by a truly great teacher with delight in exposition and debate.

56. Walsh, Chad. *C. S. Lewis: Apostle to the Skeptics*. New York: The Macmillan Company, 1949. 176 pp.

Bibliographic notes: (1) "C. S. Lewis, Apostle to the Skeptics," *Atlantic Monthly* 178 (September 1947): 115–119, is distributed throughout the book; (2) "A Variety of Writers—and How They Rediscovered God." *New York Times Book Review* (§ 7), 18 July 1948, p. 6, is reshaped into Chapter 21, "One Straw in the Wind"; (3) Chapter 12, "Last Things, First Things," first appeared as "Last Things First Things: The Eschatology of C. S. Lewis" in *Theology Today* 6 (April 1949): 25–30; (4) Chapter

13, "Reason and Intellectual Climate," first appeared as "C. S. Lewis: Champion of Reason," *Christian Century* 66 (19 January 1949): 76–77; (5) Chapter 14, " 'Romance,' " first appeared in *Advance*, March 1949 [n.p.]; (6) Chapter 15, "The Christian Day by Day," first appeared as "C. S. Lewis and the Christian Life," *Catholic World* 168 (February 1949): 370–375; (7) Chapter 19, "The Word-Weaver," first appeared as "C. S. Lewis: The Word-Weaver," *Living Church* 118 (20 February 1949): 17–18; (8) Chapter 20, "A Bird's-Eye Retrospect," first appeared as "The Pros and Cons of C. S. Lewis," *Religion in Life* 18 (Spring 1949): 222–228. These essays are not listed separately.

Written when Lewis had fourteen years of active authorship remaining, this book nevertheless represents one of the best sustained studies of him. The first chapter is biographical (including information Lewis later elaborated on in *Surprised by Joy*)—and, preceding Lewis's autobiography, it is pleasant in that it is not the currently standard paraphrase. The second chapter is a personality sketch. Walsh proceeds then to an analysis of apologetics through *Miracles*.

However, Walsh regards Lewis a "better myth-maker" than expository writer. He summarizes the trilogy and concludes "Lewis has baptized the solar system and filled it with the radiant presence of Maleldil." He considers *Pilgrim's Regress* "mediocre" but of interest as Lewis's intellectual biography. In *Screwtape Letters* "he rivaled Bunyan" but *Great Divorce* is "disturbing." Walsh interprets *Dymer* as symbolizing spiritual rebirth. He considers Lewis an undistinguished poet except in the genre of adult nonsense verse where, Walsh believes, "he rivals Lewis Carroll." Walsh summarizes Lewis's scholarly works to date, considering (along with most critics) *Allegory of Love* his best. He ranks *Preface to "Paradise Lost"* second, though he regards Lewis's defense of Milton's orthodoxy in the epic unconvincing.

Writing in the theological climate of the late 1940s, Walsh thinks Lewis's theology is that of "Classical Christianity" rather than "Modernism" or "Fundamentalism" though if he leans slightly to one side "it is perhaps more often in a slightly Fundamentalist direction." "Unpopular" doctrines which Lewis defends include original sin, heaven, hell, and the orthodox Christian eschatology.

Walsh analyzes Lewis's two roads to Christian commitment:
reason and his theory of romanticism. Walsh provides a chapter on
Lewis's "influences" and another with careful refutation of the
charge that Lewis is anti-science.

In an over-all assessment, Walsh finds Lewis's style lucid and
witty, his imagination baptized; but he provides no adequate
consideration of Christianity and society, and in his work as a
whole "one does detect a certain trace of patness." Walsh thinks
of all the writers of "Classical Christianity" in the second quarter
of the twentieth century, Lewis ranks first in combining versatility,
literary skill, and psychological insight.

Cf. also Walsh's later re-evaluation of Lewis in his prefatory
remarks to the William Luther White book, *The Image of Man
in C. S. Lewis*, immediately below.

57. ————. Foreword to *The Image of Man in C. S. Lewis*, by
William Luther White, pp. 7–9. Nashville: Abingdon
Press, 1969.

Walsh analyzes three stages of his reactions to Lewis: an initial
adulation (during which *C. S. Lewis: Apostle to the Skeptics* was
written); an uneasy reaction to a certain, occasional shrill and
sharp-edged quality especially in writings on morality; and a still
later counter-reaction into a more mature appreciation of the
sophisticated subtleties in Lewis's use of language, metaphor, and
myth. Walsh commends White's book to readers in the third
stage appreciation of Lewis. (White's volume is listed in this
section.)

58. Weathers, Winston. "The Rhetoric of Certitude." *Southern
Humanities Review* 2 (Spring 1968): 213–222.

One of the four modes of modern rhetoric is certitude (the others
are judiciousness, involvement, and absurdity); among others
showing the characteristics of this mode is C. S. Lewis. (Based on
Abstracts of English Studies 12 [May 1969]: Item 1699.)

59. White, William Luther. *The Image of Man in C. S. Lewis*.
Nashville and New York: Abingdon Press, 1969. 239 pp.

This book, which began life as a dissertation in systematic theology,
is really about two subjects: Lewis's philosophy and use of

religious language, and his philosophical-theological anthropology. These are bridged by a chapter surveying Lewis's critics. Rhetorically, White focuses on Lewis's presentation of the Christian doctrines of Creation, Fall, and Redemption in relation to men, and (after the chapter on Lewis's aesthetics) on how Lewis presents these as images in his fiction.

White's handling of Lewis on myth and religious language adequately summarizes ideas in such sources as *Miracles*, "Bluspels and Flalansferes," and elsewhere in the Lewis canon, but breaks little new ground. Placing Lewis alongside such contemporary theologians as Paul Tillich and Rudolf Bultmann on "myth" is interesting, but he fails to distinguish adequately between their differing definitions of myth. To Lewis ("Is Theology Poetry?") Christianity was myth become fact; as Chad Walsh puts it in his preface (and White tends to ignore), "Where Lewis differs from many students of religious language is his unceasing insistence that such discourse has a real objective correlative." White's discussion of Lewis on figurative language is also marred by a gratuitous assumption of extreme, naive literalism on the part of the "common reader" and the "fundamentalist," a term he uses broadly for all conservative evangelical Christians.

In the chapter on criticism, White defends Lewis from the following patterns of misunderstanding (along lines similar to those used by Chad Walsh): Lewis as too rationalist; his works as primarily allegorical; an exaggeration of his apologetic motives; a lack of compassion; hostility to science; and the view that Lewis is a fundamentalist.

White's chapters on *imago dei*—man as he was intended, as he has become, and as he is yet to be—cast a wide net over Lewis's views on reason, morality, miracles, the problem of pain, *Sehnsucht*, the Fall, grace, faith, the nature of choice, love, government, social relationships, the church, prayer, and eschatology, adding little new to Lewisian criticism on these topics.

White largely ignores Lewis's careful attention to the subjective-objective problem, deals inadequately with his attitude toward modern psychology, and fails to distinguish clearly Lewis's writings on morality and ethical theory as normative, natural law, opposed to relativist or antinomian views. The book is characterized throughout by a lack of careful distinctions, i.e., though Lewis did not affirm belief in a literal, historical Adam, he also was no contemporary theological Pelagian. White's chief motivation seems to be to separate Lewis from possible association with "fundamentalism"; it distorts his handling of Lewis.

The fifth appendix has an important letter from J. R. R. Tolkien about the origin of the name of the Inklings. A large bibliography; the index is poor. (Walsh's "Foreword" to the volume is listed in this section.)

60. Wilhelm, Marie. "Realisme, Romantikk, Mystikk." *Santiden* 68 (1958): 546–556.

Since the command of Danish of the bibliographer who looked at this essay is based primarily on a small knowledge of Old English, he can not claim full evaluation. The title seems to be a paraphrase of the subtitle of *The Pilgrim's Regress: An Apology for Reason, Romanticism, and Christianity*. The author takes up these aspects of Lewis's world view in order: Reason (pp. 547–550), with MacPhee of *That Hideous Strength* as an example; Romanticism or *Sehnsucht* (pp. 550–553), with an explanation based on Lewis's preface to *The Pilgrim's Regress*; and Christianity (pp. 553–555), with a discussion of Mother Kirk in *The Pilgrim's Regress*. The author lists some Danish translations of Lewis's works in a footnote on p. 546 (she seems amused in the text by the fact that these works are published in a series called Christian Realism—or, at least, she keeps asking how realistic these romances are), and she concludes with a quotation in Danish translation from Lewis's Cambridge Inaugural in which he compares himself to a dinosaur.

II. Biographical Essays, Personality Sketches, and News Items

Note: standard reference works, such as *The International Who's Who*, and brief death notices are omitted.

1. Anderson, George C. "C. S. Lewis: Foe of Humanism." *Christian Century* 63 (25 December 1946): 1562–1563.

   Anderson reports on an hour's visit to Lewis at Oxford and the theological subjects on which their conversation touched.

2. Babbage, Stuart Barton. "To the Royal Air Force." In *C. S. Lewis: Speaker and Writer*, ed. Carolyn Keefe, pp. 65–76. Volume listed in this section.

   An account of Lewis's speeches "to the men of the heavy bomber squadrons in Norfolk" (p. 65) one weekend in 1941; particularly memorable for Lewis's comments on the reactions he had encountered at Oxford because of his Christian activities (pp. 75–76).

3. Bailey, George. "In the University." In *C. S. Lewis: Speaker and Teacher*, ed. Carolyn Keefe, pp. 79–92. Volume listed in this section.

   A fuller version of Bailey's essay in *The Reporter* (listed immediately below)—fuller but also different in some of its anecdotes. The rumor of Lewis's period of being a stagedoor Johnny in London is dropped in the book version. Some of the new material, about Lewis's weaknesses as a teacher particularly, is biographically valuable.

4. ———. "My Oxford Tutor: C. S. Lewis." *Reporter* 30 (23 April 1964): 37–38, 40.

Bailey produces a pleasant, anecdotal remembrance of his years in Oxford immediately after the Second World War, quoting several examples of Lewis's wit and describing something of his personality (this may be the best description of Lewis as a tutor in print). The final page suggests that Lewis's love of allegory (and, thereby, his scholarship) and his Christianity were "inseparably connected."

5. Balsdon, Dacre. *Oxford Now and Then*. New York: St. Martin's Press, 1970. 267 pp. [125, 143].

Two anecdotes about Lewis, the first about Betjeman's reaction to him as a tutor, the second about Lewis gaining his Fellowship at Magdalen College. Students of the Inklings will also want to check the Nevill Coghill anecdotes (pp. 154, 240).

6. Barfield, Owen. "C. S. Lewis." An address given at Wheaton College, Wheaton, Illinois, on 16 October 1964.

A typewritten ms. exists in the C. S. Lewis Collection at the college. Some anecdotes about Lewis, some discussion of his poetry and *Till We Have Faces*, and a description of the Great War between Lewis and Barfield when Lewis was a subjective idealist.

7. ———. "In Conversation." In *C. S. Lewis: Speaker and Teacher*, ed. Carolyn Keefe, pp. 95–108.

Volume listed in this section.

Barfield, Lewis's antagonist in their "great debate," here records his generalized memories of Lewis's conversation. He mentions "the combined effect of Lewis's substantial voice, the solemnity inherent in his large, inexpressive, curiously unlined face, and the abiding flow of his imperturbably analytical judgments" (p. 108), in addition to the humor which played above his seriousness.

8. ———. "Introduction." In *Light on C. S. Lewis*, ed. Jocelyn Gibb, pp. ix–xxi.

The volume is listed in § I.

Barfield discusses his friendship with Lewis and the psychic split he saw between Lewis's public (and to some degree Christian) personality and his private self. The suggestions are tentative and phrased generally.

9. ———. *Romanticism Comes of Age.* London: Rudolf Steiner Press, 1966; Middletown, Conn.: Wesleyan University Press, 1967, p. 17.

Lewis is mentioned as passing hearsay judgment on Rudolf Steiner. (Lewis was not mentioned in the original edition, 1944.)

10. Bateson, F. W. "C. S. Lewis." *New Statesman* 66 (6 December 1963) : 835.

Obituary. Lewis's creative writing is thin and immature perhaps because of an arrested childhood emotional development, but he was a first-rate literary critic who helped make English literature into a "humaner discipline."

11. Beaton, Cecil W. H., and Kenneth Tynan. *Persona Grata.* London: Allan Wingate, 1953; New York: Putnam and Co. 1954, pp. 68–69.

In this book Beaton took photographs of people, and Tynan wrote character sketches, which are arranged in alphabetical order. (But there is no photograph of C. S. Lewis.) In a combined sketch of C. Day Lewis and C. S. Lewis, the latter "combines the manner of Friar Tuck with the mind of St. Augustine." Tynan seems to have heard Lewis lecture or been one of his pupils, for he mentions among Lewis's failings that "his passion for ritual art ('applied art,' as he calls it) is such that one sometimes wonders by what right lyric poetry ever came into existence at all." Tynan calls Lewis a "direct descendant of the robust Macaulay school of literary criticism: . . . His principal intellectual weapon is gusto." (The majority of the people in the book, by the way, seem to be connected with the theater.)

12. Bechtel, Paul M. "Clyde S. Kilby: A Sketch." In *Imagination and the Spirit*, ed. Charles Huttar, pp. 467–477 [471–474, 475–476].

The volume is listed in § I.

This biographical account of Kilby includes his friendship with Lewis, his editing of books by Lewis, and his work on the C. S. Lewis Collection at Wheaton College.

13. Bennett, J. A. W. " 'Grete Clerk.' " In *Light on C. S. Lewis,* ed. Jocelyn Gibb, pp. 44–50.

The volume is listed in § I.

Almost all of this essay can be found in Bennett's *The Humane Medievalist* (listed immediately below), although the pamphlet considers also the present state of Medieval and Renaissance studies which is beyond this more personal essay. The largest addition of the essay to the pamphlet is a paragraph on Lewis's "pleasure in 'animated relaxation' " (p. 48), which included "composing, and enacting, a libretto for a mimic opera" one evening.

14. ———. *The Humane Medievalist: An Inaugural Lecture.* Cambridge: Cambridge University Press, 1965.

The second Professor of Medieval and Renaissance English in the University of Cambridge discusses, among other things, the scholarship of his predecessor, with praise. A recasting of the portions on Lewis appears as "Grete Clerk" in Jocelyn Gibb's *Light on C. S. Lewis.* The 32–page pamphlet includes a survey of the state of medieval and renaissance scholarship in the present, and concludes with some thoughts on the paperback revolution.

15. Bertram, James. "C. S. Lewis." *Comment* [New Zealand], 5 (April–May 1964): 11–12.

Obituary. Success as religious writer "largely due to his ability to retain and even to indulge the coarser basic perceptions of the average sensual man within the fabric of his beautifully spun dialectic." Oxford history volume and *Allegory of Love* landmarks of scholarship which "will be returned to as long as their subject is studied." Remarks on Lewis as tutor and his relations at Cambridge. "It is hard to believe, when two or three may be gathered together on any of the cornices of Mount Purgatory, that assertive and challenging voice will ever be stilled."

16. Brady, Charles A. "Unicorns at Oxford." *Books on Trial* 15 (October 1956): 59–60, 101–103.

    On Williams, Lewis, and the "Oxford Circle"; Lewis's approach to religion as the "way of imagination."

17. Bredvold, Louis I. "The Achievement of C. S. Lewis." Listed in § VI-A.

18. C., G. A. "Prof. C. S. Lewis." *Times*, 29 November 1963, p. 14f.

    A letter. Tribute to Lewis's work on Psalter revision committee.

19. "Cambridge Chair for Mr. C. S. Lewis." *Times*, 10 June 1954, p. 8d.

    Announcement of professorship.

20. Cameron, Eleanor. *The Green and Burning Tree*.

    Listed in § V-G; contains a biographical study of Lewis as a writer of children's books.

21. Carnell, Corbin Scott. *The Dialectic of Desire: C. S. Lewis' Interpretation of "Sehnsucht."* Ph.D. dissertation: University of Florida, 1960; University Microfilms, No. 60-1897.

    Carnell discusses the sensation which Lewis, in his autobiography, calls *joy*, pointing out the shadings of longing, melancholy, etc., which appear throughout literature, and connecting this with awe of the numinous (although Lewis does not claim so much for it). He defines Lewis's *Sehnsucht* as a "combination of joy and melancholy" or a joy which prevented him from behavioristic psychology and a reaction against romanticism. Lewis's fiction and poetry abound in images conveying *Sehnsucht*, especially the Narnia books, the trilogy, and *Till We Have Faces*; the nature of myth facilitates *Sehnsucht* because of its quality of numinous awe. He finds the dominant images in Lewis's fiction for *Sehnsucht* to be far-away hills, exotic gardens, distant islands, and special music (pp. 103–109).

    Carnell uses *Sehnsucht* as an instrument of literary analysis and also to examine ontological implications in Lewis's theological works. Despite the unpopularity of Romantic machinery, he believes contemporary literature has a preoccupation with this kind of longing. Lewis's "interpretation clarifies both the vitality and the danger of Romanticism as a source of vision." Extensive bibliography.

22. Carter, Lin. *Tolkien: A Look Behind "The Lord of the Rings."* New York: Ballantine Books, 1969, pp. 1, 5, 16–21, 85–86, 87, 88, 148.

    Discussion of the Inklings, slight (pp. 16–21); mention of Lewis's praise of E. R. Eddison (p. 148); and *passim*.

23. Cassell, George F. *Clive Staples Lewis*. Chicago: Chicago Literary Club, 1950. 27 pp. [Limited edition of 215 copies.]

    A paper read at the club 28 November 1949. A basic introduction to Lewis with long quotations from *Screwtape Letters* and several of his nonfiction religious books.

24. Cassidy, Katherine. "The Woman's Circle: C. S. Lewis, a Picture of the Man." *Twin Circle*, 20 September 1970, p. 9.

    A light biographical piece on Lewis based on materials in *Surprised by Joy, Letters to An American Lady, A Grief Observed,* and the memoir by his brother in *Letters of C. S. Lewis.*

25. Christopher, Joe R. "Who Were the Inklings?" *Tolkien Journal*, No. 15 (Summer 1972): 5, 7–10, 12–13.

    A survey of the materials on the founding, membership, and dissolution of the Inklings. Although the essay is colloquial in style, having been intended for reading at the First Tolkien Conference in 1968, it also has forty footnotes and a 1972 Addendum, bringing its biographical material up to date.

26. Coghill, Nevill. "The Approach to English." In *Light on C. S. Lewis*, ed. Jocelyn Gibb, pp. 51–66.

    The volume is listed in § I.

    Coghill offers a personal reminiscence of Lewis, starting from the beginning of their friendship in a discussion class in 1922. Their mutual love of much literature, their differences over

Restoration comedy, Lewis's formidableness and Ulster Protestant certainties, his wit, his Christianity in later days, his bearing of his wife's pain, his traditionalism in *Dymer* and other works, his style—all are briefly but specifically sketched.

27. "Commission on Revision of Psalter: Translation Errors to be Removed." *Times*, 28 November 1958, p. 6c.

Lewis listed as member of revision committee along with T. S. Eliot and six others.

28. "C. S. Lewis Dead; Author, Critic, 64." *New York Times*, 25 November 1963, p. 19.

Obituary; good précis of life, career; final paragraph a summary of Joy Davidman Gresham's life. Accompanied with a poor photograph of Lewis.

29. "C. S. Lewis Dies; Wrote 'The Screwtape Letters.'" *New York Herald Tribune*, 26 November 1963, p. 26.

Obituary; "not all its [*Screwtape Letters*'] readers were able to derive the meanings of his subsequent work, despite the clarity and wittiness of his prose."

30. Davies, Horton. "C. S. Lewis and B. L. Manning: Lay Champions of Christianity." *Religion in Life* 31 (Autumn 1962): 598–609. Reprinted as Chapter 7, "Distinguished Lay Preaching: B. L. Manning and C. S. Lewis," in *Varieties of English Preaching: 1900–1960*, pp. 164–193. Englewood Cliffs, N. J.: Prentice-Hall, 1963; London: Student Christian Movement Press, 1963.

Comparison between Lewis and a Cambridge historian who died in 1941. Similarities: scholarly eminence, use of their fields to show Christian contribution to culture; espousal of classical and orthodox Christianity; use of satire. Lewis's sermons more topical, intellectual, explicitly apologetical, less attached to church as institution; engage mind, not heart. (Oddly, Davies discusses "Learning in War-Time" rather than more typical sermons, "Transposition" and "The Weight of Glory," when he analyzes Lewis's sermonizing.)

31. "Defender of the Faith," *Time* 82 (6 December 1963) : 57.
Reprinted: *Bulletin of the New York C. S. Lewis Society*
2 (July 1971) : 5–6.

An obituary notice (with a reproduction of the 1947 cover
picture) : "C. S. Lewis was one of the church's minor prophets, a
defender of the faith who with fashionable urbanity justified
an unfashionable orthodoxy against the heresies of his time."

32. [Demarest, Michael.] "Editor's Preface."

Listed in § III-H; some comments on Lewis's personality and his
ability to lecture.

33. "Don *v.* Devil," *Time* 50 (8 September 1947) : 65–66, 68,
71–72, 74. Reprinted: *Bulletin of the New York C. S.
Lewis Society* 2 (July 1971) : 2–5.

Cover story; good précis of Lewis's career to date, some human
interest, discussion of books, and quoted excerpts.

34. Douglas, J. D. "The Legacy of C. S. Lewis." *Christianity
Today* 8 (20 December 1963) : 27.

Obituary; favorable assessment of career as lay theologian,
apologist. *Reflections on the Psalms* indicate Lewis had the
equipment of a "profound biblical and patristics scholar."

35. Doyle, Brian. *The Who's Who of Children's Literature*.
New York: Schocken Books, 1968. 380 pp. [178-179].

A biographical sketch with a few details about the Chronicles of
Narnia; a photograph of Lewis appears opposite p. 188. Among
other authors in the book are George MacDonald and J. R. R.
Tolkien—as well as such surprises as Bram Stoker. A section in
the back discusses illustrators, Pauline Baynes being on pp. 307–308.

36. Fuller, Muriel. "C. S. Lewis." In *More Junior Authors*,
p. 140. New York: H. W. Wilson, 1963.

Brief biography; some comments on *Screwtape Letters, Surprised
by Joy,* and the Narnia books.

37. Gardner, Helen. "Book Reviews."

Listed in § VI-B-44; nominally a review of *The Discarded Image*.

38. ———. *Clive Staples Lewis, 1898–1963*. London: Oxford University Press (from the *Proceedings of the British Academy*, Volume 51 [1965], 417–428), n.d.

Excellent brief biography (in a 12–page pamphlet) with discussions of several major books, especially *The Allegory of Love, Preface to "Paradise Lost,"* and the Oxford history volume. Gardner found Lewis a man who distrusted powerful emotions, including his own, so they tended to break out and color his work as apologist and scholar. Lewis gave impression of a powerful personality, arousing strong loyalties and antipathies. She discusses his intellectual development, his "northern" imagination and reliance on intensely personal imaginative responses to reading and introspection rather than extra-literary considerations as both a strength and a weakness. She mentions that Lewis and Tolkien established the syllabus for "The Final Honour School" in English literature at Oxford; claims resentment of other dons at his "hot-gospelling" deprived him of an Oxford chair; believes his writings after the move to his Cambridge chair more slight but also more balanced and genial in tone.

39. Fox, Adam (The Rev. Canon). "C. S. Lewis at the Breakfast Table." *CSL: The Bulletin of the New York C. S. Lewis Society* 3 (May 1972): 4–7.

An ancedotal account of a breakfast table in Magdalen College, Oxford—where ate Paul Benecke, J. A. Smith, C. S. Lewis, and Fox, before World War II. Also Fox recounts how Lewis ran him to be Professor of Poetry in 1938 (Fox won).

40. GoodKnight, Glen. "The Social History of the Inklings, J. R. R. Tolkien, C. S. Lewis, Charles Williams, 1939–1945." *Mythlore* 2 (Winter 1970): 7–9.

A description of the Inklings—their membership, their meetings, *etc.*—based primarily on Lewis's *Letters* (with W. H. Lewis's "Memoir"). The author gives no evidence for saying Dorothy Sayers attended any of the meetings (p. 7).

41. Gould, A. E. *Changed Men of Our Time: The Damascus Road in the Twentieth Century* (subtitle on the cover: *Eight Studies in Christian Conversion*). Derby: Peter Smith, 1964.

The second chapter tells the story of C. S. Lewis's conversion to Christianity, based primarily on Lewis's *Surprised by Joy* (pp. 14–25). The other chapters are on Douglas Hyde, C. E. M. Joad, John Rowland, Leonard Cheshire, Hugh Redwood, D. R. Davies, and "Vernon Charles" (stage name of Vernon Symonds). Interestingly, the summary of Joad's conversion mentions that Lewis's *The Abolition of Man* played a part in it (p. 33, citing a reference in Joad's *Recovery of Belief*).

42. Green, Roger Lancelyn. *Authors and Places: A Literary Pilgrimage*. London: B. T. Batsford, 1963; New York: Putnam, 1964.

A personal guide to authors and their locales in Britain, particularly but not exclusively authors of children's books. C. S. Lewis and J. R. R. Tolkien are mentioned on pp. 147–148, particularly for dragons and the setting of Tolkien's *Farmer Giles of Ham* on the Berkshire and Oxfordshire Downs. Two authors who influenced Lewis, E. Nesbit and George MacDonald, receive (as should be expected) more space.

43. ———. "C. S. Lewis: 1898–1963." *Aryan Path* 35 (March 1964): 98–103.

A memorial essay, which surveys Lewis's scholarly, religious, and fictional writings. Two paragraphs are given to Lewis's scholarship, one to his poetry, seven to his religious works (including *The Screwtape Letters* and *The Great Divorce*), four to his adult fiction, and four to The Chronicles of Narnia.

44. Griffiths, Dom Bede, O.S.B. *The Golden String*. London: Harvill Press, 1954; New York: P. J. Kenedy and Sons, 1955, pp. 30, 44, 49, 52, 56-57, 80.

This is Griffiths' autobiography and conversion story, extending through his priesthood as a Catholic monk. The onetime pupil and later friend of Lewis remarks on his influence and literary recommendations.

45. ———. "Light on C. S. Lewis."

Listed in § VI-C-2; a review containing some reminiscences.

46. Hart, Jeffrey. "C. S. Lewis: 1898–1963." *National Review* 16 (24 March 1964): 240, 242–243.

Obituary essay; stress on the process of Lewis's conversion and the difference between a convert and a person who always believed. The kind of authors the early Lewis turned to showed reality in its fulness as opposed to the thin, tinny quality of atheists like Shaw. Also reviews *Letters to Malcolm*.

47. Hooper, Walter. "Katherine Farrer." *CSL* 3 (April 1972): 6-7.

An obituary of one of Lewis's friends which turns into a description of the friendship between Austin and Katherine Farrer and "Jack" and Joy Lewis.

48. ———. "Preface." In C. S. Lewis, *Poems*.

Listed in § III-A; some biographical background.

49. ———."Preface." In C. S. Lewis, *Selected Literary Essays*, ed. Walter Hooper, pp. vii–xx. London and New York: Cambridge University Press, 1969.

Valuable biographical background on Lewis's days as Oxford student and his early career, using unpublished Lewis family papers as source. Quotation of verse notes by Nevill Coghill describing a student paper by Lewis on Spenser done for Professor George Gordon's discussion class.

50. ———. "Preface." In C. S. Lewis, *Studies in Medieval and Renaissance Literature*, ed. Walter Hooper, pp. vii–x. London and New York: Cambridge University Press, 1966.

Remarks on Lewis's habits as lecturer and the background of this collection, some previously unpublished. Some comments on Lewis's methods as scholar, and on what he had planned to write at the time of his death.

51. ————. "To the Martlets." In *C. S. Lewis: Speaker and Teacher*, ed. Carolyn Keefe, pp. 37–62.

Volume listed in this section.

The Martlets Society (1892–present) is an Oxford literary group, consisting of twelve undergraduates. Lewis was elected secretary in 1919, and president later that year (which position he held until the middle of 1921). Hooper surveys all of the minutes of the Society which refer to Lewis's papers (his last were in 1940), as well as making some comments on Lewis's lectures on philosophy in 1924. In Lewis's *Letters* comments to supplement this account of the Martlets may be found in those letters of 21 January 1921 (Geoffrey Bles edition, p. 53), 1 July 1921 (p. 63), and undated—between 22 November 1923 and February 1924 (p. 91).

52. Huttar, C. A. "Apostle to Twentieth Century Skeptics." *Eternity* 15 (February 1964): 35-37.

Obituary, with a favorable analysis of Lewis's apologetic message on five issues of contemporary faith.

53. *Illustrated London News* 243 (27 July 1963): 120.

Portrait with biographical caption.

54. Kawano, Roland M. "The Impact of Charles Williams' Death on C. S. Lewis." In *Mythcon I Proceedings*, ed. Glen GoodKnight, pp. 27–28.

The volume is listed in § I.

A gathering together of various sources on the Lewis-Williams friendship and the effect of Williams's death on Lewis's idea of death. A misreading of one source turns Williams into an abstainer from liquor in paragraph five.

55. Keefe, Carolyn. "A Case Study of C. S. Lewis' Ten Radio Talks on Love." Unpublished M.A. thesis: Temple University, 1968. x + 275 pp.

An excellent thesis (in Speech), much more like a dissertation than the usual M. A. work. There are five chapters: I. The Life of C. S. Lewis (pp. 1–18), II. Production of C. S. Lewis' Talks on Love (pp. 19–29), III. Rhetorical Criticism of C. S. Lewis' Talks on Love (pp. 30–156), IV. Presentation of C. S. Lewis' Talks on Love (pp. 157–161), and V. Summary and Conclusions (pp. 162–166). The Appendix (pp. 167–267) is an elaborate and full comparison of the two texts involved: a printed version of Lewis's tapes and the tapes as cut for radio use. Bibliography (pp. 270–275). *Note*: Three parts of this thesis appear in Keefe's *C. S. Lewis: Speaker and Teacher* (immediately below). The "Bibliography of Oral Material" in the book (pp. 143–144) is based on a list in the "Preface" to the thesis (pp. iv–v). The second part, "Broadcasting to America," of Keefe's "On the Air" in the book (pp. 122–127) is taken without much change from two subsections of chapter II of the thesis, "Initiating the Talks" and "Taping the Talks" (pp. 19–25). And "Notes on Lewis's Voice" in the book (pp. 131–136) is a much condensed and nontechnical version of a sub-subsection of chapter III of the thesis: one of the major divisions of this chapter is "Pronuntiatio: Delivery of the Speeches"; the subdivision of this division used for the essay in the book is titled "Lewis' Use of His Voice" (pp. 126–156), which is in turn (in the thesis) divided into seven sub-sub-subsections.

56. —— (ed.). *C. S. Lewis: Speaker and Teacher*. Grand Rapids, Michigan: Zondervan Publishing House, 1971.

Contents: Thomas Howard, "Foreword"; "Preface"; Clyde S. Kilby, "The Creative Logician Speaking"; Walter Hooper, "To the Martlets"; Stuart Barton Babbage, "To the Royal Air Force"; George Bailey, "In the University"; Owen Barfield, "In Conversation"; Carolyn Keefe, "On the Air"; Carolyn Keefe, "Notes on Lewis's Voice"; "Notes"; "Bibliography of Oral Material."

The seven essays (called chapters in the book) are listed separately in this section. The bibliography of oral material is *not* a list of Lewis's recordings (none are listed) but a list of books by him which contain material originally presented orally. Thomas Howard's brief foreword contains an account of his one "brief visit to [Lewis's] house at Headington Quarry a few months before he died" (p. 7).

57. ———. "Notes on Lewis's Voice." In *C. S. Lewis: Speaker and Teacher*, ed. Carolyn Keefe, pp. 131–136.

Volume listed in this section.

An analysis, based on the recording for "The C. S. Lewis Program" (the radio talks which were published as *The Four Loves*), of the rate of Lewis's speech, his volume, his pitch and resonance, and his breathing.

58. ———. "On the Air." In *C. S. Lewis: Speaker and Teacher*, ed. Carolyn Keefe, pp. 111–127.

Volume listed in this section.

The essay is subdivided into two sections. The first, "Broadcasting to Britain," deals with the four series of broadcast talks made during World War II, which were collected as *Broadcast Talks* (*The Case for Christianity* in the United States), *Christian Behaviour*, and *Beyond Personality*. The author surveys the reviews and the letters to BBC's *The Listener*. The second section, "Broadcasting to America," discusses the 1958 radio talks which appeared in print (in somewhat different form) as *The Four Loves*. Here the information is mainly biographical, about Lewis's taping of the talks.

59. Kilby, Clyde S. "The Creative Logician Speaking." In *C. S. Lewis: Speaker and Teacher*, ed. Carolyn Keefe, pp. 15–34.

Volume listed in this section.

Dr. Kilby begins with an account of his one meeting with Lewis (pp. 15–16), moves to a sketch of Lewis's appearance and personality, including his speaking dialect (pp. 17–19), discusses his imaginative abilities (pp. 19–21) and his rationalistic side, including much of the argument which led to Lewis's conversion (pp. 21–29), and finally suggests a fusion of imagination and reason (pp. 30–34). Although a number of the examples used in the essay involve speech in one way or another, the author is attempting more of an introduction to Lewis's thought than to his talk.

60. ————. "Preface." In C. S. Lewis, *A Mind Awake: An Anthology of C. S. Lewis*, ed. Clyde S. Kilby, pp. 7–18. London: Geoffrey Bles, 1968; New York: Harcourt, Brace & World, 1969.

Biographical, including some human interest: an affectionate portrait of Lewis, likened by Kilby to Aslan of the Narnia stories. Remarks on the compilation of the anthology.

61. ————. "Tolkien, Lewis, and Williams." In *Mythcon I Proceedings*, ed. Glen GoodKnight, pp. 3–4.

The volume is listed in § I.

A consideration of the personal relationships between Tolkien, Lewis, and Williams; of the literary relationships between them; and of the common elements of their friendship and work. "The two elements common to all three of these men are a deep-seated Christianity and a vivid imagination." The address contains a few citations from unpublished letters.

62. ————. "A Visit with C. S. Lewis." *Kodon* [Wheaton College literary magazine], 8 (December 1953): 11, 28, 30.

Account of Kilby's first visit with Lewis in his rooms at Oxford.

63. Kranz, Gisbert. "C. S. Lewis." In *Europas christliche Literatur 1500–1960*, pp. 425–432. Aschaffenburg: Paul Pattloch Verlag, 1961. Reissued as *Europas christliche Literatur von 1500 bis heute*, pp. 425–432; bibliography, 600–601. Paderborn: Verlag Ferdinand Schöningh, 1968. Also pp. 119, 229, 337, 341, 342, 421, 424.

Following a section on Chesterton, Lewis is said to be in Chesterton's tradition. Lewis's conversion is traced, and his fundamental Christian position is established with quotations from *Mere Christianity*, *The Great Divorce*, and other works. The main themes of Lewis's imaginative writing are said to deal with temptation and the struggle with the devil—especially in his "scientific" and "technical" guises. The simplicity and directness of Lewis's style is praised. The essay ends on Lewis's emphasis on common, not sectarian, Christianity. (We wish to thank Henry Noel for help in preparing this summary.)

64. ———. "C. S. Lewis." *Hochland* 60 (1968): 772–779.

A general survey of Lewis's life and works, much like the same author's more limited survey, "Neue Schönheit und neue Tragik" listed below. The biography comes first; the fiction is discussed briefly, then the scholarly works, and finally the Christian. (We wish to thank Henry Noel for help in preparing this summary.)

65. ———. "Neue Schönheit und neue Tragik: C. S. Lewis nach 1954." *Wort und Wahrheit* 24 (January–February 1969): 55-63.

This essay—"New Beauty and New Tragedy"—is a survey of Lewis's later life and works, much like (and occasionally in the same language as) Kranz's more general survey, "C. S. Lewis" in *Hochland*, listed in this section. The biographical opening has a minor error, that Joy Davidman's husband was dead before she remarried. Based on a quotation from *Il Paradiso* in *A Grief Observed*, Kranz compares Joy to Beatrice. This is followed by a survey of the later fiction, scholarly works, and religious writings.

66. ———. "Die Stillbare Sehnsucht: Der Dichter und Essayist, C. S. Lewis." *Stimmen der Zeit* 85 (July 1960): 286–301.

"The Secret Longing." At first, a survey of Lewis's techniques in presenting Christian truths: modest, appealing to his own personal experience, and satiric toward liberalism, humanism, and the teachings of Freud and Marx. Then a biographical approach through Lewis's accounts of his longing and resulting joy (Sehnsucht and Freude). The fiction reflects these feelings, although the fantasy might mislead the reader about Lewis's seriousness—about man's responsibility for his salvation or damnation. But the magnetic quality of Lewis's works lies in the way they speak to man's deepest longing and show him in whom his longing may be satisfied. (We wish to thank Carol J. Kraft of Wheaton College for help in preparing this summary).

67. Kruener, Harry H. "A Tribute to C. S. Lewis." *Religion in Life* 34 (Summer 1965): 451–461.

The first of four sections of this obituary is a summary of Lewis's life (the author seems not to have heard of Lewis's appointment at Cambridge) ; the following three sections are a survey, and in part a summary, of Lewis's religious writings. Kruener puts emphasis on Lewis's fight against naturalism and theological liberalism.

68. Kuhl, Rand, "Owen Barfield in Southern California." *Mythlore* 1 (October 1969) : 8–10.

A report of Barfield's talk on "C. S. Lewis and His Friends," given at Redlands University in the Spring of 1969. Partially anecdotal, the talk also suggested some of the unifying ideas of the Inklings.

69. Lawlor, John. "The Tutor and the Scholar." In *Light on C. S. Lewis*, ed. Jocelyn Gibb, pp. 67–85.

The volume is listed in § I.

Lawlor begins with his impressions of Lewis the tutor as Lewis's pupil (pp. 68–77) : Lewis's impersonality, his dialecticalism (learned from the Great Knock), his conservatism, and his dislike for tutoring. Assessing Lewis's scholarship (pp. 77–80), Lawlor suggests that *The Allegory of Love* is his best, and one with Bradley's *Shakespearian Tragedy*, Ker's *Epic and Romance*, and Lowes's *Road to Xanadu* in that it handles a large and important subject in a way to establish the basic questions for debate. *English Literature in the Sixteenth Century* he finds cramped in topic by its chronological limits, and *A Preface to "Paradise Lost"* outside of evaluative criticism and partaking of what Lewis himself called the personal heresy. The essay concludes with a few brief remarks about Lewis's fiction (p. 81) and an outline of the interest in medievalism in England (pp. 82–84).

70. Lewis, W. H. "Letters of C. S. Lewis." *Saturday Review*, 4 April 1964, p. 22.

A letter asking for copies of C. S. Lewis's letters—an early step in W. H. Lewis's editing of his brother's letters.

71. ———. "Memoir of C. S. Lewis." Prefacing *Letters of C. S. Lewis*, ed. W. H. Lewis, pp. 1–26. London: Geoffrey Bles, 1966; New York: Harcourt, Brace and World, 1966.

Excellent personal memoir by Lewis's older brother giving insight into Lewis's childhood, his relations with his father, the strange menage he set up with a surrogate mother, his personal habits during his scholarly years at Oxford, and his warmly happy marriage to Joy Davidman; a description of him as tutor by a student, and a description of his literary circle of friends, the "Inklings."

72. Lindskoog, Kathryn. "Farewell To Shadowlands: C. S. Lewis on Death."

Listed in § I; some biographical references including reports of Lewis's appearances after death.

73. ———. "Introducing C. S. Lewis: Sincerity Personified." In *Mythcon II Proceedings*, ed. Glen GoodKnight, pp. 29–32.

The volume is listed in § I.

Note: The material in this essay was used by Lindskoog, with the same title and in much the same form, as Chapter 1 of her *C. S. Lewis: Mere Christian* (Glendale, California: Regal Books, 1973), which appeared after the terminal date for this Checklist.

A summary of Lewis's life, based primarily on *Surprised by Joy* and *Letters of C. S. Lewis* (including W. H. Lewis's "Memoir"). Some additional facts appear, and Lindskoog recounts her one meeting with Lewis.

74. "Marriages." *Times* [London], 24 December 1956, p. 8b.

Announcement of the Lewis and Mrs. J. Gresham marriage; mentions Mrs. Lewis is "now a patient in the Churchill Hospital, Oxford," and requests no letters be sent.

75. McNaspy, C. J. *America*.

Listed in § VI-B-45; a review of *Letters to Malcolm* which is also an obituary.

76. Masterman, Margaret. "C. S. Lewis: the Author and the Hero." *Twentieth Century* [London], 158 (December 1955): 539–548.

In this essay based on *Surprised by Joy*, Mrs. R. B. Braithwaite points out the amount of hatred and fear which Lewis absorbed from his environment (which appears in his later writings) and also the mystical parallels to his experience of joy; her title indicates the distinction between the author of the autobiography and the hero of it.

77. Oury, Scott. "The Value of Something Other . . ."

Listed in § I; some discussion of *Sehnsucht*.

78. "Paperback Publications: University Presses in the Field." *Times Literary Supplement*, 4 March 1960, p. 147.

Contains a comment that Lewis has no original work in paperback, although his *Allegory of Love* has been reprinted.

79. "People." *Time* 74 (4 August 1959) : 31.

Lewis among those setting up a grant for Biblical or classical studies at Trinity College, Oxford, in memory of Msgr. Ronald Knox.

80. Phillips, J. B. *Ring of Truth: A Translator's Testimony*. New York: Macmillan Company, 1967. 125 pp.

In the section near the end, "Some Personal Experience," pp. 117–119 (part of the last chapter, "The Truth of the Resurrection"), Phillips tells of C. S. Lewis appearing to him twice after Lewis's death: ". . . he 'appeared' sitting in a chair within a few feet of me, and spoke a few words which were particularly relevant to the difficult circumstances through which I was passing" (p. 118).

81. ————. "Translator's Foreword." In *The New Testament in Modern English*. New York: Macmillan Company, 1960, p. xi.

Lewis is given credit for early encouragement of Phillips's work and for supplying the title *Letters to Young Churches* for the first published part of Phillips's translation.

82. "Poetry and Politics." *Time* 77 (24 February 1961) : 58.

Oxford poetry election which C. Day Lewis won and C. S. Lewis lost.

83. "Prof. C. S. Lewis: Scholar and Christian Apologist."
    Times, 25 November 1963, p. 14c.

    A full-column death notice, accompanied by a picture. The notice
    is more personal than most such announcements, with this
    conclusion: "He was prodigally generous with his money, and with
    his time in scholarly matters; he was indomitably courageous and
    vulnerably proud. He was not easy to know, hiding reserve under a
    manner bluff, hearty, sometimes hectoring, occasionally clumsy
    in personal relationships." An earlier comment about his poor
    abilities in committee work is also interesting. But most of the
    notice is, of course, factual—and one fact, that Lewis had served
    at one time as Vice President of Magdalen College, Oxford, is not
    widely known.

84. Raine, Kathleen. "From a Poet." In *Light on C. S. Lewis*,
    ed. Jocelyn Gibb, pp. 102–105.

    The volume is listed in § I.

    A pleasant, anecdotal account of Raine's friendship with Lewis
    in his Cambridge days: his imagining of how Dryden would have
    written Blake's "The Tyger," his view of literary criticism
    (entirely useless), his (and Raine's) view of the ends of art as
    religious.

85. Ready, William. *The Tolkien Relation*. Chicago: Henry
    Regnery, 1968, pp. 12, 17, 19–34, 38, 41, 44, 58, 67, 73,
    78–79.

    Discussion of the Inklings, stressing their differences (pp. 19–32).
    Sees Lewis as an unhappy man—"the scape of his own goat
    since childhood"—with *The Allegory of Love* his only first-class
    book. Other remarks *passim*. Slight.

86. "Report Card." *Time* 59 (19 May 1952): 72.

    Report with quotations on Lewis's remarks at meeting of Britain's
    Library Association on the controversy of fairy tales versus
    "realistic" stories.

87. "Scholarships at Oxford." *Times*, 14 December 1916, p. 5d.

    Lewis, listed as C. L. Lewis (Malvern), given as winning a classics
    scholarship to University College.

88. "Scholar to Be Honored." *New York Times*, 23 July 1958, p. 11.

    Lewis joins appeal at Trinity College, Oxford, to establish a prize or scholarship in Biblical or classical studies in memory of Msgr. Ronald Knox.

89. Simpson, Ashley. "C. S. Lewis: A Crusading Intellect." *Southern Churchman* 112 (14 December 1946): 5–6.

    Personal sketch, quotations, based on one or more interviews.

90. Soper, David Wesley. "An Interview with C. S. Lewis." *Zion's Herald*, 14 and 21 January 1948, pp. 28-29, 43, 60-61, 71.

    An account of a pleasant if superficial conversation: after opening compliments, Soper discusses with Lewis such topics as reunion with Rome and Lewis's methods for getting so much writing done.

91. Starr, Nathan C. "C. S. Lewis: A Personal Memoir." *Unicorn* 2 (Spring 1972): 8–11.

    Starr recounts his meetings with Lewis in 1948, 1960, and 1963. Included in the essay is a photograph of Lewis and Starr taken by Starr's wife, and a note from Lewis to her. On p. 8, as a frontispiece to the essay, is a portrait of Lewis by Tim Kirk.

92. Thompson, Claude H. "The Unmaking of an Atheist." *Emory University Quarterly* 12 (October 1956): 148–156.

    A brief summary of Lewis's biography, ideas, and books, occasioned by the publication of *Surprised by Joy*. Sometimes the facts are misleading—for example, the confusion of Lewis's real and adopted mothers, on p. 155.

93. "University News: Prof. Lewis Resigns Cambridge Chair." *Times*, 14 October 1963, p. 12d.

    Resignation from Magdalene College; quotations from Lewis on his heart problem.

94. Wain, John. *Sprightly Running*: *Part of an Autobiography*.
London: Macmillan and Co., 1963; New York: St.
Martin's Press, 1963.

The latter part of the chapter titled "Oxford" describes Lewis
(Wain's tutor), Charles Williams, and some others (pp. 136–157);
"A Literary Chapter" includes an account of Wain's ideologically
awkward membership in the Inklings (pp. 179–185). Cf.
Lewis's letter, "Wain's Oxford," *Encounter* 20 (January 1963):
81 [Hooper's Bibliography, G45], for distinctions between his
personal friendship with Dorothy Sayers and R. L. Green, his
differences with Roy Campbell, and the Inkling circle; with
Wain's reply immediately following.

95. Walsh, Chad. "C. S. Lewis: The Man and the Mystery." In
Shadows of Imagination, ed. Mark R. Hillegas, pp. 1–14.
The volume is listed in § III-A.

This essay is a revision of "The Elusively Solid C. S. Lewis"—see
that title (next in this section) for annotation. This revision omits
two paragraphs, substantial parts of two others, and a few phrases.

96. ———. "The Elusively Solid C. S. Lewis." *Good Work* 30
(Winter 1967): 17–24.

This essay is a psychological probe of Lewis on the basis, primarily,
of the *Letters of C. S. Lewis* and Gibb's *Light on C. S. Lewis*
(the latter listed in § I). Letters show the Lewis we've known all
along and the "predominantly static quality" of his faith. Agrees
with Owen Barfield's essay that Lewis deliberately set himself
in opposition to today's subjective emphasis with great success in
clarity and logic but paying a certain price in occasional shrillness, a
lacking of awareness in the subtle sense of paradox, and a certain
tender vagueness in his mythopoesie. *A Grief Observed* indicates a
possible change; it is a raw cry of grief. (For the revised form
of this essay, see immediately above.)

97. West, Richard, (ed.). "Letters of C. S. Lewis to E. Vinaver."
Orcrist, No. 6 (Winter 1971–1972): 3–6, 24.

While Vinaver was a Visiting Professor at the University of
Wisconsin, Madison, he gave West six letters which Lewis had

sent him or his wife—one of 1935, five of 1959. West introduces
each letter and footnotes all obscurities. The material discussed
relates primarily to Malory. On p. 24 the first of the letters is
photographically reproduced.

98. ———. "Tolkien in the Letters of C. S. Lewis." *Orcrist* 1
(March 1968): 2–16.

As the title indicates, this essay discusses J. R. R. Tolkien by
means of passages in C. S. Lewis's letters which mention him; most,
but not all, of the letters are those collected by W. H. Lewis in
Letters of C. S. Lewis.

III. Fiction and Poetry

A. General

1. Barfield, Owen. "C. S. Lewis."
   Listed in § II; contains some brief comments on Lewis's poetry and on *Till We Have Faces*.

2. Beattie, Sister Mary Josephine. *The Humane Medievalist.*
   Listed in § V-B; some discussion of Lewis's lyric verse.

3. Brady, Charles A. "Introduction to Lewis." *America* 71 (27 May 1944): 213–214; "C. S. Lewis: II" (10 June 1944): 269–270. Reprinted respectively in *The Bulletin of the New York C. S. Lewis Society* 3 (November and December 1971): 6-8 and 6-7.
   An allusive study of Lewis's works up to 1944, neatly phrased, analogue-filled. It discusses the psychology of damnation in *Screwtape* and *Pilgrim's Regress*; teleology in *Perelandra*; it disagrees with critics who label Lewis Calvinist. The second installment discusses the trilogy and his literary "whispering gallery." Considers Lewis's eldila more artistically successful than Milton's angels, and Weston's transition into the Un-Man the most terrifying instance of diabolical possession since Benson's *Necromancers*. Perhaps the two unique suggestions of the author are that *Out of the Silent Planet* is an orthodox *Candide* and that the green color of Lewis's Venerians is due to that of Edgar Rice Burroughs's Martians. See also Lewis's letter to Brady of 29 October 1944 (in *Letters of C. S. Lewis*) which denies the latter suggestion.

4. Braude, Nan. "Sion and Parnassus: Three Approaches to Myth." *Mythlore* 1 (January 1969): 6-8.

Lewis is an allegorist; Tolkien, a myth-maker; and Williams, a symbolist using religious symbols from this world.

5. Christopher, J. R. "In the C. S. Lewis Tradition: Two Short Stories by Anthony Boucher." *Mythlore* 2 (Winter 1971): 25.

An eight-paragraph note discussing the relationship of Boucher's "The Quest for St. Aquin" and "Balaam" to Lewis's *The Screwtape Letters* and *Out of the Silent Planet,* respectively. These are listed in § III-I below.

6. ———. *The Romances of Clive Staples Lewis.* Ph.D. dissertation: University of Oklahoma, 1969; University Microfilms, No. 70-4462.

A study of Lewis's narratives, from the verse *Dymer* on. Using the terminology of Northrop Frye—romance, anatomy, novel, confession—it attempts to place each work as to type or combination of types, to discuss the generic tradition of each work, and to analyze its artistic structure. It concludes that *Out of the Silent Planet* and *Till We Have Faces* are Lewis's most successful works as art. Several appendices, including one on Lewis's short stories. The annotated bibliography is, of course, subsumed in the present work.

7. ———. "A Theological Triolet." *Bulletin of the New York C. S. Lewis Society,* 2 (September 1971): 4–5.

An introduction on the triolet form, with some English examples, followed by an explication of Lewis's "Divine Justice."

8. Courtney, Charles R. "The Religious Philosophy of C. S. Lewis."

Listed in § IV-B; two literary comments cited.

9. Cunningham, Don Roger. "D. H. Lawrence and C. S. Lewis: A Study in Contrasts."

Listed in § V-A; contains some discussion of *The Pilgrim's Regress, Perelandra,* and *That Hideous Strength.*

10. Detambel, Linda. "J. R. R. Tolkien and C. S. Lewis: A Personal Perspective." Student honors paper: Wheatoon College (Illinois), 1972; [Available in the C. S. Lewis Collection at Wheaton College.]

Parallels in the theories of the meaning of fairy stories in Tolkien and myth in Lewis, and in the moral actions of *The Lord of the Rings* and *Perelandra*; a consideration of the Christian elements of the Chronicles of Narnia follows, in which it is suggested that "The reason that the children cannot return to Narnia when they get 'too old,' and the reason that Susan ceases to be a friend of Narnia[,] is that whoever does not 'receive the Kingdom of God like a child shall not enter it' (Mark 10:15)" (p. 33)—Detambel doubts that Lewis consciously intended the application but finds it never-the-less valuable.

11. Fowler, Helen. "C. S. Lewis: Sputnik or Dinosaur?" *Approach*, No. 32 (Summer 1959): 8–14.

A highly generalized comparison of Lewis's writing to those that are literarily acceptable at the present: the two main differences are his impersonal art (that is, Lewis is not concerned with art which spends all its time in reflecting inner, emotional twinges) and his tone which conveys none of the division between the artist and society which is typically modern (*tone* seems an odd approach to this point, but the author justifies it).

12. Frye, Northrop. *Anatomy of Criticism: Four Essays.* Princeton, N. J.: Princeton University Press, 1957, p. 117.

Frye comments that "the sophisticated allegories of Charles Williams and C. S. Lewis . . . are largely based on the formulas of the Boy's Own Paper." This is in the context of mythopoeic writers basing their works on naive dramas or naive romances. Mythopoeic writing itself Frye sees as a product of a recondite mind, as an allegory designed to reveal, not disguise myth, and as an example of one type of literature which is an "important source of supply for archetypal criticism."

13. Fuller, Edmund. *Books with Men Behind Them.* New York: Random House, 1962.

Over two-fifths of this book of essays is of interest to the student of the Inklings: "A Note on the Fantastic" (pp. 135–142), "The Christian Spaceman: C. S. Lewis" (pp. 143–168), "The Lord of the Hobbits: J. R. R. Tolkien" (pp. 169–196), and "Many Dimensions: the Images of Charles Williams" (pp. 197–234). The essay on Lewis (as its title implies) emphasizes the Ransom trilogy: a general introduction to the plots and the Christian message (pp. 143–145, 151–163). More briefly the essay touches on Lewis's life and ideas (pp. 145–151) and, in two afternotes, the Chronicles of Narnia (pp. 163–165) and *Till We Have Faces* (pp. 165–167). (An earlier form of this chapter on Lewis appeared as an essay in *Horizon*; listed in § III-D.)

14. ———. "Speaking of Books." *New York Times Book Review*, 12 January 1964, § 7, p. 2.

Beginning from the fact of Lewis's death, Fuller discusses fantasy generally (with quotations from Tolkien's "On Fairy Stories"), ending with praise for Lewis, Williams, Tolkien, George Macdonald, and Walter M. Miller, Jr. The right column of the page has three quotations from Lewis (from *Out of the Silent Planet, Perelandra,* and *An Experiment in Criticism*); the left column quotes two poems by George Macdonald and one by Tolkien.

15. Gibbons, Stella. "Imaginative Writing." In *Light on C. S. Lewis*, ed. Jocelyn Gibb, pp. 86–101.

This volume is listed in § I.

An impressionistic and superficial survey of Lewis's major fiction: the Ransom Trilogy, *Till We Have Faces,* and the Chronicles of Narnia. The section on the Ransom Trilogy (pp. 87–94) appreciates Lewis's inventiveness and faults his implicit attitude toward women. That on *Till We Have Faces* (pp. 94-97) retells the plot and comments, "the severity is apparent on every page, and I do think that it prevented the book from having a wide appeal." Gibbons also finds the symbolic meaning puzzling. The section on the Chronicles of Narnia (pp. 98–101) appreciates the coziness of *The Lion, the Witch and the Wardrobe*, and comments that "the allegory is much stronger and more plain" in the following books (evidently Gibbons did not see the point of the death and rebirth of Aslan).

16. Gleason, Philip. "Our New Age of Romanticism." Listed in § V-A.

17. Green, Roger Lancelyn. *C. S. Lewis*. London: Bodley Head, 1963.

This Bodley Head Monograph is part of a series of small books on authors of children's books. Green gives a biography with emphasis on childhood and the reading of children's books (drawn, for the most part, from *Surprised by Joy*) and then discusses the first two books of the Ransom trilogy and the Chronicles of Narnia. The major critical interest lies in the sources suggested for some of the fictional devices and ideas, and some of Lewis's comments on his fiction—for example, that the Narnia books were not planned as a unit (pp. 47–48). A selective bibliography lists some librarians' papers on the Narnian sequence.

18. ———. "Introduction."

Listed in § V-G; an introduction to *Alice's Adventures* which includes two passing references to Lewis as a writer.

19. ———, and Alastair Fowler. "Notes to *After Ten Years*." In C. S. Lewis, *Of Other Worlds: Essays and Stories*, ed. Walter Hooper, pp. 146–148. London: Geoffrey Bles, 1966; New York: Harcourt, Brace and World, 1966.

Notes by two friends of Lewis (based on conversations with him) about his possible intentions for the unpublished, incomplete novel included in this book.

20. Haigh, John D. "The Fiction of C. S. Lewis." Unpublished Ph.D. dissertation: The University of Leeds, 1962. 443 pp. [Available in the Wheaton College (Ill.) C. S. Lewis Collection.]

One of the two or three best studies of Lewis's fiction, if not *the* best: weak only in its discussion of *Till We Have Faces*, which is considered an allegory. Haigh normally spends one chapter on an introduction to the fictional genre and then one on Lewis's example—for instance, "The Planetary Romance" (pp. 143-164) precedes three chapters (one to each volume) on the Ransom Trilogy. In his literary analyses of works, he often has a firm sense of structure, as in the division of *The Screwtape Letters* into sections on the World (Letters 10-13), the Flesh (Letters 17-22), and the Devil (Letters 23-28) (p. 81). Close critical readings appear, as in the discussion of the syntax and imagery of the passage in *Perelandra* in which Ransom is recovering after coming out of the caverns (pp. 206-210). The next-to-last chapter compares Lewis to Mauriac and Greene as a religious novelist, but perhaps more interesting is an earlier listing of likenesses between Lewis and J. R. R. Tolkien: (1) "a distinctive sense of values" in which honor is more important than the typically modern emphasis on sincerity, (2) "a fondness for populating an invented world with 'a diversity of creatures,' " (3) "a taste for the 'peculiar flavour or quality' of places and objects"—a quality in Lewis which Haigh brings out clearly elsewhere, and (4) "the use made of traditional narrative patterns" (p. 124). Twenty-one chapters, six appendices, notes, and bibliography.

21. Hannay, Margaret. "C. S. Lewis' Theory of Mythology." *Mythlore* 1 (January 1969): 14–24.

This essay, an introduction to her three essays on the Ransom Trilogy (listed in § III-D) and her one on *Till We Have Faces* (in § III-H) is only slightly modified from the introductory chapter of her M. A. thesis (listed immediately below). Hannay discusses Lewis's approaches to myth—from a Christian perspective, from the point of view of literary criticism (a "higher form of allegory"), and as it is based on *Sehnsucht*.

22. ———. "Mythology in the Novels of C. S. Lewis." M.A. thesis: College of St. Rose (Albany, N. Y.), 1970. 101 pp.

Analyzes Lewis's theory of myth and its operation in the four adult novels. Contrasts Lewis's insistence on objective correlative to Bultmann's view. Regards *Till We Have Faces* as his best novel and most pure myth. See Hannay's essays related to this material: in § III-D, "The Mythology of *Out of the Silent Planet*," "The

Mythology of *Perelandra*, and "Arthurian and Cosmic Myth in *That Hideous Strength*"; and in § III-H, "Orual: The Search for Justice."

23. Hart, Lida Dabney Adams. *C. S. Lewis's Defense of Poesie.*
Listed in § V-A; a good survey of the verse and fiction is included.

24. Hillegas, Mark R. (ed.) *Shadows of Imagination: The Fantasies of C. S. Lewis, J. R. R. Tolkien, and Charles Williams.* Carbondale and Edwardsville: Southern Illinois University Press (Crosscurrents/Modern Critiques series), 1969.
Contents: Harry T. Moore, "Preface"; Mark R. Hillegas, "Introduction"; Chad Walsh, "C. S. Lewis: The Man and the Mystery"; J. B. S. Haldane, "Auld Hornie, F.R.S."; Robert Plank, "Some Psychological Aspects of Lewis's Trilogy"; Mark R. Hillegas, "*Out of the Silent Planet* as Cosmic Voyage"; Charles Moorman, " 'Now Entertain Conjecture of a Time'—The Fictive Worlds of C. S. Lewis and J. R. R. Tolkien"; Clyde S. Kilby, "Meaning in *The Lord of the Rings*"; Daniel Hughes, "Pieties and Giant Forms in *The Lord of the Rings*"; Gunnar Urang, "Tolkien's Fantasy: The Phenomenology of Hope"; George P. Winship, Jr., "The Novels of Charles Williams"; Alice Mary Hadfield, "The Relationship of Charles Williams' Working Life to his Fiction"; W. R. Irwin, "Christian Doctrine and the Tactics of Romance: The Case of Charles Williams"; Patricia Meyer Spacks, "Charles Williams: The Fusion of Fiction"; Notes; Index.
The essays on Lewis are listed as follows: Walsh, § II; Haldane, Plank, and Hillegas, § III-D; and Moorman, § III-G. Occasional references to Lewis in the other essays may be traced through the book's index.

25. Hook, Martha Boren. "Christian Meaning in the Novels of C. S. Lewis." M. A. thesis: Southern Methodist University, 1959. 95 pp.
A thesis which has a number of errors but also moments of insight. Most of it involves paraphrases, stressing Christian and moral meaning (as the title suggests). Examples of errors: *Dymer*

is called Lewis's first book (p. 2), *Phantastes* is called a book of poetry (p. 4), Macdonald in *The Great Divorce* is called an angel (p. 50). Also, the term *allegory* is used loosely throughout. On the other hand, the author has a good analysis of John's statement to Mother Kirk in *The Pilgrim's Regress*, "I have come to give myself up" (p. 22); and she suggests the reason for the name *Maia* in *Till We Have Faces* is that the Hindu *maya* stands for the illusion of physical reality—thus Orual/Maia (physical reality, the finite) is set in contrast to Psyche (soul, the infinite) (p. 80). A number of Biblical allusions are also pointed out. 6-page bibliography.

26. Hooper, Walter. "C. S. Lewis." *The Franciscan* 9 (September 1967): 162–176. Excerpts reprinted in *The Bulletin of the New York C. S. Lewis Society* 3 (February 1972): 5–6.

    Discussion of Lewis's better-known books, with an emphasis on *Perelandra* and the Narnia books. Mention of still-unpublished materials, especially juvenilia.

27. ———. "Preface." In C. S. Lewis, *Of Other Worlds: Essays and Stories*, ed. Walter Hooper, pp. v–x. London: Geoffrey Bles, 1966; New York: Harcourt, Brace and World, 1966.

    Discussion by Hooper of Lewis's boyhood stories on "Boxen" and other unpublished juvenilia, and its relation to later Lewisian writings. Speaks of an adult unpublished [and unfinished] romance about Dr. Ransom falling chronologically between *Out of the Silent Planet* and *Perelandra* but which, according to Hooper, has no theological theme. Remarks on the volume's essays and stories.

28. ———. "Preface." In C. S. Lewis, *Poems*, ed. Walter Hooper, pp. v–ix. London: Geoffrey Bles, 1964; New York: Harcourt, Brace and Co., 1965.

    Discusses Lewis's poetry, his ambition from boyhood to be a poet, and the background of the book's compilation. Remarks on Lewis's philosophy of poetic style and the role of poetry.

29. Kawano, Roland Mamoru. "The Creation of Myth in the Novels of C. S. Lewis." M. A. thesis: University of Utah, 1969. 75 pp.

A competent but not especially profound handling of Lewis's adult novels. Most interesting is the chapter on *Till We Have Faces* (pp. 46–61) where Kawano says "the use of myth is an acknowledgment of the failure of rationalism itself" and reflects "the rationalist, empiricist struggles Lewis himself underwent."

30. King, James Roy. "Christian Fantasy in the Novels of C. S. Lewis and Charles Williams." *Journal of Religious Thought* 11 (Autumn-Winter 1953–1954) : 46–60.

A discussion of how symbols and fantasy are able to present Christianity without smugness or sentiment.

31. Kranz, Gisbert. "Die Abschaffung des Menschen."

Listed in § IV-F; some discussion of "Screwtape Proposes a Toast," *The Silver Chair*, and *That Hideous Strength*.

32. ————. "Mythos und Weltraumfahrt: Zum Werk von C. S. Lewis." *Antaios* 11 (1969) : 562–577.

The main title means "Myth and Spaceflight." The study begins with Lewis's interest in myths as a boy and young man, particularly the northern myths. Kranz explains Lewis's later reconciliation of myths (as real but unfocused gleams of God's truth) and Christian faith. Turning to Lewis's fiction, Kranz points out that *The Pilgrim's Regress* is the only allegory which Lewis wrote; the rest—The Ransom Trilogy, The Chronicles of Narnia, *Till We Have Faces*—are myths. (We wish to thank Henry Noel for help in preparing this summary.)

33. ————. "Sexualist nach C. S. Lewis."

Listed in § IV-A; contains some discussion of *Dymer*, *The Pilgrim's Regress*, *The Great Divorce*, *That Hideous Strength*, and "Ministering Angels."

34. Kuhn, Daniel K. "The Joy of the Absolute: A Comparative Study of the Romantic Visions of William Wordsworth and C. S. Lewis."

   Listed in § IV-A; contains discussions of the Ransom Trilogy (pp. 192, 197, 200, 206–213), *The Great Divorce* (pp. 206–207, 213), and *Till We Have Faces* (pp. 192, 201).

35. Lawlor, John. "On Romanticism in the 'Confessio Amantis.'"

   Listed in § V-B; the romanticism of the Ransom trilogy, the Chronicles of Narnia, and *Till We Have Faces* is briefly discussed in the fourth section of the essay.

36. ———. "The Tutor and the Scholar."

   Listed in § II; a brief appreciation of *Perelandra*, *That Hideous Strength*, and *Till We Have Faces* appears.

37. ———. " 'Rasselas,' Romanticism and the Nature of Happiness."

   Listed in § I; *Spirits in Bondage* and *The Pilgrim's Regress* are discussed.

38. Lindskoog, Kathryn. "Farewell to Shadowlands: C. S. Lewis on Death."

   Listed in § I; contains citations from *The Screwtape Letters*, *The Great Divorce*, *Out of the Silent Planet*, *The Last Battle*, *The Voyage of the "Dawn Treader,"* and *The Silver Chair*.

39. Manlove, Colin N. "The Fairy Tale: And Its English Development, 1850-1960." Unpublished dissertation: Pembroke College (Oxford University), 1967. 139 pp. [Available in the Wheaton College (Ill.) C. S. Lewis Collection.]

   Chapter Seven, "Charles Williams, C. S. Lewis, J. R. R. Tolkien" (pp. 100-126), is of main interest, although references to Lewis appear earlier—e.g., in Chapter Five, George Macdonald" (p. 83). The specific subsection on Lewis covers pp. 109-120. Interesting is the contrast between Lewis and Williams on pp. 110-111:

for Williams, the Incarnation, through Co-inherence, can raise each man to God now; for Lewis, the Incarnation is the moral goal of men (to be Sons of God), for achivement in the future. Manlove comments that Williams asks the reader "to *believe* in the relation of the supernatural to his own world" while Lewis asks him to *desire* it, with *Sehnsucht* (pp. 114-115). Finally, Williams finds numinous Images in the mundane world, while Lewis "finds them only in remote times and places, and in worlds at least partially golden" (p. 116)—although Manlove here seems to be thinking mainly of the fiction, rather than Lewis's personal moments of *Sehnsucht* in nature. The author goes on to suggest a "dissociation of sensibility" in Lewis, between reason (this world) and joy (the next)—and applies this to *Perelandra* (an argument sandwiched between a joyful opening and closing), *The Voyage of the "Dawn Treader"* (a didactic re-education of Eustace in the middle of the Quest for the Heart's Desire), and *The Great Divorce* (George MacDonald's theology discussed in the midst of a mythic landscape) (pp. 117-119). Manlove's analysis of Tolkien is poor, by the way.

40. Moorman, Charles. *The Precincts of Felicity: The Augustinian City of the Oxford Christians*. Gainesville: University of Florida Press, 1966, pp. vii, ix–xi, 4, 14–15, 17–29, 65–85, 91, 95, 97–99, 101, 103, 109, 137–139.

A good, suggestive study of a pattern of extended imagery in Lewis, Williams, T. S. Eliot, Tolkien, and Dorothy Sayers, using the Augustinian idea of two cities with its implied cosmology, theology, and theory of history. Moorman begins by explicating Augustine; the second chapter is an extended discussion of the Inklings and their relations. Chapter IV, "*Logres and Britain*: C. S. Lewis" (pp. 65–85), falls into four parts: a comparison of the styles of Williams and Lewis (pp. 65–67); a study of the Image of the City in *The Great Divorce* as parallel to that in *All Hallow's Eve* (pp. 67–70); a study of the Logres vs. Britain theme, or City of God vs. City of Earth, in *That Hideous Strength* (pp. 70–79); and a tracing of an Augustinian, evangelical insistence on the present moment as a moment of crisis, in *That Hideous Strength* and elsewhere in Lewis's writings (pp. 79–81). There is a strong emphasis on Williams's influence throughout the chapter.

41. Myers, Edward D. "The Religious Works of C. S. Lewis."

    Listed in § IV-C; *The Pilgrim's Regress, The Screwtape Letters, Out of the Silent Planet,* and *Perelandra* are included in the survey.

42. Norwood, William Durward, Jr. "The Neo-Medieval Novels of C. S. Lewis." Ph. D. dissertation: University of Texas at Austin, 1965; University Microfilms, No. 65-10,756.

    Norwood regards Lewis as a man whose thought is more akin to medievals' than our day, a fact which must be understood and related to his fiction. This study considers the Ransom trilogy on four levels: narrative, satiric, mythic, and archetypal, the latter relating to Lewis's Christian faith as the archetypal myth. These four levels are close to the four levels of allegorical interpretation in medieval Biblical criticism. Norwood considers subthemes such as faith, reason, death, hope, love, mysticism, and choice woven into the novels. He finds the Ransom trilogy an intricately unified artwork worthy of re-evaluation. His essay, "Unifying Themes in C. S. Lewis' Trilogy," listed in § III-C of this bibliography, is a highly condensed summary of the content of Chapters II–IV, which deal with the Ransom Trilogy. Norwood's approach to *Till We Have Faces* is dissimilar: after a summary of the plot (pp. 187–211), he sums up other critical views of the book (pp. 212–220) and then states his own opinions (pp. 221–255), with emphasis on the theme of naturalism *vs.* supernaturalism (a summary from *Miracles* covers pp. 236-248) and Charles Williams's Doctrine of Exchange. Selective bibliography.

43. Reilly, R. J. *Romantic Religion: A Study of Barfield, Lewis, Williams, and Tolkien.* Athens, Georgia: University of Georgia Press, 1971.

    Although C. S. Lewis and his works are mentioned in many places (and luckily the volume has a good index of works mentioned), the main discussion is in Chapter Three, "C. S. Lewis and the Baptism of the Imagination" (pp. 98–147). The biographical opening of this chapter traces how *Sehnsucht* led Lewis to Christianity, with comments on the mental nature of the universe and the truth of myth (both ideas influenced by Owen Barfield's

Anthroposophism, Reilly believes). An analysis of *Till We Have Faces* follows (pp. 116–129), in terms of Barfield's belief in the unself-consciousness of the individual mind before the Incarnation. Third is a discussion of the Ransom trilogy, where the three books are "seen as attempts to do what Macdonald had done, to Christianize romance" (pp. 129–137). Finally, Reilly discusses Lewis's nonfiction, Christian books and sermons—*Mere Christianity, The Abolition of Man, The Problem of Pain, Miracles,* "The Weight of Glory," "Transposition," *Reflections on the Psalms, The Four Loves,* and *Letters to Malcolm*—as being in the tradition of Kant and Coleridge, particularly their distinction between the understanding, the pure or speculative reason, and the practical reason (pp. 137–147). Reilly's thesis of Barfield's major influence on Lewis is controversial—Clyde S. Kilby in *The Christian World of C. S. Lewis* (listed in § I), in summarizing Reilly's 1960 dissertation on the same topic, denies the influence of Anthroposophism while admitting some Barfieldian influence (pp. 204–205).

44. Rogers, Deborah Webster. "The Use of Medieval Material in the Fiction of J. R. R. Tolkien and C. S. Lewis: A Proposal for a Doctoral Dissertation." *Orcrist*, No. 4, combined with *The Tolkien Journal* 4 (1969–1970): 21–23.

An elaborate proposal for a dissertation in the Department of Comparative Literature, The University of Wisconsin at Madison (accepted 19 May 1970); the Lewis materials will concentrate on the Ransom Trilogy and the Chronicles of Narnia.

45. Rothberg, Ellen. "The 'Hnau' Creatures of C. S. Lewis." In *Mythcon I Proceedings,* ed. Glen GoodKnight, pp. 49–53.

The volume is listed in § I.

Much of the essay is simply descriptive of the invented rational creatures of Lewis, those of the first two books of the Ransom Trilogy and Aslan and Shift of the Chronicles of Narnia. Various (fictional) human reactions to these creatures are given, and an extended comparison with Swift's *Gulliver's Travels* concludes the essay. The latter part is marred by taking the Yahoos to stand completely for mankind; the author shows no knowledge of the tradition of Swift through H. G. Wells to Lewis traced in Hillegas's *Future as Nightmare* (p. 135; the volume is listed in § III-D).

46. Sale, Roger. "England's Parnassus: C. S. Lewis, Charles Williams and J. R. R. Tolkien."

Listed in § V-A; brief mention of Lewis's fiction.

47. Scott, Nathan A., Jr. "Poetry and Prayer." *Thought* 41 (Spring 1966): 61–80.

Modern poetry, reaching toward our private selves, may, in the work of T. S. Eliot, C. S. Lewis, J. R. R. Tolkien, and Charles Williams, be religious and be a preparation for prayer. (Based on *Abstracts of English Studies* 10 [November 1967]: Item 3240.)

48. Trowbridge, Clinton W. "The Twentieth Century British Supernatural Novel." Ph.D. dissertation: University of Florida, 1958; University Microfilms, No. 58-1540.

The first four chapters of this study are surveys of "The Gothic and Nineteenth Century Background" (I) and three types of modern novels—the psychic and spiritualistic (II), the occult (III), and the tale of terror (IV). At this point the dissertation turns to the Inklings: Charles Williams (V), C. S. Lewis (VI), and J. R. R. Tolkien (VII). The chapter on Lewis (pp. 274–396) discusses the Ransom Trilogy (pp. 279–365), particularly the Christian framework, the possible influences of Charles Williams upon it, and the development of Ransom through the series; the Chronicles of Narnia (pp. 366–389); and *Till We Have Faces* (pp. 389–396), suggesting that it is Lewis's best novel, but not his best myth.

49. Urang, Gunnar. *Shadows of Heaven: Religion and Fantasy in the Writings of C. S. Lewis, Charles Williams, and J. R. R. Tolkien*. Philadelphia: A Pilgrim Press Book (United Church Press), 1971.

Although Lewis is discussed throughout the book, Chapter One, "C. S. Lewis: Fantasy and the Metaphysics of Faith" (pp. 5–50), is the major study. Urang considers all of Lewis's book-length, adult prose fiction. His interpretative criticism is, as a whole, familiar, although there are some nice passages: e.g., Tinidril "informs [Ransom] of the one prohibition. She lives on the islands, the floating lands which undulate with the waves; she is not to dwell on the Fixed Land. The image operates, in an almost Spenserian manner, to suggest the contrast between living by faith and seeking a rigid kind of security" (p. 17). But the author's concern is elsewhere: his survey of the fiction through *That Hideous Strength* (pp. 5–28) is followed by a study of Lewis's religious books (pp. 28–40), in which he suggests Lewis's emphasis on God's Otherness and on man's sinfulness explain part of what is wrong with his fiction; then, in a study of *Till We Have Faces* and the later autobiographical and religious works (pp. 40–50), he finds a greater understanding of man and a greater (though not perfect) artistry. For the earlier fiction, note the author's five-point summary of Lewis's rhetorical strategy (pp. 37–38). Although Urang suggests material which needs fuller development (particularly the artistic flaws), this study is very important as nonbenevolent criticism of Lewis's novels by someone who also understands them. (Chapter 4, "Conclusion: Fantasy and the 'Motions of Grace,' " pp. 131–170, indicates openly Urang's predilection for theology based on a modern world view.)

50. von Puttkamer, Annemarie. "Clive Staples Lewis." In *Christliche Dichter im 20. Jahrhundert*, ed. Otto Mann, pp. 227–239. Bern: Franke Verlag, 1968.

A survey of Lewis the Christian fiction-writer, which suggests the preacher has the upper hand over the novelist—for the depth of characterization is shallower than and method of approach is different from other modern Christian novelists. The anti-Wellsian nature of the Ransom Trilogy is mentioned, and *That Hideous Strength* is considered more pessimistic in its view of earthly evil than Orwell's *1984* or Gheorghiu's *25 Uhr* (*25 O'Clock*). Ungit and Merlin are compared, and von Puttkamer finds a Gnostic bent in Lewis's depiction of ancient evil. The essay ends with a quotation from the epilogue to *Experiment in Criticism* concerning the purpose of literature. (We wish to thank Carol J. Kraft for help in preparing this summary.)

51. Walsh, Chad. "Aldous Huxley and C. S. Lewis: Novelists of Two Religions." *The Living Church* 112 (28 April 1946) : 9–11; reprinted, *The Journal of Bible and Religion* 14 (August 1946) : 139–143.

After dismissing the Established Religion (an odd term for a sort of optimistic evolutionism, which Walsh derives from H. G. Wells and John Dewey) and Marxism, Walsh considers the beliefs and didactic fictions of Aldous Huxley and C. S. Lewis in turn. He finds them in agreement on the dangers of science, but otherwise opposed: Huxley has a mouthpiece character in two of his novels illustrating the Perennial Philosophy while Lewis makes his Christian beliefs more a part of the background of the Ransom trilogy; Huxley dislikes the body and physical life while Lewis celebrates it; Huxley dislikes individual personality while Lewis assigns it a place in a spiritual hierarchy; and, finally, Huxley is more quietistic than Lewis, more filled with despair.

52. Williams, Jane. "The Use and Meaning of Myth in Literature." Unpublished student paper: Wheaton College, 1963. 39 pp. [Available in the Wheaton College (Ill.) C. S. Lewis Collection.]

After a 19-page introduction on myth, Williams summarizes Lewis's views of myth (pp. 19-22) and then discusses the Ransom Trilogy (pp. 22-28) and *Till We Have Faces* (pp. 28-29) as myths, finding the latter closest to Lewis's view in *Reflections on the Psalms*. Not of scholarly significance.

53. Wright, Marjorie Evelyn. *The Cosmic Kingdom of Myth: A Study in the Myth-Philosophy of Charles Williams, C. S. Lewis, and J. R. R. Tolkien.* Ph.D. dissertation: University of Illinois, 1960; University Microfilms, No. 60-4025.

A study of the making of myth to find and express basic truths in an artistically created cosmology that is both ordered and open-ended. Wright finds the kingdoms are not static, but are full of life and movement. They combine a broad, unchanging structure ("geography") with movement inside the structure ("commerce," especially vertical since all three authors insist on the principle of social order). Wright traces the archetypes used by the three authors, including the remote or mysterious land beyond the sea, the city, the quest, and the saving remnant; and she analyzes the forces of evil which threaten each author's cosmos. She finds the myths of all three authors satisfy the requirements for living myth: They have correspondence with man's condition in the modern world, yet serve all times and all conditions; they are set in eternal mobility; and they invite further development. No bibliography.

54. ————. "The Vision of Cosmic Order in the Oxford Mythmakers." In *Imagination and the Spirit*, ed. Charles Huttar, pp. 259–276.

The volume is listed in § I.

A chapter reprinted from Wright's dissertation (listed immediately above). The cosmic order here considered involves hierarchy in The Ransom Trilogy (pp. 261–262) and the Chronicles of Narnia (pp. 264–265), the principle of correspondences in the Trilogy (pp. 266–267), and in Narnia (pp. 267, 268–269), the exchange of rule and obedience in the Trilogy (pp. 269–270), the principle of substitution in Narnia (p. 273) and *Till We Have Faces* (p. 273), the action of courtesy in the Trilogy (p. 274) and in The Great Snow Dance in Narnia (p. 275), and Merlin's magic in the Trilogy as a lesser example of correspondences (p. 276).

B. *Dymer* and *Narrative Poems*

1. Christopher, J. R. "A Study of C. S. Lewis's *Dymer.*" *Orcrist*, No. 6 (Winter 1971–1972): 17–19.

   A discussion of the structure, romance tradition, and meaning of *Dymer*. Identical to the chapter on the poem in Christopher's dissertation, *The Romances of Clive Staples Lewis* (listed in § III-A).

2. Coghill, Nevill. "The Approach to English."

   Listed in § II; the essay contains a 2-page discussion of *Dymer*.

3. Hooper, Walter, ed. "Preface." In C. S. Lewis, *Narrative Poems*, ed. Walter Hooper, pp. vii–xiv. London: Geoffrey Bles, 1969.

   Valuable preface to a volume containing *Dymer* and three previously unpublished narrative poems. Hooper gives the personal historical background of them (and some juvenilia) with quotations from Lewis's unpublished personal papers. Hooper thinks *The Queen of Drum*, the writing of which spanned both his atheist and Christian years, is Lewis's best poem.

4. Linden, William. "New Light on Narnia; or, Who Beat the Drum?"

   Listed in § III-G; a nonserious combining of the histories in the Chronicles of Narnia and "The Queen of Drum."

5. Milne, M[arjorie]. "Dymer: Myth or Poem?" *Month* 194, n.s. 8 (September 1952): 170–173.

   Milne interprets Dymer as the Romantic Poet who at first finds his Muse in the palace of Romantic Tradition set in nature, but only after suffering can he see his Muse as she really is—that is, find his true relationship to nature, tradition, and the cosmos: The end of the poem signals the transformation/rebirth of the Romantic poetic vision. Although the author claims no special authority from Lewis for her views, his dedication of *Dymer* to her lends them particular interest.

C. The Pilgrim's Regress

1. "Books." *Bulletin of the New York C. S. Lewis Society* 2 (February 1971): 15–16.

   A list of books mentioned or alluded to in *The Pilgrim's Regress*, alphabetized by author; sixty-two items appear.

2. London, Kenneth. "C. S. Lewis and I: The Bible and Existentialism."

   Listed in § IV-A; compares John's leap into the pool with Kierkegaard's leap of faith.

3. Noel, Henry. "A Guide to C. S. Lewis's *The Pilgrim's Regress* (London: J. M. Dent, 1933)." *Bulletin of the New York C. S. Lewis Society* 2 (February 1971): 4–15.

   "Part I. A Book Out of Time" (p. 4) is an introductory statement of what the book meant to Lewis when he wrote it, of its metaphysical basis, and its noncontemporary orientation. "Part II. The Chronology and the Schools of Thought Leading to Lewis's Reconversion" (pp. 4–5) contains a list of the steps in Lewis's mental development—Childhood Christianity, Popular Realism, Philosophical Idealism, Pantheism, Theism, Christianity—keyed to pages in *The Pilgrim's Regress* and *Surprised by Joy*, with definitions of the terms. "Part III. The Characters of the Allegory and What They Stand For" (p. 5) is a list of 41 characters. "Part IV. Lewis's Own Running Headlines Printed Consecutively" (pp. 6–7) is something of a summary of the book's meaning. "Part V. Footnotes" (pp. 7–13) is a long series of identifications of foreign phrases, unusual terms, and allusions in the book, keyed to page numbers (of the Third Edition). "Part VI. Published Opinions of *The Pilgrim's Regress*" (pp. 13–15) is a summary with excerpts of five books and pamphlets (mostly negative) and five reviews of the first edition (mainly favorable). For the critic, the most valuable section of this "Guide" is Part V; the material in Part II has been done in Christopher's *The Romances of Clive Staples Lewis* (listed in § III-A), but this is a more convenient listing. At least Part V of this paper was distributed at the sixteenth meeting of the New York C. S. Lewis Society; cf. the report of the meeting in the *Bulletin*, pp. 1–2.

4. Ostling, Joan K. "A Forthcoming Annotated Bibliography of CSL." *Bulletin of the New York C. S. Lewis Society* 2 (February 1971): 3.

   Under this misleading title appears a bibliography of ten reviews of *The Pilgrim's Regress*; this was a supplement to Henry Noel's "A Guide to C. S. Lewis's *The Pilgrim's Regress*" in the same issue (listed in this subsection).

5. Sadler, Glenn Edward. "The Fantastic Imagination in George MacDonald."

   Listed in § V-E; parallels of MacDonald's works to Lewis's, especially *The Pilgrim's Regress*.

6. Walsh, Chad. "A Pilgrim's Progress."

   Listed in § III-I.

D. The Ransom Trilogy

1. Adams, Frank Davis. "The Literary Tradition of the Scientific Romance." Ph. D. dissertation: University of New Mexico, 1951.

   Adams surveys science-fiction from its beginnings (with Lucian) into the twentieth century. The basic division is that between the adventure tale (Jules Verne and his followers) and meaningful story (in the satiric and utopian traditions, such as H. G. Wells and his followers). The Ransom trilogy is discussed (pp. 311–323), with the emphasis on the first two novels. Adams sums up the meaning of the two books well, particularly of *Perelandra* (which he does not care for).

2. Atkins, John. *Tomorrow Revealed.* New York: Roy Publishers, 1956.

   According to Schmerl's *Reason's Dream* (p. 121) listed in this subsection, this book on pp. 159–160 analyzes the Unman of *Perelandra* as part of a future development of man; Schmerl indicates that Atkins's book is attempting some sort of narration of the future.

3. Atheling, William, Jr. *The Issue at Hand: Studies in Contemporary Magazine Science Fiction.* Chicago: Advent Publishers, 1964, pp. 53, 54, 65.

   Chapter Five, "Cathedrals in Space," discusses the original magazine version of James Blish's *A Case of Conscience* (with an appendix on the book version), Robert Lowndes's *Believer's World*, and Robert A. Heinlein's *Stranger in a Strange Land*. Three passing references to the Ransom trilogy appear. Since "Atheling" is the pseudonym used by James Blish for his magazine reviews—and later some book reviews—and since Blish's *A Case for*

Conscience refers to the Ransom Trilogy and his *Black Easter* is dedicated, posthumously, to Lewis, his comments on religious science-fiction are of particular interest.

4. Bailey, J. O. *Pilgrims Through Space and Time: Trends and Patterns in Scientific and Utopian Fiction.* New York: Argus Books, 1947, pp. 123–124, 196, 198, 203, 214, 220–221, 224, 242–244, 259, 275. Facsimile edition, with a new foreword by Thomas D. Clareson: Westport, Connecticut: Greenwood Press, 1972.

   This is Bailey's 1934 doctoral dissertation at the University of North Carolina, brought (with some omissions) up to 1945. A series of comparisons of *Out of the Silent Planet* to other cosmic voyages may be found here and there in the book. (The other volumes of the Ransom trilogy are not mentioned.)

5. Bergier, Jacques. *Admirations.*

   Listed in § I; some discussion of the Ransom Trilogy.

6. Bond, Brian C. "The Unity of Word: Language in C. S. Lewis' Trilogy." *Mythlore* 2 (Winter 1972): 13–15.

   Based on the linguistic theories of Owen Barfield's *Poetic Diction*, Bond's paper distinguishes between the unfallen language, Old Solar (equivalent to primitive language in Barfield's book), and modern language, such as the uses of newspapers and speeches by N.I.C.E.

7. Borges, Jorge Luis, with Guerrero, Margarita. *The Book of Imaginary Beings.* Revised, enlarged, and translated by Norman Thomas de Giovanni in collaboration with the author. London: Jonathan Cape, 1969. [The Spanish version appeared in 1967.] 256 pp.

   "An Animal Imagined by C. S. Lewis" (pp. 27-29): a reprint of the description of the Singing Beast in *Perelandra.* "A Creature Imagined by C. S. Lewis" (pp. 73-74): the insect-crustacean in the cave in *Perelandra.*

8. Braude, Nan. "The Two-Headed Beast: Notes toward the Definition of Allegory."

Listed in § V-B; contains a brief analysis of some allegory in *Perelandra* and *The Lion, the Witch and the Wardrobe*.

9. Burleson, Lyman E. "An Analysis of Major Christian Doctrines in C. S. Lewis' Space Trilogy." M.A. thesis: East Tennessee State University, 1967. 65 pp.

Rather superficial handling of Lewis's theology; information in it is easily available elsewhere.

10. Butor, Michel. "Science Fiction: The Crisis of Its Growth." (Translated from the French by Richard Howard.) *Partisan Review*, Fall 1966, pp. 595-602.

A brief mention of Lewis's "curious antimodern trilogy" appears on p. 599.

11. Callahan, Patrick J. "The Two Gardens in C. S. Lewis's *That Hideous Strength*." In *SF: The Other Side of Realism*, ed. Thomas D. Clareson, pp. 147–156. Bowling Green, Ohio: Bowling Green University Popular Press, 1971.

The emphasis of the Ransom Trilogy is moral, not religious or theological. Specifically, in *That Hideous Strength*, St. Anne's has images of flowers (some of the people who live there are named Camilla, Ivy, and Ironwood), with Ransom tied to sun imagery. On the other hand, Belbury—the name may come from one of King Arthur's battles, but it is used here to suggest a cemetery, something its garden reflects, in a manner like Spenser's Bower of Bliss. Also the characters' names—such as Frost and Wither—reflect its anti-garden, anti-life bias. Other materials, such as the emphasis on language, also back up this dichotomy. In short, Lewis writes out of a background of Natural Law, and the result is more like Swift's *Gulliver's Travels* and Johnson's *Rasselas* than a specifically religious work. (An intriguing misprint appears in note 7 on p. 156: *anagram* for *epigraph*.)

12. Carleton, Jim. "Wondelone." *Parma Eldalamberon* 1 (Autumn 1971): 7–8.

   Contains an addition of four words to Christopher's "Glossary of Old Solar" (below) and a discussion of seven of Christopher's definitions.

13. Christopher, Joe R. "A Glossary of Old Solar." *Parma Eldalamberon* 1 (Autumn 1971): 4–7.

   A list of the invented words in the Ransom Trilogy, with grammatical form, meaning, and (often) citation of example. See Jim Carleton's "Wondelone" above for some corrections. Compare R.H.M.'s suggestions for the derivations of *Malacandra, Thulcandra, Viritrilbia, Perelandra, Glundandra, Lurga, Neruval, Maleldil, Arbol,* and *Sulva,* in *The Bulletin of the New York C. S. Lewis Society* 1 (October 1970): 4–5; and Henry Noel's more elaborate suggestions (disagreeing with R.M.H.) for possible derivations of *Maleldil,* settling upon Anglo-Saxon for "the lord of the agreement" (i.e., the Lord of the Covenant), in *The Bulletin of the New York C. S. Lewis Society* 2 (November 1970): 6–7.

14. Clarke, Arthur C. "Science Fiction: Preparation for the Age of Space." In *Modern Science Fiction: Its Meaning and Its Future,* ed. Reginald Bretnor, pp. 197–220. New York: Coward-McCann, 1953.

   Concerned mainly with technical concepts of space flight, Clarke mentions the Ransom Trilogy only in passing (pp. 200, 201, and 204). (It is amusing, by the way, that Gerald Heard— H. F. Heard—can discuss "Science Fiction, Morals, and Religion" in the same anthology without mentioning Lewis; but then Heard mentions no science-fiction writer except H. G. Wells.)

15. ———. "Space and the Spirit of Man." *Horizon* 1 (January 1959): 27–31, 122–123 [122].

   Lewis is given two paragraphs for his pessimism about man's moral fitness for space travel—both Lewis's Ransom trilogy (the first two volumes) and "Will We Lose God in Outer Space?" are mentioned.

16. Clarke, I. F. *The Tale of the Future: From the Beginning to the Present Day: A Checklist . . .* London: The Library Association, 1961.

    That Hideous Strength is listed on p. 87.

17. Como, James T. "The Rhetoric of Illusion and Theme: Belief in C. S. Lewis' Perelandra."

    Listed in § V-A; a theory of literary criticism, with extended applications to *Perelandra*.

18. Deasy, Phillip. "God, Space, and C. S. Lewis." *Commonweal* 68 (25 July 1958): 421–423.

    After an introductory mention of Lewis's essay "Will We Lose God in Outer Space?" Deasy moves to a discussion of the Ransom trilogy, first as fiction of ideas (he lists some of the Christian topics touched on), then as antiscientific propaganda, contrasted with views of Pope Pius and Romano Guardini.

19. de Camp, L. Sprague. *Science-Fiction Handbook: The Writing of Imaginative Fiction.* New York: Hermitage House, 1953, pp. 82–83.

    De Camp gives a concise summary of and commentary on "the Ransom trilogy" in two pages. His use of the term "the Ransom trilogy" is its first use, so far as we have discovered; he also points out that Horace Jules is a caricature of H. G. Wells (but Theodore Spenser, in a review, first saw that in 1946).

20. Dowie, William John, S.J. *Religious Fiction in a Profane Time: Charles Williams, C. S. Lewis, and J. R. R. Tolkien.* Ph. D. dissertation: Brandeis University, 1970; University Microfilms, No. 70-24,624.

    What can a religious novelist do in a nonreligious period? Dowie studied the Inklings to find out. He decides that Lewis is too explicit in his Christian message in *Out of the Silent Planet* and *Perelandra*, and that he does not develop the characterizations well enough in *That Hideous Strength* to suggest the ultimate religious relationship to a Person. Williams is also faulted in his fiction; Tolkien is praised. (This account is based on the summary in *Dissertation Abstracts* 31 [1970]: 2911A.)

21. Egoff, Sheila A. "Tomorrow Plus X: Some Thoughts on Science Fiction." *Ontario Library Review* 45 (May 1962): 77–80.

A defense of science-fiction as being, at its best, a serious form of literature which emphasizes not characterization but social problems. Lewis's Ransom trilogy is given one paragraph, pp. 79–80, as dealing with the problem of man's enslavement of others and as being memorable for the creation of alien races.

22. Farley, Karen. "Philology in *Out of the Silent Planet.*" *Bulletin of the New York C. S. Lewis Society* 2 (October 1971): 3.

A nine-paragraph survey of the various emphases on language in the first of the Ransom trilogy.

23. Fitzpatrick, John F. "From Fact to Fantasy: A Study of C. S. Lewis' Use of Myth." Unpublished M.A. thesis: City College of the City University of New York, 1972. 95 pp.

A good passage on Lewis looking for "a steep hillside covered with firs where Mime might meet Sieglinde," as described in *Surprised by Joy*: ". . . the curious thing about that statement is that there is no such scene in [Wagner's] Ring. . . . [The words, pictures, and music] merely served as a stimulus to a budding romantic imagination" (p. 15). But primarily a discussion of two types of myth in the Ransom Trilogy: (1) the anti-myth (so called by Fitzpatrick) of humanistic evolution and scientific progress, and (2) the Lewis-invented (or Lewis-combined) myth of the three planets. The postscript to *Out of the Silent Planet* is defended in that it is "an entirely justifiable development of the 'myth became fact' theme" (p. 71). On the function of the planets at the end of *That Hideous Strength*: "Under the spell, the company of St. Anne's becomes successively mercurial, venereal, martial, jovial, and saturnine—but not lunatic for it is the N.I.C.E. that worships the powers of the Moon" (p. 79). Of the Trilogy, *Perelandra* is held to be the best as myth (pp. 81-82), and *That Hideous Strength*, to dilute its myth with too many other things (pp. 82-85).

24. Frank, Josette. *Your Child's Reading Today*.

Listed in § III-G; *Out of the Silent Planet* is recommended.

25. Fuller, Edmund. "The Christian Spaceman: C. S. Lewis." *Horizon* 1 (May 1959): 64–69, 125–127.

An earlier form of the chapter which appears in Fuller's *Books with Men Behind Them* (listed in § III-A); pp. 68–69 contain a handsome painting of Ransom meeting Perelanda's Lady, by James Lewicki.

26. Gerber, Richard. *Utopian Fantasy: A Study of English Utopian Fiction since the End of the Nineteenth Century*. London: Routledge and Kegan Paul, 1955, pp. 31–32, 36, 38, 57–58, 97–98, 105, 108, 112, 114, 116–117, 154.

This study views the modern utopian genre as rising from a quasi-religious belief in the miraculous power of evolutionary progress and moving to a more moderate, realistic utopianism with "sociological forecasts." Gerber treats *Out of the Silent Planet* as both allegorical and utopian, *Perelandra* as an ecstatic vision. He neglects *That Hideous Strength* and what Chad Walsh (in *From Utopia to Nightmare*) calls the "dystopic" tradition. Lewis is not considered in the last section of the last chapter, "Literary Achievements"—which discusses mainly Orwell's *1984* and Huxley's *Brave New World*. There is an annotated list of over one-hundred Utopian books, by year, on pp. 143-157.

27. [GoodKnight, Glen.] "Editorial: Lewis, Power, and Science." *Mythlore* 2 (Winter 1971): 27.

A brief discussion (four paragraphs) of Lewis's attitude toward science, mainly in terms of the Ransom trilogy. "Science isn't bad or dangerous. What's dangerous is the moral and ethical relativity of those who might use the power of science." Cf. "CSL and Science" in § IV-E.

28. Green, Roger Lancelyn. *Into Other Worlds: Space-Flight in Fiction, from Lucian to Lewis*. London: Abelard-Schuman, 1957; New York, 1958, pp. 9–10, 173–176, 181–184.

This volume, which the author calls more descriptive than critical, concludes with an appreciation of the first two books of the

Ransom trilogy: *Perelandra,* pp. 173–176, and *Out of the Silent Planet,* pp. 181–184.

29. Grennan, Margaret R. "The Lewis Trilogy: A Scholar's Holiday." *Catholic World* 167 (July 1948): 337–344.

Grennan, in this early essay on the Ransom trilogy, generally introduces the romances, and points out (among other things) how Ransom on Malacandra often resembles Gulliver defending men to the emperor of Brobdingnag (p. 340), how Perelandra parallels "the Celtic paradise of many ancient *imrama*" (p. 341), and how Ransom in the last book resembles "Anfortas—even to an incurable wound" (p. 342).

30. Haldane, J. B. S. "Auld Hornie, F.R.S." *Modern Quarterly,* n. s. 1 (Autumn 1946): 32–40.

Reprinted in (1) *Haldane's Everything Has Got a History* (London: George Allen and Unwin, 1951); and (2) Mark R. Hillegas, ed. *Shadows of Imagination,* pp. 15–25. The latter volume is listed in § III-A.

A study of the Ransom Trilogy, with references to *The Great Divorce* and *Christian Behaviour.* An interesting and generally valid commentary from Haldane's scientific and Marxist orientation, which indicates how meaningless fantasy can become when taken more literally than it was intended. Some of his points reappear in many critiques of Lewis, such as Lewis's anti-scientific bias (not actually a rationale). Lewis's answer to this essay is "A Reply to Professor Haldane" in *Of Other Worlds.*

31. Hamm, Victor M. "Mr. Lewis in Perelandra." *Thought* 20 (June 1945): 271–290.

Hamm, writing before the publication of *That Hideous Strength,* discusses the first books of the Ransom Trilogy. Calling *Perelandra* a "Paradise Retained," he compares the ideas of the novel and *Preface to "Paradise Lost"* (§ IV, pp. 278–283) and finds, in artistry, that Lewis sometimes surpasses Milton (as in the length of the temptation, and its three-fold development: first, to think on the fixed land; then, to feel pride in being independent of Maleldil; and third, to feel the pathos and tragedy of being a martyr to what one felt was right). Other points discussed by

Hamm include what the future of the Fall-less world is to be (§ V, pp. 283–287, based on *Out of the Silent Planet*) and Lewis's influences (§ II, pp. 273–276—Shelley, Keats, Blake, and Dante are treated the most extensively).

32. Hannay, Margaret. "Arthurian and Cosmic Myth in *That Hideous Strength*." *Mythlore* 2 (Autumn 1970): 7–9.

"In *That Hideous Strength* Lewis has joined his own cosmic mythology to the Grecian planetary deities, the Fisher-King of the Grail legend, and Merlin and the Pendragon of the Arthurian legend" (p. 9). The author faults the explanation of the name Fisher-King, but otherwise finds the fusion successful. Most of the materials are drawn from Moorman's *Arthurian Triptych* and Wright's *The Cosmic Kingdom of Myth* (both listed in § I of this bibliography), although the differentiation between Ransom and Christ (p. 9) is probably unique.

33. ————. "Evil in Eden: A Study in *Paradise Lost* and *Perelandra*." Unpublished student paper: Wheaton College (Ill.), 1966. 64 pp. [Available in the C. S. Lewis Collection, Wheaton College, Illinois.]

A study of critical views of *Paradise Lost* as much as a study of *Perelandra* (with briefer references to other works by Lewis); better than many M.A. theses.

34. ————. "The Mythology of *Out of the Silent Planet*." *Mythlore* 1 (October 1969): 11–14.

A summary of Lewis's use of a science-fictional background for a presentation of the Christian myth of Satan's fall. Although there is nothing in the essay which had not been said by other writers, the presentation is clear and useful as a summing up.

35. ————. "The Mythology of *Perelandra*." *Mythlore* 2 (Winter 1970): 14–16.

A discussion of the Eden, Redeemer, and Apocalyptic Myths of the book. The first is the myth of the Fall of Adam and Eve— or, here, the near-Fall of Tinidril. The second involves the parallels between Ransom and Christ (a better summary than most). The third myth is the post-Un-man celebration (the author suggests parallels to the New Heaven and New Earth). A final section discusses some classical and Biblical allusions, and, with them, Lewis's view of myth as here expressed.

36. Hay, Evelyn. "C. S. Lewis's Idea Novel: *That Hideous Strength*." Unpublished student paper: Wheaton College (Ill.), 1968. 49 pp. [Available in the C. S. Lewis Collection, Wheaton College, Illinois.]

An approach through (1) Merlin and myth, (2) the conflict of Belbury and St. Anne's, (3) the lives of the Studdocks, and (4) *That Hideous Strength* as literature. Better than some M.A. theses, but containing nothing which has not been said elsewhere.

37. Heinlein, Robert A. "Science Fiction: Its Nature, Faults, and Virtues." In *The Science Fiction Novel*: *Imagination and Social Criticism*, intro. Basil Davenport, pp. 24, 41, 52. Chicago: Advent Publishers, 1959.

Heinlein refers to *Out of the Silent Planet* on pp. 24 and 52 as a fantasy, not as science-fiction (according to his definition); rather inconsistently, on p. 41 he refers to Lewis as a science-fiction writer.

38. Herzfeld, Charles M. "Space Year I."
Listed in § IV-E.

39. Highet, Gilbert. "From World to World." In *People, Places, and Books*, pp. 130-137. New York: Oxford University Press, 1953; London: Oxford University Press, 1954.

Highet finds the Ransom Trilogy the best example of "scientifiction" because it deals with moral and religious ideas, and he briefly explains the Christian assumptions behind the first two books. *That Hideous Strength* "often passes the point where mysticism changes into sheer nonsense."

40. Hillegas, Mark R. *The Future as Nightmare*: H. G. Wells *and the Anti-Utopians*. New York: Oxford University Press, 1967.

Chapter VII (pp. 133-144) traces the influences of and reactions to H. G. Wells in the Ransom Trilogy (the influences are in the science-fiction trimmings, the reactions are to Wells's ideas—and person); also considered in the reaction are the ideas of two other writers—those in the essays of J. B. S. Haldane and the fiction of Olaf Stapledon.

41. ———. "*Out of the Silent Planet* as Cosmic Voyage." In *Shadows of Imagination*, ed. Mark R. Hillegas, pp. 41–58.

The volume is listed in § III-A.

An excellent generic consideration of *Out of the Silent Planet* in terms of earlier cosmic voyages, the popular "myth" of Mars when the book was written, and the book's own artistry.

42. ———. "Science Fiction and the Idea of Progress." *Extrapolation* 1 (May 1960): 25–28.

A brief discussion of Lewis's views on the relationship of technology and humanity, as reflected in the Ransom Trilogy, is included (pp. 27–28).

43. ———. "Science Fiction as Cultural Phenomenon: A Re-evaluation." *Extrapolation* 4 (May 1963): 26–33. (Publication of a paper read at the ASA general meeting at MLA, Washington, D. C., in December 1962.)

Lewis's *Out of the Silent Planet* and Wells's *The First Men in the Moon* are given a paragraph (pp. 30–31) as examples of the use of plausible other worlds to show aspects of the earth's society by comparison.

44. Hilton-Young, Wayland. "The Contented Christian." *Cambridge Journal* 5 (July 1952): 603–612.

An allegorical interpretation of the Ransom trilogy which sees (1) in *Out of the Silent Planet* "the three communities of inhabitants" of Mars as "the three parts of man": the *hrossa*, emotion; the *séroni*, reason; and the *pfifltriggi*, will; (2) in *Perelandra* and *That Hideous Strength* the myths of the beginning and ending of the human race, the Creation and the prelude to the Second Coming. Hilton-Young ends with a comparison of Lewis, contented and speaking of contentment, to other modern religious novelists— Sartre, Mauriac, Greene.

45. Hodgens, Richard. "Star-Begotten on the Silent Planet."
    Bulletin of the New York C. S. Lewis Society 3 (February
    1972) : 7.

    A comparison of Lewis's *Out of the Silent Planet* (1938) and
    H. G. Wells' *Star Begotten* (1937). Hodgens finds such similarities
    as both books mentioning the popular view of the Martians as
    monsters and both imagining good Martians with "smooth wise-
    looking heads of seals" (to quote Wells). He also points out
    Wells's Utopian hopes as a contrast to Lewis's view of society.

46. Irwin, W. R. "There and Back Again: The Romances of
    Williams, Lewis, and Tolkien." *Sewanee Review* 69
    (Autumn 1961) : 566–578.

    The author sees an interplay between the romantic and the familiar
    in these romances—the novels of Williams, *The Lord of the
    Rings*, the Ransom Trilogy—in plot movement, as his title, the
    subtitle of *The Hobbit*, suggests (pp. 568–570, 577); through
    language (pp. 571–573); and through myths (pp. 574–576). A
    convenient, brief summing up of a number of similarities between
    these writers. One of the bibliographers finds the author's
    Hegelian frame of reference helpful, one does not.

47. Kaufmann, V. Milo. "Brave New Improbable Worlds:
    Critical Notes on 'Extrapolation' as a Mimetic Technique
    in Science Fiction." *Extrapolation* 5 (December 1963) :
    17–24.

    Readers find it hard to accept Ransom as saintly while he kills
    the Un-man on Venus (pp. 22-23).

48. Kirk, Tim. "The Country Around Edgestow." *Mythlore* 2
    (Autumn 1970), 8.

    A map which accompanies Hannay's "Arthurian and Cosmic Myth
    in *That Hideous Strength*" (listed in this section of this
    bibliography), but which has little connection to her content
    except that of being drawn from the same book.

49. Knight, Damon (pseud.). *In Search of Wonder: Essays on Modern Science Fiction*. Chicago: Advent Publishers, 1956; 2nd ed., 1967.

A passing reference to the Ransom trilogy (p. 153) states one thing which it signifies: that *evil* and *meaning* are opposite terms. In the second edition, this reference is on p. 259; two other references to Lewis appear: (1) a mention of his autobiography during a discussion of *Sehnsucht* (p. 267), and (2) a brief comparison of the Objective Room in *That Hideous Strength* to some of the rooms in Shirley Jackson's *The Haunting of Hill House* (p. 226).

50. Lewis, Arthur O., Jr. "The Anti-Utopian Novel: Preliminary Notes and Checklist." *Extrapolation* 2 (May 1961): 27–32.

That Hideous Strength is listed (p. 30).

51. Lobdell, Jared C. "C. S. Lewis, Distributist: His Economics as Seen in *That Hideous Strength*." *Orcrist*, No. 6 (Winter 1971–1972): 20-21.

Beginning from the description of Arthur Dennison in *That Hideous Strength* as a Distributist, Lobdell traces the ideas of the doctrine in G. K. Chesterton's *Outline of Sanity* (1926), applies them to Lewis's comment on economics in *Mere Christianity*, and discusses St. Anne's in the novel as a Distributist model.

52. ———. "Petty Curry: Salvation by a Taste for Tripe and Onions." *Orcrist*, No. 6 (Winter 1971–1972): 11–13.

A discussion of the preservation of Curry, the Sub-Warden of Bracton College, in *That Hideous Strength*. Lobdell suggests the influence of Julien Benda's *La trahison des clercs* (English translation, 1928) on Lewis's conception of N.I.C.E., and Curry's inability to descend to such evil.

53. Moorman, Charles. *Arthurian Triptych: Mythic Materials in Charles Williams, C. S. Lewis, and T. S. Eliot*. Berkeley and Los Angeles: University of California Press, 1960, pp. vii-ix, 38–40, 48, 69, 102–126, 152–153, 154–155, 156.

A good study of Lewis's use of Arthurian myth as an example of myth's function in modern literature. After discussing Lewis's apologetic style and the development of his own myth mingled with old myths (*Till We Have Faces*, the trilogy), Moorman concentrates on *That Hideous Strength*. In that novel Lewis uses the Arthurian myth as a backdrop for the world of Bracton College and N.I.C.E., adding a dimension of grandeur and archetypal strength. Lewis was highly selective in his use of the Arthurian legends, taking the Fisher-King, Pendragon, Merlin, and the notion of Logres (the latter in dichotomy with Britain, an idea first developed by Charles Williams) while suggesting the larger myths and a comparison to modern England. Williams, T. S. Eliot, and Lewis all used myth for order, coherence, and meaning to pattern their vision of twentieth century life; all three sensed increasing materialism, a loss of certainty and point to a way out of the dilemma. For Lewis this was by a call to orthodoxy.

Note: Chapter 4, "C. S. Lewis" (pp. 102–126), covers essentially the same material as the author's essay, "Space Ship and Grail" (listed below), although the chapter does not trace Lewis's views of literary myths (elsewhere in the book) and it does have the addition of an introductory paraphrase of *Till We Have Faces*.

54. ———. "Space Ship and Grail: The Myths of C. S. Lewis." *College English* 18 (May 1957): 401–405.

In the Ransom Trilogy, Lewis uses an invented mythology in the first two novels (which is parallel to Christian doctrine) and certain aspects of the Arthurian mythology in the third (which is dovetailed with the cosmic myth of the first two); Moorman adds some comments on the function of these myths in the fiction, based on Lewis's statements about myths. (This essay is nearly identical to the chapter on Lewis in Moorman's *Arthurian Triptych*, listed above.)

55. Moskowitz, Sam. *Seekers of Tomorrow: Masters of Modern Science Fiction*. New York: Ballantine Books, 1967. (This paperback edition has an index which the earlier hardback edition by The World Publishing Company did not have.)

The contribution of Lewis to science-fiction is briefly assessed on pp. 407–408 (with three factual errors on the two pages); the general idea is that Lewis brought the concepts of religion into space travel. (Moskowitz's discussion of religious science-fiction here and on the two pages immediately following is not intended to be complete: there are other references in the discussions of individual writers previously in the book. Nevertheless, it should be noted that he misses Lewis's short story, "Ministering Angel," and he very oddly omits what most critics believe to be the best religious science-fiction short story, Anthony Boucher's "The Quest for St. Aquin.")

56. Myers, Doris T. "Brave New World: The Status of Women according to Tolkien, Lewis, and Williams." *Cimarron Review*, No. 17 (October 1971): 13–19.

A very interesting analysis of the fictional worlds created by the Inklings. Myers establishes three medieval views of women: (1) "the essentially womanless world of heroic poetry," (2) "the chivalric world of the Arthurian romance," and (3) "the hierarchial world of *The Clerk's Tale* or *Paradise Lost.*" In her analysis, Myers shows Tolkien using all three types in *The Lord of the Rings*, Lewis using the first in *Out of the Silent Planet* (the society of the hrossa) and the third in the other books of the Ransom Trilogy, and Williams generally escaping the medieval view into an equality of sexes. She concludes, "[T]he fictional world of Charles Williams is better for women—for people—than the worlds of Tolkien and Lewis."

57. Nicolson, Marjorie Hope. *Mountain Gloom and Mountain Glory: The Development of the Aesthetics of the Infinite.* New York: W. W. Norton and Company (Norton Library, N-204), 1963. (First published in 1959.)

Ransom's experiences on seeing the Malcandran landscape are cited on p. 33 as an analogy to the experiences of "eighteenth-century Englishmen who discovered the Sublime in the external world."

58. ———. *Voyages to the Moon.* New York: The Macmillan Company, 1960. (The book was first published in 1948; 1960 is the date of the Macmillan Paperback edition.)

§§ IV and V of the Epilogue (pp. 251–256) discuss the first two books of the Ransom Trilogy; a brief appreciation of Lewis's additions to the space-flight tradition. There are a few earlier references to Lewis, such as the conjecture of Kepler's influence (p. 47).

59. Norwood, W. D., Jr. "C. S. Lewis, Owen Barfield and the Modern Myth." *Midwest Quarterly* 8 (Spring 1967): 279–291.

Norwood sums up Barfield's and Lewis's comments on the result of Galileo's insistence that the Copernican theory of the solar system was the one true model: a gradual de-mythologizing of nature. He compares to this Lewis's attempt to overcome the standard mechanistic and Wellsian view of the solar system and space in *Out of the Silent Planet.*

60. ———. "Unifying Themes in C. S. Lewis' Trilogy." *Critique* 9 (n.d.): 67–80.

A highly condensed version of the chapters on the Ransom Trilogy in Norwood's *Neo-Medieval Novels of C. S. Lewis* (listed in § III-A). At the mythic level of interpretation, *Out of the Silent Planet* presents false myth (Wells's view of a mechanistic universe), *Perelandra* presents true myth (where Perelandra is the Christian Heaven, as well as having some obvious mythic real-occurences), and *That Hideous Strength* presents emergent myth (where, as the pagan and Jewish myths become reality in Christ, so the romantic fantasies of the first two volumes shift to historical realism). At the archetypal level of interpretation, *Out of the Silent Planet* portrays a confirmation in Christian experience (Ransom learns to see the eldila, for example), *Perelandra* portrays a baptism (Ransom's coffin voyage, plunge into water, descent to a cave with an incarnate devil, re-emergence, and physical health upon emerging from his coffin), and *That Hideous Strength* a new life (Ransom becomes the Fisher-King and the Pendragon, a little Christ). In addition to a satiric level of interpretation (not so novel as these outlined), an interlocking set of subthemes is traced.

61. O'Brien, Edward. "Outer Space and C. S. Lewis." *Christian Herald* 92 (November 1962): 51–55.

    General piece on the space fantasies by a science-fiction buff.

62. Patterson, Nancy-Lou. "Anti-Babels: Images of the Divine Centre in *That Hideous Strength*." In *Mythcon II Proceedings*, ed. Glen GoodKnight, pp. 6–11.

    The volume is listed in § I.

    A discussion of the two *horti conclusi* in the novel: Bragdon Wood, with Merlin's Well at its core; and St. Anne's Manor, with its walled garden. The literary allusions associated (by Jane Studdock) with the latter are traced and analyzed, partially on the basis of Freud and Jung. And the use of such images in the other books of the Trilogy and in the Chronicles of Narnia is pointed out.

63. Phelan, John M. "Men and Morals in Space." *America* 113 (9 October 1965): 405–407.

    This brief study of the "exo-ethics" of the Ransom trilogy is largely summary of action with moral points, but there are some other comments—e.g., "Deep Heaven is heavily populated by creatures Lewis calls Eldils, who are fascinating hybrids of angels (to use the Christian term) or intelligences (the Greek term) and mythological creatures of light. . . . Like angels, they are the servants and messengers of God; like intelligences, they are the operative principles of the ordered movement of the planets" (p. 405).

64. Philmus, Robert M. "C. S. Lewis and the Fictions of 'Scientism.'" *Extrapolation* 13 (May 1972): 92–101.

    Arguing from Lewis's description of Science and Magic as twins in purpose, Philmus traces Lewis's development of scientism's lust for power in the Ransom Trilogy. Partially this revelation of scientism's nature is made by the education of Ransom in *Out of the Silent Planet* (for example, his new view of space), partially by the development of Weston in the first two books. Also see Philmus's note on p. 101, where he comments that "Earth is ultimately the Silent Planet because man has lost the 'language' [literally, Old Solar] that articulates cosmic harmony."

65. Plank, Robert. *The Emotional Significance of Imaginary Beings: A Study of the Interaction Between Psychopathology, Literature, and Reality in the Modern World.* Springfield, Illinois: Charles C. Thomas, Publisher, 1968, pp. 8, 15, 22, 33–35, 50, 83, 94.

The seven references are general ones to the Ransom Trilogy and a specific one to *Perelandra*, and discussions using Lewis's essay "The Seeing Eye" (under its magazine title, "Onward Christian Spacemen"; the essay is available in Lewis's *Christian Reflections*). Plank commented more clearly on his intention in a letter to *The Bulletin of the New York C. S. Lewis Society*, 1 (October 1970): 8, than he does in his book: "I quoted the famous passage from *Perelandra*, 'He was a man obsessed with the idea . . .' in my book . . . in order to present the dissident viewpoint on space travel clothed in the splendor of Lewis's words. In general, . . . the aim of my writings has been psychological analysis rather than appreciation of Lewis's work."

66. ————. "Some Psychological Aspects of Lewis's Trilogy." In *Shadows of Imagination*, ed. Mark R. Hillegas, pp. 26–40.

The volume is listed in § III-A.

Plank reconstructs Lewis's "confession" in his fiction. "We see the bonds of ordinary relationships loosened, sex mechanized and short of its attractions, the energies thus freed poured into the apotheosis of the hero and into the joy of imaginary worlds closer to the heart's desire" and much like those of drug experiences.

67. "Pop Theology: Those Gods from Outer Space" [in the Religion Section]. *Time*, 5 September 1969, p. 64.

Included is a section (three long paragraphs) on science-fiction speculations about God/gods. In addition to the Ransom Trilogy, the following items were mentioned: Erich von Däniken's *Chariots of the Gods?*, Nelson Bond's "The Cunning of the Beast," Lester del Rey's "For I Am a Jealous People," Ray Bradbury's "The Fire Balloons," a *Star Trek* script, and Philip José Farmer's "Prometheus."

68. Presley, Horton Edward. "Fantasy, Allegory, and Myth in the Fiction of C. S. Lewis." M.A. thesis: University of Illinois, 1952. 63 pp.

After three chapter-long, historical definitions of *fantasy*, *allegory*, and *myth*, the author spends another chapter on each term as applicable to the Ransom Trilogy. He has a few minor errors in the early chapters—for example, saying that *myth* was first used to mean *plot* in the Middle Ages (pp. 22, 26–27). The chapter on "Allegory in the Trilogy" (pp. 38–47) is interesting for its identification of Scriptural phrases used in the book (although not every Scriptural parallel is an allegory, as the author seems to think, despite allegory being based on parallelism) and for its discussion of Devine as a type character (which the author also considers allegorical). The "Conclusion" (pp. 57–61) has an interesting chart of eight characteristics of fantasy, allegory, and myth (p. 58), indicating the varying degrees to which each characteristic is typical of each mode. This section decides that myth is the predominant mode in the Ransom Trilogy. (The footnote page for the "Conclusion" is omitted in the copy which the University of Illinois circulates.) The other chapters contain nothing which has not been said elsewhere in a more thorough manner.

69. Ringer, David K. "C. S. Lewis' Use of the Christian World-View as Structure in the Science Fiction Trilogy." M.A. thesis: McNeese State College (Lake Charles, La.), 1968. 81 pages.

Discusses Lewis's understanding of the sovereignty of God and its operation, Providence, freedom of man, moral law, and several other major doctrines. Contains little not easily available elsewhere.

70. Rockow, Karen. "The Hunting of the Hnakra." *Orcrist*, No. 6 (Winter 1971–1972): 23–24.

A humorous identification of the *hnakra* of *Out of the Silent Planet* with the quarry in Lewis Carroll's *Hunting of the Snark*.

71. Rose, Lois, and Stephen Rose. *The Shattered Ring: Science Fiction and the Quest for Meaning*. Richmond, Virginia: John Knox Press, 1970, pp. 60–67, 76, 80, 94.

Two subsections of Chapter 3, "Humanum: What Manner of Men Are We?" discuss the Ransom Trilogy: "C. S. Lewis's 'Bent' World" and "A Dostoevskian Diversion" (pp. 60–67). The authors find the major failing of Lewis's work (both theologic and artistic) is its failure to realize that a redeemed man is different from an unfallen man. (No index.)

72. Russell, Mariann Barbara. *The Idea of the City of God.* Ph.D. dissertation: Columbia University, 1965; University Microfilms, No. 65-9174.

The content is on the same Augustinian topic as Moorman's *Precincts of Felicity* (listed in § III-A) : a consideration of the Heavenly City and the Earthly City (often the Good Company and the Evil Company) in the writings of Charles Williams, C. S. Lewis, and J. R. R. Tolkien. Russell gives a fuller history of the dualistic concept (in Chapter Two) than does Moorman, and her discussion of Lewis's writings is limited to the Ransom Trilogy, Ransom's "Company" being tied to "the celestial commonwealth of 'Deep Heaven.' "

73. Samaan, Angele Botros. "C. S. Lewis, The Utopist, and His Critics." *Cairo Studies in English,* no vol. no. (1963–1966) : 137–166.

This essay, one of the best which has dealt with the Ransom Trilogy, appears to be based on Samaan's dissertation (listed immediately below), cited in a footnote on p. 138. Pp. 137–158 are a sensitive survey of the three books, discussing how they fit into the modern Utopian tradition (which is not entirely the modern science-fiction tradition) and offering symbolic interpretations of various events; pp. 158–166 discuss the British reception of the books in terms of the reviews (both the George Orwell and Graham Greene reviews of *That Hideous Strength* are mentioned, for example).

74. ———. *The Novel of Utopianism and Prophecy: With Special Reference to Its Reception.* Ph.D. dissertation: University of London, 1963.

Not seen; the material on Lewis presumably appears in "C. S. Lewis, The Utopist, and His Critics" (listed immediately above).

75. Sayers, Dorothy L. "The Writing and Reading of Allegory."
    Listed in § V-B; includes an anecdote about a review of *Perelandra*.

76. Schmerl, Rudolf Benjamin. *Reason's Dream: Anti-Totalitarian Themes and Techniques in Fantasy*. Ph. D. dissertation: University of Michigan, 1960; University Microfilms, No. 60-6931.

    Schmerl studies the following works: *Brave New World* and *Ape and Essence* by Aldous Huxley; the Ransom Trilogy by C. S. Lewis; *The Wild Goose Chase*, *The Professor*, *The Aerodrome*, and *Men of Stone* by Rex Warner; and *Animal Farm* and *1984* by George Orwell. The Ransom Trilogy is discussed primarily in Chapter Three (the attempts to establish a totalitarian state), rather than in Four (the attempts to overthrow one); also see Part B of Chapter Two, on totalitarian motivations. The latter passage (pp. 60–69) discusses the demonic impulses and Lewis's depiction of them in terms more moral than social (as the other writers use), but it also suggests (p. 78) that the end of *That Hideous Strength* where outside forces are introduced [*dei ex machina*] harms the moral point. The former passage (Chapter Three, pp. 113–128) traces Lewis's anti-scientific attitudes throughout the Trilogy (as a unifying theme, which emphasizes that science is amoral and amorality leads to immorality) and repeats that the Christian framework removes the books from modern immediacy. Dr. Schmerl finds the Ransom Trilogy better than Warner's books (p. 193) because it at least has a clear meaning. (He finds *Animal Farm* the best of the books considered.)

77. "SF in the Classroom." *Extrapolation* 13 (May 1972): 106–118.

    This title covers three essays on science-fiction teaching: "Opportunities and Limitations" by Patrick G. Hogan, Jr. (pp. 106–111); "Teaching Religion through Science Fiction" by Andrew J. Burgess (pp. 112–115), and "USAFA: 'English, Special Topics 495': Spring 1971" by John R. Pfeiffer (pp. 116–118). In the first essay, two paragraphs are spent on Lewis on p. 109, listing some of his familiar titles and discussing a student's enthusiasm for *Till We Have Faces*; in the second, Lewis's trilogy was read as part of a background for creating an imaginary world and "translating" religious truths for its inhabitants (Lewis is mentioned on pp. 112–113); in the third, Lewis's *That Hideous Strength* is only listed as a text (p. 116) in a discussion of a science-fiction course given at the Air Force Academy.

78. Shumaker, Wayne "The Cosmic Trilogy of C. S. Lewis." *Hudson Review* 8 (Summer 1955): 240–254.

Regarding the trilogy as a unit, Shumaker traces the plan for the work, the theological thesis of man's alienation from God's will, as a three-fold repetition on an old, unfallen world, on a young, tempted world, and on man's fallen world. As an example of Lewis's use of symbolism to indicate theology, he points to the use of *eldila* (or angels) in the first volume—where the heavens are first felt as glorious during the space trip, then the eldila are found everywhere on Malacandra, finally the eldila are heard and felt in the heavens during the return trip; thus, as with the weighty pressure of God Himself on Perelandra, is indicated not only the doctrine of plentitude but the omnipresence of God in the universe. Penultimately, Shumaker gives a symbolic reading of Ransom's entrance into the Rise (first and second chapters of the first volume) and of Wither's appearance (in the third volume). Finally, as another example of Lewis's ability to present theological truth without overt statement, he points to Tinidril's childlike reactions combined with great intellectual capabilities.

79. Spacks, Patricia Meyer. "The Myth-Maker's Dilemma: Three Novels by C. S. Lewis." *Discourse* 2 (October 1959): 234–243.

Spacks first traces the Christian meaning, then the use of both Christian and classical myths ("The stories of the Bible often have the same quality as the tales of Greek gods and goddesses: one gets precisely the same thrill of recognition from Weston's body throwing back its head and crying, *'Eloi, Eloi, lama sabachthani,'* as from the sudden perception of the dragon coiled around the tree of golden fruit." [p. 239]), and finally suggests the science-fictional framework trivializes the Christian meaning for the non-Christian reader.

80. Starr, Nathan Comfort. *King Arthur Today*: *The Arthurian Legend in English and American Literature, 1901–1953.* Gainesville: University of Florida Press, 1954, pp. 14, 135, 142–143, 168, 179, 181–188.

    Discussion of *That Hideous Strength* as a book which deserves to be better known (pp. 142–143); includes a summary, emphasizing the novel's moral aspects and comparing it briefly to Williams's *War in Heaven* (pp. 181–187). Moorman's *Arthurian Triptych* (listed in this section) treats the Arthurian materials in this novel more thoroughly.

81. Underhill, Evelyn. *The Letters of Evelyn Underhill*, ed. Charles Williams. London: Longmans, Green, and Company, 1943.

    There are three letters to C. S. Lewis, two about *Out of the Silent Planet* (pp. 268–269) and one about *The Problem of Pain* (pp. 300–302). The two on the romance are "fan" letters, although the second suggests that Lewis was wondering if he had presented the Cosmic Rays scientifically enough; the letter on the other book praises most of it but argues with Lewis's human-centered salvation of animals.

82. Wallis, Ethel. "Surprising Joy: C. S. Lewis' Deep Space Trilogy." *Mythcon I Proceedings*, ed. Glen GoodKnight, pp. 21–23.

    The volume is listed in § I.

    After giving five characteristics of *joy*, as Lewis uses the word in his autobiography, Wallis traces analogous moments in all three volumes of the Ransom Trilogy.

83. Walsh, Chad. "Attitudes Toward Science in the Modern 'Inverted Utopia.'" *Extrapolation* 2 (May 1961): 23–26. (The publication of a paper read at the meeting of General Topics 7: Literature and Science, at the MLA meeting, 1960.)

    That Hideous Strength receives a half paragraph on p. 26.

84. ———. *From Utopia to Nightmare*. New York and Evanston: Harper and Row, 1962; London: Geoffrey Bles, 1962, pp. 28, 139, 147n, 163, 165.

A book on the genre of the dystopia, the negative or "inverted" utopian fiction; remarks on *That Hideous Strength* as typical of the type (pp. 139, 165); euthanasia theme in religious utopias such as *Out of the Silent Planet* (p. 147n); Lewis on use of language in *Abolition of Man* (p. 163).

85. Warren, Eugene. "All Lies in a Passion of Patience." *Bulletin of the New York C. S. Lewis Society* 2 (May 1971): 4.

A brief (six-paragraph) but valuable sketch of the resemblances of the household of Taliessin, in Charles Williams's poetry, and the company at St. Anne's in *That Hideous Strength*: "Both companies are gathered providentially and save the kingdom of Logres in eschatological battle."

86. ———. "Venus Redeemed." *Orcrist*, No. 6 (Winter 1971–1972): 14-16.

A valuable discussion of the marital problems of Mark and Jane Studdock in *That Hideous Strength*, often on the basis of Lewis's comments about marital love in *The Four Loves*. The emphasis is on Jane's change in attitude (and belief), but Mark's change in marital attitude is also indicated.

87. Wollheim, Donald A. *The Universe Makers: Science Fiction Today*. New York: Harper and Row, Publishers, 1971.

The Ransom Trilogy is given one paragraph (pp. 51–52) during a discussion of Philip José Farmer's *The Maker of Universes* and its sequels: *Out of the Silent Planet* is described as "an allegorical depiction of the conflict between materialistic science and moralistic theology." The other two volumes are not considered science-fiction, and so are quickly passed over by the author.

E. *The Screwtape Letters* and "Screwtape Proposes a Toast."

Note: see § III-I for several imitations of *The Screwtape Letters*.

1. Churchill, R. C. "Mr. C. S. Lewis as an Evangelist."
   Listed in § IV-C.

2. Fremantle, Anne (ed.). *The Protestant Mystics*.
   Listed in § IV-A; Letter XXXI from *The Screwtape Letters* is included.

3. Fuller, Muriel. "C. S. Lewis."
   Listed in § II; brief comments on *Screwtape Letters*.

4. Gordan, John D. "New in the Berg Collection: 1957–1958."
   Bulletin of the New York Public Library 58 (March 1959), 134–147.
   Lewis's ms. of *The Screwtape Letters* is one of the works acquired. (Based on *Abstracts of English Studies* 2 [November 1959], item No. 1603.)

5. Hough, Graham. "The Screwtape Letters." *Times*, 10 February 1966, p. 15.
   This essay is no. 6 in the series "How Well Have They Worn?" Professor Hough suggests several deficiences in *The Screwtape Letters* as an imaginative work: It seems trivial in light of the concentration camps when it was written, as an *apology* it assumes a world view which a post-Christian generation does not accept and it assumes that reason will lead one to faith (in a Chesterton-sort of way) which existentialists and absurdists would deny, and the conclusion, when the human dies doing his duty, does not

seem to illustrate anything which non-Christians have not also done. However, Hough praises "the ingenuity, the wit, and the shrewd observation in satirizing the weaknesses and the self-deceptions of common life." (Walter Hooper answers the first of the above objections to *The Screwtape Letters* in his preface to *Christian Reflections* [Grand Rapids, Michigan: Eerdmans, 1967], pp. viii-ix.)

6. Johnson, Mary E. "Dialogues of Devils." *Congregational Quarterly* 23 (January 1945): 47–52.

   Contrasts *Screwtape Letters* with Rev. John Macgowan, *Infernal Conference or Dialogues of Devils, concerning the many vices which abound in the Social, Civil, and Religious World* (1862).

7. Kirkpatrick, Hope. "*The Screwtape Letters*: A Personal View." *Bulletin of the New York C. S. Lewis Society* 3 (November 1971): 2-3.

   A brief consideration of Lewis's Christianity centering in the Will, which is reflected in *The Screwtape Letters*.

8. Landers, Joyce. "Scattered Thoughts on Screwtape Letters." *Chronicle of the Portland C. S. Lewis Society* 1 (5 May 1972): 5-7.

   The author begins with the difficulties of reading *The Screwtape Letters*: their approach (through an evil point of view) and style (the didacticism of the epistolary novel). She then considers the characterization of Wormwood, Screwtape, and "the patient."

9. Loughlin, Richard L. "Time Out." *English Record* 16 (April 1966): 2–8.

   A study of aphorisms about the paradoxes of time—C. S. Lewis's *Screwtape Letters* is one of the sources considered. (Based on *Abstracts in English Studies* 10 [September 1967]: Item 2341.)

10. Mondrone, Domenico. "Berlicche e l'Arte di Dannare gli Uomini." *La Civiltà Cattolica*, 26 Luglio 1947, quaderno 2331.

    Not seen; presumably a review-essay on *Le Lettere di Berlicche* (the Italian translation of *The Screwtape Letters*) which appeared with an introduction by Alberto Castelli in 1947.

11. Soth, Connie. *Valley Times* [Beaverton, Oregon]. Reprinted as "The Screwtape Letters" in *Chronicle of the Portland C. S. Lewis Society* 1 (5 May 1972): 4–5.

    Primarily an account of the author's first reading of Lewis's book, with some comments on the inverted point of view and the depiction of salvation.

F. *The Great Divorce*

1. Christopher, J. R. "Considering *The Great Divorce*, Parts I and II." In *Mythcon I Proceedings*, ed. Glen GoodKnight, pp. 40–48.

   The volume is listed in § I.

   "Part I: The Medieval Analogues" discusses primarily the Dantean parallels with Lewis's work. "Part II: The Modern Analogues" discusses Rudyard Kipling's " 'The Finest Story in the World,' " Algernon Blackwood's "The Wood of the Dead," E. M. Forster's "The Celestial Omnibus," J. R. R. Tolkien's "Leaf by Niggle," and Charles Williams's *All Hallows' Eve*. Both of these parts are expansions of material in Christopher's dissertation, *The Romances of Clive Staples Lewis*, listed in § III-A.

2. ———. "Considering *The Great Divorce*: Parts III, IV, and V." In *Mythcon II Proceedings*, ed. Glen GoodKnight, pp. 12–21.

   The volume is listed in § I.

   "Part III: The Various Versions" is a comparison of the three versions of *The Great Divorce*: the magazine serial and the British and American hardcovers. The text seems fairly sound, but the incidentals and the chapter divisions have no authority. "Part IV: The Generic Artistry" is an analysis of (and attack on) the organization of the book. "Part V: The Religious Application" suggests a seventeenth-century meditative approach for the Christian's use of the book. Part IV is an expansion of material in Christopher's dissertation, *The Romances of Clive Staples Lewis* (listed in § III-A); the other two parts are new.

98

3. Prudentius. "Hymn for the Lighting of the Lamp" (excerpt).
   Bulletin of the New York C. S. Lewis Society 2 (April
   1971): 5.

   Full "title" as it appears in the *Bulletin*: "A passage from the
   'Hymn for the Lighting of the Lamp,' from *Liber Cathemerinon*
   ('The Daily Round'), by Aurelius Prudentius Clemens (ca.
   348-410 A.D.)" Translated into English prose; translator not given.
   This is the passage referred to by George Macdonald in *The
   Great Divorce* which mentions the "refrigerium"—the releasing of
   souls from Hell for a brief period.

4. Sayers, Dorothy L., (trans.). *The Comedy of Dante Alighieri
   the Florentine: Cantica I, Hell*. Baltimore, Maryland:
   Penguin Books, 1949.

   The Great Divorce is cited in a note on p. 83, concerning the feeling
   of the saved for the damned.

5. ———. "The Meaning of Heaven and Hell." 1948. In
   Introductory Papers on Dante, pp. 44–72 [61]. London:
   Methuen and Company, 1954.

   "A . . . point that many people find difficult about Dante's Heaven
   is that although the blessed remain very closely and intimately
   concerned with the affairs of earth, and are indeed continually
   denouncing the sins of mankind, they remain untroubled in their
   ecstasy" (p. 60). Sayers cites from the discussion between George
   Macdonald and Lewis on Sarah Smith being untroubled in her
   joy over her husband's damnation the "admirable phrase" (Sayers's
   terminology): "The action of pity will live for ever, but the
   passion of pity will not." Sayers does not explain the full context
   of the phrase she uses.

G. The Chronicles of Narnia

1. Adams, Bess Porter. *About Books and Children: Historical Survey of Children's Literature.* New York: Henry Holt, 1953, pp. 183–184.

   Brief discussion of *The Lion, the Witch and the Wardrobe* as a "gay little story"; no mention of its meaning.

2. Arbuthnot, May Hill. *Children's Reading in the Home.* Glenview, Ill.: Scott, Foresman and Company, 1969, pp. 143, 144, 161, 203, 205.

   Resumé and favorable review of the Narnia books (p. 205).

3. Aymard, Elaine. "C. S. Lewis's Narnian Chronicles or On the Other Side of the Wardrobe Door." Thesis for the Diplôme D'Etudes Supérieures d'Anglais (master's degree): Université de Toulouse, Faculte des Lettres et des Sciences Humaines, Juin 1967. 179 pp. [Available at the Wheaton College (Ill.) C. S. Lewis Collection.]

   Thesis is in English. A study of Lewis's balance of the familiar and the fantastic in the children's books. The author notes in Part II that Lewis's understanding of "myth become fact" is contrary to the concept of myth in modern theology (i.e., Bultmann). The thesis contains an interview with Walter Hooper on Lewis's working habits and literary approach to children's stories.

4. ————. "On C. S. Lewis and the *Narnian Chronicles.*" *Caliban,* 5, i: 129–145.

   Not seen. The *1968 MLA Bibliography* (June 1969) identifies the item as an "Interview with Rev. Walter Hooper, Wadham College, Oxford"; thus this seems to be the publication of the interview in Ayward's thesis, listed immediately above.

5. Beattie, Sister Mary Josephine. *The Humane Medievalist.*
   Listed in § V-B; some discussion of the Chronicles of Narnia.

6. Beversluis, John. "The Chronicles of Narnia." *Reformed Journal* 10 (November 1960): 20-21.

   This review-essay praises the Chronicles for not being the typical preachy fiction of Christian books for children, for fusing natural and supernatural concerns, and for presenting in Aslan a truthful picture of the Incarnation.

7. Brady, Charles A. "Finding God in Narnia." *America* 96 (27 October 1956): 103–105. Reprinted: *CSL* 3 (April 1972): 3–6.

   Brady calls the seven-volumed Chronicles of Narnia (Angria + Norns?) a juvenile *Faerie Queene*, and indicates in a general way a number of the sources: the books of Nesbit and Macdonald, the Greek, Norse, Celtic, and Arabian myths and romances. He suggests the best things (for the children reading) are the sense of the numinous, the understanding of death (in *The Last Battle*), the introduction to traditional literary concepts (i.e., of the epic rather than the novel), and, of course, the religious meaning behind the symbols.

8. Braude, Nan. "The Two-Headed Beast: Notes toward the Definition of Allegory."

   Listed in § V-B; contains a brief analysis of some allegory in *Perelandra* and *The Lion, the Witch and the Wardrobe*.

9. Brophy, Brigid, Michael Levey, and Charles Osborne. *Fifty Works in English* (* *and American*) *Literature We Could Do Without*. New York: Stein and Day, 1968, pp. 147-148.

   A more-or-less chronological listing, from such works as *Beowulf* and *The Faerie Queene* to *A Farewell to Arms*. *The Silver Chair*, which is the most recent work listed, appears just before Hemingway's volume. This Narnian volume, as typical of the series, is attacked as a falsification of myth, with flat language and imagination, Walt Disney characters, and personal prejudices instead of "the ambiguous morality of myths." Passages are cited as evidence to sustain the two-paragraph attack.

10. Cameron, Eleanor. *The Green and Burning Tree.*

Listed in § V-G; discusses Lewis as a writer of children's books without much emphasis on the Narnian books in themselves.

11. Cenit, Gloria Alfoja. " 'The Christian Life—A Warfare:' A Curriculum Unit based on C. S. Lewis' *The Lion, the Witch, and the Wardrobe.*" M.A. thesis in Christian Education, Wheaton College, 1968. 94 pp.

"This thesis is a course of study for sixth graders aimed to make the Christian Junior realize that the Christian life is a constant battle and to help him participate successfully in this warfare. To achieve these purposes, the symbolism in C. S. Lewis' *The Lion, the Witch, and the Wardrobe* is used as the starting point leading into the inductive study of Bible portions pertinent to the theme of the curriculum" (p. 1). "A secondary aim of this thesis is that the Junior who studies curriculum will be aided in developing a taste for good literature" (p. 6). *Very* evangelical. Arranged as a series of ten Sunday School lessons, but also intended for Vacation Bible schools or other similar situations. Some of Lewis's chapters are dramatized. No emphasis on the book as literature, except some comments about the students' enjoyment of it (in a Sunday School trial).

12. Christopher, J. R. "An Introduction to Narnia, Part I: The Chronology of the Chronicles." *Mythlore* 2 (Autumn 1970): 23-25.

This essay, the first in a proposed series of twelve, discusses (1) the order of publication of Lewis's children's books, followed by a digression on "Narnian Suite"; (2) the order of composition; and (3) the internal chronologies of the books. *Note:* this essay is a fuller discussion of material which appears in the Narnian chapter of the author's *The Romances of Clive Staples Lewis* (which is listed in § III-A.); the internal chronology has been outdated by Hooper's publication of Lewis's chronology for the series in "Past Watchful Dragons" (listed in this section).

13. ———. "An Introduction to Narnia, Part II: The Geography of the Chronicles." *Mythlore* 2 (Winter 1971): 12-14, 27.

A survey of the cosmography of Narnian heavens and the geography of the Narnian world (the latter done by means of discussion of Pauline Baynes's maps in the various books), followed by two thematic suggestions: first, that Narnia (the country proper) resembles in different ways both England and Israel, and, second, that the geography of the Narnian world resembles that in *The Pilgrim's Regress*. See Tim Kirk's map listed in this section.

14. ———. "An Introduction to Narnia, Part III: The Genre of The Chronicles." *Mythlore* 2 (Winter 1972): 17-20.

A history of the folk tale (as collected) and the imitation folk tale, with parallels to folk ballads and imitation folk ballads: specifically, the folk tales of Charles Perrault and the Brothers Grimm, and the imitation folk tales of Hans Christian Andersen, George MacDonald (with a digression on the German Romantics), E. Nesbit, and C. S. Lewis.

15. ———. "On the CSL Theory of Composition of the Chronicles of Narnia." *Bulletin of the New York C. S. Lewis Society* 2 (August 1971): 4.

A reply to Shramko's "Composition of the Chronicles of Narnia" and Linden's "New Light on Narnia" (both in this subsection). Christopher suggests a "J" source be added to Shramko's "CSL" sources, and advances some suggestions about Narnian prehistory.

16. Cook, Elizabeth. *The Ordinary and the Fabulous: An Introduction to Myths, Legends, and Fairy Tales for Teachers and Storytellers*. Cambridge: Cambridge University Press, 1969, pp. 2, 23, 45-46, 118, 132, 134, 139, 150.

As the author indicates in her preface, this book is intended as a survey "for the ignorant, the unconverted, or the recent convert [to fairy tales], not for the initiate" (p. viii). She includes invented fairy tales in her survey: Hans Christian Andersen's, of course, but also George Macdonald's, J. R. R. Tolkien's, and C. S. Lewis's. The list of books at the back lists the Chronicles of Narnia (No. 122, p. 139) and *Surprised by Joy*, the latter included for its description of Lewis's childhood reading (No. 150, p. 144)—as well as Charles Williams's *Arthurian Torso*, edited by Lewis (No. 81, p. 132), an item not listed under Lewis in the index. The references to the Chronicles and to *Surprised by Joy* in the text are of an obvious nature, although she does comment that Lewis's White Witch derives from Andersen's Snow Queen (p. 46).

17. Crouch, Marcus S., (ed.). *Chosen for Children: An Account of the Books Which Have Been Awarded the "Library Association Carnegie Medal," 1936-1965*. London: The Library Association, revised edition 1967. (The 1957 edition also included—in fact, closed with—Lewis's book.)

On pp. 83–87 is the account of Lewis's *The Last Battle*; first a page-and-a-half introduction (presumably by Marcus Crouch who is credited on p. vii with "compiling" the book), with one of Pauline Baynes's illustrations on the second page; then an excerpt from Chapter VIII on the third page; finally, an excerpt from Lewis's "On Three Ways of Writing for Children" entitled "One Way of Writing for Children" on pp. 86–87. There is a photograph of Lewis opposite p. 56.

18. Crouch, Marcus S. "Chronicles of Narnia." *Junior Bookshelf* 20 (November 1956): 244–253.

An essay written after Lewis's completion of the Chronicles, it points to the flat characterization and poor style (particularly in dialogue) in the series, but also points to memorable scenes and excellent fusion of moral and action. "Sombre, melancholy, thrilling, gay, the scenes and the events have an actuality, a three-dimensional quality, which marks them as the work of a first-rate inventive genius." The essay also outlines the chronological sequence of the series and describes the geography of Narnia. Over all, a good short treatment of the Chronicles.

19. ———. *Treasure Seekers and Borrowers: Children's Books in Britain, 1900–1960*. London: The Library Association, 1962, pp. 103, 115–116, 133.

References to Lewis, to Tolkien, and to Roger Lancelyn Green (once as a writer of "a fantasy of the school of Tolkien and Lewis"). Crouch identifies the George Macdonald-E. Nesbit tradition of Lewis, and briefly comments on the combination of the sublime and trival in plot and style.

20. Doyle, Brian. *The Who's Who of Children's Literature*.

Listed in Section II; only a few details on the Chronicles of Narnia.

21. Ellis, Alec. *How to Find Out About Children's Literature*. Oxford: Pergamon Press, 1966, pp. 83–85.

Summary and some evaluation of the Narnia books.

22. Ellwood, Gracia Fay. "A High and Lonely Destiny." *Mythcon I Proceedings*, ed. Glen GoodKnight, pp. 23–27.

The volume is listed in § I.

"The idea that certain persons with supernatural powers have a destiny that sets them apart from the crowd in [an amoral] way is an old one." The discussion begins with Andrew Ketterley and Jadis in *The Magician's Nephew*; a later allusion to the Macrobes in *That Hideous Strength* appears in a discussion of Hitler (p. 26). The conclusion: "Digory's judgment on the Magician with a High and Lonely Destiny is well borne out by the comparison with others in the tradition. Most of them are driven by inner hunger and are self-deceived. Those who come closest to greatness . . . are those who master themselves and do not claim to be free from the common restrictions."

23. ———. "The Mirror of Galadriel." *Mythprint* 6 (July 1972): 3.

After three paragraphs by Laura Ruskin, Ellwood replies, rejecting dualism: "It is interesting to note that Lewis who consciously rejected the union of ultimate good and ultimate evil and satirized it in 'Tashlan,' himself used the concept in the image of Aslan's

shadow at the Door. Lewis is quite practical in his rejection,
however. . . . people who consciously serve Tashlan tend to end up
serving only Tash."

24.————. " 'Which Way I Flie is Hell.' " *Narnia Conference
Proceedings*, ed. [Glen GoodKnight), pp. 11–14.
The volume is listed in this subsection.
Ellwood begins with Milton's Satan, summarizing his position as
"Pride asserts itself, first through forgetfulness and later through
suppression, of some very basic facts." She then applies this to
Edmund in *The Lion, the Witch and the Wardrobe*; Eustace in
The Voyage of the "Dawn Treader"; Uncle Andrew in *The
Magician's Nephew*; and the dwarfs in *The Last Battle*.

25. Fisher, Margery. *Intent Upon Reading: A Critical
Appraisal of Modern Fiction for Children*. Leicester:
Brockhampton Press, 1961; New York: Franklin Watts,
1962, pp. 11, 14, 80-84, 95, 98-99, 123, 128, 130.
Discussion of the Narnia books as poetically beautiful; the
allegorical meaning considered a bit difficult for children
(pp. 80-84); favorable mention of Lewis's views on writing for
children; recommendation of Narnia books and trilogy.

26. Foulon, Jacqueline. "The Theology of C. S. Lewis'
Children's Books." Master of Religious Education thesis:
Fuller Theological Seminary, 1962.
This is very much an educationally oriented thesis, pointing out
how Lewis's books may be used to teach Christian concepts to
children (by reading the Narnian books in Sunday School, *etc.*).
This teaching is in the fourth chapter, the practical application
of the survey of Lewis's theological and moral ideas in the books
in the first two chapters, and the summary of these ideas in the
third.
Despite the title, more comments on Christian life-style and
more discussion of Aslan as parallel to Christ than pure theology
appear in the chapters of analysis, which take the form of a précis
of each book followed by an examination. In the third chapter
the author faults Lewis on his presentation of God the Father and

God the Holy Spirit; she also notes some differences in application of the Passion in Narnia and in the human world; finally, she points out "the Doctrine of Scripture and the Doctrine of the Church" do not appear in any clear or extended way in the Narnian stories.

27. Fuller, Muriel. "C. S. Lewis."

Listed in § II; brief comments on the Chronicles of Narnia.

28. GoodKnight, Glen. "A Comparison of Cosmological Geography in the Works of J. R. R. Tolkien, C. S. Lewis, and Charles Williams." *Mythlore* 1 (July 1969): 18–22.

A comparison of the geography of Tolkien's Middle Earth, Lewis's Narnia (especially the Eastern Ocean), and Williams's Arthurian poems, which suggests a basic pattern of Mortal Lands, an Intermediate State, and Undying Lands. A diagrammatical set of maps appears on p. 20.

29. ————. "Lilith in Narnia." *Narnia Conference Proceedings*, ed. [Glen GoodKnight], pp. 15-19.

The volume is listed in this subsection.

A brief history of the Lilith legend, with comparisons drawn to Jadis in *The Magician's Nephew*; the White Witch—Jadis again—in *The Lion, the Witch and the Wardrobe*, who is said in the book to be a descendant of Lilith; and the Green Witch in *The Silver Chair*. George Macdonald's *Lilith* is mentioned in the history, but Charles Williams's Mrs. Lily Sammile in *Descent into Hell* is omitted.

30. [GoodKnight, Glen], ed. *Narnia Conference Proceedings.* Maywood, California: The Mythopoeic Society, 1970. 40 pp.

Contents: "Narnia Conference" (information on the conference on 29 November 1969); Doris Robin, "An Introduction to Middle Earth and Narnia"; Laura A. Ruskin, "What Is Narnia?"; Bruce McMenomy, "Arthurian Themes in the Narnia Books"; Gracia Fay Ellwood, " 'Which Way I Flie is Hell' "; Glen GoodKnight, "Lilith in Narnia"; Eugene Warren, "Utter East";

David Hulan, "Narnia and the Seven Deadly Sins"; Nancy-Lou Patterson, "Lord of the Beasts: Animal Archetypes in C. S. Lewis"; David Ralph, "A Comparison of the Calormenes with the Arabs, Turks, and Ancient Babylonians"; Peter Kreeft, "Narnia as Myth"; and "A Short Bibliography of Narnia Criticism" (a list of five articles and three books, presumably chosen by the editor). All of these titles, except the first and the last and Eugene Warren's, are separately annotated in this subsection; Eugene Warren's "Utter East" appears in § III-I.

31. Green, Carole A. "Observations on *The Magician's Nephew.*" *Chronicle of the Portland C. S. Lewis Society* 1 (3 March 1972): 3–4.

After a short survey of Lewis's comments on writing for children, Green considers such topics in *The Magician's Nephew* as humor, the contrast of the present and the past, male and female characteristics, pride, blindness to God, the acceptance of responsibility for sin, and opposite reactions of Aslan or God—all very briefly discussed.

32. Green, Roger Lancelyn. *Tellers of Tales: An Account of Children's Favorite Authors from 1839 to the Present Day, Their Books and How They Came to Write Them, Together with an Appendix and Indexes Giving the Titles and Dates of These Books.* London: Edmund Ward, 1953, pp. 258-260, 282. Revised edition, as *Tellers of Tales: British Authors of Children's Books from 1800 to 1964.* London: Edmund Ward, 1965; New York: Franklin Watts, 1965, pp. 39, 167, 192, 232, 277–279, 299.

The original edition has a favorable if minor discussion of the Narnia books (pp. 258–260); the revised edition contains a brief mention of Lewis's ideas of writing for children and his Chronicles of Narnia (mainly) (pp. 277-279). Neither edition contains anything which Green does not discuss more thoroughly in his *C. S. Lewis* (listed in § III-A).

33. Helson, Ravenna. "Fantasy and Self-Discovery." *Horn Book Magazine* 46 (April 1970): 121–134.

Fantasies are classified into six groupings, three by masculine authors, three by feminine. *The Lion, the Witch and the Wardrobe,* as well as Tolkien's *The Hobbit,* fits the group of masculine heroism: "the heroic or patriarchal fantasy."

34. Higgins, James E. *Beyond Words: Mystical Fancy in Children's Literature.* New York: Teachers College Press (Teachers College, Columbia University), 1970, pp. vii, 8, 18, 27, 32-47, 57, 62, 68, 81, 84, 104, 106, 108–109, 111.

After defining his terms in his first chapter, Higgins spends most of one chapter each on Tolkien, Lewis, George MacDonald, W. H. Hudson, and Antoine de Saint-Exupéry. The chapter on Lewis—"How These Books Are Written," pp. 32–48—is based on a passage in a letter from Lewis to the author mentioning four ways in which the writing of juvenile fiction differed from his usual writing.

35. ———. "A Letter from C. S. Lewis." *Horn Book Magazine* 42 (October 1966): 533–539.

The author quotes a letter from Lewis which answers seven questions he had posed about writing for children; the rest of the essay is an expansion of these answers. Nothing in the letter adds anything to Lewis's comments elsewhere on the Narnian stories (which form the main topic of the questions), but Lewis does mention that he had never met G. K. Chesterton.

36. Hooper, Walter. "CSL's Own Map of Narnia." *Bulletin of the New York C. S. Lewis Society* 2 (April 1971): 13.

A report on the publication of the map of Narnia drawn by C. S. Lewis for Pauline Baynes; published by the Bodleian Library on postcards (in black and white instead of Lewis's color), April 1971.

37. ———. "Past Watchful Dragons: The Fairy Tales of C. S. Lewis." In *Imagination and the Spirit,* ed. Charles Huttar, pp. 277-339.

The volume is listed in § 1.

This is the most important essay on the Chronicles of Narnia so far published, both for its content and for the original material by Lewis which it includes. Among the latter is Lewis's chronology of the history of Narnia (pp. 298–301); the "Lefay Fragment"—a non-Narnian version of some material later used in *The Magician's Nephew* (pp. 304–307); Lewis's map of Narnia (p. 310); and his sketch of two Monopods (p. 313). Hooper's essay is divided into nine sections. The first is a brief biography through Lewis's conversion, with emphasis on humanized animals, mythology, and *Sehnsucht*. The second section traces Lewis's later, Christian thinking about these three elements of his life. The third section gives Lewis's thoughts on the value of fairy tales. The fourth section gives the order in which the books were written, their chronology as Narnian history, and a plot summary of the books in the order they were published. The fifth section gives Lewis's chronology of Narnian history and a discussion of other Narnian fragments in Lewis's notebooks. The sixth section discusses several subjects, beginning with Pauline Baynes's work in illustrating the Narnia books; then it moves to the humanized animals, speaking of their unaltered animal characters, and to the psychological value in fiction of such type characters; next it takes up the relationship between the Narnian animals and humans, which leads into a discussion of Lewis's ideas about modern education and of the medieval aspects of the Narnian society—in short, Lewis's depiction of hierarchy in Narnia. The seventh section discusses the relationship of the Chronicles of Narnia and the Christian religion, pointing to both parallels and nonparallels in the relationship of Aslan and Christ; Hooper suggests the Chronicles were written to give pleasure and to unconsciously prepare the imagination for Christian belief, *not* to teach any thorough doctrinal beliefs. The eighth section discusses Lewis's attitude toward pagan myth and his use of pagan deities in Narnia. And the ninth section discusses the desire for God (or God's seeking of the individual), death, and salvation, both in Narnian terms and (so far as death is concerned) in terms of Lewis's biography.

38. Huck, Charlotte S., and Doris A. Young. *Children's Literature in the Elementary School*. New York: Holt, Rinehart and Winston, 1961, pp. 16, 305.

   Plot synopsis of the Narnia series with no mention of religious or philosophical meaning (p. 305).

39. Hulan, David. "Narnia and the Seven Deadly Sins." *Narnia Conference Proceedings*, ed. [Glen GoodKnight], pp. 21–23.

The volume is listed in this subsection.

A suggestion that Lewis accidently illustrated one of the Seven Deadly Sins in each book of the Narnia series; forcing of the thesis is admitted.

40. Hutton, M. "Writers for Children: C. S. Lewis." *School Librarian* 12 (July 1964): 124, 126, 129–132.

Discussion of the Narnia books, which Hutton regards as deliberately undramatic (i.e., Lewis does not have a gift for representing action) but a good imaginative vehicle for the inner meaning in them.

41. Kirk, Tim. An untitled map of Narnia. *Mythlore* 2 (Winter 1971): 15–16.

This fold-out map accompanies J. R. Christopher's "An Introduction to Narnia, Part II: The Geography of the Chronicles" (listed above).

42. Kreeft, Peter. "Narnia as Myth." *Narnia Conference Proceedings*, ed. [Glen GoodKnight], pp. 35–39.

The volume is listed in this subsection.

An application of four senses of *myth* to the Narnian Chronicles: first, a story of primitive divinity—*myth* as used by anthropologists and folklorists; second, a created Secondary World reflecting some truth in the Primary World—terms taken from Tolkien's "On Fairy-Stories"; third, a story echoing the truth of some other world outside our space-time continuum; and, fourth, a Platonic myth, as here, where Narnia is but a copy of the real Narnia (shown at the end of *The Last Battle*). As Kreeft says in his first paragraph, "[This paper] is more about myth than about Narnia; but Narnia is a perfect example of what it means by myth."

43. "The Light Fantastic." *Times Literary Supplement: Children's Books Section* 57 (21 November 1958): x.

A review of Roger Lancelyn Green's *The Land of the Lord High*

Tiger (along with eight other books). The reviewer suggests that this depicts a second-rate Narnia; Lewis replies in the next issue, p. 689 ("Books for Children," Hooper's Bibliography G-37), saying that the Tiger predated Aslan and was not derivative. (Cf. also Lewis's essay, "Modern Theology and Biblical Criticism," in *Christian Reflections*, p. 160, with Hooper's footnote quoting Lewis's letter.)

44. Linden, William. "New Light on Narnia; or, Who Beat the Drum?" *Bulletin of the New York C. S. Lewis Society* 2 (April 1971): 9–10.

   A reply to Shramko's "The Composition of the Chronicles of Narnia" (listed in this subsection); Linden nonseriously combines Lewis's "The Queen of Drum" with the Chronicles for a political analysis of various events in Narnia.

45. Lindskoog, Kathryn. *The Lion of Judah in Never-Never Land*. Grand Rapids, Michigan: Eerdmans Publishing Company, 1973.

   The publication, after the cut-off date of this checklist, of Kathryn A. Stillwell's M.A. thesis, which is listed below in this subsection; the book form appears under her married name.

46. McMenomy, Bruce. "Arthurian Themes in the Narnia Books." *Narnia Conference Proceedings*, ed. [Glen GoodKnight], pp. 8–10.

   The volume is listed in this subsection.

   A comparison of Arthur and Caspian; the points of the comparison are generally unfounded.

47. Montgomery, J. W. "The Chronicles of Narnia and the Adolescent Reader." *Journal of Religious Education* 54 (September–October 1959): 418–428. Excerpts printed: *Bulletin of the New York C. S. Lewis Society* 2 (April 1971): 10–13.

   A discussion of Aslan as Christ, of the proper age for children to read the Narnia books, and of Tolkien's essay on fairy tales (the parallel between the happy ending of the fairy tale and Christian belief).

48. Moorman, Charles. " 'Now Entertain Conjecture of a Time'—The Fictive Worlds of C. S. Lewis and J. R. R. Tolkien." In *Shadows of Imagination*, ed. Mark R. Hillegas, pp. 59–69.

The volume is listed in § III-A.

Moorman begins with the critical positions of Lewis in "Sometimes Fairy Stories May Say Best What's to Be Said" and Tolkien in "On Fairy-Stories," finding Lewis didactically Christian and Tolkien not, and then considers the Chronicles of Narnia and *The Lord of the Rings* as showing Christian optimism and pagan heroism respectively.

49. "The Myth Makers." *Times Literary Supplement*: *Children's Book Section*, 1 July 1955, pp. i-ii.

A survey of the Chronicles of Narnia (the reviewer has some knowledge of *The Last Battle*, which was to appear that fall), with a valuable brief study of Lewis's indebtedness to George Macdonald's children's books.

50. "Narnia Crossword Puzzle." *Mythril* 1 (Fall 1971): 15.

A crossword puzzle of a nonstandard sort, involving Narnian terms. The solution appeared as "Answer to Narnian Crossword Puzzle," *Mythril* 1 (Winter 1972): 17.

51. Patterson, Nancy-Lou. "Anti-Babels: Images of the Divine Centre in *That Hideous Strength*."

Listed in § III-D; some discussion of "divine centres" in the Chronicles of Narnia appears.

52. ———. "Lord of the Beasts: Animal Archetypes in C. S. Lewis." In *Narnia Conference Proceedings*, ed. [Glen GoodKnight], pp. 24–32.

The volume is listed in this subsection.

An anthropological sketch of man-beast identifications, with applications to Narnia, and also with brief comments on animals in fables and on Lewis's belief in animal salvation. This essay is a valuable aid in reading the Chronicles of Narnia as "vast *kōans*" (Chad Walsh's phrase, quoted on p. 30).

53. Ralph, David. "A Comparison of the Calormenes with the Arabs, Turks, and Ancient Babylonians." In *Narnia Conference Proceedings*, ed. [Glen GoodKnight], pp. 33–34.

The volume is listed in this subsection.

The title is indicative of the content; the actual comparisons are fairly obvious ones of types of clothing, social organizations, architecture, *etc.* Not scholarly.

54. Rajan, J. S. "German Mythology Applied: The Extension of the Literary Folk Memory." *Folklore* 77 (Spring 1966): 45–59 [45, 46, 54].

Analysis of the Germanic and Old English folk myth traditions, and their influence on Tolkien with some notes on Lewis's uses of a similar imaginative world.

55. Robin, Doris. "An Introduction to Middle Earth and Narnia." In *Narnia Conference Proceedings*, ed. [Glen GoodKnight], pp. 2–3.

The volume is listed in this subsection.

A brief comparison of the inner consistency, themes, and styles of Tolkien and Lewis; personal and impressionistic rather than scholarly.

56. Ruskin, Laura A. "What Is Narnia?" In *Narnia Conference Proceedings*, ed. [Glen GoodKnight], pp. 4–7.

The volume is listed in this subsection.

A comparison of Tolkien's Middle Earth, L. Frank Baum's Oz, and Narnia; the map of Oz promised on p. 4 does not appear. Not scholarly.

57. Sayers, Dorothy L. "Chronicles of Narnia." *Spectator* 195 (22 July 1955): 123.

A letter replying to the review of *The Magician's Nephew* by Amabel Williams-Ellis (listed in § VI-B-32) in which the reviewer said, "Surely Mr. Lewis should, all along, have had the courage of his convictions, and given Aslan the shape as well as the nature

and functions of an archangel." Sayers replies, ". . . the Lion
Aslan . . . has most emphatically *not* the 'nature and functions' of
an archangel, and for that reason has not been given the form
of one. In these tales of Absolutely Elsewhere, Aslan is shown as
creating the worlds (*The Magician's Nephew*), slain and arisen
again for the redemption of sin (*The Lion, the Witch, and the
Wardrobe*), incarnate as a Talking Beast among Talking Beasts
(*passim*), and obedient to the laws he has made for his own
creation (*The Voyage of the Dawn Treader*, p. 146). His august
archetype—higher than the angels and 'made a little lower' than
they—is thus readily identified as the 'Lion of the Tribe of Judah'.
Apart from a certain disturbance of the natural hierarchies
occasioned by the presence in the story of actual human beings,
Professor Lewis's theology and pneumatology are as accurate and
logical here as in his other writings. To introduce the historical
'form' of the Incarnation into a work of pure fantasy would, for
various reasons, be unsuitable."

58. Shramko, Richard. "The Composition of the Chronicles of
Narnia." *Bulletin of the New York C. S. Lewis Society* 2
(April 1971): 7–9. Reprinted in *Mythprint* 4 (September
1971): 2.

A parodic discussion of the Chronicles of Narnia in terms of
Higher Criticism, finding the various sources which were combined
in the Chronicles as published. The essay started a number of
replies: in the *Bulletin* appeared Linden's "New Light on Narnia"
and Christopher's "On the CSL Theory of Composition of the
Chronicles of Narnia" (both listed in this subsection); and in
Mythprint appeared a series of increasingly juvenile items which
have not been annotated here: "Dissent" by Dick Grundy, vol. 4
(October 1971): 6; "More on Narnia," vol. 4 (November 1971):
7; "More on Narnia," vol. 4 (December 1971): 4; and "Letters"
and "On a White Twig," vol. 5 (January 1972): 3-5.

59. ———. "Reflections on Narnia: Comments Desired."
Dittoed single sheet dated 1 May 1970. Untitled dittoed
five or six sheets dated 4 July 1970.

For the explanation of these separately printed materials, see the
note in § I on *The Bulletin of the New York C. S. Lewis Society*
about the Society's early separate publications.

The original sheet makes a few comments on the effects of myth and applies these to the Chronicles of Narnia. The subsequent pages contain letters of comments from Hope Kirkpatrick, Eugene Warren, Jared Lobdell, Richard Hodges, Dick Shramko, and (on the sixth page which appears in some copies) Maureen Kirkpatrick. Most of the comments are more religious than mythic.

60. Smith, Lillian H. "News from Narnia." *Canadian Library Association Bulletin* 15 (July 1958): 36–38. Reprinted in *Horn Book Magazine* 39 (October 1963): 470–473.

The note surveys *The Magician's Nephew* and *The Lion, the Witch and the Wardrobe*; mentions the memorable characters of Trufflehunter, Reepicheep, Puddleglum, and Aslan; and concludes that the books teach children "there is something to which [they] can lay hold: belief in the essential truth of their own imaginings."

61. Stillwell, Kathryn A: "The Lion of Judah in Never-Never Land: The Theology and Philosophy of C. S. Lewis Expressed in His Fantasies for Children." Unpublished M. A. thesis: Long Beach Teachers College, 1957. 113 pp.

A study of Lewis's conception of nature and supernature as operating in the children's books; Lewis's concept of God as symbolized by Aslan (see the essay immediately below); his concept of man as seen in the Narnia creatures. The thesis is bound with a letter from Lewis complimenting her work. *Note*: after its reorganization as Long Beach State College, the school lost or discarded this thesis; a copy is available in the Wheaton College C. S. Lewis Collection. See Lindskoog's book above in this subsection.

62. ———. "The Lion of Judah in C. S. Lewisland." *HIS: Magazine of Campus Christian Living* 19 (March 1959): 36-40.

After a brief introduction to the Chronicles, and an identification of Aslan in Biblical terms as "the Lion of the Tribe of Judah" (Revelation 5:5), the various aspects of Aslan, with parallels drawn to Christ, are discussed in a thorough survey.

63. Thomas, Mary Burrows. "The Fairy Stories of C. S. Lewis."
M. A. thesis: University of Oklahoma, 1964.

Mrs. Thomas beings with a 24-page survey of "The Fairy Story
as an Instructive Work" (her chapter title), which includes
analyses of "The Juniper Tree" (collected by the Brothers Grimm),
Hans Christian Andersen's "The Girl Who Trod on a Loaf," and
George Macdonald's *The Princess and Curdie* (oddly, she does
not mention *The Princess and the Goblin*, nor does she consider
E. Nesbit's books, which are in the tradition Lewis is using).
The second half of the thesis, 37 pages, discusses the meaning and
sources of the Chronicles of Narnia, and does it quite well. The
author's allegorical interpretation is sometimes, one suspects, far
more thorough than Lewis consciously intended, but it is generally
successful.

64. Townsend, John Rowe. *Written for Children: An Outline
of English Children's Literature*. London: Garnet Miller,
1965, pp. 122-123.

Discussion of the Narnia books as fantasy. Finds Aslan's sacrifice
and the end of *The Last Battle* moving. Suggests that some of the
magic machinery (as the rings in *Magician's Nephew*) is not
equal to the size and scope of the theme, and that the characterization of the children is inadequate to sustain their roles as the
ruler of Narnia or the betrayer of Christ.

65. Wallace, Robert. "Kids' Books: A Happy Few Among the
Junk." *Life* 57 (11 December 1964): 112-114, 116, 118,
120, 121-122, 125-126, 128, 129, 130 [116, 130].

Mentions Lewis as an example of writing with respect for children;
recommends *The Lion, the Witch, and the Wardrobe*.

H. *Till We Have Faces*

1. [Demarest, Michael]. "Editors' Preface" to *Till We Have Faces: A Myth Retold*, by C. S. Lewis, pp. vii-xi. New York: Time, Inc., 1966. [Time Reading Program special edition reprinted by arrangement with Harcourt, Brace & World.]

   Lewis was "superbly endowed" with wit, wisdom, warmth, erudition, imagination, and a deep understanding of human nature. This is his only "straight" novel and perhaps his most powerful: "austere, opaque." An appreciation also of Lewis as trail-blazing literary historian, popular campus lecturer. [The preface is anonymously written by a *Time* senior editor, a one-time Oxford pupil of Lewis.]

2. Griffiths, Bede. *Christian Ashram: Essays towards a Hindu-Christian Dialogue*. London: Darton, Longman, and Todd, 1966.

   This volume by a close friend of Lewis, while it has no reference to Lewis, is of interest because of its discussion of the Hindu word *maya* (cf. Orual's nickname of Maia in *Till We Have Faces*). The word is usually translated as "illusion" but "Sankara, when he describes the world as *maya*, does not mean that it has no being at all. He describes it as 'neither being nor not-being at all.' What he was principally concerned to do was to deny that the world has the same kind of being as the Brahman, that is absolute being. The world has relative being; it may even be said to have being 'by participation,' or at least that is what his thought seems to imply" (p. 203). See also pp. 33, 170, 186, 210–211.

3. Hannay, Margaret. "Orual: The Search for Justice." *Mythlore* 2 (Winter 1971): 5–6.

   "One essential difficulty of the novel is understanding in what way Orual is Psyche and in what way she is Ungit" (p. 5)—the essay is an extended discussion of these likenesses.

4. Hogan, Patrick G., Jr. "Opportunities and Limitations."

Listed under "SF in the Classroom" (no author) in § III-D; a report of a student's enthusiasm for *Till We Have Faces*.

5. Kilby, Clyde S. "An Interpretation of *Till We Have Faces.*" *Orcrist*, No. 6 (Winter 1971–1972): 7–10.

Kilby summarizes the plot of the novel with Christian applications, and then spends a paragraph each on the Fox, Ungit, transformations, Bardia, Redival, and Lewis's use of Apuleius.

6. Kranz, Gisbert. "Amor and Psyche: Metamorphose eines Mythos bei C. S. Lewis." *Arcadia: Zeitschrift für vergleichende Literaturwissenschaft* 4 (1969): 285–299.

"Cupid and Psyche: The Metamorphosis of a Myth as seen by C. S. Lewis." Part I is a study of Apuleius's story of Cupid and Psyche: is it a myth or an allegory? Part II is a précis of Lewis's book—the scene where Orual reads her complaint is compared to Ransom, Weston, and Devine before the Oyarsa in *Out of the Silent Planet*. Part III is an elaborate, exhaustive comparison of the stories by Apuleius and Lewis. Allegorical readings of episodes—for example, the collecting of the grains of wheat— are suggested. Finally, Kranz suggests that the original of Orual may be Mrs. Moore, Lewis's "mother."

7. Matthews, T. S. "Introduction" to *Till We Have Faces: A Myth Retold*, by C. S. Lewis, pp. xii–xvii. New York: Time, Inc., 1966. [Time Reading Program special edition reprinted by arrangement with Harcourt, Brace & World.]

Time's former managing editor summarizes story line and literary sources. Though "religious fiction," Matthews says this novel has "not a trace of Christian propaganda."

8. Moorman, Charles. *Arthurian Triptych.*

Listed in § III-D; some discussion of myth in *Till We Have Faces*.

9. Norwood, W. D., Jr. "C. S. Lewis' Portrait of Aphrodite."
   Southern Quarterly 8 (1970): 237-272.

   An essay taken directly from Norwood's treatment of the book in
   his dissertation; see the summary in § III-A of Norwood's
   Neo-Medieval Novels of C. S. Lewis.

10. Ruskin, Laura A. "Three Good Mothers: Galadriel, Psyche
    and Sybil Coningsby." In *Mythcon I Proceedings*, ed.
    Glen GoodKnight, pp. 12-14.

    The volume is listed in § I.

    "Galadriel [of Tolkien's *Lord of the Rings*] personifies the
    fundamental Mother Moon of the primitive man, from whom
    flow blessings and good gifts. From the Moon Mother grows
    World Soul, or Psyche [of Lewis's *Till We Have Faces*], innocent
    and girlish. From Psyche's disobedience came the Weeping Mother,
    or *Mater Dolorosa*, endlessly searching for her child. At last
    Psyche matures into Sybil [of Williams's *Greater Trumps*], while
    Isis merely ages into the mad Joanna [also a character in
    Williams's novel]."

11. Starr, Nathan Comfort. *C. S. Lewis's "Till We Have Faces"*:
    Introduction and Commentary. New York: Seabury Press,
    Religious Dimensions in Literature pamphlet series, 1968.

    A 24-page pamphlet. A brief biographical section; a discussion of
    the view of myth in *Experiment in Criticism*; a summary of
    plot; and a skillful introduction to the book, emphasizing Lewis's
    explanation of the book in a letter to Professor C. S. Kilby
    (pp. 11–12); the various types of love, as explained in *The Four
    Loves* (pp. 13–15); and the spiritual death and rebirth motifs
    (pp. 15–17). Professor Starr also points out Lewis's use of
    Williams's "coinherence" (p. 16) and the likenesses of Psyche to
    Christ (p. 19). He regards the novel "the most powerful
    expression of Lewis's religious belief to be found in any of his
    novels" and "no period piece" but "triumphantly a tract for the
    times."

I. Poems and Fiction not by Lewis

Note: this section does not try to enter the tangled briars of cross-influences among the Inklings, but simply records a few clear references to Lewis or his works in later creative literature.

1. Another Clerk. "Letters to a Great-Nephew." *Bulletin of the New York C. S. Lewis Society* 3 (November 1971) : 4–5.

   The winner of the Society's Screwtape imitation competition. Screwtape advises Flibbergib about his female "patient" who is thinking about entering a convent.

2. Barfield, Owen, and C. S. Lewis. *Mark vs. Tristram: Correspondence between C. S. Lewis and Owen Barfield.* Ed. Walter Hooper. Cambridge, Massachusetts: The Lowell House Printers, 1967. 16 pp. [This pamphlet appeared in an edition of 126 numbered copies.]

   In "The *Morte Darthur*" (*Times Literary Supplement*, 7 June 1947, pp. 273-274), Lewis wrote, ". . . how different such nobility may be from the virtues of the law-abiding citizen will appear if we imagine the life of Sir Tristram as it would be presented to us by King Mark's solicitors" (p. 273). Owen Barfield wrote a letter from Barfield and Barfield, Solicitors, acting for H. M. King Mark I of Cornwall; Lewis replied for Blaise and Merlin on behalf of Sir T. de Lyonesse K. T. R.; two letters from Barfield and Barfield followed; and a final one from Maistre Bleyse.

3. Berrigan, Daniel J., S.J. "Failure." *Atlantic Monthly* 181 (May 1948) : 107.

   A poem (mentioned in Walsh's *C. S. Lewis: Apostle to the Skeptics*) which uses the phrase "a lost perelandran lane." The poem is not otherwise specifically Lewisian. (It seems to be by one of the Berrigan brothers, known for the burning of draft-board records and other acts of war protest.)

4. Betjeman, John. "May-Day Song for North Oxford." In *Collected Poems*, pp. 110–111. Boston: Houghton Mifflin, 1959. Originally published in *New Bats for Old Belfries* (1945).

   A reference to "St. C. S. Lewis's Church" appears in 1. 10.

5. Blish, James. *Black Easter.* Garden City, New York: Doubleday and Company, 1968.

   Not seen. This science-fiction novel is dedicated to Lewis, includes a quotation from *The Screwtape Letters,* and involves a dualistic theology. Blish wrote a sequel, *The Day After Judgment,* which also has not been seen.

6. Booth, Wayne C. "The College as Church: or, Screwtape Revived." In *Now Don't Try to Reason with Me.* Chicago: The University of Chicago Press, 1970, pp. 175–185. Previously printed in *The Earlham Review,* Summer 1967.

   Beginning with a note on the modern tendency to look to the university for values, Booth appends eight letters from Screwtape to Dr. Harley P. Sellout, Vice-President of Surrogate University, giving him advice to advance optimism *about the future,* to keep courses from making contact with reality, *etc.*

7. Boucher, Anthony. "Balaam." In *Far and Away,* pp. 25–39. New York: Ballantine Books, 1955.

   A science-fiction short story set on Mars which refers to Lewis by name (calling him an Anglo-Catholic) and which uses his Old Solar term *hnau* in a theological discussion, "What is man?" The story is a "first contact" story not between humans and Martians but between humans and another group of *hnau* visiting Mars; it also echoes the Biblical story of Balaam and his ass.

8. ————. "The Quest for St. Aquin." In *New Tales of Space and Time,* ed. Raymond J. Healy. New York: Henry Holt, 1951.

   A brief allusion to Screwtape appears in a dialogue between a Catholic priest and a robot ass.

9. Braude, Nan. "A Shy Proposal." *Yandro* 17 (November 1969) : 13.

A mock educational essay about a Master of Oligarchy and Coercion degree being offered by Mandeville College, "aided by a grant from the National Institute of Coordinated Experiments." Except for this one allusion to *That Hideous Strength*, no Lewisian matter appears.

10. Burgeon, G. A. L. [pseudonym of Owen Barfield]. *This Ever Diverse Pair*. With an introduction by Walter de la Mare. London: Victor Gollancz, 1950. 144 pp.

A small, fictional book, possibly autobiographical, about a psychological split of a solicitor into a poet (Burgeon) and a businessman (Burden). Ramsden, mentioned in Chapter VI, "The Things That Are Caesar's!," seems to be a portrait of Lewis—this is presumably the chapter "founded irresponsibly on fact," according to the note on p. 8; Barfield has, in other discussions of Lewis, also mentioned Lewis's failure to pay income tax on his royalities at first. ". . . I thought of Ramsden, with his morale in the skies and his mind blowing steadily out of them, a strong mind edged like a razor" (p. 66).

11. Chambers, Whittaker. "The Devil." *Life* 24 (2 February 1948), 76–85 [77–78, 80].

A dialogue between Satan and a young pessimist during a New Year's party. C. S. Lewis, as one of those not taken in by Satan's disappearance from the modern world, is mentioned in the text (p. 78) and given a box with photograph and quotation from *The Screwtape Letters* (p. 80).

12. Christopher, Joe R. "Loss of Vision: A Sequence of Five Median Odes." *Mythril* 1 (Summer 1972) : 11.

Five sonnets, on the author's experiences of *Sehnsucht* compared with those of Wordsworth, Coleridge, Shelley, and Lewis.

13. Forsyth, James. *Dear Wormwood: A Play in Three Acts Based Upon C. S. Lewis's Book 'The Screwtape Letters.'* Chicago: The Dramatic Publishing Company, 1961.

Approved by C. S. Lewis for publication and performance, this
116-page adaptation of Screwtape Letters is designed for 17 actors
playing on an uncluttered stage. Lewis's epistolary format is
dropped; in Forsyth's version Screwtape and Wormwood confer
face-to-face on how to corrupt Michael Average, a young
architect.

14. Fowkes, Robert W. "A Christmas Tale." *Living Church*
161 (20 December 1970) : 10–12.

A report of a meeting of "the lowerarchy of hell" in 1800, in a
general imitation of *The Screwtape Letters* and "Screwtape
Proposes a Toast." Wormwood is the only Lewisian character to
appear. The lowerarchy plots Clement Clarke Moore's writing
of "A Visit from St. Nicholas"; an allusion appears to Dr. Seuss's
"How the Grinch Stole Christmas."

15. Grant, Myrna. "A Radio Adaptation of *The Lion, the Witch
and the Wardrobe.*" Unpublished M.A. thesis: Wheaton
College (Ill.), 1971. 64 pp. + nine separately numbered
scripts of approximately a dozen pages each.

Some light analysis of the connotations of names in *The Lion, the
Witch and the Wardrobe*—part of the preparation for radio
characterization (pp. 36-38). The adaptations are into fifteen-
minute scripts; most of them seem nicely done.

16. Green, Roger Lancelyn. "Logres." *Oxford Magazine* 67
(18 November 1948) : 161.

An Italian sonnet subtitled "To C. W. and C. S. L." in which "a
young knight in the Waste Land" (presumably Green) finds
Arthur's realm and begins his search for the Grail under the
direction of Taliessin (Charles Williams) and Merlin (C. S.
Lewis).

17. Hooper, Walter. "Hell and Immortality." *Breakthrough*,
no vol. no. or date, 6-8.

Hooper attempts a Screwtape letter to damn the cult of anti-hero
but lacks Lewis's wit.

18. Lawson, Craig. Untitled "Screwtape Letter." *Bulletin of the New York C. S. Lewis Society* 3 (November 1971) : 5-6.

    Screwtape writes Drainscum about tempting a young man who is planning to attend a theological seminary.

19. McMurtry, Larry. *All My Friends Are Going to Be Strangers.* New York: Simon and Schuster, 1972. 286 pp.

    A novel about the sex life and other adventures of a Texas writer; at one point (p. 90) he meditates on being a scholar "like George Saintsbury or C. S. Lewis."

20. Morris, Richard Melvin. "C. S. Lewis as a Christian Apologist." *Anglican Theological Review* 33 (July 1951) : 158-168.

    A Lewis puff written as a series of Screwtape letters describing him and several major religious writings.

21. Myra, H. L. *No Man in Eden.* Waco, Texas, and London: Word Books, 1969.

    In the preface, "Beyond Space Operas," Myra writes, ". . . unfortunately, with a few exceptions such as C. S. Lewis' works, modern science-fiction writers both good and bad depict a universe in which God is irrelevant" (p. 9). He also "acknowledges his debt to many writers and speakers, among them C. S. Lewis . . ." (p. 2). The story is reminiscent of the Ransom Trilogy, involving (1) an unfallen visitor to earth from another part of the universe (via a flying saucer), (2) a married couple with marital problems, and (3) a plot to corrupt young people by a pop music company. A later trip to space by the hero shows a progressive, unfallen race: a couple and their descendents are turning a barren world livable. (Myra has odd ideas about the hero of antimatter visiting the rest of the universe of matter without an explosion.) After some ritual meetings which are slightly reminiscent of Lewis's works, a return trip involves a visit to Hell where the demons feed on negative human emotions, rather like Screwtape, but otherwise without Lewisian imagery. (Two minor allusions: the hero reads Tolkien's *Lord of the Ring* on p. 79, and the image of Christ's birth as an invasion—which Lewis used in his wartime *Case for Christianity*—appears on p. 125:) The whole work, as fiction, is better than this list of derivations would suggest. (We wish to thank Mrs. Vicki Cate for drawing our attention to this novel.)

22. "The Origin of the Wasp." *Good Work* 28 (Winter 1965): 20-21.

   A light satire with political overtones in a Screwtape vein. An editor's note maintains it originated in a conversation between Lewis and an unidentified pupil in summer, 1963.

23. Preston, Trevor (adaptor). "The Lion, the Witch and the Wardrobe." 1967.

   A television serialization run in Britain in the summer of 1967. Cf. Norman Hare's review listed in § VI-A-3.

24. Swann, Donald, and David Marsh. *Perelandra.*

   An opera with a score by Swann and lyrics by Marsh. See Pepper's "New Opera 'Discovers' a Campus Diva" and Sargent's "Musical Events: As It Was in the Beginning" in § VI-A-3.

25. Walsh, Chad. "A Pilgrim's Progress." *University of Kansas City* 13 (Summer 1947): 328–329.

   A poem with apparent reference to Walsh's personal reaction to *Pilgrim's Regress.*

26. Warren, Eugene. "Utter East." In *Narnia Conference Proceedings*, ed. [Glen GoodKnight], p. 20. Reprinted in *Mythlore* 2 (Winter 1970): 10.

   The volume is listed in § III-G.

   Twelve or fourteen lines of free verse, describing the effect of the conclusion of *The Voyage of the "Dawn Treader"* upon the author.

IV. Religion and Ethics

A. Miscellaneous Items

1. Allen, Jimmy R. " 'Geraldine theology' sign of the times."
   Brownwood Bulletin, 8 May 1972, p. 4.

   A religious editorial beginning from Flip Wilson's portayal of
   Geraldine, with "her" phrase, "The devil made me do it." It
   develops into a discussion of current Satanism and ends with quoting
   Lewis on two attitudes toward Satan of which the devil approves.
   (Probably a syndicated column; we wish to thank Mrs. Joyce
   Greenlee for giving us this copy.)

2. Auden, W. H. "The Corruption of Innocent Neutrons."
   New York Times Magazine, 1 August 1965, § 6,
   pp. 18-19 [18].

   Lewis is cited and discussed in Auden's article as dealing with the
   "emotional faith in Progress."

3. Barfield, Owen. "Either : Or." In *Imagination and the Spirit*,
   ed. Charles Huttar, pp. 25-42 [33-35, 41-42].

   The volume is listed in § I.

   Barfield discusses Coleridge's concept of polarity (a central truth
   which manifests itself in opposite forms) : in his discussion he
   regrets the failure of the romantic theologians—C. S. Lewis and
   Charles Williams—to avail themselves of the unifying nature
   of Coleridgean thought. Lewis's particular irreconcilable opposites
   were self and the Absolute, joined (but not unified) by longing,
   just as the Romantic were selves divided from nature.

4. Bergier, Jacques. *Admirations*.
   Listed in § I.

5. Carnell, Corbin Scott. "C. S. Lewis on Eros as a Means of Grace." In *Imagination and the Spirit*, ed. Charles Huttar, pp. 341-351.

The volume is listed in § I.

In a discussion based primarily on *The Four Loves* but drawing on many of Lewis's writings, Carnell traces "four basic emphases concerning the benefits of married love": first, "one has the opportunity to develop a disciplined awareness of another person, to get to know that person in his or her uniqueness" (pp. 342-343); second, "the opportunity [marriage] affords to celebrate sexuality as a kind of pagan sacrament" (p. 343); third, "a . . . gift . . . in the way one person completes the other, helping to heal the wounds encountered in living, helping to overcome the limitations of being one person sealed in one skin" (p. 347); and fourth, "earthly love as a reflection of divine love" (p. 348).

6. Cassells, Louis. "Preconceptions determine most of your beliefs." *Fort Worth Press*, c. 23 February 1972 (no page numbers on the clipping given one of the editors). [United Press International release.]

A discussion of the ideas in "Miracles," a Lewis essay in *God in the Dock*, with quotations from the first paragraph.

7. Every, Edward. "Doctrine and Liturgy." *Church Times* 132 (8 July 1949): 445-446; and "Invocation of Saints," *ibid.* (22 July 1949): 481-482.

Letters. Cf. also Lewis's letters, "The Church's Liturgy," *ibid.* (20 May 1949): 319; *ibid.* (1 July 1949): 427; "Invocation," *ibid.* (15 July 1949): 463–464; and *ibid.* (5 August 1949): 513. Every takes issue with Lewis over liturgy and Lewis's restricted use of the word "devotion." See also Hughes's "The Church's Liturgy" in this subsection for another correspondent at the same time on the same topics.

8. Fowler, Albert. "The Lost Relevance of Religion." *Approach*, No. 32 (Summer 1959): 3-7.

A brief study of the post-Christian present, focused through Lewis's *De Descriptione Temporum*, which compares Lewis's lecture with Toynbee's notion of post-Christian man. Fowler believes Lewis gives the idea "concentrated impact" but the sooner "the remnant of practicing Christians who live uneasily in the church's hollow shell" give it up, the better.

9. Fremantle, Anne (ed.). *The Protestant Mystics*. With an Introduction by W. H. Auden. Boston: Little, Brown and Company, 1964. 396 pp. [7-8, 349-354, 386-389, 395, 396].

In addition to a citation of Lewis on Renaissance history in Auden's Introduction (pp. 7-8), a selection from *Surprised by Joy* and Letter XXXI from *The Screwtape Letters* appear on pp. 349-354, and a selection from N. W. Clerk's *A Grief Observed* on pp. 386-389. (Clerk is identified only as "a distinguished contemporary writer and theologian.") Note also Auden's mention of Charles Williams (p. 29) and the selections from George Macdonald (pp. 260-265).

10. Fuller, Edmund. *Man in Modern Fiction: Some Minority Opinions on Contemporary American Writing*. New York: Random House, 1958, pp. 13–14, 59, 79, 119.

In a discussion of James Jones's *Some Came Running*, Lewis's *The Abolition of Man* is cited (pp. 13–14). In a discussion of John Aldridge's *In Search of Heresy*, Fuller includes Lewis (and Tolkien, Charles Williams, and Dorothy Sayers) in a list of writers meant to counteract the suggestion that acceptance of a religious belief inhibits the creative mind—T. S. Eliot and W. H. Auden are also listed (p. 59). Tolkien, Williams, and Lewis are again mentioned in a discussion of writers who describe the demonic (p. 79). And the final mention of Lewis is a quotation on sex from *Mere Christianity*, meant (by Fuller) as an answer to D. H. Lawrence (p. 119).

11. Glasson, T. Francis. "C. S. Lewis on St. John's Gospel: A correction and a protest." *Theology* 71 (June 1968): 267–269.

The essay refers to the fifth paragraph of "Modern Theology and Biblical Criticism" (collected in *Christian Reflections*). There Lewis quotes from a commentary which sums up the view of James

Drummond's *An Inquiry into the Character and Authorship of the Fourth Gospel*, saying that Drummond holds the Gospel to be a romance of the type of *Pilgrim's Progress*. (Walter Hooper's footnote on p. 154 of *Christian Reflections* gives the full citations.) Glasson shows that the commentary distorted Drummond's meaning, that the word *romance* appeared in Drummond only in a quotation from Macaulay about classical historians and was agreed to by Drummond only in connection to the parts of the Old Testament, and that Drummond, although not taking the Fourth Gospel to be precise history, nevertheless thought it accurate on the date of the Last Supper and believed it written by the Apostle John.

12. Hamilton, C. J. "Christian Myth and Modern Man." *Encounter* [Butler University College of Religion, Indiana], 29 (Summer 1968): 246–255.

A contrast of Lewis and Bultmann on myth. Bultmann is subjective, demands existential encounter and relevance, and brackets factual questions; Lewis is rational, sees Christianity as myth-fulfillment, and, Hamilton says, believes one can accept the facts and not become personally involved. Discussion interesting but slight.

13. Hart, Jeffrey. "The Rebirth of Christ" (subtitle on the cover only: "The Oxford Don Who Went to Bethlehem"). *National Review* 17 (28 December 1965): 1192–1196.

Beginning from Lewis's treatment of the contemporary world as a "period" like past periods, the author comments about Higher Criticism (which formed the non-Christian modern attitudes) now being proven wrong by specialized studies; then he returns to Lewis as being the modern equivalent to Church tradition.

14. Hooke, S. H. "Basic Fears." *Times Literary Supplement*, 27 January 1945, p. 43; and *ibid.*, 10 February 1945, p. 67.

Letters. Cf. Lewis's letters, *ibid.*, 2 December 1944, p. 583; and *ibid.*, 3 February 1945, p. 55. A dispute over Hebrew translation and interpretation of creation.

15. Hooper, Walter. "Preface." In *Christian Reflections*, by
    C. S. Lewis. London: Geoffrey Bles, 1967; Grand Rapids,
    Mich.: William B. Eerdmans, 1967, pp. vii-xiv.

    Hooper discusses Lewis's theology; he regards as central to his
    thought his belief in man's immortality and the solid either-or of
    his Christian faith. Hooper remarks on the background of the
    essays and addresses in this collection, some published for the
    first time.

16. Howard, Thomas. *An Antique Drum: The World as Image.*
    Philadelphia and New York: J. B. Lippincott Company,
    1969.

    The book is dedicated to Clyde S. Kilby, and it is prefaced with
    this acknowledgment: "While there are no footnotes in the
    following pages, it will be perfectly obvious to many readers that a
    hundred acknowledgments are due to Charles Williams, J. R. R.
    Tolkien, C. S. Lewis, and T. S. Eliot. If there is anything here
    which makes sense, it probably derives from something which one
    or another of these gentlemen has said somewhere. Any woolly-
    mindedness and bad workmanship are mine." The most obvious
    reference to the ideas of the Inklings is that to Gomorrah in
    connection with a discussion of masturbation (p. 129), which
    recalls Williams's *Descent into Hell*. One image which may come
    from Lewis (but, like many in Lewis, it is a traditional one) is
    that of Heaven or salvation as a Dance (p. 157). The basic
    argument of the volume is a contrast between the scientific world
    view in which factual knowledge has no meaning outside itself
    and man's personal view which involves ritual actions for the
    sake of pleasure and meaning.

17. Hughes, W. D. F. "The Church's Liturgy." *Church Times*
    132 (24 June 1949): 409.

    A letter. The exchange began with E. L. Mascall's article on
    liturgical development, "Quadringentesimo Anno," *ibid.*, (6 May
    1949): 282. Lewis wrote a 20 May 1949 letter in response. Hughes
    wonders if Lewis is against Scriptural enrichments of the liturgy
    (as the first part of "Hail Mary") because of doctrinal implications.
    Lewis's reply, 1 July 1949, says such enrichment does imply

doctrinal changes but "the individual priest is not the judge of such a doctrinal change." See also Every's "Doctrine and Liturgy" in this subsection for another correspondent at the time on the same topics.

18. Joad, C. E. M. *The Recovery of Belief: A Restatement of Christian Philosophy*. London: Faber and Faber, 1952, pp. 24, 81.

Joad disagrees with Lewis and others on the cosmic Fall postulated "as a result of which the whole of life is infected with sin" (as a way of dealing with the problem of evil; p. 24); and discusses the influence of *Abolition of Man* in changing Joad's view toward the problem of evil and moral responsibility (p. 81).

19. King, James Roy. "Christian Fantasy in the Novels of C. S. Lewis and Charles Williams."

Listed in § III-A.

20. Kranz, Gisbert. "Sexualität nach C. S. Lewis." *Begegnung* 24 (October 1969): 156-164.

"Sexuality according to C. S. Lewis" in six sections. The first is biographical: the homosexuality of schoolboys described in *Surprised by Joy*, and Lewis's (or John's) relations to the brown girls in *The Pilgrim's Progress*; Lewis's late marriage is also noted. The next four sections are a survey of Lewis's statement on sexual matters in various books: *The Allegory of Love*, *Studies in Words* (the passages dealing with D. H. Lawrence), *Dymer*, *Mere Christianity*, *The Four Loves*, *That Hideous Strength* ("Venus at St. Anne's" chapter), *A Preface to "Paradise Lost,"* "Ministering Angels," and *The Great Divorce*. Finally, the conclusion is drawn that Lewis, like Aquinas, sees sexuality as good. (We wish to thank Henry Noel for help in preparing this summary.)

21. Kuhn, Daniel K. "The Joy of the Absolute: A Comparative Study of the Romantic Visions of William Wordsworth and C. S. Lewis." In *Imagination and the Spirit*, ed. Charles Huttar, pp. 189-214.

The volume is listed in § I.

"If for Wordsworth sensations of Spirit come to man from nature and find a corroborating affinity with his own spirit within the mind, for Lewis the impact of absolute Spirit is to raise man to a higher, mythological level. It is a renovation of man's natural being into the godlike echelon of life. For Wordsworth transcendental consciousness actualizes the inherent potential for goodness in man, intensifying his perspicacity of soul and energizing it to communicate its depth more creatively. But for Lewis the divine Spirit imparts godlikeness *to* man" (p. 198). This quotation is typical of Kuhn's style and sums up the essential distinction he is making, but a number of other points are made: a comparison of Wordsworth's and Lewis's views to Bergson's vitalism (pp. 194–196), a comparison of Wordsworth's and Lewis's explanations of evil (pp. 198–201), and a comparison of their views of the universe, especially in connection to science (pp. 210–211) and love (pp. 213-214).

22. Lambert, Byron C. "Reflections on *Reflections on the Psalms." Bulletin of the New York C. S. Lewis Society* 2 (November 1970): 2-4.

Lambert begins with his first impressions upon reading the book and his thoughts on his second reading, together with some comments on the English reviews; he then makes three points: first, that Lewis is "a luminous teacher of poetry" in the book; second, that he is "an ideal scholar" in that he does not lose the essential point under a heap of erudition; and, third, that the book provides a "harrowing moral experience" because of the moral judgments it leads its reader to pass upon himself. The end of the paper digresses onto the psychology of Jews as suggested by Lewis and as applied to the modern era by Lambert (who seems to think they are mostly radicals).

23. Lander, Joyce; Phyllis Talbott; and Terri Williams. "Panel Discussion on *Reflections on the Psalms." Chronicle of the Portland C. S. Lewis Society* 1 (2 June 1972): 3-4.

The "panel discussion" actually consists of three statements on the book read by the panelists. Phyllis Talbott's comments compare the Cursing Psalms to current child-raising practices which allow the child to express his feelings but not to act on the destructive ones. Joyce Lander's comments were epitomizing except for her summary: the volume "is for me the least appealing of Lewis' books. I find it difficult to accept his interpretation of the so-called cursing and judgmental psalms. . . ." I "have not found that his experience corresponded in any important way with mine. . . ." Terri Williams's comments listed six points on which Lewis praised the psalmists' attitudes vs. four points on which he condemned them.

24. Lindskoog, Kathryn. "Farewell to Shadowlands: C. S. Lewis on Death."

Listed in § I; contains citations from *Miracles, Mere Christianity, The Four Loves,* "The Weight of Glory," "Membership," and "The World's Last Night."

25. London, Kenneth. "C. S. Lewis and I: The Bible and Existentialism." Student honors paper: Wheaton College (Ill.), n.d. 52 + 33 pp. [Available in the C. S. Lewis Collection, Wheaton College, Illinois.]

The study consists of two papers (with separate pagination): "Lewis and I: Modern Theology, God, the Bible, *Genesis* and the Fall" and "Lewis and Existentialism." The style is lively (some may call it *undergraduate*); the second essay is based largely on *The Pilgrim's Regress,* with John's leap into the black pool paralleled to Kierkegaard's leap of faith (II, p. 20). Not of scholarly importance.

26. Malania, Leo. "One Eucharist: Different Forms." *Living Church* 164 (6 February 1972): 10-11 [11].

Malania uses Lewis's *An Experiment in Criticism* to suggest that users of the Episcopal *Services for Trial Use* should (and have to) surrender themselves to the trial use before they judge it, and that they avoid judging the style by arbitrary rules rather than its power to communicate. A letter from Hope M. Kirkpatrick, Secretary of the New York C. S. Lewis Society, *ibid.* (5 March 1972): 4, while not disputing the application made of Lewis's criticism, clarifies his thought on liturgical change, based on *Letters to Malcolm,* first letter.

27. Merchant, Fr. Robert. "An Appraisal of *Malcolm*." *Bulletin of the New York C. S. Lewis Society* 3 (February 1972): 2-4.

Merchant begins with two criticisms of *Letters to Malcolm*, that the literary convention of epistles seems too clever in its tossing of topics back and forth and that there is much padding in the fictionalizing. He then summarizes or quotes Lewis on a number of topics, and concludes by raising a question about Lewis's understanding of the corporate nature of the Church. An account of the meeting of the Society at which this paper was read appears on pp. 1–2.

28. Myers, Doris T. "Brave New World: The Status of Women according to Tolkien, Lewis, and Williams."

Listed in § III-D; the medieval view of women's status in the Ransom Trilogy.

29. Oury, Scott. "The Value of Something Other . . ."

Listed in § I; some discussion of Natural Law.

30. Phillips, J. B. "Translator's Foreword."

Listed in § II; Lewis's encouragement of Phillips's New Testament translation.

31. Routley, Erick. "Correspondence with an Anglican Who Dislikes Hymns." *Presbyter* 6 (1948): 15-20.

An excerpt from the first of Routley's two letters is reprinted (with all of Lewis's two letters) in *God in the Dock* (Grand Rapids: Eerdmans, 1970), 330.

32. Scott, Nathan A., Jr. "Poetry and Prayer."

Listed in § III-A.

33. Urang, Gunnar. *Shadows of Heaven: Religion and Fantasy in the Fantasy in the Writings of C. S. Lewis, Charles Williams, and J. R. R. Tolkien.*

Listed in § III-A.

34. Vincent, P[aul]. "C. S. Lewis as Amateur Philosopher."

A 4-page mimeographed address, dated July 1970 but mailed to members of the New York C. S. Lewis Society in October; see listing of *The Bulletin of the New York C. S. Lewis Society* in § I for the explanation of these early separate publications.

Vincent does not seem to know that Lewis taught philosophy for one year at Oxford—hence the "Amateur." The content is basically a discussion of the first part of *Miracles*, "Transposition," and *The Abolition of Man*.

35. Walsh, Chad. "Aldous Huxley and C. S. Lewis: Novelists of Two Religions."

Listed in § III-A; despite the *novelists* in the title, much emphasis on the religious ideas simply.

36. Warren, Eugene. "Venus Redeemed."

Listed in § III-D; a comparison of the comments on marital love in *The Four Loves* with the Studdocks in *That Hideous Strength*.

B. General Surveys of Lewis's Theology

1. Allen, E. L. "The Theology of C. S. Lewis." *Modern Churchman* 34 (January–March 1945): 317–324.

   From the theological viewpoint of the Broad Church, with praise for Albert Schweitzer, in appreciation of Jesus as a challenger of tradition, Allen attacks Lewis's theological works as dogmatic, unhistorical (in the Schweitzerian sense), and crude. That is, Lewis treats a supposed central tradition in Christianity as authority when there is no central tradition. He concentrates on the Pauline epistles as the "norm" of Christianity and seems to "regard any other view as reducing Christ to the level of a mere moral teacher." He ignores Scriptural scholarship, such as the differences between the Synoptics and John. "He takes the thought-forms of an earlier period and insists on interpreting them in a grossly literal fashion." His demonology is awful, his Christology "docetic."

2. Boss, Edgar W. *The Theology of C. S. Lewis.* Ph. D. dissertation: Northern Baptist Theological Seminary, Chicago, 1948.

   This dissertation consists largely of paraphrases of Lewis's writings (to 1948) arranged under appropriate theological headings (pp. 37-266), which paraphrases sometimes show confusion of genres (see the apple of *Paradise Lost* in Lewis's discussion which becomes the fruit in *Genesis* on p. 42). Dr. Boss faults Lewis on his theistic evolutionism, his liberal higher criticism, and his "example theory" of the Atonement, and dislikes his sacramentalism and belief in Purgatory (summed up on p. 269), but appreciates his advocacy of supernaturalism in naturalistic times. As a study of Lewis's beliefs, this paper is not profound.

3. Courtney, Charles R. "The Religious Philosophy of C. S. Lewis." Master of Arts thesis: the University of Arizona, 1955.

Courtney's thesis is unusual as a study for an English degree in that it is a summary of Lewis's theological thought rather than a literary analysis. It is pleasantly written, but its iv + 36 pages obviously offer no competition in completeness to Cunningham's *C. S. Lewis: Defender of the Faith* (listed immediately below). Two statements of interest to the literary critic are (1) that Mother Kirk in *Pilgrim's Regress*, because she helps man to cross the gulf by Original Sin, is symbolic of the Holy Spirit (p. 20), and (2) that Mark in *That Hideous Strength*, being asked to trample the cross, finds himself in the situation described in Hebrews 10:29, ". . . shall he be thought worthy, who hath trodden under foot the Son of God . . . ?" (p. 19).

4. Cunningham, Richard B. *C. S. Lewis: Defender of the Faith.* Philadelphia: Westminster Press, 1967. 223 pp.

Cunningham reworks the familiar materials of Lewis's intellectual biography, touches briefly on Lewis's views of psychology, natural science, education, government, and society. He provides a competent discussion of Lewis's epistemology. Evaluating Lewis's theology and apologetic arguments as traditional and orthodox, he defends Lewis against the charges of Docetic Christology and Manichean moral theology. He correctly interprets Lewis's bibliology as broader than that of conservative evangelicals ("fundamentalists"). He regards Lewis's "Sorge" (care or concern) as "his finest Christian apology," transcending his wit and scholarship. Assessing Lewis as prose artist, Cunningham prizes his brilliant use of the vernacular, his freshness, his stylistic mastery, and his imaginative writings. He faults Lewis's occasional substitution of bludgeon for needle, presentation of forced choice without alternatives, and violation of technical rules of logic.

But most of this territory has been covered by previous Lewis scholars (especially Chad Walsh, Clyde S. Kilby, and the authors of several unpublished Ph. D. dissertations). Where Cunningham's book is the "original study" promised in the preface, it betrays the author's "chronological snobbery." Regarding Lewis's concept of timeless eternity as "a boy's approach to difficult problems," he suggests Lewis should have read Cullmann or the later Barth. Lewis's view of time is, however, firmly rooted in the Augustinian tradition. When he faults Lewis for his "inexcusable neglect of the results of the best Biblical scholarship," he sheds more light on his own critical perspective than on Lewis. An example is his charge that Lewis's failure to distinguish between John and the Synoptics weakened the thrust of *Miracles*—though *Miracles* was written as a philosophical defense for the possibility of miracles, not as a work of biblical criticism. The omission of the Doctrine of Exchange (Charles Williams's concept) is unfortunate.

5. Hoff, Jacobo E., S. J. "The Idea of God and Spirituality of C. S. Lewis." Unpublished dissertation: Pontificia Universitas Gregoriana Facultas Theologica (Roma), 1969. 270 pp. [Available at the Wheaton College (Ill.) C. S. Lewis Collection.]

A 4-chapter dissertation on Lewis's theology of God. The first chapter is biographical material on Lewis's own religious experience, his atheism, and his conversion. Chapter two is an analysis of Lewis's concept of God, revelation, the purpose of God's involvement in history, and the problem of evil. (This chapter has been published. See below.) Chapter three discusses man's response to God: surrender, sanctification, prayer, love. The concluding chapter studies Lewis's views of characteristics of secular man, of how to care for this world in the light of faith, of human activity and the full life, of knowledge sacred and secular, of autonomous man and freedom, and of hope and understanding.

6. ———. *The Idea of God and Spirituality of C. S. Lewis.* Rome: Pontificia Universitas Gregoriana Facultas Theologica, 1969. 105 pp.

Chapter two of Jacobo E. Hoff's unpublished dissertation. The author analyzes Lewis's working concept of God, his use of Scripture, and his view of inspiration. Hoff regards Lewis as middle-of-the-road on Biblical criticism: no literalist, but also not agreeable to wholesale demythologizing. He notes Lewis made little use of form criticism and no mention of redaction criticism. Hoff emphasizes that Lewis's God was both transcendent and involved in history. In dealing with God and the problem of pain, Hoff believes that Lewis thought the Christ event explained this by transposition, the law of the cross and the pattern of descent and re-ascent. He interprets *Out of the Silent Planet* as a portrayal of the Christian meaning of death, a recurring theme elsewhere in Lewis. In discussing Lewis on the God of revelation and redemption, Hoff emphasizes his idea of the numinous, his acknowledgment of conscience, and the identification of the numinous and morality. Aslan and the *Zoe* of *Mere Christianity* are examples of the God of redemption. Though Lewis "spent much of his time trying to make the Christian faith understandable, reasonable, and acceptable, still he himself after all the words always returned to belief in the face of mystery and to the practical problem of living the clear implications of faith."

7. Kilby, Clyde S. "C. S. Lewis: Everyman's Theologian." *Christianity Today* 8 (3 January 1964): 11-13.

An abstract of *The Christian World of C. S. Lewis* (listed in § I).

8. Springer, J. Randall. "Beyond Personality: C. S. Lewis' Concept of God." M. A. thesis: Wheaton College, Ill., 1969. 119 pp.

Broader than its title suggests, the thesis analyzes Lewis on natural theology; the Christian concept of divine and human personality; God, freedom, and evil; salvation; and religious language. The chapter on religious language stresses Lewis was a literature professor, forgetting Lewis's expertise as philologist; the author seems unaware Lewis did teach philosophy a year at Oxford.

C. Apologetics

1. Adams, Dr. E. W. "The Problem of Pain as a Doctor Sees It." *Hibbert Journal* 42 (January 1944): 145–151.

   Adams disagrees with a number of Lewis's basic theses in *The Problem of Pain*: that men cause most of the suffering of their fellow men, that one person does not suffer through another's suffering, that animals do not suffer as humans do; and he explains why he disagrees in a clear, simple style.

2. Anscombe, G. E. M. "A Reply to Mr. C. S. Lewis' Argument that 'Naturalism' is Self-refuting." *Socratic Digest*, No. 5 [?] (1948?): 7–15.

   Part of a sequence of articles listed under H. H. Price's "Reply" in this subsection; also see Price for an explanation of the question marks in the listing above. Anscombe offers a refutation of third chapter in *Miracles* where Lewis wrote, "no thought is valid if it can be fully explained as the result of irrational causes." Anscombe says "such an argument is based on a confusion between the concepts of cause and reason" and between grounds and cause. "A causal explanation of a man's thought only reflects on its validity as an indication, if we know that opinions caused in that way are always or usually unreasonable." He says Lewis's terms are ambiguous. (Lewis later revised *Miracles* to eliminate this failing.)

3. Barrington-Ward, Simon. "The Uncontemporary Apologist." *Theology* 68 (February 1965): 103-108.

   Lewis's personal, emotional reticence is a key to his isolation from the modern world, including existentialism, psychology, "secular gospel." But his vision of joy is infectious.

4. Binns, Harold. "Mr. C. S. Lewis on Christianity." *Listener* 31 (9 March 1944): 273.

A letter. Binns disputes Lewis's historical explanation of doctrine of the Trinity. This letter is part of the reactions to Lewis's radio broadcasts in Britain on Christian topics; *The Listener* is or was a B. B. C. publication. See also the letters under the same title by Childe and Webb, listed in this subsection.

5. "Books." *Bulletin of the New York C. S. Lewis Society* 2 (April 1971): 4–5.

"Books and authors that Lewis quotes or mentions in *Miracles*. . . ." It is not clear from the *Bulletin* whether or not this list was made by Fr. Fisher as part of his synopsis of *Miracles* (see his listing in this subsection).

6. Cassels, Louis. "Christian Belief Supports Prayer." *New York World Telegram and Sun.* 9 September 1961, p. 9. [UPI column.]

Uses Lewis in dealing with the possibility of answered prayer.

7. Childe, W. R. "Mr. C. S. Lewis on Christianity." *Listener* 31 (2 March 1944): 245; and *ibid.* (16 March 1944): 301.

Letters. Cf. Lewis's letter, *ibid.* (9 March 1944): 273. Childe charges Lewis is a potential persecutor in the name of religion; Lewis demurs; Childe refuses to retreat. This exchange was part of the reactions to Lewis's radio broadcasts in Britain on Christian topics; *The Listener* is or was a B. B. C. publication. See also the letters under the same title by Binns and Webb, listed in this subsection.

8. Christopher, J. R. "A Brief Study in Implied Disjunctive Syllogisms." *Bulletin of the New York C. S. Lewis Society* 2 (January 1971): 8.

A consideration of the argument in the first three chapters of "What Christians Believe" (which in turn is the second half of *Broadcast Talks* or—in the United States—*The Case for Christianity*). Christopher argues that Lewis is implying a series of disjunctive syllogisms in these chapters, that the first syllogism is faulty in its major premise, and that a step in the series is missing between second and third syllogisms proper (there is a digressive syllogism between them, but it is not on the topic). *Note*: this essay is a revised version of an appendix which appeared in Christopher's dissertation, *The Romances of Clive Staples Lewis*, listed in § III-A.

9. Churchill, R. C. "Mr. C. S. Lewis as an Evangelist." *Modern Churchman* 35 (January-March 1946): 334-342.

Churchill mounts a spirited attack upon Lewis's early theological works, pointing (most effectively) to Lewis's ignorance of modern Biblical studies. For example, first, in *The Screwtape Letters* Screwtape says modern writers "conceal the very substantial agreement between [Christ's] teaching and those of all other great moral teachers" when they don't; second, Lewis argues in *Mere Christianity* that Jesus either was what he said he was or he was mad or he was a devil, which ignores the problems of the validity of Biblical texts. Churchill's less effective points ignore genres, complaining that Screwtape does not back up his devilish delight in modern attitudes with arguments, or that the method of the *Broadcast Talks* is oversimplified.

10. Corbishley, Thomas. "C. S. Lewis." *Month* 15 (January 1956): 9-13.

A general favorable evaluation of Lewis's nonfiction Christian writings.

11. Daniel, Jerry L. "A Rhetorical Analysis of the Apologetic Works of C. S. Lewis." Unpublished M.A. thesis in Speech: University of Wyoming, 1969. 150 pp.

Daniel, after background chapters on Lewis's life, the occasion of Lewis's apologetic works, and some of Lewis's major themes, offers a fifty-seven page analysis of Lewis's rhetorical strategies and style in *Mere Christianity*, *The Problem of Pain*, and *Miracles* (with occasional citations of other works). Perhaps his most effective analysis is of Lewis's simplicity of diction, involving contrasts of Lewis and other modern theologians on the same topics; but the analyses are thorough (if often obvious) throughout. Daniel also lists some flaws in Lewis's apologetics: Lewis's failure to thoroughly discuss modern Biblical criticism, for example, and his imaginative digressions in theology. The selective bibliography at the end does not, unfortunately, list all the items which appear in the footnotes. Overall, a satisfactory work.

12. Donnelly, M. J. "Church and Law and Non-Catholic Books." *American Ecclesiastical Review* 114 (June 1946): 403-409 [406-408].

   A discussion of Canon 1399, 4⁰ (which requires Catholics to gain permission to read books written *ex professo* on religious matters by a non-Catholic) with special reference to Lewis and *Beyond Personality*. Donnelly lists points where Lewis departs from Catholic doctrine and states Catholic reviews should not recommend such books.

13. Donnelly, Philip, S. J. "Protest on C. S. Lewis." *America* 73 (30 June 1945): 263.

   A letter referring to G. D. Smith's review of *Beyond Personality* (listed in § VI-B-16), criticizing Lewis's erroneous theological views. See also Gardiner's "Protest on C. S. Lewis" in this section.

14. Driberg, Tom. "Lobbies of the Soul." *New Statesman and Nation* 49 (19 March 1955): 393-394.

   Driberg writes an essay on the religious revival in England at that time, balancing C. S. Lewis and Billy Graham against the Social Gospel and preferring the latter.

15. "Dung and Scum." *Christianity Today* 1 (8 July 1957): 20-21.

   Lewis is cited in a discussion on the proper approach to debate.

16. Edwards, David L. *Religion and Change*. London: Hodder and Stoughton, 1969; New York: Harper and Row, 1969, p. 361.

   Edwards takes issue with Lewis's opinion that no one has been converted from skepticism to liberal Christianity.

17. Farrer, Austin. "The Christian Apologist." In *Light on C. S. Lewis*, ed. Jocelyn Gibb, pp. 23–43.

The volume is listed in § I.

"Lewis was an apologist from temper, from conviction, and from modesty. From temper, for he loved an argument. From conviction, being traditionally orthodox. From modesty, because he laid no claim either to the learning which would have made him a theologian or to the grace which would have made him a spiritual guide" (p. 24). Farrer judges Lewis's two most direct examples of apologetics to be *Miracles* and *The Problem of Pain* (p. 31), and he offers an extended analysis of the type of arguments Lewis used in the latter, both the effective ones (pp. 31-40) and the eccentric ones (pp. 40-42). A good, objective essay.

18. Feinberg, Barry, and Ronald Kasrils (eds.). *Dear Bertrand Russell: A Selection of His Correspondence with the General Public, 1950-1968*. London: George Allen and Unwin, 1969, pp. 50-51.

A woman writes that her lack of faith has been disturbed by Lewis's *Mere Christianity*; Russell replies (26 April 1958) that she should not sacrifice her family to "a form of glorifying masochism" and recommends his *Why I am Not a Christian*.

19. Fisher, James, C. S.P. "AMDG: A synopsis of *Miracles* . . . ." *Bulletin of the New York C. S. Lewis Society* 2 (April 1971): 3-4.

A brief outline of the "Structure of the argument," followed by a list of the chapters with a basic quotation chosen from each. This was prepared for the eighteenth meeting of the New York C. S. Lewis Society; see the report of the discussion of *Miracles* in the same issue, pp. 1-3.

20. Gaebelein, Frank E., and Clyde S. Kilby. "What About C. S. Lewis and His Writings?" *Sunday School Times* 100 (1 March 1958): 158.

Gaebelein finds Lewis's books "very persuasive" and his approach useful in dealing with nonbelievers who shy from the Bible. Kilby finds Lewis superb in thought and expression, giving fresh views by turning ideas upsidedown.

21. Gardiner, Harold C., S. J. "Protest on C. S. Lewis." *America* 73 (30 June 1945): 263.

    See Donnelly's letter, "Protest on C. S. Lewis," in this subsection; Gardiner accepts the points Donnelly makes.

22. Gerstner, John H. *Reasons for Faith.* New York: Harper and Brothers, 1960, pp. 6, 218.

    Gerstner includes a mention of enthusiastic response to Lewis's broadcasts (p. 6), and a brief discussion of Lewis on Christian development of character (p. 218).

23. Haldane, J. B. S. "God and Mr. C. S. Lewis." *Rationalist Annual for the Year 1948*, ed. Frederick Watts, pp. 78-85. London: Watts and Co., 1948.

    Haldane turns each of Lewis's arguments for the existence of God, based on Moral Law (in *Broadcast Talks*), upsidedown. "His arguments . . . definitely muddy the stream of human thought." Haldane feels the idea of levels of morality does not imply the concept of an absolute standard, nor that of moral obligation a superhuman personal being. On Lewis and the nature of reason: "I don't expect that anyone will be able to give even a moderately satisfactory account until a lot more is known about our brains."

24. Hartshorne, Charles. "Philosophy and Orthodoxy." *Ethics Journal* 54 (July 1944): 295-298.

    The title is footnoted, "Reflections upon C. S. Lewis' *The Problem of Pain* and *The Case for Christianity* . . . ." In a carefully reasoned essay, Hartshorne says Lewis does not understand the meaning or implications of being and nonbeing as related to the impassivity, completion, or immutability of God and the question of whether existence has a religious answer. Disputes Lewis's arguments against the "sum of human misery" and sees the orthodox answer to individual suffering as undercutting the doctrine of the substitutionary atonement. Says theology and philosophy must synthesize, for theology is in large part the philosophy of an earlier age.

25. Hordern, William. *A Layman's Guide to Protestant Theology*. New York: Macmillan, 1960, pp. 192, 209.

The work remarks on Lewis and the idea that facts can be interpreted only within a framework (p. 192); it has a discussion of Lewis as example of rebirth of theology written by laymen (p. 209).

26. Joad, C. E. M. *God and Evil*. New York and London: Harper and Brothers, 1943, pp. 64, 86-88, 91, 92, 207, 249–250, 284–292, 296, 299–300, 321–323.

Joad uses Lewis as a major source (especially *Problem of Pain*) in discussing the orthodox view of the Atonement, Hell, the idea of a good God willing evil, a personal God, the unique importance of Jesus's birth and resurrection, and the problem of evil. The book is a criticism of Christian orthodoxy.

27. ———. "The Pains of Animals: A Problem in Theology." *Atlantic* 186 (August 1950): 57–59. Also published in *Month* 189, n.s. 3 (February 1950): 95–99, under the title "The Pains of Animals: An Inquiry and a Reply."

Joad takes issue with Lewis's *Problem of Pain,* ninth chapter, asking how animals, who have no souls, can be permitted by a good God to suffer pain for which they have no moral responsibility. Or how, if they have souls, a line is drawn between animals and man, and how one then explains the moral corruption of animals. Lewis's reply follows.

28. Kilby, Clyde S. "C. S. Lewis and His Critics." *Christianity Today* 3 (8 December 1958): 13–15.

A critique of Norman Pittenger's views on Lewis (listed in this subsection). Kilby believes Pittenger's views relate to his own doctrinal (or naturalistic) assumptions, and that he does not understand Lewis's use of deliberate metaphoric discussion nor realize adequately the audience Lewis addressed.

29. Kruener, Harry H. "A Tribute to C. S. Lewis."

Listed in § II; contains an extended survey and summary of the religious works through 1965.

30. Lee, Ernest George. *C. S. Lewis and Some Modern Theologians*. London: The Lindsey Press, 1944. (This is the second pamphlet in a series: "Religion in a Changing World: Unitarians State Their Faith.")

Lee investigates the works of three wartime theologians: Lewis's *Problem of Pain* (pp. 10–16), Dr. J. S. Whale's *Christian Doctrine* (pp. 16–20), and Canon L. Hodgson's *The Doctrine of the Trinity* (pp. 20–24), and finds them part of a conservative reaction against modern reason. The specific passages he faults in Lewis's book are Lewis's description of unfallen man and Lewis's presentation of the old disjunction: Either Christ was whom he said he was, or he was mad. The first Lee considers a nonrational "exploitation of surprise and wonder" (p. 12); the second he dismisses as not giving all the alternatives, after mentioning textual problems briefly (pp. 13–16).

31. Lynch, John L. "Forbidden Reading." *Books on Trial* 15 (March 1957): 297-298, 344-350 [346].

A treatment of Canon 1399 (limitations on books for Catholics) and warnings about Lewis.

32. Martell, Clare Lorinne. "C. S. Lewis: Teacher as Apologist." Unpublished M. A. thesis: Boston College, 1949. 91 pp.

The author thinks Lewis's effectiveness as an apologist stemmed from his understanding of the learning process. She stresses Lewis's simplicity, his clever use of analogy, and his use of such pedagogical techniques as repetition and anticipating problems.

33. McCully, Dale. "C. S. Lewis: An Unorthodox Champion of Orthodoxy." *Christian Herald*, (November 1947): 69-71.

On Lewis's conversion and religious writings.

34. Morris, Richard Melvin. "C. S. Lewis as a Christian Apologist."

Listed in § III-I; the discussion is in the form of *The Screwtape Letters*.

35. Myers, Edward D. "The Religious Works of C. S. Lewis."
    Theology Today 1 (January 1945): 545-548.

    A brief survey of seven of Lewis's books: *The Pilgrim's Regress,
    The Screwtape Letters, The Problem of Pain, The Case for
    Christianity, Christian Behaviour, Out of the Silent Planet,* and
    Perelandra; each book receives one or two paragraphs of summary
    and appreciation.

36. Nott, Kathleen. *The Emperor's Clothes.* London:
    Heinemann, 1953; Bloomington: Indiana University Press
    (A Midland Book: MB9), 1958, pp. 2, 8, 43, 48, 59, 68,
    76, 106, 175, 211, 231, 254-285, 299.

    An extremely hostile, sarcastic polemic; Nott is chiefly concerned
    to vindicate the scientific method and dislikes Lewis largely
    because he was an unabashed Christian and also popular. She
    regards him as vulgar (p. 8) and coarse (p. 43), a "funda-
    mentalist" popularizer ready with answers from a bag of tricks
    (p. 254), whose sense of sin is curiously obsessed with sex (p.
    231) and who places little stress on the joys of salvation (p.
    297). In her discussion of *Miracles* in Chapter IX, "Lord Peter
    Views the Soul" (pp. 254-285), Nott says the argument is
    essentially circular and analogical and Lewis confuses the meaning
    of "rational" and "irrational." She thinks he has an inadequate
    understanding of Freud, Marx, and Hume.

37. Pittenger, W. Norman. "Apologist versus Apologist: A
    critique of C. S. Lewis as 'defender of the faith' " (called
    simply "A Critique of C. S. Lewis" on the cover). *Christian
    Century* 75 (1 October 1958): 1104–1107. Reprinted in
    The Bulletin of the New York C. S. Lewis Society 3
    (January 1972): 3–6.

    A detailed hostile critique of Lewis as an apologist: Lewis's
    Christology is Docetic or Gnostic; he substitutes "smart
    superficiality for careful thought"; he understands the
    Bible literally as an "irrational fideism"; his view of sexuality is
    "sub-Christian"; the naturalism knocked down in *Miracles* is a
    straw man; he ignores modern biblical scholarship; his metaphors

are crude. Lewis replies in a "Rejoinder to Dr. Pittenger," *ibid.*
(26 November 1958): 1359-1361; an exchange of letters
followed: Van Heerdon *et al*, "Pittenger-Lewis" 75 (24 December
1958): 1485-1486 (listed in this subsection), and Lewis,
"Version Vernacular," 75 (31 December 1958): 1515. See also
Kilby's "C. S. Lewis and His Critics" in this subsection.

38. Price, H. H. "The Grounds of Modern Agnosticism."
Phoenix Quarterly I (Autumn 1946): 10–30.

Price indicates how the scientific *attitude* has undermined
religious belief, as well as scientific facts discrediting some
religious details (the creation story in Genesis I, for example).
He suggests that theism (a belief in God and a belief in
immortality) may be retained when more people accept the
evidence for telepathy and related phenomena (because they show
that the personality is not simply physical and thus limited to
the body). His essay does not mention C. S. Lewis, but it is listed
here because Lewis answered it in the same issue, "A Christian
Reply to Professor Price," pp. 31-44 (Hooper's Bibliography,
D-65).

39. ———. "Reply." *Socratic Digest*, No. 4 (1948): 94–102.

This is part of a sequence of articles listed in Hooper's
Bibliography, D-70:
   (1) C. S. Lewis, "Religion without Dogma?" *Socratic
   Digest*, No. 4 (1948): 82–94.
   (2) The above article.
   (3) G. E. M. Anscombe, "A Reply to Mr C. S. Lewis'
   Argument that 'Naturalism' is Self-refuting," [No. 5?—
   Hooper says simply "*ib.*"], pp. 7–15.
   (4) C. S. Lewis, "Reply," *ib.* [*sic*], pp. 15–16.
This reply discusses immortality, mythology, the relevance of
psychical research, the self-refutation of naturalism, and the
alleged insufficiency of "minimal religion."

40. Reilly, R. J. *Romantic Religion: A Study of Barfield, Lewis,
Williams, and Tolkien.*

Listed in § III-A; nine nonfiction works are discussed, usually
one to a paragraph.

41. Robinson, John. *Honest to God*. London: Student Christian Movement Press; 1963; Philadelphia: Westminster Press, 1963, p. 15.

Robinson calls Lewis "boldly anthropomorphic" in use of language, writing (with J. B. Phillips and Dorothy Sayers) for a "ready-made public" which is enough to "make us hesitate to pull it down or call it into question."

42. Stillwell, Kay. "C. S. Lewis: Modern Christian Writer." *HIS: Magazine of Campus Christian Living* 17 (January 1957): 12-14.

A general piece on Lewis's Christian writings.

43. Thompson, Claude H. "The Unmaking of an Atheist." Listed in § II.

44. Trueblood, David Elton. *Philosophy of Religion*. New York: Harper and Brothers, 1957, pp. 9–10, 107n, 177, 231n, 245–247, 254, 262, 270.

Trueblood draws on *The Problem of Pain* to clarify the concept of God's omnipotence as it relates to the problem of evil (pp. 245-247, 254); he discusses Lewis's distinction between enjoyment and contemplation (pp. 9–10); and he recommends *The Case for Christianity* (pp. 107n, 262).

45. Underhill, Evelyn. *The Letters of Evelyn Underhill*. Listed in § III-D; contains one letter on *The Problem of Pain*.

46. van Heerden, L., John M. Scott, R. A. Ramseth, and Norman Pittenger. "Pittenger-Lewis." *Christian Century* 75 (24 December 1958): 1485–1486.

See W. Norman Pittenger, "Apologist versus Apologist," in this subsection for the beginning of this controversy. This item is a group of four separate letters; the first three favor Lewis in his "Rejoinder to Dr. Pittenger" (*ibid.*, 26 November 1958, pp. 1359–1361). Pittenger's lengthy letter differs with Lewis on the meaning of God's "transcendence" as related to contemporary understanding; he also disagrees with Lewis on the simplification of the Christian message, and refuses Lewis's gambit on counting numbers of conversions. Lewis replies to one portion of Pittenger's letter in "Version Vernacular," *ibid.*, 31 December 1958, p. 1515. Lewis's "Rejoinder to Dr. Pittenger" and "Version Vernacular" are reprinted in *God in the Dock* (Grand Rapids: Eerdmans, 1970), pp. 177–183 and 338 respectively.

47. Vidler, Alec. "Unapologetic Apologist."

Listed in § VI-A; nominally a book review.

48. Walsh, Chad. "Impact on America." In *Light on C. S. Lewis*, ed. Jocelyn Gibb, pp. 106–116.

The volume is listed in § I.

Walsh, writing on the topic of the impact of Lewis's religious works on America, discusses his own introduction to Lewis's writings through *Perelandra*; contrasts the British and American views of Lewis (the British seeing him as a scholar gone into religion, the Americans meeting him first as a religious writer); speaks of Lewis's appeal to educated, humanistically oriented readers searching for some orthodoxy; suggests Lewis was lucky in his timing in America, reaching it after the social concern of the 1930's had dwindled; and mentions other matters more briefly.

49. Webb, M. J. "Mr. C. S. Lewis on Christianity." *Listener* 31 (9 March 1944): 273.

A letter, which disagrees with Lewis that man can reason from human to the suprahuman and must accept the theological superstructure thereon. This letter is part of the reactions to Lewis's radio broadcasts in Britain on Christian topics; *The Listener* is or was a B. B. C. publication. See also the letters under the same title by Binns and Childe, listed in this subsection.

50. Watts, Alan W. *Behold the Spirit: A Study of the Necessity of Mystical Religion*. New York: Pantheon Books, 1947.

Unfortunately lacking an index, this book refers to Lewis on p. 57 as a supporter of the basic doctrines of Catholicism, on p. 185n as a clever defender of the *status quo* in Christian belief, and on p. 251 in the bibliography (*Pilgrim's Regress* and *The Screwtape Letters* are all that are listed). We include this book because Owen Barfield quotes from the footnote cited above on p. xi of *Light on C. S. Lewis*, ed. Gibb (listed in § I), and, without checking, one might expect more mention of Lewis than this.

51. Williams, Terri. Untitled paper on *Mere Christianity*. *Chronicle of the Portland C. S. Lewis Society* 1 (4 February 1972): 3–5.

A brief survey of the organization of *Mere Christianity*, followed by three, briefly analyzed examples of Lewis's writing skills.

D. Culture

1. Bethell, S. L. "Christianity and Culture: Replies to Mr Lewis, I." *Theology* 40 (May 1940): 356–362.

   See Every, "The Necessity of *Scrutiny*" in this subsection for the full listing of the controversy of which this formed a part. This essay restates Bethell's thesis that poets reveal both conscious and unconscious attitudes in their work. He suggests also that no one can avoid such subconscious cultural influences, for no one can entirely cut himself off from his culture; hence, works which are thoroughly Christian are meritorious in that they help, or at least do not hinder, the Christian in finding salvation.

2. ———. "Poetry and Belief." *Theology* 39 (July 1939): 24–35.

   See Every, "The Necessity of *Scrutiny*" in this subsection for the full listing of the controversy of which this formed a part. This essay begins with a discussion of belief in the poet (with a distinction between conscious and unconscious beliefs), discusses the effect of common beliefs between the poet and reader, and ends with a history of poetry which suggests the effect different types of belief have had upon the writers of the eras.

3. Carritt, E. F. "Christianity and Culture: Replies to Mr Lewis, II." *Theology* 40 (May 1940): 362–366.

   See Every, "The Necessity of *Scrutiny*" in this subsection for the full listing of the controversy of which this formed a part. This essay attacks Lewis's essay which preceded it partly because it used authorities instead of relying on conscience for answers and partly because it used "choplogic."

4. Conn, Harvie M. "Literature and Criticism." *Westminster Theological Journal* 23 (November 1960): 16–32 [26–31].

Lewis made objective value the basis of all judgment but did not claim this made it necessarily an indirect argument for theism. In this, says Conn, he sacrifices his whole argument. In his critical works, Lewis settles for humanism, separating it from his Christian ground motive, destroying the normative value he tries to defend in his religious writings. He should have integrated a more-self-conscious Christian motivation in his aesthetic theory.

5. Derrick, Christopher. "C. S. Lewis: A Philosophy of Letters." Listed in § V-A.

6. ———. "The Cult of Culture." *Triumph* 3 (October 1968): 30–33.

An analysis of Lewis as an able opponent of the "religion of culture" prophesied by Matthew Arnold. Lewis's own literary philosophy "is soundly rooted . . . in a Christian's necessary scale of values; it can save us from spoiling the whole business by taking it with the wrong kind of seriousness."

7. Every, George, S. S. M. "In Defence of Criticism." *Theology* 41 (September 1940): 159–165.

See Every, "The Necessity of *Scrutiny*" (immediately below) for the full listing of the controversy of which this formed a part. This essay replies to Lewis's previous essay, saying that in a modern industrial society people *do* read, and thus there is a problem of what they read. For Christians to read second-rate writers like Dorothy Sayers simply because the writers are Christians is often a waste of time (we may "find Christian authors who are satisfactory so far as they go, but tell us nothing that is worth the trouble of reading"); hence, Christian critics are needed to distinguish both artistic merit and moral worth in both Christian and non-Christian writers (in "the great tradition of Christian education, which made Virgil and Sophocles 'classical' ")—at the present time, the best model of this sort of criticism, although not Christian, is that found in *Scrutiny*.

8. ———. "The Necessity of *Scrutiny*." *Theology* 38
   (March 1939) : 176–186.

> This is the first in a series of essays:
>   (1) George Every, S. S. M.: "The Necessity of *Scrutiny*."
>   (2) S. L. Bethell: "Poetry and Belief." *Theology* 39 (July
>   1939): 24–35.
>   (3) C. S. Lewis: "Christianity and Culture." *Theology* 40
>   (March 1940): 166–179.
>   (4) S. L. Bethell and E. F. Carritt: "Christianity and
>   Culture: Replies to Mr Lewis." *Theology* 40 (May 1940):
>   356–366.
>   (5) C. S. Lewis: "Christianity and Culture" (a letter).
>   *Theology* 40 (June 1940): 475–477.
>   (6) George Every, S. S. M.: "In Defence of Criticism."
>   *Theology* 41 (September 1940): 159–165.
>   (7) C. S. Lewis: "Peace Proposals for Brother Every and Mr
>   Bethell." *Theology* 41 (December 1940) : 339–348.

> The essays by Lewis are collected in *Christian Reflections*.
> Hooper in his preface to that volume lists the last five of these
> articles, and the first two are referred to in the various texts.
> Brother Every refers to a "little book" of his in his second
> essay which develops his ideas further, but we have not tried to
> trace it, for it presumably was written before the essay and
> thus does not bear on Lewis directly.

> In this first essay Brother Every suggest there is something wrong
> when Christians prefer to read Dorothy Sayers (one of his
> examples) instead of E. M. Forster; he suggests that the goals of
> F. R. Leavis (however poorly carried out at times) are valuable
> in reminding readers which works are masterpieces and why.
> (There is also a discussion of Leavis's comparisons of T. S. Eliot
> and D. H. Lawrence which was not picked up in the following
> essays.)

9. Ives, Robert B. "Christianity and Culture: An Interpretation
   of C. S. Lewis."

> Listed in § V-A.

10. Weatherby, H. L. "Two Medievalists: Lewis and Eliot on Christianity and Literature." *Sewanee Review* 78 (Spring 1970): 330–347.

A contrast of C. S. Lewis and T. S. Eliot on what appealed to them in medieval literature, what they believed the relationship between Christianity and literature to be, and what types of religious experiences they had. Eliot sought in the middle ages a period before the modern "dissociation of sensibility" set in, while Lewis sees a distinction between the images the medieval poet used and the belief behind it (indeed, until Lewis could make the distinction between his experience of Joy and its origin, he was not converted). Further, Eliot's attempt to return to earlier belief contrasts with Lewis's sophisticated acceptance of gap between the image and the reality, which does not (to the sophisticated mind) destroy the enjoyment of the image. Weatherby concludes by questioning the historicity of Lewis's view of medieval poets but suggesting Lewis's approach to the "dissociation of sensibility" is "the more valuable for the future."

E. Science

1. Clarke, Arthur C. "Space and the Spirit of Man."
   Listed in § III-D; "Will We Lose God in Outer Space?" is included.

2. Crowell, Faye Ann. "The Theme of the Harmful Effects of Science in the Works of C. S. Lewis." Master of Arts thesis: Texas A&M University, 1971.

   An excellent and well-written summary of Lewis's philosophic fears of the amorality of "scientism" as expressed in the Ransom Trilogy, this thesis investigates these three books in light of *The Abolition of Man* and "A Reply to Professor Haldane." (One incidental observation of critical interest is that the sexual imagery of "Prelude to space, an Epithalamium" probably derives from the conclusion of Olaf Stapledon's *Last and First Men*, where the "last men" send minute particles of life-bearing matter to distant planets, p. 17, n. 12.) The thesis does not discuss evolution—what Lewis called "Wellsianity"—in other works than the trilogy. The final chapter (pp. 72–82) discusses essays by current writers dealing with the same moral questions which Lewis raised.

3. "CSL and Science." *Bulletin of the New York C. S. Lewis Society* 2 (May 1971): 5.

   A brief report of a meeting of the New York Metropolitan Section of The American Scientific Affiliation on 1 May 1971, when the topic was "Science and C. S. Lewis." Nathan C. Starr addressed the group on his friendship with Lewis, and Henry Noel gave two speeches: in the afternoon, "C. S. Lewis and Science," and one on *The Pilgrim's Regress* in the evening. Accompanying this notice in the *Bulletin* is the bibliography Noel prepared to Lewis's references to science in his works (page references given for twenty-four books): see Noel's essay, "CSL on Science," below in this subsection.

4. Derrick, C. H. "C. S. Lewis and the Evolutionary Myth." Listed in § VI-B-45.

5. Farnum, George R. "Foreword." In *Vivisection*, by C. S. Lewis. Boston: New England Anti-Vivisection Society, 1947.

   Not seen; an 11–page pamphlet. Compare Fielding-Ould's "Foreword" immediately below.

6. Fielding-Ould, R. "Foreword." In *Vivisection* by C. S. Lewis. London: National Anti-Vivisection Society, 1948.

   Not seen; the English edition of the pamphlet listed under Farnum's "Foreword" immediately above.

7. [GoodKnight, Glen.] "Editorial: Lewis, Power, and Science."

   Listed in § III-C.

8. Herzfeld, Charles M. "Space Year I." *Commonweal* 69 (26 September 1958): 632–634 [634].

   Lewis is cited as an example of the problem of men standing in the way of scientific progress. Lewis's portrait of the power-mad scientist in the Ransom Trilogy is false and "obscures the real problems."

9. Noel, Henry. "CSL on Science." *Bulletin of the New York C. S. Lewis Society* 2 (October 1971): 4–5.

   Noel reorganizes the most important of the 113 passages which appeared in the *Bulletin* earlier (see "CSL and Science" above in this subsection). He cites Lewis's most important comments on science under the headings of Validity, Metaphysics, Agency, Scientism, Progress, Misapplications, Magic, and Pneumatology.

10. Plank, Robert. *The Emotional Significance of Imaginary Beings*.

    Listed in § III-D; "The Seeing Eye" is considered.

11. "Space, History and God: Christians Are Armed with His Love for New Adventure of the Human Mind" (editorial). *Life* 44 (7 April 1958): 37.

    Among other comments on the impending lunar probes is one sentence: "Toward the sentient inhabitants (if any) of other planets, C. S. Lewis warns us against 'theological imperialism,' since they might even prove to be an 'unfallen race' in no need of redemption."

F. Society and Education

Note: Several essays on Lewis as a tutor appear in § II.

1. Babbage, Stuart Barton. "Current Religious Thought."
   Christianity Today 3 (19 January 1959): 39–40.

   Discussion of Lewis's article "The Humanitarian Theory of
   Punishment" (Hooper's Bibliography, D-75; reprinted in *God in
   the Dock*). Favorable. See also Morris and Buckle's "Reply
   to C. S. Lewis" and Smart's "Comment: The Humanitarian
   Theory of Punishment" (all listed in this subsection).

2. Brett-James, Norman G. "C. S. Lewis's 'Notes on the Way.'"
   Time and Tide 25 (25 March 1944): 264.

   A letter. A public schoolmaster takes issue with Lewis on
   "appreciative" cultural education. Cf. Lewis's "Notes on the
   Way," *ibid.* (11 March 1944): 213.

3. Davis, Claude. "Capital Punishment." *Church Times* 144
   (8 December 1961): 14.

   A letter. Cf. Lewis's letters, "Capital Punishment," *ibid.* (1
   December 1961): 7; and "Death Penalty," *ibid.* (15 December
   1961): 12. Davis takes issue with Lewis's distinction between
   "society" and "individual."

4. Hallowell, John H. *Main Currents in Modern Political
   Thought.* New York: Holt, Rinehart and Winston, 1950,
   pp. 543–544, 651–652, 745–746.

   Hallowell uses *Miracles* to discuss the contemporary tendency
   to use arguments by reason to persuade men that man is irrational
   (pp. 543-544); cites Lewis on progress, in the beginning of a
   discussion on Christianity and social order (pp. 651-652); discusses

161

"first principles" and *Abolition of Man* (p. 745, n.2); and recommends several of Lewis's books (pp. 745–746, n.3).

5. ———. *The Moral Foundation of Democracy.* Chicago: University of Chicago Press, 1954; Cambridge: Cambridge University Press, 1954, pp. 5-6, 11, 98–99.

A leading scholar in political theory cites Lewis in a discussion of reason as necessary for democracy (pp. 5–6); remarks on *That Hideous Strength* favorably as a depiction of demonic forces resulting from a lack of distinction between good and evil, truth and falsity, based on rationality of man (p. 11); discusses Lewis (*Abolition of Man, Miracles*) on the danger of the power of the conditioners over the conditioned as the outcome of a philosophy of ethics denying a transcendent moral law (pp. 98–99).

6. Hodgens, Richard. "Notes on *The Abolition of Man.*" *Bulletin of the New York C. S. Lewis Society* 2 (January 1971): 3–6.

The paper begins with a summary of the content of the book and a discussion of the concept of the Tao, with emphasis on how basic to Lewis's thought the Tao (or Natural Law) is; then it compares *The Abolition of Man* with "On Ethics" and "The Poison of Subjectivism" (both in *Christian Reflections*); third, it briefly traces the concept of the Tao in the Ransom Trilogy, in *A Preface to "Paradise Lost,"* and in some of Lewis's apologetics; and, fourth, the paper considers objections to the book—the use of the term *Tao,* and Lewis's discussion of science, the latter of which leads into a digression on eschatological fiction and essays. This paper was prepared for the fifteenth meeting of the New York C. S. Lewis Society; cf. the discussion reported in the same issue, pp. 1–2.

7. Kerns, Joan Elaine [Joan K. Ostling]. "Fighting Western Anomie: The Social and Ethical Philosophy of C. S. Lewis." Master's thesis (Master of Arts in Political Science): University of Illinois, 1966. 128 pp.

"This paper will include three chapters. The first two chapters will be mainly expository and interpretative, discussing Lewis' ideas on the nature of reason, the possibility and importance of a normative ethic, the relationship of a normative ethic to social order, and his ideas on the organization of ideal and actual society. The final chapter will be evaluative" (p. 4). This final "evaluative" chapter is primarily a comparison of Lewis's views to other political theorists who also see the materialism of the West as leading to meaninglessness in society. Bibliography. This thesis is the fullest available discussion of Lewis's social ideas.

8. Kranz, Gisbert. "Die Abschaffung des Menschen: C. S. Lewis über moderne Erziehung." *Neue Sammlung: Göttinger Zeitschrift für Erziehung und Gesellschaft* 9 (1969): 548–552.

"The Abolition of Man: C. S. Lewis on Modern Education." The essay begins with a survey of Lewis's comments on modern education in *Surprised by Joy*, "Screwtape Proposes a Toast," and *The Silver Chair*. A summary of the ideas of *The Abolition of Man* makes up the majority of the essay, with some discussion of the fictional presentation of these ideas in *That Hideous Strength* as a conclusion. (We wish to thank Henry Noel for help in preparing this annotation.)

9. Leavis, Q. D. " 'The Discipline of Letters': A Sociological Note." *Scrutiny* 12 (Winter 1943): 12–25 [14n, 20n, 22–23].

An extended attack on triviality on the part of some literature professors (mainly at Oxford): Sir Walter Raleigh (1879-1922), George S. Gordon, and others in passing. Lewis, on the basis of his essay on the English School at Oxford in *Rehabilitations*, is placed in this reactionary tradition.

10. Lobdell, Jared C. "C. S. Lewis, Distributist: His Economics as Seen in *That Hideous Strength*."
Listed in § III-D.

11. ———. "Petty Curry: Salvation by a Taste for Tripe and Onions."

Listed in § III-D; an influence of Julien Benda's *La trahison des clercs* on *That Hideous Strength* is suggested.

12. McGovern, Eugene. "*The Greening of America* and *The Abolition of Man*." *Bulletin of the New York C. S. Lewis Society* 2 (January 1971): 6.

McGovern begins with the disagreement between Charles Reich (author of *The Greening of America*) and Herbert Marcuse in the *New York Times* over Reich's "old-fashioned" commandments for the future. McGovern traces Lewis's argument in *The Abolition of Man* that no new moral values can exist, and examines some new "values" in euthanasia, abortion, and genetic control of future children; he returns to *The Greening of America* to attack what he considers the implications of the second commandment: "No one judges anyone else." This paper was read at the fifteenth meeting of the New York C. S. Lewis Society; cf. the report of the meeting in the same *Bulletin* on pp. 1–2.

13. Martell, Clare Lorinne. "C. S. Lewis: Teacher as Apologist."

Listed in § I; on common techniques.

14. Molnar, Thomas. *The Decline of the Intellectual*. Cleveland: Meridian Books, World Publishing, 1961, p. 181.

Mention of the tone of Lewis and a few others as "that of the last lonely man, engaged in a losing battle with . . . the Modern World."

15. Morris, Norval, and Donald Buckle. "Reply to C. S. Lewis." *Twentieth Century: An Australian Quarterly Review* 4 (Summer 1952): 20–26; reprinted in *Res Judicatae* 6 (June 1953): 231–237.

A rejection of Lewis's retributive theory of punishment in "The

Humanitarian Theory of Punishment" (Hooper's Bibliography, D-75; reprinted, with Lewis's reply to the above article, in *God in the Dock*). See also Smart's "Comment" and Babbage's "Current Religious Thought" in this subsection.

The authors feel Lewis's theory fails to account for the potential victims of crime, as in the question of indeterminate sentences for certain types of sex offenders and criminally insane; also it fails to account for the more complex social causes of crime. Overall, they point out that Lewis is advocating punishment, not cure, and that he ignores (1) the protection of society as a legal goal and (2) the possibility of having public supervision of the curative process.

16. Noel, Henry. *"Quid Est Veritas? Est Vir Qui Adest."* *Bulletin of the New York C. S. Lewis Society* 2 (January 1971): 7–8.

   Noel begins with an imaginary dialogue of a husband and wife where he suggests and she rejects abortion of their unborn child; then Noel outlines five methods of "the abolition of man," including (as number five) murder; he connects murder with abortion, then considers the little that C. S. Lewis wrote which might be applied to the subject, and finally joins his opening dialogue with his title. This paper was read at the fifteenth meeting of the New York C. S. Lewis Society; cf. the discussion reported in the same *Bulletin*, p. 1-2.

17. Perrin, Noel. *Dr. Bowdler's Legacy: A History of Expurgated Books in England and America.* New York: Atheneum, 1969. [Pp. 237-238.]

   Lewis's note in favor of printing the unexpurgated text of Pepys' diaries (*Letters of C. S. Lewis*, 17 June 1960) is discussed in an account of the expurgated editions.

18. "Professor C. S. Lewis and the English Faculty." *Delta: The Cambridge Literary Magazine,* no vol. no. (October 1960): 6–17 [6–9, 17].

   Editorial criticism of Lewis's piece in *Broadsheet* [Cambridge], 9 March 1960, in which Lewis faulted undergraduate criticism as being too emotional, unbalanced and ignorant of the Bible and classics. *Delta* editors lament Lewis's contempt for the undergraduate and lack of concern for personal relevance of literary interpretation; the item then launches into an attack on Cambridge's English Tripos examination system.

19. Rodway, Allan, and Mark Roberts. "English in the University: II: 'Practical Criticism' in Principle and Practice." *Essays in Criticism* 10 (January 1960): 1–18 [2–8, 15, 17–18].

An essay on the values of the discipline of "practical criticism" to the English literature student. In the first half of the essay the authors quote and discuss Lewis, especially his views in *Rehabilitations*, as a contrasting view of criticism, literature, and education based on such philosophical difficulties as the nature and status of value judgments.

20. Sayers, Dorothy L. "The Teaching of Latin: A New Approach." 1952. In *The Poetry of Search and the Poetry of Statement, and Other Posthumous Essays on Literature, Religion, and Language*, pp. 177–199 [198]. London: Victor Gollancz, 1963.

Near the end of an argument for the teaching of medieval Latin in schools, Sayers quotes a two-paragraph note from Lewis suggesting secular texts for classroom use.

21. Skinner, B. F. *Beyond Freedom and Dignity*. New York: Alfred Knopf, 1971. Passage quoted in *The Bulletin of the New York C. S. Lewis Society* 2 (June 1971): 7.

Skinner quotes Lewis's fears about some men controlling other men's futures in *The Abolition of Man*, and comments, with anticipation, "We have not yet seen what man can make of man." (His phrasing implies a rejection of Wordsworth, as well as Lewis.)

22. Smart, J. J. C. "The Humanitarian Theory of Punishment." *Res Judicatae* 6 (February 1954): 368–371.

A reply to Lewis's "The Humanitarian Theory of Punishment"

(Hooper's Bibliography, D-75; reprinted, with Lewis's reply to the above article, in *God in the Dock*). See also Morris and Buckle's "Reply to C. S. Lewis" and Babbage's "Current Religious Thought" in this subsection. Smart distinguishes between social (or Utilitarian) and personal (or Intuitive) moral questions, and suggests that much of Lewis's argument depends on a confusion between these levels.

23. Snow, C. P. "Is Progress Possible? – 1. Man in Society." *Observer*, 13 July 1958, p. 12.

This is the first of five articles on progress, suggested by the hundredth anniversary of the publication of Darwin's *Origin of the Species*. Snow writes of the possibilities for social progress (elimination of hunger throughout the world, for example) but denies that individuals may find psychic progress ("each of us . . . has to die alone"). The second article ("Is Progress Possible? – 2. Willing Slaves of the Welfare State," *Observer*, 20 July 1958, p. 6) is by C. S. Lewis and is, in part, a reply to Snow: Lewis states the fear which appears in several of his essays—that social progress can be gained only by the loss of personal freedom, that corruptible men should not be given control of the personal lives of others. (Lewis's essay is accompanied by a photograph of Lewis, his wife, and their dog.)

24. Thompson, William Irwin. *At the Edge of History: Speculations on the Transformation of Culture.* New York: Harper and Row, 1971. 180 pp. [126-127, 158, 159].

"Lewis' and Tolkien's Oxford attack on the modern machine age is not novel, but it is subtle and clever" (p. 127); later, Lewis's views and other writers' are blended to make "the universal myth of human nature" (p. 158). Thompson's basic thesis is that western culture is drawing to a close.

25. Tillyard, E. M. W. "Lilies or Dandelions?" *Cambridge Review* 77 (12 November 1955): 148–149. Collected in *Essays, Literary and Educational* (London: Chatto and Windus, 1962), pp. 204–208.

Tillyard disagrees with Lewis's extreme stress on spontaneity in aesthetic appreciation in the essay "Lilies that Fester"; also he feels

Lewis does not distinguish sufficiently between schoolboys and scholars-in-training in his discussion of compulsion.

26. ———. *The Muse Unchained: An Intimate Account of the Revolution in English Studies at Cambridge.* London: Bowes and Bowes, 1958, pp. 135, 137.

In his last chapter, "Wider Implications," Tillyard uses Lewis's essay, "Lilies that Fester," as a foil to set off his defense of the Cambridge School of English and the American New Criticism; Tillyard's more thorough treatment of Lewis's essay is in his "Lilies or Dandelions?" (listed immediately above).

G. Lewis's Religious Influence upon Others

1. *Encounter with Light*. Lynchburg, Va.: Church of the
   Covenant (United Church of Christ), no date. Reprinted
   in *Eternity* 19 (December 1968): 21–23; and in *HIS*
   29 (December 1968): 6–11.

   A pamphlet relating the influences leading to a Christian
   conversion; Lewis's books were an important persuasion. The
   author includes a correspondence with Lewis, two letters from each.

2. Kilby, Clyde S. "Preface." In C. S. Lewis, *Letters to An
   American Lady*, ed. Clyde S. Kilby, pp. 5–9. Grand Rapids,
   Mich.: William B. Eerdmans, 1967; London: Hodder, 1969.

   Kilby remarks on Lewis's approach to and philosophy of writing
   letters to people he never met, and offers some analysis of the
   letters in this volume as advice which shares the path of a
   pilgrim with a fellow Christian. Some background of the
   correspondence and of the recipient of Lewis's letters is given.

3. Soper, David Wesley (ed.). *These Found the Way:
   Thirteen Converts to Protestant Christianity*. Philadelphia:
   Westminster Press, 1951, pp. 17, 22, 76–77, 82, 91,
   118, 127, 147.

   Several of the essayists mention or discuss the influence of
   Lewis's books on their conversions to Christianity. The essayists
   include Joy Davidman (later Lewis's wife, pp. 7–26); William
   Lindsay Gresham (Joy Davidman's first husband, pp. 63–82);
   and Chad Walsh (pp. 117–128).

V. Literary Criticism

A. General

1. Auden, W. H. *Secondary Worlds.*

    Listed in § I; one reference to Lewis's criticism.

2. Bateson, F. "The Genuine Text."

    Listed in § V-C; a series of letters by Lewis, Bateson, J. Dover Wilson, M. R. Ridley, and W. W. Greg, which argue bibliographic theory on the basis of the text of *Hamlet.*

3. Bennett, J. A. W. *The Humane Medievalist: An Inaugural Lecture.*

    Listed in § II; includes an assessment of Lewis's scholarship.

4. Bush, Douglas. "Book Reviews."

    Listed in § VI-B-48; a survey of Lewis as a critic, although nominally a review of *Studies in Medieval and Renaissance Literature.*

5. Como, James. "The Critical Principles of C. S. Lewis." *Bulletin of the New York C. S. Lewis Society* 2 (March 1971): 5-10.

    A survey of Lewis's major critical writings, some application of Lewis's critical principles to his own writings, a brief attempt to establish classical critical principles ("classical" meaning down to the nineteenth century), and finally, climaxing a discussion of myth, the labelling of Lewis as a Platonist in criticism. This last point does not mean that Lewis would outlaw poets, but that (like Socrates) he saw this world as a reflection of supernatural Forms, and that he believed the best poets caught sight also of those Ideas/Images. The paper was read at the seventeenth meeting of the New York C. S. Lewis Society; cf. the report of the discussion in the same *Bulletin*, pp. 1-3.

6. ———. "The Rhetoric of Illusion and Theme: Belief in C. S. Lewis' *Perelandra*." Unpublished M.A. thesis: Queens College, The City University of New York, 1970. 100 pp.

A fairly abstract discussion of literary criticism and mythic criticism, which is then applied to *Perelandra*. The literary criticism is based upon an analogy to calculus: "The X-axis may be called Meaning, with calibrations corresponding to Sense, Feeling, Tone, and Intention. Our Y-axis may be called Types of Narration, with calibrations corresponding to the various relationships observed and analyzed by [Wayne C.] Booth [in *The Rhetoric of Fiction*]. The Z-Axis . . . must be the Reader," with calibrations based on Lewis's *An Experiment in Criticism* (pp. 34-35). The mythic (or archetypal) chapter rests heavily on the works of Carl Jung. Como considers his work more a contribution to criticism than an analysis of *Perelandra*.

7. Cunningham, Don Rodger. "D. H. Lawrence and C. S. Lewis: A Study in Contrasts." Unpublished M.A. thesis: Indiana University, 1972. 80 pp.

An interesting thesis, unfortunately without subdivisions in the text (pp. 1-75). Cunningham suggests that both authors begin from an awareness of the numinous in life, but move in different directions from that point; he indicates Lawrence's different meanings of the word *life*, and Lewis's criticism of Lawrence which applies only to part of Lawrence's position (Lewis associated Lawrence with the Bergsonian school of the Life Force). Further, Cunningham supplies Owen Barfield's criticisms of Lawrence, since the Barfield-Lewis friendship suggests some affinities of point of view. The analysis of Lewis is mainly in terms of *The Pilgrim's Regress*, *Perelandra*, *That Hideous Strength*, and *The Abolition of Man*; not all of Lewis's references to Lawrence are cited; such a one being omitted as the brief attack at the end of "What Chaucer Did to 'Il Filostrato,' " and it is unfortunate that Cunningham does not seem to know of Ungit in *Till We Have Faces* (the book is not listed in his bibliography).

8. [Demarest, Michael.] "Editor's Preface."

   Listed in § III-H; some appreciation of Lewis's scholarship.

9. Derrick, Christopher. "C. S. Lewis: A Philosophy of Letters."
   Good Work 27 (Summer 1964): 68-72.

   On the relation between Lewis's critical views and his
   Christianity. Derrick discusses Lewis's dislike of literary activity
   raised to a semi-religious function, and of the snobbery of
   litterateurs. He sees Lewis's greatest contribution as his "emphasis
   upon the imagination as the organ of meaning, and hence upon
   'myth' as a vehicle of objective wisdom."

10. Every, George. "The Necessity of *Scrutiny*."

    Listed in § IV-D; this begins a controversy in a series of articles
    over the relationship of Christianity and culture.

11. Fairchild, Hoxie Neale. *Religious Trends in English
    Poetry*: *Volume VI*: *1920-1965*: *Valley of Dry Bones*.
    New York and London: Columbia University Press, 1968,
    pp. 24-25, 35-36, 174, 204, 260-261, 371, 484-485.

    On Lewis and the language of poetry and science (pp. 24-25,
    204); the "personal heresy" and the role of the poet (pp. 34-35,
    260-261, 371); Lewis's esteem of David Jones's poem *In
    Parenthesis* (p. 174); importance of Lewis's interpretation of
    Charles Williams's poetry (pp. 484-485).

12. Goldberg, S. L. "C. S. Lewis and the Study of English."
    Melbourne Critical Review 5 (1962): 119-127.

    An attack on Lewis's rejection of evaluative criticism.
    (Based on *Abstracts of English Studies* 6 [May 1963]: Item 1103.)

13. Green, Roger Lancelyn. "Rudyard Kipling: 1865-1936."
    Aryan Path 36 (December 1965): 553-557.

    C. S. Lewis's essay on Kipling is one of the five critical works
    which prepared the way for the present appreciation of Kipling's
    work. (Based on *Abstracts of English Studies* 10 [November
    1967]: Item 2943.)

14. Hannay, Margaret. "C. S. Lewis' Theory of Mythology."
    Listed in § III-A; cf. her M.A. thesis summary in the same
    subsection.

15. Hart, Dabney Adams. *C. S. Lewis's Defense of Poesie.* Ph.D.
    dissertation: University of Wisconsin, 1959; University
    Microfilms, No. 59-3194.

    Most critics of this "controversial" writer, according to Hart,
    are dealing with individual books and not the literary theory
    underlying all the critical and imaginative writing. Yet Lewis's
    "chief contribution to contemporary literature" is his unity within
    diversity. Lewis has "upset the conventions of literary history"
    because of his major premise, that myth is fundamental to the
    human imagination: he repudiates the "personal heresy" and
    emphasizes medieval romances as the central English tradition.
    (Unfortunately Hart's summary of Lewis's critical theory predates
    his most extended statement of his position: *An Experiment in
    Criticism,* 1961.)

    Hart regards Lewis's novels, poetry and fairy stories as never
    completely successful because of "unresolved conflict between his
    theories and his talents" though of the various mythopoetic
    experiments, the children's stories are the best. Of her many other
    valuable critical comments, perhaps the most interesting is
    the thesis that Lewis is most successful in fiction (not as myth)
    when he is able to restrict the point of view. However, to Hart,
    Lewis's development and application of mythopoeia "establishes a
    significant basis for contemporary literary criticism." Extensive
    bibliography.

16. Holbrook, David. *The Quest for Love.* University:
    University of Alabama, 1965, p. 20n.

    "In this book I try to make connections between recent findings
    of psychoanalysis about love and our dealings with reality, and
    the poet's preoccupation with these" (p. 9). The footnote on p. 20
    is suspended from the statement that "Much academic
    criticism . . . is anti-life." Holbrook cites as his example Lewis's
    comment on D. H. Lawrence's *Sons and Lovers* in *Experiment
    in Criticism* (p. 126): that the scene "where the young pair
    copulating in the wood feel themselves to be 'grains' in a

great 'heave' " of Life is an example of "Bergsonian biolatry."
Holbrook's comment: ". . . Lewis . . . used the cold word
'copulate,' typically—for it is life that he hated, rather than
the art which 'worships' it."

17. Hooper, Walter. "Preface." In *Poems*, by C. S. Lewis.

Listed in § III-A; comments on Lewis's theory of poetry.

18. ————. "Preface." In *Studies in Medieval and Renaissance Literature*, by C. S. Lewis.

Listed in § II; contains some comments on Lewis's methods as a scholar.

19. Ives, Robert B. "Christianity and Culture: An Interpretation of C. S. Lewis."

A 7-page mimeographed address given 9 January 1970 to the New York C. S. Lewis Society; revised in June 1970 and mailed to members. See the listing of *The Bulletin of the New York C. S. Lewis Society* in § I for the explanation of these early separate publications.

A survey of Lewis's ideas expressed in various works on the relationship of Christianity and culture: "Christianity and Literature," "Learning in Wartime," "Christianity and Culture," and (on twentieth-century literature) "*De Descriptione Temporum*."

20. Kuhn, Daniel K. "The Joy of the Absolute: A Comparative Study of the Romantic Visions of William Wordsworth and C. S. Lewis."

Listed in § IV-A; not on Lewis's criticism.

21. Lawlor, John. "The Tutor and the Scholar."

Listed in § II; an extended discussion of Lewis's scholarly works is included.

22. Malania, Leo. "One Eucharist: Different Forms."

Listed in § IV-A; an application of *Experiment in Criticism* to the Episcopal Church's *Services for Trial Use*.

23. Nassar, Eugene Paul. "Metacriticism." In *The Rape of Cinderella*: *Essays in Literary Continuity*, pp. 133-140. Bloomington: Indiana University Press, 1970.

   In "Metacriticism," Nassar mentions Lewis as one of three examples of critics "of great ability" for whom it would be good to have a guide to their basic critical orientation when beginning to read their critical works.

24. Norwood, W. D., Jr. "C. S. Lewis, Owen Barfield, and the Modern Myth."

   Listed in § III-D; begins from Lewis's and Barfield's ideas of myth.

25. Oury, Scott. "The Value of Something Other. . ."

   Listed in § I; some discussion of myth and the personal heresy.

26. Pott, Jon. "The Poet, the Vision, and the Fires of Irony." *Reformed Journal* 19 (January 1969): 15-19 [17-18].

   Pott discusses Lewis's *Personal Heresy* and the relation of biography to criticism in a piece on the "new critics" and religious interpretation of art.

27. Raine, Kathleen. "From a Poet."

   Listed in § II; contains some references to Lewis's view of literary criticism and the ends of art.

28. Rauber, D. F. "Observation on the Biblical Epic." *Genre* 3 (December 1970): 318-339 [319-320].

   A discussion of the themes of the *comitatus* and of honor in the Biblical narratives; Lewis's *Preface to "Paradise Lost"* is cited to establish the underlying principles of the heroic age.

29. Robson, W. W. "C. S. Lewis" or "The Romanticism of C. S. Lewis."

   Listed in § VI-C-2; a summary of Lewis's achievements, although nominally a review of *Light on C. S. Lewis*.

30. Sale, Roger. "England's Parnassus: C. S. Lewis, Charles Williams and J. R. R. Tolkien." *Hudson Review* 17 (Summer 1964): 203-225 [203-214].

The basic discussion of Lewis (pp. 205-210) is about his approach to criticism: helpful as a guide to "lost" works but not helpful to understanding them. Lewis's fantasies are "tinny." Of the two other members of "Anglo-Oxford," Sale finds Williams's Arthurian poems filled with private iconography and Tolkien's *Lord of the Rings* very good in the parts dealing with Frodo's quest toward death.

31. "The Scholar's Tale." *Times Literary Supplement.*

Listed in § VI-B-45. Nominally a review of *Poems*; actually an analysis of Lewis's blend of scholarship and historical imagination.

32. "The Stock Responses." *Times Literary Supplement*, No. 2131 (5 December 1942): 595.

Leading Article (central essay), agreeing with Lewis's thesis of stock responses being valuable (in *Preface to "Paradise Lost"*). Lewis's diagnosis says much about contemporary verse and criticism, which is often shaky.

33. Suckling, Norman. "Molière and English Restoration Comedy." In *Restoration Theatre*, ed. John Russell Brown and Bernard Harris, pp. 92-107 [101]. New York, Capricorn Books, 1967.

"The moral objection to Restoration comedy has almost always proceeded from a conscience afraid of any enquiry into its own foundations; and the objectors, in the seventeenth century as later in Victorian times, were of the kind who could rest content, like the complacently paradoxical C. S. Lewis in our own day, with 'stock response' to a situation as morally adequate to the treatment of it, but who—whether it were Collier or Macaulay—had no answer that a civilised intelligence could accept to what the dramatists had observed of the life about them."

34. Sundaram, P. S. "C. S. Lewis: Literary Critic." *Quest* (Bombay), Issue 60 (January-March 1969): 58-66.

Professor Sundaram (of Rajastham University, Jaipur) writes a pleasant, informal survey of Lewis's "criticism" (literary histories, introductions to works, comments in letters), with some emphasis on Lewis the man (his hours as a tutor, for example). No attempt is made to find any weaknesses; the sources are well documented.

35. Tillyard, E. M. W., and C. S. Lewis. *The Personal Heresy: A Controversy.* London and New York: Oxford University Press, 1939, pp. 31-48, 70-94, 122-145.

A literary debate begun by Lewis and answered by Tillyard carried to six essays with additional postscript by Lewis. The first three essays appeared originally in *Essays and Studies.* See Tillyard's first reply, "The Personal Heresy in Criticism: A Rejoinder," *Essays and Studies by Members of the English Association* 20 (1935): 7-20. See also John Lawlor's "The Tutor and the Scholar," p. 65 (listed in § II), for a brief account of the final face-to-face debate on the topic between Lewis and Tillyard.

Lewis's aim is to eliminate personal interest in the poet and the poet's privately subjective state of mind (including his psychology) from the enjoyment and study of poetry. Tillyard, in his first essay, contends the personality of a poet has something distinctive and worth knowing, that art is not just communication but experience communicated. He suggests Lewis's idea includes some Platonic notion of essence.

In his second essay, Tillyard thinks Lewis "presses the distinction between art and life too far." He maintains artistic sharing of experience can heighten apprehension; communicating his mental pattern is part of the author's work, and to enjoy it, part of the reader's privilege. In Tillyard's closing essay he opposes Lewis's view that the ordinary man and the poet are not on different levels of feeling. Tillyard says Lewis is not clear what poetry is *about* and goes on to discuss the categories of states of mind which are subject matter of poetry.

The debate is stimulating, though certain basic differences in definition (i.e., "personal," "personality") are never resolved.

36. " 'Translation from Hatred': Classics in Modern Dress
Condemned." *Times*, 8 August 1958, p. 5c.

Report on Lewis's speech to conference of classical teachers.
Lewis against modern translations of classics as reflecting poetics
of this age and hostility to poetics of earlier ages. Main target
is Homeric translation work of W. H. D. Rouse.

37. Trodd, Kenneth. "Report from the Younger Generation."
Essays in Criticism 14 (January 1964): 21-32 [23].

A comment on Lewis's reaction to the world of Leavis and
Scrutiny: he prefers to "create straw men caricatures and then stab
them from behind."

38. "University of Cambridge" ("The State of English"
series, No. 3). *Times Literary Supplement*, No.
3,652 (25 February 1972): 215.

The discussion begins from the Lewis-*Delta* controversy of 1960
over the goals of criticism.

39. Viswanatham, K. "Metaphor and Modernity in Metaphor."
Aryan Path 35 (July 1964): 298-304; 35 (August
1964): 355-362.

C. S. Lewis is referred to among other moderns who recognize the
true value of metaphors as basic to expression. (Based on
Abstracts of English Studies 10 [November 1967]: Items 2922
and 2925.)

40. Wain, John. "Leavis on Lawrence."

Listed in § VI-A-3; contains a brief contrast of Leavis and Lewis.

41. Warburton, Robert W. "Fantasy and the Fiction of Bernard
Malamud." In *Imagination and the Spirit*, ed. Charles
A. Huttar, pp. 387-416 [392-393, 402].

The volume is listed in § I.

In a discussion of Malamud's fantasies, Lewis's discussion of
fantasy in *An Experiment in Criticism* is used—"Lewis has
perhaps been the most lucid in attempting to distinguish between
psychological and literary fantasy" (p. 393); "On Stories" is
quoted also (p. 402).

42. Watson, George. *The Literary Critics: A Study of English Descriptive Criticism.* London: Chatto and Windus, 1964. 222 pp. [99, 149, 172, 202, 209].

Several comments on Lewis, but the most extended is on p. 202, which traces a tradition (W. P. Ker, R. W. Chambers, and C. S. Lewis) of Christian literary history.

43. Watt, Ian. "Robinson Crusoe as a Myth." *Essays in Criticism* 1 (July 1951): 313.

A letter. Cf. Lewis's letter, "Letter on 'Robinson Crusoe as a Myth,' " *ibid.* (July 1951): 313, in response to Watt's article, "Robinson Crusoe as a Myth," *ibid.* (April 1951): 95-119. Watt responds to Lewis's questioning his use of Midas and Rheingold stories.

44. Williams, Jane. "The Use and Meaning of Myth in Literature."

Listed in § III-A; contains a summary of Lewis's views on myth.

B. Allegory, Medieval Literature, and Spenser

1. Atchity, Kenneth John (ed.). *Eterne in Mutabilitie*: *The Unity of "The Faerie Queene"*: *Essays Published in Memory of Davis Philoon Harding, 1914-1970.* Hamden, Connecticut: Archon Books, 1972. 209 pp. No index.

Contents: Eugene M. Waith, "Davis Philoon Harding, 1914-1970" (pp. ix-xii); K. J. A[tchity], "Introduction" (pp. xiii-xxvii); Judith Cramer, "Motif and Vicissitude in *The Faerie Queene*" (pp. 1-19 [4-6, 11-12, 19n]); Susan C. Fox, "Eterne in Mutabilitie: Spenser's Darkening Vision" (pp. 20-41 [20-21, 23-25, 41n]); Janet Gezari, "Borne to Live and Die" (pp. 42-59 [43, 53, 59n]); Gerald Grow, "Form or Process?" (pp. 60-64); Jean McMahon Humez, " 'This Richly Patterned Page' " (pp. 65-104 [65-66, 68, 70, 72-75, 80, 102, 102n-103n]); Paula Johnson, "Literary Perception and *The Faerie Queene*" (pp. 105-126 [110-111, 122, 125n-126n]); Susanne Murphy, "Love and War in Spenser's *The Faerie Queene*" (pp. 127-143 [131, 136, 143n]); John E. O'Conner, "Prince Arthur: The Cohesive, Tempering Grace" (pp. 144-157); Richard Pindell, "The Mutable Image: Man-in-Creation" (pp. 158-179 [162, 179n]); Sherry L. Reames, "Prince Arthur and Spenser's Changing Design" (pp. 180-206 [196, 206n]); "Works Cited" (bibliography, pp. 207-209 [208]).

According to the "Introduction" (p. xxiv), D. P. Harding regularly assigned his Yale students the topic of the unity of *The Faerie Queene*, and the ten papers of this volume are revised versions of such essays. He seems to have started his students from a contrast of Lewis's view in *The Allegory of Love* of Spenser's poem as incomplete and Graham Hough's defense in *A Preface to "The Faerie Queene"* of its unity—at least, several of these essays begin from that point. The most considered comparison on strictly these lines is by Humez, where Lewis's views are considered on pp. 65-74 and Hough's on pp. 74-80; Murphy has an extended discussion of the Bower of Bliss and the Garden of Adonis, which does not precisely follow Lewis's celebrated contrast (pp. 136-141). The bibliography lists *The Allegory of Love*, but misses *English Literature in the Sixteenth Century* (cited by Fox) and *Spenser's Images of Life* (cited by Murphy).

2. Barfield, Owen, and C. S. Lewis. *Mark vs. Tristram*.

Listed in § III-I; an exchange of fictionalized letters between Barfield and Lewis over a passage in Lewis's review of Vinaver's edition of Malory.

3. Bayley, P. C. "Order, Grace and Courtesy in Spenser's World." In *Patterns of Love and Courtesy*, ed. John Lawlor, pp. 178-202.

Volume listed in this subsection.

Believing that Lewis's Irish background interfered with his understanding of Book V of *The Faerie Queene*, as given in *The Allegory of Love*, Bayley offers an interpretation of Books V and VI as a unit, which also involves a different approach to the dance of the Muses in Book VI and to "The Mutabilitie Cantos" from Lewis's.

4. Beattie, Sister Mary Josephine, R. S. M. *The Humane Medievalist: A Study of C. S. Lewis' Criticism of Medieval Literature*. Ph. D. dissertation: University of Pittsburgh, 1967; University Microfilms, No. 68-1967.

The writer describes recurring themes in Lewis's criticism to show his contribution to twentieth century medieval studies is not only enjoyable but important. Lewis reconstructs the "medieval model" of a former universe with order and value not given by man, and then develops an aesthetic response to this. Lewis is the first twentieth century critic to contribute extensively to re-evaluation of medieval allegory (a mode of

representing the psychological reality of the soul), which he
distinguishes from symbol.

The author studies Lewis's explication of the allegory *Romance
of the Rose*; his tracing of the courtly love tradition from
medieval sources through allegory to Spencer's *Faerie Queene*;
his interpretation of *Troilus* as a poem of courtly love; and
his later writing extending the love ethos an Western society.
She sees Lewis as joining the modern revival of interest in
Arthurian romances, with his seeking to reinvigorate for moderns
the deep imagination of man in the universe. To this end
Lewis uses the medieval model in his children's novels and
poems; he was in the broadly humanist tradition and wanted to
make medieval literature's appeal available to modern readers,
and to help those readers be fully human in response.

Chapter Six, "A Note on Medieval Themes and Genres in Lewis'
Creative Writing" (pp. 161-175), as mentioned above,
indicates how Lewis used his medieval learning in some of his
fiction and poems. The Chronicles of Narnia are discussed
(pp. 162-172), with emphasis on plentitude and hierarchy, as well
as the more obvious elements of medieval romances—quests,
for example. The lyrics which are discussed (pp. 172-175) come
from both *Spirits in Bondage* and *Poems*: the author points to
French verse forms and themes, to the alliterative poem describing
the astrological influences of the planets, and to a poem
about the ennobling quality of love.

5. Bennett, J. A. W. "Gower's 'Honeste Love." In *Patterns
   of Love and Courtesy*, ed. by John Lawlor, pp. 107-121.
   Volume listed in this subsection.

   Bennett concludes, " 'Honeste love' in wedlock, *caritas* in the
   commonwealth, are wholly compatible ideals, and it is Gower's
   distinctive achievement to have harmonized them in a single
   poem, whilst still setting forth the graces and 'gentilesse' of
   courtoisie" (p. 121)—as a series of comments in his essay
   indicates, this interpretation differs greatly from Lewis's
   emphasis on *courtoisie* in *Confessio Amantis*, on the poem as being
   a Courtly Love production almost entirely.

6. Berger, Harry Jr. *The Allegorical Temper: Vision and
   Reality in Book II of Spenser's "Faerie Queene."* New
   Haven: Yale University Press, 1957, pp. 4n, 68n,
   177-178, 181, 211, 212-213, 215, 218-219, 224, 226-227.

   Scholarly citations of *The Allegory of Love.* The passages on pp.
   177-178, 181, 211, and 224 cite or discuss Lewis's definition
   of *allegory.* The passage on pp. 226-227 disagrees with Lewis's
   famous antithesis between the Bower of Bliss and the Garden of
   Adonis.

7. Bliss, A. J. "The Appreciation of Old English Metre."
   In *English and Medieval Studies: Presented to
   J. R. R. Tolkien on the Occasion of his Seventieth
   Birthday,* ed. Norman Davis and C. L. Wrenn, pp. 27-40
   [28-29, 33-37]. London: George Allen and Unwin,
   1962.

   In a discussion of the poetic quality of Old English alliterative
   verse and its influence on later verse, Lewis's "The
   Fifteenth-Century Heroic Line" (collected in *Selected Literary
   Essays*) is used as an authority on some points.

8. Braude, Nan. "The Two-Headed Beast: Notes toward
   the Definition of Allegory." In *Mythcon I Proceedings,*
   ed. Glen GoodKnight, pp. 32-35.

   The volume is listed in § I.

   The first part of the discussion separates allegory proper and
   allegorism, the latter being a reading of nonliteral meanings into
   literary works. Allegorism is identified with symbolism, as
   Lewis used the term in *The Allegory of Love* (three different
   current senses of *symbolism* are distinguished). Finally, the works
   of the Inklings are discussed: Tolkien is said to use natural
   symbols but not allegory; Williams uses allegorism, which is
   unusual as a mode of expression; and Lewis uses allegory. "He
   has certainly the greatest allegorical imagination since Bunyan."
   Examples from *The Lion, the Witch and the Wardrobe* and
   Perelandra are briefly examined.

9. Brewer, D. S. "The Present Study of Malory." In *Arthurian Romance: Seven Essays*, ed. D. R. Owen, pp. 83-97 [87, 90-91, 93, 97]. New York: Barnes and Noble, 1971.

Lewis's comments on Malory's character, realism, and moral intentions are cited; a more general comment: "Marvels can be presented realistically; that is, by a literary technique of a kind to emphasise plausible appearances, plausible cause-and-effect, and Lewis loved this kind of effect in relating marvels, which is a little like serving ice-cream with hot chocolate sauce" (p. 91).

10. Brooke, N. S. "C. S. Lewis and Spenser: Nature, Art and the Bower of Bliss." *Cambridge Journal* 2 (April 1949): 420-434.

A thorough and convincing attack on one of Lewis's most famous critical antitheses—that between art and nature in the Bower of Bliss and the Garden of Adonis respectively. Brooke says Elizabethans did not view relation of nature and art as Lewis's exposition defines it in *Allegory of Love*; also he disagrees with Lewis's definition of what Spenser meant by nature. Brooke defines Spenserian "nature", analyzes three levels of meaning in the Bower of Bliss, and concludes the imagery of the bower is full of imagery not of perverted sex but of perverted order.

11. Coghill, Nevill. "God's Wenches and the Light that Spoke (Some notes on Langland's kind of poetry)." In *English and Medieval Studies: Presented to J. R. R. Tolkien on the Occasion of his Seventieth Birthday*, ed. Norman Davis and C. L. Wrenn, pp. 200-218 [202]. London: George Allen and Unwin, 1962.

Coghill quotes Lewis's distinction between allegory and symbolism from *The Allegory of Love* as "the most trenchant and authoritative description of allegory I know"; he spends the rest of the essay showing that *Piers Plowman* combines allegory and symbolism in the same figures.

12. ————. "Love and 'Foul Delight': Some Contrasted
    Attitudes." In *Patterns of Love and Courtesy*, ed.
    John Lawlor, pp. 141-156.

    Volume listed in this subsection.

    Section one of this essay (pp. 141-149) is a consideration of the
    attitude toward his material held by Andrea Capellanus in
    De Arte Honeste Amandi; Coghill suggests that Capellanus has
    "an unhealthy hatred of sexuality, especially in women" (p.
    142), which is revealed only in his third book, but which underlies
    his contemplation of sexual love in the first two books—an *odi-amo*
    attitude. In his brief introduction, Coghill sets up as contrast
    Lewis's serious, nonpsychiatric approach to Capellanus in
    The Allegory of Love.

13. Deneef, A. Leigh. "Robertson and the Critics." *Chaucer
    Review* 2 (Spring 1968): 205-234 [226].

    In a discussion of D. W. Robertson's "Chaucerian Tragedy,"
    Deneef contrasts C. S. Lewis's poor explanation of Troilus's
    soliloquy on free will (in "What Chaucer Really Did to *Il
    Filostrato*") with Robertson's explanation.

14. Donaldson, E. Talbot. "The Myth of Courtly Love."
    Ventures 6 (Fall 1965): 16-23.

    Donaldson disagrees with the "adultery" part of Lewis's definition
    of courtly love in *The Allegory of Love*, saying Lewis misread
    Andreas the Chaplain, a major source, by approaching him
    with solemnity when Andreas intended to be funny, and he claims
    that adultery played no greater part in "courtly" love in the
    Middle Ages than in any other era. Lewis's definition is thus
    made the basis of an attack on the common modern critical view
    of medieval love.

15. Dunning, T. P. "God and Man in *Troilus and Criseyde*." In
    *English and Medieval Studies: Presented to J. R. R.
    Tolkien on the Occasion of his Seventieth Birthday,*
    ed. Norman David and C. L. Wrenn, pp. 164-182
    [164-166]. London: George Allen and Unwin, 1962.

    Although *The Allegory of Love* is quoted or cited only on the first three pages of this study, yet the whole essay is a contradiction of Lewis's thesis of "a return to high seriousness" (Dunning's phrase) at the end after "a temporary truancy" (Lewis's phrase) in the love affair. Dunning argues that Pandarus's view of love is that of the Courtly Love tradition but that Troilus's view is an idealistic one, based on his "sincere natural religion" (p. 168). A discussion of this thesis, followed through the poem, occupies the rest of the essay.

16. Grunwald, Henry Anatole. "The Disappearance of Don Juan." *Horizon* 4 (January 1962): 57-65 [57].

    Grunwald mentions Lewis's concept of romantic love as a revolution in human sentiment (cf. *The Allegory of Love*, Chapter One).

17. Fletcher, Angus. *Allegory: The Theory of a Symbolic Mode.* Ithaca, New York: Cornell University Press, 1964, pp. 12n, 20-21, 36n, 84n, 121n, 151n.

    The first note on Lewis cites the chapter on allegory in *The Allegory of Love* and refers to Lewis's "several fables," including *"The Chronicles of Narcion"* (*sic*). The other references are to *The Allegory of Love*, except for 121n, which refers to the style of Milton as discussed in *A Preface to "Paradise Lost."*
    Fletcher, over all, does not disagree with Lewis especially, but rather ignores him; his conclusion—"allegories are the natural mirrors of ideology" (p. 368)—is not unusual, although he is far more concerned with psychological aspects of allegory writing than was Lewis.

18. Fowler, Alastair. "Preface." In C. S. Lewis, *Spenser's Images of Life*, ed. Alastair Fowler, pp. vii-ix. Cambridge and New York: Cambridge University Press, 1967.

    Remarks on the posthumous preparation of the manuscript from Lewis's notes.

19. ———. *Spenser and the Numbers of Time.* London: Routledge and Paul, 1964; New York: Barnes & Noble, 1965, pp. 72, 136-137.

    Remarks on Lewis's interpretation of R. Ellrodt's Spenserian criticism (pp. 136-137).

20. Gunn, Alan M. F. *The Mirror of Love: A Reinterpretation of "The Romance of the Rose."* Lubbock, Texas: Texas Tech Press, 1951, pp. x, 11-12, 19, 26, 42, 91n, 104-105, 145, 151-152, 166-167, 175, 177n, 186n, 201, 203, 297, 318, 333n, 401n.

Though Gunn acknowledges Lewis as a major influence (p. x), his book is in large part a defence of the *Romance of the Rose* against some of Lewis's negative criticisms. In general, Gunn thinks Jean de Meun fused his ideas better than Lewis thought.

21. Hardie, Colin. "Dante and the Tradition of Courtly Love." In *Patterns of Love and Courtesy,* ed. John Lawlor, pp. 26-44.

Volume listed in this subsection.

Hardie argues that Dante's *La Vita Nuova* does not reflect the same religious attitude toward Beatrice that *La Divina Commedia* does, in contrast to Lewis's position in *The Allegory of Love.*

22. Hough, Graham. *A Preface to "The Faerie Queene."* New York: W. W. Norton, 1963, pp. 6, 83, 93, 101-103, 152, 179, 203.

Scholarly citations of *The Allegory of Love* and *English Literature in the Sixteenth Century.* The author acknowledges his "greatest debt" to Lewis (p. 6). He agrees with Lewis's emphasis on the incompleteness of the poem (p. 83) and its unity of atmosphere (p. 93); he regards Lewis's distinction between allegory and symbolism or sacramentalism as a useful one (pp. 101-102). This extended discussion of allegory and symbolism leads to Hough's famous adaptation of Northrop Frye's theory of a scale between allegory and realism—here the circular scale on p. 107. Though Hough agrees in general with Lewis's interpretation of the Garden of Adonis and the Bower of Bliss, he thinks Lewis should have stressed the sterility rather than the artificiality of the Bower (p. 179).

23. Jordan, Robert M. *Chaucer and the Shape of Creation:
The Aesthetic Possibilities of Inorganic Structure.*
Cambridge, Massachusetts: Harvard University, 1967,
pp. 31, 40, 81.

All three references are to *The Allegory of Love*: Lewis on
allegory, Aristotle, and the *Roman de la Rose*—Jordan dissenting
from Lewis's emphases on the latter two.

24. Kinneavy, Gerald B. "The Poet in *The Palice of Honour.*"
Chaucer Review 3 (1969): 280-303 [280, 299].

Kinneavy cites Lewis's views of Gavin Douglas's poem in *The
Allegory of Love* and *English Literature in the Sixteenth
Century* at the first of his essay, in a summary of critical views;
later, he cites and agrees with a critical interpretation of a
passage discussed by Lewis in *The Allegory of Love*.

25. Lawlor, John. "On Romanticism in the 'Confessio
Amantis.' " In *Patterns of Love and Courtesy*, ed. by
John Lawlor, pp. 122-140.

Volume listed in this subsection.

Lawlor begins with a definition: "The essential characteristic
of the romantic would seem to lie in giving new significance to that
which has ceased to command belief in terms of its actual or
possible existence"—with an illustration from Coleridge's
The Rime of the Ancient Mariner (p. 123). He then surveys the
passages in the *Confessio Amantis* which Lewis found romantic
in *The Allegory of Love*, finding that none of them fit his
definition. He suggests finally that Lewis's romantic tastes, as
displayed in the Ransom trilogy, the Chronicles of Narnia, and
Till We Have Faces, were the cause of his critical misreading:
Lewis was seeing what he wanted to see, not what there.

26. Lawlor, John (ed.). *Patterns of Love and Courtesy: Essays
in Memory of C. S. Lewis.* London: Edward Arnold,
1966; Evanston: Northwestern University Press, 1967, pp.
1, 26-28, 86-87, 107-109, 117, 120-123, 130,
132-135, 138-140, 141, 142, 144, 178, 182-183,
191-192, 197, 199, 200.

Contents: John Lawlor, Preface; John Stevens, "The *granz biens* of Marie de France"; Colin Hardie, "Dante and the Tradition of Courtly Love"; Gervase Mathew, "Ideals of Friendship"; D. S. Brewer, "Courtesy and the *Gawain*-Poet"; Elizabeth Salter, "*Troilus and Criseyde*: a Reconsideration"; J. A. W. Bennett, "Gower's 'Honeste Love' "; John Lawlor, "On 'Romanticism' in the *Confessio Amantis*"; N. K. Coghill, "Love and 'Foul Delight': some contrasted attitudes"; R. T. Davies, "The Worshipful Way in Malory"; and P. C. Bayley, "Order, Grace and Courtesy in Spenser's World"; Index.

Lawlor writes in his preface: "These essays are all in a field which the late C. S. Lewis made very much his own. It is hoped they extend and vary some of the considerations advanced in his writings, notably *The Allegory of Love*" (p. unnumbered). One of the essays does not mention Lewis or his writings (that by Mathews); two more have only *pro forma* opening references (those by Stevens and Brewer); and another one has only two passing references to one of Lewis's essays (that by Davies). The other essays are annotated in this subsection.

27. Loomis, Roger Sherman. "Literary History and Literary Criticism: A Critique of C. S. Lewis." *Modern Language Review* 60 (October 1965): 508-511.

A reply to Lewis's criticism of Loomis's Grail studies in Lewis's "The Anthropological Approach." Loomis says Lewis misrepresents his position on the Grail stories and Lewis's view of the development of Arthurian scholarship is "strangely inaccurate."

28. MacNeice, Louis. *Varieties of Parable*. Cambridge: Cambridge University Press, 1965, pp. 3-5, 8, 22, 24, 42-43, 48, 59-60, 94-95, 106.

MacNeice refers to Lewis primarily as an expounder of allegory and a critic of *The Faerie Queene* in *The Allegory of Love* and as a critic of George Macdonald's works. The publishers, who added the bibliography after MacNeice's death in 1963, did not list the source of the latter material: Lewis's "Preface" to his *George Macdonald: An Anthology* (partially reprinted as an

"Introduction" to George Macdonald, *"Phantastes"* and *"Lilith"* [London: Victor Gollancz, 1962], 7-11). As criticism of Lewis's criticism, the passage on pp. 3-5 is the most important, for it points out an inconsistency in Lewis's comments about allegory.

29. Manzalaoui, Mahmoud. "Lydgate and English Prosody." *Cairo Studies in English,* no vol. no. (1960): 87-104.

    A technical piece on medieval prosody in which Manzalaoui attempts to harmonize the empirical analysis by Joseph Schick *(Lydgate's Temple of Glas.* London: published for E. E. T. S. by K. Paul, Trench, Trubner and Co., 1891) with the one suggested by Lewis *(Essays and Studies* 24 [1939]: 28-41) and a more recent one by Catherine Ing *(Elizabethan Lyrics.* London: Chatto and Windus, 1951). Manzalaoui is trying to develop a broader theory of prosody to accomodate what Lewis calls metrical irregularities in the fifteenth century heroic verse. Lewis's response to a draft of Manzalaoui's essay is included.

30. Milward, Peter, S. J. "C. S. Lewis on Allegory." *Bigo Seinen: The Rising Generation* [Tokyo] 114 (April 1968): 227-232.

    Lewis, in correspondence with Milward, ultimately went beyond his usual restrictive definition of allegory to agree that allegorical interpretation can validly go beyond conscious intent of the author. At this point, says Milward, literary questions enter the sphere of religious belief; literature, though no substitute for religion, is ultimately dependent.

31. Moorman, Charles. *The Book of King Arthur: The Unity of Malory's "Morte Darthur."* Lexington: University of Kentucky Press, 1975, pp. xxi-xxii, xxv, 74, 99n.

    Moorman feels Lewis denied historical unity of medieval writers because of their "differentness" from modern writers; he argues for the unity of Malory.

32. ———. *A Knight There Was: The Evolution of the Knight in Literature.* Lexington: University of Kentucky Press, 1967, pp. 16, 17, 110, 133, 155n, 163n, 164n.

    Citations of Lewis on courtly love, on Malory, and on Spenser.

33. Murrin, Michael. *The Veil of Allegory: Some Notes toward a Theory of Allegorical Rhetoric in the English Renaissance*. Chicago: University of Chicago Press, 1969. 224 pp. [99, 123, 191].

   Lewis's definition of myth as a story which has value in itself, independent of how it is told, is cited and illustrated (p. 99), in a discussion of the interpretation of allegory; Lewis is also cited on the confusion of poetry (epics in particular) and encyclopedias (pp. 123, 191).

34. Nassar, Eugene Paul. "The Rape of Cinderella." In *The Rape of Cinderella: Essays in Literary Continuity*, p. 6. Bloomington: Indiana University Press, 1970.

   Nassar argues for the creation of a world by the artist "of a certain complex tonality"; the critic judges the success of the art by the development and maintenance of this tone. He cites the break in tone in the fifth book of *Troilus and Criseyde*, and comments that Lewis's explanation of why Criseyde fell (in *The Allegory of Love*), while persuasive, is beside the artistic point of Chaucer's failure to maintain the narrative mode used in the earlier books.

35. Piehler, Paul. *The Visionary Landscape: A Study in Medieval Allegory*. Montreal: McGill-Queen's University Press, 1971, [pp. vii, 11n, 24n, 33n, 34, 42-45, 70, 101, 107, 132n, 142n, 148n.]

   Piehler rejects Coleridge's distinction between allegory and symbolism, and hence Lewis's reformulation of it in *The Allegory of Love* (pp. 11n, 42-45). Lewis is also cited on Statius (p. 24n), Boethius (pp. 33n, 34), Guillaume de Lorris (pp. 70, 101), Jean de Meun (p. 107), Dante (pp. 132n, 142n), and the Pearl Poet (p. 148n).

36. Richmond, H. M. *The School of Love: The Evolution of the Stuart Love Critic*. Princeton: Princeton University Press, 1964, pp. 97, 250-251, 254.

   Mention of *The Allegory of Love* as showing Spenser's

adjustment of adulterous courtly love to institution of marriage (p. 97); also discussion of Lewis's view of Tudor lyricism (pp. 250-251).

37. Sale, Roger. *Reading Spenser: An Introduction to "The Faerie Queene."* New York: Random House (Studies in Language and Literature, SLL–20), 1968, pp. 14-15, 21, 26-27, 35, 59, 99, 151-152, 201-202.

Scholarly citations of *The Allegory of Love* and *English Literature in the Sixteenth Century.* Sale is approaching *The Faerie Queene* from a humanistic rather than religious point of view, so he disagrees often with Lewis's tone; he also believes the last two books, V and VI, show an important change in Spenser's orientation, which Lewis does not see.

38. Salter, Elizabeth. " 'Troilus and Criseyde': a Reconsideration." In *Patterns of Love and Courtesy*, ed. John Lawlor, pp. 86-106.

Volume listed in this subsection.

After beginning with two pages of praise of *The Allegory of Love* and "What Chaucer really did to *Il Filostrato*," Salter offers what seems to be intended as a complementary view of what Chaucer was doing with *Troilus and Criseyde*, suggesting a number of inconsistencies and unpreplanned developments in Chaucer's adaptation of Boccaccio's poem. Lewis in his essay certainly does not consider any such possibilities.

39. Sayers, Dorothy L. " '. . . And Telling You a Story': A Note on *The Divine Comedy*." In *Essays Presented to Charles Williams*, ed. C. S. Lewis, pp. 1-37 [5]. 1947. Grand Rapids: William B. Eerdmans Publishing Company, 1966. Reprinted without the subtitle in *Further Papers on Dante*, pp. 1-37 [5]. London: Methuen and Company, 1957.

Lewis is cited on the ritual or incantatory style of Virgilian and Miltonic epics in order to point a contrast with the Dantean opening of *The Divine Comedy*.

40. ———. "Dante's Imagery: I—Symbolic." 1947. In
Introductory Papers on Dante, pp. 1-20 [4-5]. London:
Methuen and Company, 1954.

"As . . . Lewis . . . has pointed out in his excellent book *The
Allegory of Love*, allegory was not, for medieval people, a
long–winded, indirect way of saying something that might have
been more plainly put: it was the quickest, most direct and
most vivid way of writing at a time when the technical vocabulary
of psychology and of the physical sciences had not yet been
perfected and popularised. And one might perhaps claim that it
still is."

41. ———. "The Writing and Reading of Allegory." 1954.
In *The Poetry of Search and the Poetry of Statement,
and Other Posthumous Essays on Literature, Religion,
and Language*, pp. 210-225 [201-202, 207]. London:
Victor Gollancz, 1963.

The essay opens with an anecdote about *Perelandra*: Lewis said it
was not an allegory in his preface, but one reviewer, who is
quoted, labeled it an allegory and so dismissed it. Also pp. 203-213
contain a history of the development of allegory which is
obviously indebted to Lewis's *The Allegory of Love* (no doubt
if Sayers had prepared the papers in this volume for publication,
some acknowledgment would have been made).

42. Sharrock, Roger. "Second Thoughts: C. S. Lewis on
Chaucer's *Troilus*." *Essays in Criticism* 8 (April 1958):
123-137.

A good critique of Lewis on *Troilus and Criseyde*. Sharrock
disagrees with Lewis's emphasis on the importance of courtly love
code and the omission of serious consideration of the concluding
stanzas. Lewis sees the poem as a hymn in praise of love;
Sharrock, as a poem about human frailty, the closing stanzas in
line with Boethian echoes and intimations scattered throughout.

43. Tindall, William York. *The Literary Symbol*. Bloomington: Indiana University Press, n.d. Originally published by Columbia University Press in 1955. Pp. 31-32, 36.

In connection with the rose as used as a symbol by Dante and Yeats, Tindall cites Lewis's discussion of *The Romance of the Rose* in *The Allegory of Love*, also mentioning and denying Lewis's distinction between allegory and symbolism.

44. Utley, Francis Lee. "Anglicanism and Anthropology: C. S. Lewis and John Speirs." *Southern Folklore Quarterly* 31 (March 1967): 1-11.

A consideration of Lewis's essay "The Anthropological Approach" as an answer to John Speirs's later books on Chaucer and the non-Chaucerian tradition in medieval literature (satisfactory) and to Roger Loomis's books (unsatisfactory). Specifically, Lewis's Christianity led him into "polemic slips and faulty judgments" as in his remarks on Roger Sherman Loomis's Grail scholarship. Speirs rejects the Christian element in medieval literature and seeks a new religion of post-Arnoldian faith manqué, Leavisite positivism.

45. Vinaver, Eugene. "On Art and Nature: A Letter to C. S. Lewis." In *Essays on Malory*, ed. J. A. W. Bennett, 29-40. Oxford: Clarendon Press, 1963.

Vinaver replies to the preceding essay by Lewis, "The English Prose 'Morte,' " pp. 7-28 (Hooper's bibliography, D-118); the essays discuss the seeming gap between Malory's intentions and his results.

46. von Hendy, Andrew. "The Free Thrall: A Study of *The Kingis Quair*." *Studies in Scottish Literature* 2 (January 1965): 141-151 [141, 143-144, 148n].

The essay opens with disagreement with Lewis's interpretation (in *The Allegory of Love*) that *The Kingis Quair* is autobiographical on the part of James I, reflecting his courtship and marriage: "one finds no hint of marriage and no wooing." von Hendy offers an interpretation in terms of the education of a prisoner by a *donna angelicata*.

47. Walker, Jan C. "Chaucer and *Il Filostrato*." *English Studies* 49 (August 1968): 318-326 [318, 320, 321].

"The problem 'what Chaucer really did to *Il Filostrato*' has been ably investigated by C. S. Lewis, and his general conclusion is that in *Troilus and Criseyde* Chaucer medievalized Boccaccio's classical treatment of the Cressida story. However, the examples of alteration adduced by him are mostly technical—under the headings of 'historical' poetry, rhetoric, doctrine and sentence, and courtly love—and a study of the more important divergences, especially those connected with the action of the English poem, may help to clarify Chaucer's attitude to his subject, and reveal his greatness as a literary artist" (first paragraph).

48. Weatherby, H. L. "Two Medievalists: Lewis and Eliot on Christianity and Literature." Listed in § IV-D.

49. West, Richard (ed.). "Letters of C. S. Lewis to E. Vinaver." Listed in § II; the six letters mainly discuss Malory.

50. "William Dunbar." *Times Literary Supplement*, 18 April 1958, p. 208.

In the course of a review of *The Poems of William Dunbar*, C. S. Lewis is cited on the superiority of Dunbar's "Nativitie" to Milton's "Ode on the Morning of Christ's Nativity." (Based on *Abstracts of English Studies* 1 [July 1958], Item 973.)

51. Wimsatt, James I. *Allegory and Mirror: Tradition and Structure in Middle English Literature*. New York: Pegasus (Western Publishing Company), 1970, pp. 33, 59, 88-90, 115, and 162.

Each chapter in the book is followed by a short bibliographic essay, and all of the citations of Lewis appear in these essays. The majority of the citations are to *The Allegory of Love*, and the majority of these citations, in turn, record disagreements.

C. The Renaissance

1. Bateson, F. "The Genuine Text." *Times Literary Supplement,*
   9 May 1935, p. 301.

   This letter is the second of a series of bibliographic observations;
   all under the same title in the same journal:
   - (1) Lewis, *ibid.*, 2 May 1935, p. 388.
   - (2) Bateson: this item.
   - (3) J. Dover Wilson, *ibid.*, 16 May 1935, p. 313.
   - (4) Lewis, *ibid.*, 23 May 1935, p. 331.
   - (5) M. R. Ridley, *ibid.*, 30 May 1935, p. 348.
   - (6) J. Dover Wilson, *ibid.*, 30 May 1935, p. 348.
   - (7) W. W. Greg, *ibid.*, 6 June 1935, p. 364.
   - (8) J. Dover Wilson, *ibid.*, 13 June 1935, p. 380.

   Bateson says that Lewis pushes a false dilemma; the original
   prompt copy might be Shakespeare's best acting version, but
   perhaps something else might be regarded as the genuine reading
   version.

2. Bennett, Joan. "The Love Poetry of John Donne: A Reply to
   Mr. C. S. Lewis." In *Seventeenth Century Studies
   Presented to Sir Herbert Grierson,* no editor listed,
   pp. 85-104. Oxford: At the Clarendon Press, 1938.
   Published again in *Seventeenth-Century English Poetry:
   Modern Essays in Criticism,* ed. William R. Keast,
   pp. 111-131. New York: Oxford University Press, 1962.

   A refutation of Lewis's essay, "Donne and Love Poetry in the
   Seventeenth Century" (pp. 64-84 in the 1938 book and pp. 92-110
   in the 1962 Keast volume). Bennett defends Donne's love
   poetry against Lewis's charges that Donne's work "retains the
   medieval view of the sinfulness of sex," that a contempt for
   women permeates the poetry, and that he wrote in a state of
   perpetual excitement.

3. Coles, Paul. "The Interpretation of More's *Utopia.*" *Hibbert Journal* 55 (July 1958): 365-370.

Coles believes *Utopia* has a serious political proposal, unlike Lewis's theory of satirical entertainment. (Based on *Abstracts of English Studies* 1 [December 1958]: Item 1773.)

4. Greg, W. W. "The Genuine Text." *Times Literary Supplement*, 6 June 1935, p. 364.

See Bateson's "The Genuine Text," in this section, for the series of letters of which this forms a part. This letter agrees with Lewis that bibliography exists to provide tools for editors, not to define the aims of editors with some notion of a text in pristine purity.

5. Hunter, G. K. "Drab and Golden Lyrics of the Renaissance." In *Forms of Lyric: Selected Papers from the English Institute*, ed. Reuben A. Brower, pp. 1-18. New York: Columbia University Press, 1970.

Hunter distinguishes between the middle-class poets of the mid–sixteenth century (Churchyard, Golding, Howells, Googe, Turberville, Gascoigne, Edwardes, and Hunnis) and the courtly poets of the time (Wyatt, Surrey, Vaux, Ralegh, Dyer, Oxford, and Essex) and later (Sidney especially). He suggests the strengths and weaknesses of each group. While using Lewis's distinction from *English Literature in the Sixteenth Century* throughout, he also is suggesting a predominate social difference which leads to a literary difference (Wyatt is an exception).

6. Kostič, Veselin. "Marlowe's *Hero and Leander* and Chapman's Continuation." In *Renaissance and Modern Essays: Presented to Vivian de Sola Pinto in celebration of his seventieth birthday*, ed. G. R. Hibbard, with the assistance of George A. Panichas and Allan Rodway. London: Routledge and Kegan Paul, 1966, pp. 25-34 [25, 27, 28].

Kostič attacks the thesis that the two parts of *Hero and Leander* are a harmonious whole, finding that Marlowe saw love as a superhuman passion and the tragedy as one of fate, while Chapman saw love as personal and the tragedy as based on the social sin of not waiting for marriage. Kostič cites Lewis's essay on the poem(s) as the most influential expression of the view he disagrees with.

7. Murrin, Michael. *The Veil of Allegory.*
   Listed in § V-B; the concern is with Renaissance allegory.

8. Richmond, H. M. *The School of Love.*
   Listed in § V-B; discusses Lewis's view of Tudor lyricism.

9. Ridley, M. R. "The Genuine Text." *Times Literary Supplement*, 30 May 1935, p. 348.
   See Bateson's "The Genuine Text," in this subsection, for the series of letters of which this forms a part. This letter is a defense of concern for what Shakespeare himself actually wrote.

10. Thompson, John. *The Founding of English Metre.* London: Routledge and Kegan Paul, 1961. 181 pp. [34, 46, 49, 172, 175].
    Lewis is cited on the poulter's measure (p. 34), and in a discussion of the meter of George Ferrers' "Tresilian," where Thompson suggests a different explanation than Lewis's (pp. 46, 49).

11. Wilson, J. Dover. "The Genuine Text." *Times Literary Supplement*, 16 May 1935, p. 313.
    See Bateson's "The Genuine Text," in this subsection, for the series of letters of which this forms a part. This letter disputes Bateson's point; it says if Lewis saw the maimed prompt copy of *Hamlet* he would see an enormous difference.

12. ———. "The Genuine Text." *Times Literary Supplement*, 30 May 1935, p. 348.
    See Bateson's "The Genuine Text," in this subsection, for the series of letters of which this forms a part. This letter feels Lewis has an inadequate grasp of bibliography. The correct text comes first, aesthetic judgment after.

13. ———. "The Genuine Text." *Times Literary Supplement*, 13 June 1935, p. 380.

See Bateson's "The Genuine Text," in this subsection, for the series of letters of which this forms a part. This letter extends a gracious acknowledgment to Greg and Lewis.

14. ———. "Text Corruptions." *Times Literary Supplement*, 10 March 1950, p. 153.

A letter. Cf. Lewis's letter, *ibid.*, 3 March 1950, p. 137. A dispute over whether certain lines are by Shakespeare or an adapter in the J. D. W. edition of *Two Gentlemen of Verona*.

D. Milton

1. Adams, Robert Martin. *Ikon: Milton and the Modern Critics*. Ithaca, N.Y.: Cornell University Press, 1955, pp. 4, 36-39, 50, 52, 124, 136-137, 149, 150, 201, 202, 205, 206, 214, 216, 222.

   A critique of modern Milton criticism by a Miltonist who believes "Milton's ideas are dead." Predictably, he dislikes Lewis's handling of Milton's theology and Satan and his idea of "Stock Response."

2. Bergonzi, Bernard. "Criticism and the Milton Controversy." In *The Living Milton*, ed. Frank Kermode, pp. 162-180 [171-172, 174, 176]. London: Routledge and Kegan Paul, 1960.

   Bergonzi questions the underlying critical assumptions of F. R. Leavis and A. J. A. Woldock (the latter listed below in this subsection) in their critical attacks on Milton. His comments on Lewis are something of a parenthesis, taking Lewis's book primarily as an introduction to Milton's historical assumptions and not a systematic refutation of Leavis (which Leavis, in 1958, had claimed had not been done). Bergonzi praises some parts of Lewis's book, but he also comments, ". . . Lewis was not able to resist the temptation to play the public moralist from time to time . . . And his characteristic manner of blandly jollying along his reader, though engaging in short stretches, becomes rather tiresome in the long run" (p. 171).

3. Broadbent, J. B. *Some Graver Subject: An Essay on "Paradise Lost."* 1960. New York: Schocken Books, 1967, pp. 47n, 135, 209n, 291.

   A discussion of a poet's presentation of God having to be

aesthetics, not religion, begins from a comment by Lewis (p. 135); and, in the "Conclusion": "the most influential book on [*Paradise Lost*] is by an Augustinian Anglican" (p. 291).

4. Burden, Dennis H. *The Logical Epic: A Study of the Argument of "Paradise Lost."* Cambridge: Harvard University Press, 1967, pp. 47, 168.

Lewis had incorrect responses to the description of Eve, with her "sweet reluctant amorous delay" (p. 47); Lewis was correct about Adam's fault in sinning simply because Eve's sin "seemd remediless" (p. 168).

5. Bush, Douglas. *"Paradise Lost" in Our Time: Some Comments.* 1945. Gloucester, Mass.: Peter Smith, 1957, pp. 14, 25, 59, 94n.

The first chapter, "The Modern Reaction against Milton" (pp. 1-57), surveys the T. S. Eliot and F. R. Leavis attacks on Milton, with a large number of fellow travellers; Lewis appears as a defender, most fully as one who answered Eliot's request for literary judgments to be made only by the major poets of the day (p. 14)—Bush supplies another answer to Eliot. Later, Lewis's thematic summary of Vergil's *Aeneid* is cited (p. 59).

6. Daiches, David. *Milton.* 1957. New York: W. W. Norton and Company [Norton Library, N347], 1966, pp. 127, 169-170, 198.

Lewis is cited for his knowledge of sixteenth and seventeenth century Puritanism (p. 127), for his analysis of the moral significance and organization of the Great Consult (pp. 169-170), and as an authority on angels (p. 198)—in the latter case, Daiches considers Lewis correct but beside the aesthetic point.

7. Eliot, T. S. "Milton II." In *On Poetry and Poets.* New York: Farrar, Straus and Cudahy, 1957, pp. 168-169.

A neutral remark on Lewis's "skilfully arguing that Milton . . . can be acquitted of heresy." Interesting in view of Lewis's own views on Eliot's opinion of Milton in his *Preface to "Paradise Lost"* and elsewhere.

8. Emma, Ronald David, and John T. Shawcross (eds.). *Language and Style in Milton: A Symposium in Honor of the Tercentenary of "Paradise Lost."* New York: Frederick Ungar Publishing Company, 1967, pp. 25n, 296, 302n, 335, 364-366, 368n.

Three of the essays here collected mention Lewis. Mario A. di Cesare, "Advent'rous Song: the Texture of Milton's Epic," comments that Lewis's "discussion of epic style remains important, despite misleading distinctions between 'primary' and 'secondary' epic" (p. 25n). Christine Brooke–Rose, "Metaphor in *Paradise Lost*: A Grammatical Analysis," includes in her summary some comments on seeing Milton's imagery in terms of modern science, and quotes Lewis's analogy from physics (pp. 296, 302n). Robert Beum, "So Much Gravity and Ease," cites Lewis approvingly on the style of the secondary epic, the *solempne* (pp. 364-366, 368n).

9. Empson, William. *Milton's God*. Norfolk, Conn.: New Directions Books, 1961; London: Chatto and Windus, 1961, pp. 9, 18-19, 25, 52-53, 62-70, 88, 89, 95, 102-109, 119, 154, 161-163, 167-169, 173, 183-195, 207.

This book is as much a polemic as a work of literary criticism. Empson is strongly negative about the Christian strain in literary criticism which, he feels, misinterprets literature, especially Milton. The reason why *Paradise Lost* is so good is because Milton makes his God so bad. Lewis, as the most famous of orthodox Christian Miltonists, is handled especially in his interpretation of God and Satan. Empson says Lewis unintentionally defends Satan.

10. Ferry, Anne Davidson. *Milton's Epic Voice: The Narrator in "Paradise Lost."* Cambridge, Massachusetts: Harvard University Press, 1963, p. 183n.

Although the Foreword (pp. xi-xii especially) places this volume in the Milton Controversy, the actual text is free from discussion of criticis. Lewis's *Preface to "Paradise Lost"* is recommended, along with two other books, for its re-education of readers in the tradition of heroic poetry (p. 183n).

11. Fish, Stanley Eugene. *Surprised by Sin: The Reader in "Paradise Lost."* London: Macmillan, 1967, pp. 6, 145, 208, 269, 300-302.

   Fish is often against Lewis's positions but not for the usual reasons: he dismisses Lewis's analysis of "the speciousness of Satan's rhetoric" in Book I because the goal of rhetoric is immediate impact and Satan manages that (p. 6), he inverts Lewis's query about why "great modern critics have missed" the very simple fact that "the Fall is simply and solely Disobedience" into a query as to why Adam and Eve missed Obedience (p. 208), and he defends the style of Books XI and XII as appropriate to the matter (pp. 300-302). Basically, Fish is arguing that *Paradise Lost* is meant to create reader involvement in the Fall, *etc.*; hence his approach is far more internal than Lewis's.

12. Gardner, Helen. "Milton's 'Satan' and the Theme of Damnation in Elizabethan Tragedy." *Essays and Studies* 1 (1948): 46-66 [46-47, 59, 62-64, 66]. Reprinted under the title, "The Tragedy of Damnation." In *Elizabethan Drama: Modern Essays in Criticism*, ed. Ralph J. Kaufmann, pp. 320-338 [320-321, 334-336, 338]. New York: Oxford University Press, 1961.

   Gardner feels the Lewis and Williams approach to Satan fails to account for the tragedy of his damnation and why the common reader finds the earlier books of *Paradise Lost* more powerful. Gardner thinks the parallels to the career of Satan lie on the English stage (character development from glorious heights to a fall). The horror of Satan's fall is its irreversibility.

13. ———. *A Reading of "Paradise Lost."* Oxford: Clarendon Press, 1965, pp. vii, 1-2, 11, 13-15, 63n, 84-85, 99-100, 113-114, 117-118, 120.

   Gardner begins with a survey of twentieth-century criticism, "*Paradise Lost* Today" (pp. 1-28), which includes the Charles Williams-C. S. Lewis position. She also cites Lewis on Milton's angels (p. 63n), and she discusses the prelapsarian sexual intercourse, contrasting her view with Lewis's (pp. 84-85).

Pages 99-120 reprint "Milton's Satan and the Theme of
Damnation in Elizabethan Tragedy" as Appendix A (see
immediately above).

14. Gilbert, Allan H. "Critics of Mr. C. S. Lewis on Milton's
    Satan." *South Atlantic Quarterly* 47 (April 1948):
    216-225.

    Gilbert discusses Hamilton's *Hero or Fool? A Study of
    Milton's Satan* and Stoll's "Give the Devil His Due," arguing
    that the first ends up in substantial agreement with Lewis and
    the second is following a Romantic tradition which does not, in
    actuality, exist. Gilbert then suggests a two-Satan theory: the
    dramatic Satan (i.e., from Milton's early plans for a drama) is a
    fool, the epic Satan is heroic.

15. Grace, William J. *Ideas in Milton.* Notre Dame:
    University of Notre Dame, 1968, pp. 100 (n. 7), 105, 122
    (n. 2), 171, 173, 188 (nn. 15, 21-24), 196.

    The two citations of more than passing critical reference are in the
    sixth chapter, "Milton as a Poet" (pp. 168-188), where Grace
    is presenting the conservative argument on Milton's style being
    decorous.

16. Hamilton, George Rostrevor. *Hero or Fool? A Study of
    Milton's Satan.* London: G. Allen and Unwin, 1944;
    New York: Haskell House, 1969.

    A 41-page monograph which argues against Lewis's and
    Williams's view of Satan as a fool by listing Satan's heroic
    qualities in *Paradise Lost* (courage, splendour of speech, etc.).
    Hamilton finds Satan a tragic figure, even his pride; the only
    element of absurdity is his boasting and lying (p. 17). He analyzes
    Lewis's and Williams's use of Milton's text and thinks they
    do not always represent the text fairly. Hamilton thinks Satan is
    "a wholly splendid rebel, a tragic figure" (p. 37).

17. Hogan, J. J. "Milton and Some Critics." *Studies* 32
    (March 1943): 25-35 [31-33].

    An account of Miltonic criticism of the preceding decades,
    which considers Lewis's work a good handling of "mistaken

comment" (as on Satan) in a new vision of the epic as "simplex et unum." Lewis has an advantage over other critics in having read such authors as Augustine and knows Milton did not invent his account of the Fall. However, Lewis makes Milton a "little too Catholic and Dantesque" and glosses over weaknesses of scenes in heaven.

18. Hughes, Merritt Y. "Beyond Disobedience." In *Approaches to "Paradise Lost": The York Tercentenary Lectures*, ed. C. A. Patrides, pp. 181-198 [189-190]. Toronto: University of Toronto Press, 1968.

In the first part of this essay, subtitled "Disobedience," Hughes cites Lewis's "short list of the crimes which were instantly spawned in Eve's mind by the forbidden fruit" (p. 189). However, Milton was not "interested in any domino theory of the sins comprised in the Fall" (p. 190).

19. ———. *Ten Perspectives on Milton*. New Haven and London: Yale University Press, 1965, pp. 32, 177, 200.

The first reference is the most interesting: Hughes discusses a critic who finds in Joyce's *Ulysses* and *Finnegans Wake* a negation of "the Protestantism, moralism, and political responsibility which underlay Milton's work" and (in the latter volume) of "the Protestant, Christian sense of a moral and meaningful human history." Hughes continues, "The reply . . . was written to the satisfaction of those of Milton's admirers who are still living in the seventeenth century by Mr. C. S. Lewis, in 1942. With a sure scent for the real peril, Mr. Lewis saw a supreme danger to Milton's literary reputation in the public response to Joyce." Hughes proceeds to a reply "to the modern distrust of Milton" on grounds he finds more acceptable. The other two references to Lewis are less fully developed, the third being simply a passing scholarly citation.

20. MacCaffrey, Isabel Gamble. *"Paradise Lost" as "Myth."* Cambridge, Massachusetts: Harvard University Press, 1959, pp. 118, 149, 223.

A phrase from *Miracles* is used in a discussion of gulf imagery (p. 118); Lewis's pointing to the "hairie sides" of Eden's mountain is cited in a discussion of Milton's organicism (p. 149).

21. Murray, Patrick. *Milton: The Modern Phase: A Study of Twentieth-Century Criticism.* New York: Barnes and Noble, 1967, pp. 9, 13, 15, 16, 20-21, 24-28, 80, 82, 86-88, 108-110, 112-113, 120, 127, 129, 135, 139, 148-151, 153, 156.

The first chapter traces the attacks on Milton's works issued by Ezra Pound, T. S. Eliot, F. R. Leavis, and A. J. A. Waldock— as well as the reaction by a number of critics, including Lewis (p. 9). The second chapter, "The Grand Style" (pp. 13-30), shows the nonliterary split between Leavis and Lewis over Milton's style, and then shows that Christopher Ricks answers Leavis in his own terms: "Future apologists for Milton's style will almost certainly follow [Ricks'] lead rather than that of C. S. Lewis" (p. 30). Lewis is also cited on Milton's ideas and his modern relevance, and on the historical approach to *Paradise Lost vs.* a modern reading; but these, and a scattering of other references, are not a basic evaluation of Lewis's criticism.

22. Parish, John E. "Milton and the Well–Fed Angel." *English Miscellany* 18 (1967): 87-109.

Lewis is one of a number of critics who has misunderstood the symbolic significance of *Paradise Lost,* V, 219-576. (Based on *Abstracts of English Studies* 12 [February 1969]: Item 394.)

23. Patrides, C. A. *Milton and the Christian Tradition.* Oxford: Clarendon Press, 1966, pp. 33n, 48n, 171n, 173n.

The first two and the last footnote references are typical critical citations of *A Preface to "Paradise Lost"* among other works; surprisingly, the third footnote, starting from St. Augustine's views of *caritas* and *cupiditas,* moves to Anders Nygren's *Agape and Eros* and suggests Lewis's *Four Loves* as a "companion volume."

24. Peter, John. *A Critique of "Paradise Lost."* New York: Columbia University Press, 1960; London: Longmans, 1960, pp. 49, 50, 52, 62, 87, 111, 127.

Peter disagrees with Lewis over the notion of Satan's smooth decline and thinks Lewis errs in equating Milton's Satan with the doctrinal equivalent. Peter also thinks the epic is not secondary but tertiary (p. 111), far removed from oral tradition.

25. ————. "Reflections on the Milton Controversy." *Scrutiny* 19 (October 1952): 2-15 [6,11].

Lewis's *Preface to "Paradise Lost"* is one of a number of works being contrasted to Leavis's essay on Milton in *The Common Pursuit.*

26. Rajan, B. *"Paradise Lost" and the Seventeenth Century Reader.* London: Chatto and Windus, 1947; New York: Barnes and Noble, 1947, pp. 13, 55, 79, 93, 109, 117, 139n, 141n, 149n, 162n, 163n.

Brief remarks stating favorably Lewis's views in *Preface to "Paradise Lost"*; Rajan disagrees with Lewis on the self-perpetuating tendency of epic diction (p. 163n).

27. ————. *"Paradise Lost*: The Providence of Style." In *Milton Studies I,* ed. James D. Simmonds, pp. 1-14 [2, 13]. Pittsburgh: University of Pittsburgh, 1969.

An acceptance of Lewis's thesis of the secondary epic's style, used here only as a beginning for the transcendence of the tradition through anticipatory metaphors and other devices.

28. Reesing, John. "An Essay for the Tercentenary of *Paradise Lost.*" In *Milton's Poetic Art: "A Mask," "Lycidas," and "Paradise Lost,"* pp. 69-86 [71, 80]. Cambridge, Massachusetts: Harvard University Press, 1968.

In a discussion of the aesthetic value of Michael's revelation to Adam of the future, Reesing notes Lewis's comment about "an untransmuted lump of futurity" at the beginning of his essay (p.

71) and Lewis's aesthetic comment about the writing being "curiously bad" just before a defense of the rhetoric (p. 80).

29. Ricks, Christopher. *Milton's Grand Style.* Oxford: at the Clarendon Press, 1963, pp. 8, 10, 17, 86-87, 90, 125, 133-134.

Ricks calls Lewis the most lively and influential of the traditionalists, though unfortunately he hands the argument to philosophers and theologians; contrasts Lewis with Leavis and Empson (pp. 8, 10). Ricks agrees with Lewis's opinion of Books XI and XII of *Paradise Lost* (p. 17), likes Lewis's handling of Milton's and English syntax (pp. 86-87) and the beauty of Paradise (p. 125), and thinks Lewis correctly interprets Book IX, 11. 439-443, as a comparison of Eve to Proserpina (pp. 133-134).

30. Sayers, Dorothy L. "Dante and Milton." 1952. In *Further Papers on Dante*, pp. 148-182 [152, 174]. London: Methuen and Company, 1957.

Lewis is cited on the Aristotelian basis for the disputation between Satan and Abdiel in the fifth book of *Paradise Lost* (p. 152) and on the archetypal nature of the Garden of Eden in the fourth book (p. 174).

31. Starkman, M. K. "The Militant Miltonist; or, the Retreat from Humanism." *ELH* 26 (June 1959): 209-228 [211, 213-217, 222, 224-225].

Starkman sees Milton as the bellwether of critical history and regards much of today's criticism as motivated by reaction to Milton via dogma. Lewis "obscured and simplified Milton because he has a theological axe to grind. . . ." In this type of criticism one sees "a progressive retreat to aestheticism and orthodoxy . . . in the general retreat from humanism."

32. Steadman, John M. *Milton's Epic Characters: Image and Idol.* Chapel Hill: University of North Carolina Press, 1968, pp. 39n, 118n, 227-231, 234, 241.

The major citations of Lewis come in Part V, "The Devil As Rhetorician," where Steadman begins from the Charles Williams-C. S. Lewis thesis that "Hell is always inaccurate," as contrasted with A. J. A. Waldock's thesis of the poetic truth of Satan's early utterances (pp. 227-231)—Steadman agrees with Williams and Lewis. Lewis is also cited on Satan's government in Hell (p. 234) and on the futility of the Great Consult (p. 241).

33. Stein, Arnold. *Answerable Style: Essays on "Paradise Lost."* Minneapolis: University of Minnesota Press, 1953; London: Oxford University Press, 1953, pp. 4, 29, 48, 56.

References to Lewis on Satan.

34. ————. "Satan's Metamorphoses: The Internal Speech." In *Milton Studies I*, ed. James D. Simmonds, pp. 93-113 [93-94, 113n]. Pittsburgh: University of Pittsburgh, 1969.

Beginning from Lewis's account of Satan's degeneration, Stein discusses the roles Satan plays and his arguments for them. Essentially, Stein makes far more subtle and less step-by-step the "progressive degeneration" of Satan than does Lewis, basing it on close textual reading.

35. Stoll, Elmer Edgar. "Give the Devil His Due: A Reply to Mr. Lewis." *Review of English Studies* (O.S.) 20 (April 1944): 108-124.

Stoll likes Lewis on Milton's style but he is "extraordinarily mistaken" on Milton's characters, especially Satan. If Milton had made his devils so despicable from the start, the poem's dramatic development would have been forestalled. Lewis robs Satan of his Titanic character. Also he disagrees with Lewis on the personalities of Adam and Eve.

36. Stroup, Thomas B. *Religious Rite and Ceremony in Milton's Poetry.* Lexington: University of Kentucky Press, 1968, pp. 67, 79n.

Stroup comments near the end of this short book: ". . . in his epics especially [Milton] achieves a high ritual. C. S. Lewis in his discussion of the style of the Secondary epic . . . observes that it requires a higher solemnity than the Primary. . . . I have been concerned throughout this study with making explicit this very point" (p. 67).

37. Summers, Joseph H. *The Muse's Method: An Introduction to "Paradise Lost."* Cambridge, Mass.: Harvard University Press, 1968, pp. 11, 34, 105-106, 187.

A balanced Miltonist disagrees with Lewis on several points, including his view that Book IX, 11. 1022-1059, and Books XI and XII were failures. Summers gives a detailed defense of them as successes in line with Milton's aim.

38. Tillyard, E. M. W. *Studies in Milton.* London: Chatto and Windus, 1951, pp. 26-27, 53-54, 141.

In "The Crisis of *Paradise Lost*" (pp. 8-52), Tillyard comments that Lewis's interpretation of Eve's words on her resolve to share the forbidden fruit with Adam misses the humor of the passage (pp. 26-27). "A Note on Satan" (pp. 53-61) begins with the Charles Williams and C. S. Lewis interpretation of Satan, finding that they make "him too cheap" (pp. 53-54)–the discussion of their views (with Williams cited) extends to p. 57. In "Theology and Emotion in Milton's Poetry" (pp. 137-168), Lewis's writing "very well on Milton and Hierarchy" (p. 141) is mentioned as an excuse not to go into the topic in the essay.

39. Waldock, A. J. A. *"Paradise Lost" and Its Critics.* London and New York: Cambridge University Press, 1947, pp. 11-12, 16-17, 26-30, 39-41, 47, 52-56, 61-62, 63, 68-76, 84, 95-96, 98-100, 107-108, 109 n.1, 110, 139, 143, 146.

A leading anti-Miltonist. He summarizes Lewis's book and thinks Lewis over-simplifies the epic (pp. 16-17). He thinks Lewis makes Adam too like Charlemagne, his conception not Milton's (pp. 26-30); Lewis defines pride too broadly in interpreting Eve's Fall (pp. 39-41); Lewis is, along with Milton, unconvincing on prelapsarian sex (pp. 61-62); Lewis ignores the nobler side of Eve (p. 63); he preaches a sermon when discussing fallen angels (pp. 95-96); and he has a silly respect for

Milton's faith in angels (pp. 107-108). He disagrees with
Lewis's condemnation of Adam (pp. 52-55) and his interpretation
of Satan (pp. 68-76, 84). Waldock thinks (p. 143) Lewis's
interpretation a smokescreen for what Milton really meant. For
Waldock, there is a basic discrepancy between what the poem
says and what it compels the reader to feel, a discrepancy
Milton could not artistically resolve.

40. West, Robert H. *Milton and the Angels*. Athens:
University of Georgia Press, 1955, pp. 2-3, 132, 187n,
200n, 202n-203n, 208n, 209n.

Lewis first appears as a modern writer who, in *The Screwtape
Letters* and the Ransom Trilogy, has treated of angels and fallen
angels openly (pp. 2-3, 187n); then he is cited on the Attendant
Spirit of *Comus* being, in manuscript, *Daemon* (pp. 132, 202n).

41. ———. "The Substance of Milton's Angels." In *SAMLA
Studies in Milton*, ed. J. Max Patrick, pp. 20-53 [21,
35, 50]. Gainesville: University of Florida Press, 1953.

Lewis is cited on the substance of Milton's angels along with a
number of other critics near the beginning of the essay and in a
critical disagreement with Waldock later (pp. 21, 50), and a
discussion of the one passage which Lewis thought might be
discrepant also appears (p. 35).

42. Whiting, George Wesley. *Milton and This Pendant World*.
Austin: University of Texas Press, 1958, pp. 83, 237.

Lewis is quoted on Milton's acceptance of hierarchial order (p.
83); Lewis's analysis of Satan's progress from Archangel to
Serpent "should have settled" the Romantic celebration of
Satan as hero (p. 237).

43. Widmer, Kingsley. "The Iconography of Renunciation:
The Miltonic Simile." In *Critical Essays on Milton from
ELH*, no editor listed, pp. 75-86 [79, 85]. Baltimore:
Johns Hopkins Press, 1969.

Lewis is incorrect in believing that Satan is self-contradictory
(p. 79), and he ignores in his discussion the disparity
between Heaven and Hell (p. 85).

44. Wright, B. A. "Above the Smoke and Stir." *Times Literary Supplement*, 4 August 1945, p. 367; and *ibid.*, 27 October 1945, p. 511.

Letters. Cf. Lewis's letters, *ibid.*, 14 July 1945, p. 331; and *ibid.*, 29 September 1945, p. 463. Disagreement over Milton's neo-Platonism and over the interpretation of *Comus*.

45. ———. *Milton's "Paradise Lost."* London: Methuen, 1962; New York: Barnes and Noble, 1962, pp. 104-106, 158, 190-191.

Wright discusses Lewis on epic similes (pp. 104-106), and cites Lewis on sex in Eden (p. 158).

E. George Macdonald

1. MacNeice, Louis. *Varieties of Parable*.

   Listed in § V-B; some discussion of Lewis's criticism of George Macdonald included.

2. "Myth and Form." *Times Literary Supplement*, No. 2303 (23 March 1946): 139.

   Leading Article (central essay), on George Macdonald.
   Lewis's anthology of pensees from Macdonald is mentioned, and his distinction between myth–making and artistry is discussed.

3. Reis, Richard H. *George MacDonald*. New York: Twayne Publishers, 1972. 161 pp. [18-22, 30-31, 71, 74, 85, 87, 121, 136, 139-140, 142-143, 156].

   The best book available on MacDonald. It calls Lewis "perhaps the most important of MacDonald's modern critics" (p. 18), citing one of Lewis's statements as "the shrewdest remark" the author has seen on MacDonald (p. 30). However, Reis finds Lewis's high ranking of *A Double Story* "unfathomable" (p. 85). In his critical theory for mythopoeic literature, Reis substitutes archetype, myth, and symbol for the character, plot, and setting of realistic fiction—and he acknowledges his use of *myth* is indebted to Lewis's (p. 121).

4. Sadler, Glenn Edward. "The Fantastic Imagination in George MacDonald." In *Imagination and the Spirit*, ed. Charles A. Huttar, pp. 215-227.

   The volume is listed in § I.
   Sadler begins from the "Holiness" which Lewis found in MacDonald's *Phantastes*, tracing its elements back through the German Romanticism of Novalis, especially in "Hyazinth und

Rosenbluetchen," and forward into Lewis's *Pilgrim's Regress*, among other works. MacDonald "will be remembered, I think, as the founder of a modern circle of fantasy writers all of whom use, in varying degrees, the parable form. *Phantastes* and *Lilith* will stand as touchstones of the fantasy craft in fiction" (p. 227).

5. Wolff, Robert Lee. *The Golden Key: A Study of the Fiction of George Macdonald.* New Haven and London: Yale University Press, 1961, pp. vii, 8-9, 14, 266, 388, 389.

Influence of Macdonald on Lewis (pp. 8-9); citations. As a study of Macdonald, the volume is poor, except for a study of the application of Freudian ideas to mythopoeic works.

F. The Inklings

Note: this section is concerned only with reactions to Lewis's criticism of his friends' works; for biographical essays on the Inklings, see § II.

1. Conquest, Robert. "The Art of the Enemy." *Essays in Criticism* 7 (January 1957): 42-55. Replies: *ibid.* (July 1957): 330-343.

   Conquest finds the Arthurian poems of Charles Williams (and Lewis's commentary upon them) to be sadomasochistic in psychology and totalitarian in politics, because the authors believe in a "closed" system of truth and ideas, an *a priori* lack of humility in the presence of the empirical. Of the replies, three are against Conquest's theses, one for him.

2. Fairchild, Hoxie Neale. *Religious Trends in English Poetry*. Listed in § V-A; contains one passage on Lewis's interpretation of Williams's Arthuriad.

3. Gigrich, John P. *Immortality for Its Own Sake*. Washington: Catholic University Press, 1954, pp. vii, 13, 67, 106, 112.

   A reproduced dissertation on Charles Williams which discusses Lewis's interpretation of Williams in *Arthurian Torso*.

4. Isaacs, Neil D., and Rose A. Zimbardo. (eds.). *Tolkien and the Critics: Essays on J. R. R. Tolkien's "The Lord of the Rings."* Notre Dame and London: University of Notre Dame Press, 1968, pp. 2, 11, 133, 135-137, 144-145, 156, 242, 244.

   Lewis's second review of *The Lord of the Rings*, "The

Dethronement of Power," appears on pp. 12-16. The references to Lewis's criticism in the other essays are all (but one) to Lewis's two reviews, and they did not seem significant enough to these bibliographers to justify listing the essays separately.

5. Morgan, Kathleen E. *Christian Themes in Contemporary Poets: A Study of English Poetry of the Twentieth Century*. London: SCM Press, 1965, pp. 65, 74n, 75, 85, 101, 105.

Contains chapters on Charles Williams, W. H. Auden, and Anne Ridler, among others. Lewis's commentary on Williams' Arthurian poems in *Arthurian Torso* is used in the chapter on Williams (pp. 65-91), with an indication that K. C. B. Allott in *An Anthology of Contemporary Verse* spends some time disagreeing with Lewis's evaluation of Williams (see p. 65); also *The Discarded Image* is cited in the discussion of Williams (p. 85). In the chapter on Auden (pp. 92-122), *Surprised by Joy* is mentioned (p. 105), and Rosetta's development in *The Age of Anxiety* is compared to that traced in *The Pilgrim's Regress* (p. 101).

6. Sayers, Dorothy L. "Charles Williams: A Poet's Critic." 1955. In *The Poetry of Search and the Poetry of Statement, and Other Posthumous Essays on Literature, Religion, and Language*, pp. 69-90 [70, 81-82, 87, 89]. London: Victor Gollancz, 1963.

Lewis is cited on the meaning of one of Williams's poems (pp. 81-82), on interpretation of modern poetry (p. 87), and on the condition of the modern poet (p. 89).

7. Shideler, Mary McDermott. *The Theology of Romantic Love: A Study in the Writings of Charles Williams*. New York: Harper and Brothers, 1962; Grand Rapids, Mich.: William B. Eerdmans, 1966, pp. 2, 84, 86-87, 91-93, 102-103, 108, 124, 129, 134, 144-145, 154, 171, 179, 181, 184, 188.

All but two of the quotations from Lewis are from his commentary on Williams's Arthurian poems in *Arthurian Torso*.

G. Children's Literature

1. Cameron, Eleanor. "The Dearest Freshness of Deep Down Things." *Horn Book* 40 (October 1964): 459-472 [463, 471].

   The topic, "Imagination vs. Realism in Children's Literature." Lewis's "On Three Ways of Writing for Children" is cited (p. 471) on the side of imagination.

2. ————. *The Green and Burning Tree: On the Writing and Enjoyment of Children's Books*. Boston: Little, Brown and Company, 1969. 377 pp. [4-6, 8-9, 11, 15, 21, 35-36, 41-43, 75, 86, 205, 206, 209, 216-218, 235, 273].

   Not a discussion of the Narnia books but of Lewis as a writer of children's books: thus, *Surprised by Joy* (and Lewis's life) is basic to the references on pp. 4-6, 8-9, 35-36, and 41 (the "Arthur Coghill" on the latter page is Nevill Coghill, of course), and the essays in *Of Other Worlds* to those on pp. 41, 43, 206, 209, and 216.

3. ————. "Why *Not* for Children?" *Horn Book* 42 (February 1966): 21-33 [22, 29-31].

   Cameron disputes the contention that famous children's writers do not deliberately write for children and uses Lewis's essay "On Three Ways of Writing for Children" to support her thesis.

4. Green, Roger Lancelyn. "Introduction." In *Alice's Adventures in Wonderland and Through the Looking-Glass*, by Lewis Carroll, pp. ix-xxv [ix-xi]. Oxford English Novels. London: Oxford University Press, 1971.

P. ix cites Lewis's "On Three Ways of Writing for Children" (collected in *Of Other Worlds*); p. x refers to Lewis as a children's author; and p. xi refers to Lewis as an adventure story author.

5. Higgins, James E. "A Letter from C. S. Lewis."

   Listed in § III-G; the letter concerns writing for children.

6. Schickel, Richard. *The Disney Version: The Life, Times, Art and Commerce of Walt Disney*. New York: Simon and Schuster, 1968, pp. 207-208, 373.

   Lewis is cited in a discussion of the appeal of fairy tales; the annotated bibliography recommends the essays in *Of Other Worlds*.

7. V., R. R. "Good Reading." *Horn Book* 38 (August 1962): 335.

   The author applies *An Experiment in Criticism* to children's reading.

VI. Selected Book and Drama Reviews

Note: some of these reviews, mostly in British newspapers and journals, were taken by one of the bibliographers from the publishers' files in England; unfortunately, these are lacking dates and page numbers in most cases. These reviews have been marked with a [PF] to indicate their origin.

A. Multiple and Miscellaneous Reviews

1. Multiple Reviews

Note: all multiple reviews are cross-referenced under the individual titles in § VI-B, so a researcher need not check this subsection against the later listings.

1. Barrows, Herbert. "A Christian Off Duty." *Washington Post Book Week*, 3 September 1965, § E, p. 8.
   Dual review of *Of Other Worlds* and *Letters of C. S. Lewis*. Resumé of the former. Of the latter: ". . . the letters present a strongly consistent portrait of a good and courageous man whose charm and force of mind captivate us entirely, whether we share his religious views or not." (W. H. Lewis's memoir "a model of what such things should be.")

2. Bredvold, Louis I. "The Achievement of C. S. Lewis."
   Intercollegiate Review 4 (January-March 1968): 116-122.

   Although nominally a review of *Studies in Medieval and
   Renaissance Literature* and *Of Other Worlds*, Bredvold uses
   materials from these books along with many others to write a fine,
   brief summary of Lewis's life and ideas. The approach is by
   means of Lewis's "several reputations among different reading
   publics" (p. 116).

3. Carter, A. H. "One About, One By." *Christian Century*
   82 (13 January 1965): 54, 56.

   Dual review of *The Discarded Image* and Kilby's *The Christian
   World of C. S. Lewis*. On the former: Useful warning
   against assuming contemporary point of view, but too readily
   convinced the modern mind could not embrace the "discarded
   image." On the latter: No point in paraphrases; not enough
   analysis of Lewis's aesthetic means; elimination of scholarly
   works from the "Christian world" arbitrary. Some value due to
   insights from personal relationship with Lewis but not enough to
   communicate the immediacy of enthusiasm.

4. Cavanaugh, H. "Two By and One About C. S. Lewis."
   Report, July 1964. [PF]

   Triple review. *Letters to Malcolm* is "valuable and entertaining"
   but at times a trifle too lofty. *The Discarded Image* "will interest
   even the non-specialist." And Kilby's *The Christian World of
   C. S. Lewis* is valuable as appetizer or explanatory aid.

5. Cooke, Alistair. "Mr. Anthony at Oxford." *New Republic*
   110 (24 April 1944): 578-580.

   A dual review of *Christian Behaviour* and *Perelandra*. Very
   hostile; ascribes Lewis's popularity to the uncertainties of
   wartime. Re *Christian Behaviour*: evaluates Lewis's skill as radio
   lecturer; criticizes his view of sex as Puritan; regards his reasoning
   as pat over-simplifications. Also manages to find a Freudian slip:
   a substitution of *pleasure* for *sin*. Calls *Perelandra* the "arid
   counterpart of 'Christian Behavior,' " a sexless fictional realm
   which would make a "magnificent analytic source-book"; finds a

riot of Freudian images. (The allusion in the title is not explained in the review.)

6. Derrick, Christopher. "Contemplation and Enjoyment." *Tablet* 24 April 1971. [PF]

Review of *Undeceptions* and White's *The Image of Man in C. S. Lewis*. On the former: Lewis's "barrel-scrapings are worth more than many people's primary work." He shows translating Christianity to modern times is much more of a "lexical problem" and less a subtle theological problem than neo-modernists believe. On the latter: White's book is earnest and able but shows Lewis's genius was presentation rather than substance. By treating Lewis as an original thinker, White "hovers on the brink of absurdity" as though orthodoxy were peculiar to Lewis.

7. "Hard, polemical, black-or-white, them-or-us." *Times Literary Supplement*, No. 3,570 (31 July 1970): 853-854.

Review of *Selected Literary Essays* and *Narrative Poems*. A general discussion of Lewis's life and works: Lewis was a first-rate teacher, a not-quite first-rate critic, a readable if didactic novelist, and an argumentative and not-completely-successful apologist. A photograph of Lewis is on p. 853.

Two letters appeared in subsequent issues. P. L. Heyworth (No. 3,572 [14 September 1970]: 903) comments as one who did not enjoy Lewis's tutorials. Owen Barfield (No. 3,574 [28 September 1970]: 951) corrects a minor factual point and asks for a clarification of *ontologies*, which the reviewer supplies.

8. Hawkins, Desmond. "The Debate Continues." *Time and Tide* 20 (10 June 1939): 760.

On *Rehabilitations*: "well worth reading"; "the reader must sharpen his wits to resist Mr. Lewis's persuasive manner. . ." On *The Personal Heresy*: Lewis "is in danger of forcing a false dichotomy between form and content"; since Donne, poets have drawn on autobiography for material, and critics cannot be divorced from aesthetic practice. Lewis does not press the point that doctrines of criticism have a parallel historical growth with doctrines of practice.

9. Haynes, Renée. "The Soothsayer." *Tablet*, 6 April 1968. [PF]

   A review of *The Discarded Image* and *A Mind Awake*. The former is "lucid and erudite"; on the latter: "The reader will be reminded of books enjoyed but blurred in remembrance, and be glad to perceive again the unerring sweep of thought, the precision of detail that characterizes them all."

10. Howard, Thomas. "Old Truths and Modern Myths." *New York Times Book Review*, 15 March 1970, pp. 40-41.

    Multiple review, including *A Mind Awake*, edited by C. S. Kilby, and White's *The Image of Man in C. S. Lewis*. On the former: thinks the anthology is "in proportion to how one would find [Lewis] if one were to read every word [he] ever published (which Kilby, I think, has done)." And on White's book: "It is not in the least turgid or pettifogging."

11. J., P. M. "Friars' Bookshelf." *Dominicana* 29 (Spring 1944): 42.

    Review of *The Pilgrim's Regress*, *The Case for Christianity*, and *Christian Behavior*. On the first title: "lucid appraisal and trenchant statement of fact" plus "imaginative quality ornamented with scholarship" found in later works. On *The Case for Christianity*: Favorable. And on *Christian Behaviour*: "unequivocal statement of truth, clarity of style."

12. Lockerbie, D. Bruce. "God in the Dock: C. S. Lewis." *New York Times Book Review*, 26 December 1971, § 7, pp. 2, 13.

    A review of Lewis's *God in the Dock* and Carolyn Keefe's *C. S. Lewis: Speaker and Teacher*. Lockerbie summarizes Lewis's career as a Christian writer, quotes a few passages from essays in *God in the Dock*, and comments that Keefe's book is of value (although occasionally misleading) in its biographical materials and of less value in its technical comments on Lewis's speech.

13. Miller, P. Schuyler. "From Numenor to Edgestow" (lead essay in a book-review section "The Reference Library"). *Astounding Science Fiction* 56 (August 1958): 134-137.

A review of the Avon paperback editions of the Ransom Trilogy. The third volume is the shortened version of *That Hideous Strength* which Lewis edited from his original book; the American version had a name change, *The Tortured Planet* (probably to make it sound more like science fiction). Miller notes the connection to Tolkien's Middle-Earth mythology; hence his title. But most of the review is a plot summary.

14. O'S., D. "Reviews: Apologetics." *Studies* 34 (September 1945): 412-413.

A multiple review of *Broadcast Talks, Christian Behaviour,* and *Beyond Personality*. On the first title: Lewis "leaves Lutheran theology very far behind" when writing on incorporation into Christ, though words "good infection" sound "uncomfortably reminiscent of extrinsic justification"; too Protestant in his view of the corporate church. On *Christian Behaviour*: "verve and sparkle"; reviewer likes much of the treatment of vice, dislikes Lewis's failure to recognize "marriage as being by nature intrinsically indissoluble."

15. *The Press*, 21 February 1970. [PF]

Review of *Selected Literary Essays* and *Narrative Poems*. On the former: "Lewis as writer deserves a place in the history of criticism independent of the literature he analyzed." On the latter: the reviewer considers "Dymer" mainly interesting for its glimpse into pre-Christian Lewis; its too-heavy elements of Romanticism are laboriously applied. He finds "Launcelot" and "The Nameless Isle" mere technical exercises but "The Queen of Drum" a "magnificent poem."

16. R., W. B. and P. M. S., "Friars' Bookshelf." *Dominicana* 31 (June 1946): 149-151.

Dual review of *That Hideous Strength* and *The Great Divorce*. On the former: "clothed in a symbolism which is profound without ever becoming obscure." On the latter: "delightful presentation of a tremendous truth" but caution needed regarding Lewis's statements on Purgatory and predestination.

17. "Religion." *Catholic World* 158 (March 1944): 604.

A review of *The Problem of Pain* and *Christian Behaviour*. On the former: "worthy of careful study by anyone whose duty it is to preach sermons." And on the latter: "emotionally stirring and mentally illuminating."

18. Schleuter, Paul. "Scholar and Wit." *Chicago Daily News*, July 1964. [PF]

Review of *The Discarded Image* and Kilby's *Christian World of C. S. Lewis*. On the former: "Solid scholarship" which is enjoyable to nonspecialists as well as specialists. On the latter: it is "What will be without doubt, for many years, the definitive analysis of Lewis' 'religious writings.' "

19. Sewell, Gordon. "The Wisdom of C. S. Lewis." *Southern Evening Echo*, 18 June 1968. [PF]

Review of *The Discarded Image* and *A Mind Awake*. The former receives a favorable summary. And the latter has an "excellent" introduction by Kilby.

20. "Two Sides of a Scholar." *Australian*, 3 December 1966. [PF]

Dual review. The critic finds *Of Other Worlds* gay but slight. He feels a "sense of indigestion" at all the Hooper collections of Lewis but finds this one—*Studies in Medieval and Renaissance Literature*—"the truest and happiest Lewis."

21. Vidler, Alec. "Unapologetic Apologist." *New York Herald Tribune Book Week*, 26 July 1964, p. 3.

Dual review on *The Discarded Image* and Kilby's *The Christian World of C. S. Lewis*, although generally on Lewis's career as apologist: "He was temperamentally dogmatic in the bad as well as in the good sense of the word." On Kilby's book: an "invaluable guide" for beginning Lewis readers and helpful for

serious students since "it tackles the task of interpretation."
The review is accompanied by a rare photograph of Lewis
which makes him look old.

22. West, Richard. "The Critics, and Tolkien, and C. S.
Lewis—Reviews." *Orcrist*, No. 5, combined with
Tolkien Journal 4 (1970-1971): 4-9.

A review of twelve books on Tolkien and Lewis. The books on
Lewis are *Shadows of Imagination*, ed. Mark R. Hillegas (listed
in § I, with the Lewisian essays separately annotated), Peter
Kreeft's *C. S. Lewis: A Critical Essay* (listed in § I), Nathan
Comfort Starr's *C. S. Lewis' "Till We Have Faces": Introduction
and Commentary* (listed in § III-H), William Luther
White's *The Image of Man in C. S. Lewis* (listed in § I), Clyde
S. Kilby's *A Mind Awake: An Anthology of C. S. Lewis*, and two
books by Lewis, *Narrative Poems* and *Selected Literary Essays*.
All of these reviews are on pp. 7-9.

Only the essays related to Lewis in *Shadows of Imagination*
will be mentioned here. The attack by J. B. S. Haldane on Lewis
was not worth reprinting since Lewis has thoroughly answered it
in "A Reply to Professor Haldane" in *Of Other Worlds*. Chad
Walsh's "The Man and the Mystery" shows his tendency to
retract his early enthusiasm for Lewis, but it does have a useful
point about Lewis's interest in external, not internal, things.
Robert Plank's "Some Psychological Aspects of Lewis' Trilogy"
reduces symbolic richness to psychological quirks. Charles
Moorman's "The Fictive Worlds of C. S. Lewis and J. R. R.
Tolkien" has an interesting topic not thoroughly handled—
Lewis is not always preaching in the Narnia books, for example.
The best of the Lewisian essays is the editor's "*Out of the Silent
Planet* as Cosmic Voyage": a thorough treatment of a
limited subject.

On William Luther White's *The Image of Man in C. S. Lewis*,
West says, ". . . a very good study . . . of the non-literal nature
of religious language (in which the reality is more, not less, than
the metaphor expressing it), of Lewis as a Christian
remythologizer for modern men, and of Lewis' dour view of the
existential human condition and his exhilarating view of human
potential." The pamphlets on Lewis, Kilby's anthology, and
Lewis's books are all given a paragraph each.

23. Williams, Kathleen. "Recent Studies in the English Renaissance." *Studies in English Literature* 8 (Winter 1968): 151-185 [154, 171-172].

On *Studies in Medieval and Renaissance Literature*: Lewis "made mistakes, but he had a rare ability to place himself at precisely the right distance from the poems he was discussing so that particularity and generality merge one into another." On *Spenser's Images of Life*: "the originality of this small book lies . . . in its adumbration of a manner of approach to fiction not suitable for textual analysis." Also see pp. 170-171 for a discussion of one essay from *Patterns of Love and Courtesy*: *Essays in Memory of C. S. Lewis*, edited by John Lawlor.

24. Woolley, Paul. "Reviews." *Westminster Theological Journal* 6 (May 1944): 210-214.

Multiple review of *The Problem of Pain, The Case for Christianity*, and *Christian Behaviour*. On the first: Criticizes Lewis for denial of the (Calvinist) doctrine of total depravity, suggesting that denial brings into question common grace and omniscience of God. Insights into the nature of spiritual experience "vivid." On *The Case for Christianity*: A "brilliant" statement of basic doctrines in nontheological language. And on *Christian Behaviour*: Weakness in treatment of sex; other chapters "volumes in nutshells."

25. Zandvoort, R. W. *English Studies* [Amsterdam] 37 (December 1956): 271-274.

Dual review of *English Literature in the Sixteenth Century* and *De Descriptione Temporum*. On the first: "fascinating reading"; reader likes Lewis's refusal to place a large gap between Medieval and Renaissance (this also applies to *De Descriptione Temporum*). Indeed, the term *Renaissance* is useless in discussing the history of English literature, as the reviewer had pointed out in 1929. Minor criticism: a little disappointed to see Sackville's *Induction* briefly dismissed. (Lists several misprints.)

2. Dramas

Note: the two dramas here reviewed are separately listed in § III-I.

1. Hare, Norman. "The Magic of C. S. Lewis Comes to Life on Screen." *Daily Telegraph* [London], 17 July 1967, p. 15. [PF]

   Very favorable review of ABC British serialization of *The Lion, the Witch and the Wardrobe* which ran in summer, 1967. Adaptor was Trevor Preston.

2. Pepper, Laning. "New Opera 'Discovers' a Campus Diva." *Sunday Bulletin* [Philadelphia], 14 December 1969, § 5, p. 6.

   Feature story on staging of the Swann and Marsh opera based on *Perelandra*.

3. Sargent, Winthrop. "Musical Events: As It Was in the Beginning." *New Yorker* 45 (6 December 1969): 196, 198-200 [196, 198-199].

   Review of opera based on Lewis's *Perelandra* with score by Donald Swann and lyrics by David Marsh, premier and only performance at Riverside Church, New York City, 24 November 1969, by the Bryn Mawr and Haverford Colleges' music and drama departments. It is "genuine opera" with a "very serious plot" and "deft score" in a musicial idiom "unabashedly old-fashioned" but "enjoyable and moving." Sargent thinks Perelandra seems to be an "awfully dull place" (no sex) but the idea of a Perelandrian ideal world has "a certain charm."

3. Other Volumes

1. Ley, Willy. "Book Reviews." *Astounding Science Fiction* 43 (August 1949): 154-156.

   Frank Davis Adams's "The Literary Tradition of the Scientific Romance" (listed in § III-D) refers to this item in such a way that it seems to be a review of *Perelandra* but it turns out to be a review of Marjorie Hope Nicolson's *Voyages to the Moon*. The reference to Lewis appears on p. 156: "The 'Epilogue' . . . deals merely with a very few typical examples of the nineteenth century: . . . and C. S. Lewis' 'Out of the Silent Planet'—plus a short, sharp and well-deserved slap at Lewis' 'Perelandra.' " Why Ley puts Lewis in the nineteenth century is not clear.

2. Simons, John W. "An Attack on the New Orthodoxy of Books." *Commonweal* 62 (22 April 1955): 83-84.

   Review of Kathleen Nott, *The Emperor's Clothes* (listed in § IV-C). A "frankly polemical book"; author is "passionately involved in a vindication of the scientific method" while her own book "is strewn with the sophistries she would foist upon others." How can she purposefully discuss theological views (as Lewis on original sin, the devil) if she believes them without content? But a useful warning to Christians who accept too readily theological comments of those in the arts.

3. Wain, John. "Leavis on Lawrence." *Spectator* 195 (7 October 1955): 457-458 [457].

   Review of *D. H. Lawrence, Novelist*, by F. R. Leavis. *English Literature in the Sixteenth Century* is mentioned in the first paragraph (with high praise) as a contrasting method of criticism.

4. "William Dunbar." *Times Literary Supplement.*

   Listed in § V-B; a review of *The Poems of William Dunbar.*

5. Williams, Kathleen. "Recent Studies in the English Renaissance."

   Listed in § VI-A-1; a review of *Studies in Medieval and Renaissance Literature, Spenser's Images of Life,* and John Lawlor's *Patterns of Love and Courtesy.*

B. Books and Pamphlets by Lewis

1. *Spirits in Bondage*: *A Cycle of Lyrics* (1919).
   Published under the pseudonym of Clive Hamilton.

1. *Times Literary Supplement*, 27 March 1919, p. 167a.
   Moderately favorable notice of Lewis's first published work.

2. *Dymer* (1926). Published under the pseudonym of
   Clive Hamilton; reissued in 1950 in the U.S. only under
   the author's own name; since collected in *Narrative Poems*
   (1969).

1. "Books in Brief." *Nation* 124 (26 January 1927): 96.
   "interesting narrative, in uninteresting verse"

2. Lazare, Christopher. "Reflections and Judgments."
   New York Times Book Review, 20 May 1951, § 7, p. 20.
   "*Dymer* demonstrates the peculiar advantages of poetry as a
   medium for Mr. Lewis' cogent moral reflections and social
   judgments."

3. "A Modern Epic." *Times Literary Supplement*, 13 January
   1927, p. 27.
   Considers the allegory and symbolism of a spiritual journey in
   this modern metaphysical epic successfully and subtly handled.

4. "The New Books: Poetry." *Saturday Review of Literature* 4 (13 August 1927): 46.

> "the symbolism is not at all clear. . . . stanzas are often reminiscent of Masefield when they are most realistic. . . . some good writing, but the poem as a whole does not 'jell'. . . ."

5. Warren, C. H. "Gems and Coloured Glass." *Spectator Literary Supplement* 137 (30 October 1926): 758.

> "Here is a little epic burnt out of vital experience and given to us through a poet's eye."

3. *The Pilgrim's Regress*: *An Allegorical Apology For Christianity, Reason, and Romanticism* (1933).

1. Conway, Rev. Bertrand L., C. S. P. *Catholic World* 143 (May 1936): 239-40.

> "caustic, devastating critique of modern philosophy, religion, politics and art"

2. J., P. M. "Friar's Bookshelf."

> Listed in § VI-A-1; a review of *The Pilgrim's Regress*, *The Case for Christianity*, and *Christian Behavior*.

3. P., A. W. *Downside Review* 54 (January 1936): 138-139.

> Finds humour, mastery of dialogue, satiric irony: "a notable contribution to Catholic literature . . ."

4. "Pilgrim's Regress." *Times Literary Supplement*, 32, No. 1640 (6 July 1933): 456.

> Allegory witty, well-written but "the romanticism of homesickness for the past not of adventure towards the future." The reviewer praises the satire and the poetry, amazing as the latter seems.

5. Pittenger, W. Norman. "Books of the Day." *Living Church* 94 (11 January 1936): 46.

"amusing allegory"; "done with a delightful lightness and wit." Pittenger mistakenly identifies Lewis as Roman Catholic.

6. Sayer, G. S. "Reviews." *Blackfriars* 17 (4 January 1936): 69-70.

"remarkable acuity" in expressing weaknesses of modern doctrines; handling of D. H. Lawrence rather bad.

4. *The Allegory of Love: A Study in Medieval Tradition* (1936; with slight corrections, 1938).

1. Bonnard, G. *English Studies* 21 (1939): 78-82.

Gift of "sympathy" helps make the first two chapters on courtly love and allegory of exceptional interest. Handling of Chaucer, Spenser "of really outstanding interest."

2. Boyce, Gray C. "Lewis: Allegory of Love." *American Historical Review* 43 (October 1937): 103-104.

"a distinguished book . . . wise erudition in criticism, and delightful felicity of style." ". . . he is as sane as he is sure, and very human."

3. Brook, G. L. "Reviews." *Modern Language Review* 32 (April 1937): 287-288.

"undoubtedly one of the best books on medieval literature ever published in this country. . . . probably the sanest and most illuminating expositions that have yet appeared on the difficult questions" of courtly love and the nature of allegory.

4. Coblentz, Stanton A. "The Songs of Love in the Middle Ages." *New York Times Book Review*, 5 July 1936, § 6, p. 12.

   "something more than the dry dust of scholarship"; shows a legacy to the future.

5. Elston, O. "Reviews." *Medium Aevum* 6 (February 1937): 34-40.

   "opulent remarkable book"; major caveat: Lewis began by "claiming too much for the historical significance of the love-allegory."

6. Empson, William. "Love and the Middle Ages." *Spectator* 157 (4 September 1936): 389.

   This review is interesting mainly because of its objections to a number of Lewis's points. For example, that courtly love in eleventh-century Provence was a great change in human sentiment; Empson points to the tenth-century Japan of the *Tale of Genji*. But Lewis is "excellent on the essential point of allegory . . ."

7. Fraser, Vera S. M. *Criterion: A Quarterly Review* 16 (January 1937): 383-388.

   A summary of the book's argument, which also says the chapter on allegory is "most profound." "Apart from its argument, the book becomes an anthology of beauty."

8. Guerard, Albert, Jr. "Courtly Love." *New York Herald Tribune Books*, 18 October 1936, § 10, p. 14.

   "two books—both excellent, but each vitiating the other"; considers the literary theory and criticism better than the history.

9. Hewitt, R. M. "Literature and Love." *Nottingham Journal*, 28 August 1936. [PF]

   Reviewer thinks the book puts the reader "in touch with the most momentous and far-reaching of all literary influences" but throws no new light on the origins of courtly love.

10. "A History of Romantic Love: Provencal Sentiment in English." *Times Literary Supplement*, 6 June 1936, p. 475.

   Long resumé; emphasis on a lucid explication of Lewis on the nature of allegory, its relation to romantic love in life, literature, and the history of human psychology; "altogether worthy of the great matter which he treats."

11. Knowlton, Edgar C. *Journal of English and German Philology* 36 (January 1937): 124-126.

   "valuable account of the territory covered" "emphasis on adultery mars the conception given of courtly love; and too much weight is given to Andreas Capellanus as an authority . . ."; sometimes oversimplified, but "supplies a serious need, and is a substantial contribution."

12. "The Library." *Notes and Queries* 171 (3 October 1936): 250-251.

   Excellent in tracing the movement towards the use of allegory but weak in its handling of the relation between personification and a living mythology; brilliant in its treatment of *The Romance of the Rose*.

13. *Speculum* (April 1937). [PF]

   "Afford excellent reading. The author has covered a wide territory, and has the gift of summarizing his documents in a manner both sensitive and illuminating . . ."

14. Tillotson, Kathleen. "Reviews." *Review of English Studies* 13 (October 1937): 477-479.

   "No one could read it without seeing all literature a little differently for ever after." In *Roman de la Rose* "for the first time the depth and delicacy of the allegory are clearly demonstrated." On Spenser "he has gaily and (one hopes) finally punctured a number of critical fallacies."

15. W[illiams], C[harles] L. *Oxford Magazine* 55 (25 February 1937): 449-450.

   "virile, fresh and important volume" [The author is said to be

Charles Williams in Sister Beattie's *The Humane Medievalist*
(listed in § V-B), p. 40; but the L. makes it doubtful.]

16. Young, G. M. *Daylight and Champaign*. London: Jonathan
Cape, 1937.

Not seen; according to J. A. W. Bennett's *The Humane
Medievalist* (listed in § II), p. 30, this volume reprints a review
of *The Allegory of Love* on pp. 160-166.

17. ————. "The World of Books—Love-in-the-Mist—A
Garland from the Middle Ages." *Sunday Times*, 28 June
1936. [PF]

"A great book . . . Mr. Lewis has one of the most precious gifts
with which a student of deceased literature can be endowed. He is
never bored."

5. *Out of the Silent Planet* (1938).

1. "Briefly Noted: Fiction." *New Yorker* 19 (2 October
1943): 79.

Brief. "almost as good as the early H. G. Wells. The writing
is miles above the usual 'scientifiction' level."

2. *Catholic World* 158 (December 1943): 314.

"Either you like scientific fantasies or you don't. . ." and after the
first twenty pages the story doesn't come off; no profound
commentary on life as in *Screwtape*.

3. Keenan, Charles. "One Universe." *America* 70 (23
October 1943): 77-78.

Resumé, some discussion; especially moved by the beauty of the
Oyarsa's history of primeval creation.

4. Kennedy, John S. "Fiction in Focus." *Sign* 23 (November 1943): 255.

"well-written but rather doughy book" with little of *Screwtape's* searching satire but too much thought for Flash Gordon enthusiasts.

5. Lewis, Elaine Lambert. "Fiction." *Library Journal* 68 (1 September 1943): 668.

Brief; uncertain as to the meaning of the book; decides it may "intrigue slumming intellectuals."

6. "Little *Hmān,* What *Hnau?*" *Time* 42 (11 October 1943): 100, 102, 104.

Long resumé, filled with Malacandrian terms, but little discussion of the allegory-myth.

7. Mascall, E. L. "Book Reviews." *Theology* 38 (April 1939): 303-304.

A perceptive four-paragraph notice in which the reviewer points to the reversal of Wellsian assumptions about aliens and praises in particular the translation of scientific humanism into one-and-two-syllable words. "an altogether satisfactory story, in which fiction and theology are so skilfully blended that the non-Christian will not realize he is being instructed in theology until it is too late."

8. Miller, P. Schuyler. "From Numenor to Edgestow."
Listed in § VI-A-1; a review of the Ransom Trilogy.

9. Morley, Christopher. "More Books of the Week." *Commonweal* 39 (29 October 1943): 45-46.

One-paragraph notice, with praise. "To me he is to this year's reading what Major Grey used to be on the pantry shelf, when chutney was still available."

10. Neider, Charles. "Novels: Fact and Fantasy." *New York Herald Tribune*, 3 October 1943, § 8, pp. 12, 14.

"a type of social criticism" "unusual descriptions and insights and a pungent style"

11. "New Novels." *Times*, 30 September 1938, p. 7c.

    Comparison to Wells; sees a moral but mainly reviews it in terms of adventure.

12. North, Jessica Nelson. "Sorns, Hrossa for the 'Bent.'" *Chicago Sun Book Week*, 19 September 1943, § 5, p. 9.

    "Escape literature . . . author himself is escaping—from the . . . necessity of checking his material against known facts—from the hard work of conceiving living characters."

13. "Novels of the Week." *Times Literary Supplement*, No. 1913 (1 October 1938): 625.

    A three-paragraph comparison of Lewis and H. G. Wells, which finds Wells the better in "dramatic sharpening . . . running characterization, other-worldly exposition and vivid incident." The reviewer liked the opening and spaceflight sections of Lewis's novel. "Alas! and alas! that Mr. Lewis, who is a capable writer with an excellent basic notion, did not learn more from his evident teacher."

14. Redman, Ben Ray. "C. S. Lewis's Magnificent Fantasy." *Saturday Review of Literature* 26 (16 October 1943): 52.

    "not Mr. Lewis's most distinguished book, but it is delightful"

15. Reynolds, Horace. "Rocket to Mars." *New York Times Book Review*, 3 October 1943, § 7, p. 16.

    Interprets *Out of the Silent Planet* as utopian fiction without metaphysical meaning; is unhappy the Oyarsa, and Lewis, "leave the problem of our deliverance from evil days among the Mysteries."

16. Swinnerton, Frank. "Our Planet and Others." *Observer*, 27 November 1938, p. 6.

    Sees *Out of the Silent Planet* as mere science fiction: "beautifully written as some of it is, does not seem quite to have grown from any conviction."

6. *Rehabilitations and Other Essays* (1939). Nine essays.

1. Blackstone, Bernard. "Rehabilitations and Other Essays." *Theology* 39 (July 1939): 73-75.

   Blackstone's review discusses the essay on Shelley for three paragraphs, and discusses the essay on Morris and mentions "Christianity and Literature" in the final paragraph; the other essays are not considered, as being not of particular interest to the readers of *Theology*.

2. Hawkins, Desmond. "The Debate Continues."

   Listed in § VI-A-1; review of *Rehabilitations* and *The Personal Heresy*.

3. Jameson, R. D. "Reviews." *Modern Language Notes* 55 (March 1940): 235-237.

   "value of the book is less in the points made than in the impulses toward dissent it arouses in the reader." Jameson checks Lewis's beginning of his essay on Shelley (which claims that T. S. Eliot has sacrificed Shelley to the fame of Dryden) against Eliot's essays on Dryden, finding no such comparison. After considering other essays, the author concludes: "Mr. Lewis wears his erudition gravely and though the horses he beats are, for the most part, dead, it is doubtless worth while to tap them occasionally when English societies meet lest they should astonish us by coming to life."

4. Knights, L. C. "Mr. C. S. Lewis and the Status Quo." *Scrutiny* 8 (June 1939): 88-92.

   Knights disagrees with "The Idea of an English School," "Our English Syllabus," and "High and Low Brows."

5. Leishman, J. B. "Rehabilitations and Other Essays." *Review of English Studies*, O. S. 16 (January 1940): 109-113.

   "a certain tendency to paradox and to the insistence upon neglected half-truths as though they were whole truths" but "it is impossible

not to be grateful for the formidable batteries of wit,
learning, and judgment with which Mr. Lewis is able to deliver
his counter-attack." Defense of Morris's prose styles "special
pleading"; essay on the English school "of really first-rate
importance"; "Bluspels and Flalansferes" is "a brilliant piece of
dialectic."

6. Sisson, C. J. "Reviews." *Modern Language Review* 34
   (October 1939): 604-605.

   Considers Lewis has the combined characteristics of Christian and
   classical scholar, which are considerable advantages for
   a modern critic of English literature.

7. Viator. "Men and Books." *Tablet* 173 (15 April 1939):
   490-491.

   Disagrees with Lewis on Shelley's word techniques; feels he has
   not adequately dealt with T. S. Eliot's views; regards him as
   insufficiently critical of Morris's workmanship.

7. *The Personal Heresy: A Critical Controversy* (1939).

Alternate essays written by E. M. W. Tillyard.

1. Bateson, F. W. "Reviews." *Review of English Studies* 16
   (October 1940): 487-489.

   Considers Lewis's case "just nonsense" in "the gratuitous
   assumption that there is a difference of kind between a poet's
   normal consciousness and the exceptional heightened consciousness
   out of which his best poems emerge." The difference is
   "no hiatus at all, but a gradual transition."

2. Boas, George. "Reviews." *Modern Language Notes* 55
   (March 1940): 233-234.

   Finds a double interest in the controversy (the subject and

dramatic development of the debate) but a basic flaw in the "*a priori* method of arguing from verbal formulas instead of from history."

3. Every, George, S. S. M. "The Personal Heresy, A Controversy." *Theology* 39 (August 1939): 151-152.

    Brother Every's review observes that both Lewis and Tillyard are often expressing their feelings rather than being concerned with the words of the poems they are discussing: that is, they do not agree with the reviewer about T. S. Eliot.

4. Gelby, Thomas, O. P. "The Man and the Work." *Tablet* 173 (27 May 1939): 685-686.

    Resumé emphasizing that the debate reaches early to the problem of literary criticism turning into the realm of philosophical "first things." Reviewer calls the debate an excellent dialogue, "not a couple of monologues."

5. Hawkins, Desmond. "The Debate Continues."

    Listed in § VI-A-1; review of *Rehabilitations* and *The Personal Heresy*.

6. "The New Books: Belles." *Saturday Review of Literature* 20 (19 August 1939): 20.

    "some extraordinarily sensitive criticism" though an "occasional tendency to indulge in sentimental rhetoric"

7. *Notes and Queries* 176 (3 June 1939): 394-395.

    Stimulating; controversialists equally matched; both seem to have tacit assumption that literature is for improvement first, delight second.

8. "The 'Personal Heresy': Style and the Man in Poetry: A Critical Controversy." *Times Literary Supplement*, 29 April 1939, p. 248.

    Special article (central essay) which makes the obvious point that Lewis and Tillyard do not mean the same thing by *personality*; it agrees with Lewis in regretting the biographical approach to writers but disagrees about his central thesis that the

reader does not make contact with the writer's personality
("the style is the man"). "Entertainment rather than enlightenment
is . . . the chief outcome of this debate. . ." Note also the brief
editorial on the opposite page (249) titled "The 'Personal
Heresy.'"

9. Temple, Ruth Z. "Pool of Bethsaida." *Sewanee Review* 47
(October-December 1939): 596-599.

Spirited argument but better at attacking "vulgar errors" than
substituting a true system; Lewis has humor, style, but separates
form from matter.

10. Tillotson, Geoffrey. "Reviews." *Modern Language Review*
35 (April 1940): 250-251.

Lewis has the more interesting debate style but has chosen the
wrong horse and presses the distinction too far.

8. *The Problem of Pain* (1940).

1. Dwyer, John F. "Book Reviews." *Thought* 19 (September
1944): 565.

Beautiful and consoling main thesis but seems to mingle orthodox
(i. e., Roman Catholic) Christianity, private Protestant
interpretation and modernist subjectivism in such things as
nature and function of the human soul, the problem of evolution,
the Fall, and Biblical inerrancy.

2. Gruenthaner, Michael J., S. J. "Book Reviews." *American
Ecclesiastical Review* 111 (October 1944): 312-313.

"The notions of the author about the elevation of man to a higher
state, and of original sin, are hazy and unsatisfactory. The
concept of the supernatural has eluded him altogether." Only
"educated" Catholics should read.

3. Johnson, Talmage C. "The Meaning and Use of Pain." *Christian Century* 60 (1 December 1943) : 1400.

   Finds much of the argument sound and well stated but marred by Lewis's low opinion of man.

4. Keenan, Charles. "Shadow of His Hand." *America* 70 (18 March 1944): 664.

   "fresh and lucid treatment of an age-old problem"; a professor of theology would question some remarks on the Fall and on animal pain but Lewis stands ready to admit mistakes and the speculation is not essential to the main thesis.

5. L., A. "Problem of Evil." *Studies* 32 (June 1943): 291-293 [291-292].

   Feels Lewis ignores the "real crux" of the problem of evil, providence and its relation to the implications of the infinity of God.

6. Marron, M. A., O. F. M. *Franciscan Studies* 26, n. s. 5 (June 1945): 209.

   "vigor, novelty, and freshness" but the book is "a strange amalgam of Orthodox Christianity, Protestant Subjectivism, and Modern Skepticism": the Bible entirely human, Hell not eternal, Paul often misunderstood, the concept of human soul and origin inadequate.

7. Moore, Francis John. "Books of the Day." *Churchman* 158 (15 February 1944): 16-17.

   "He is not always convincing—as in the Chapter on Animal Pain—but he is always interesting; and no one can read him without being both instructed and mentally provoked."

8. Moore, John M. "Book Reviews: Philosophy and Theology." *Journal of Bible and Religion* 12 (May 1944): 123-124.

   Five paragraphs of summary, with the final paragraph spent on the reviewer's unanswered questions: (1) about the intensity and distribution of pain, if pain is educative; and (2) about the lack of striving to remove pain, if pain is felt to be God-given.

9. "Religion." *Catholic World.*

Listed in § VI-A-1; a review of *The Problem of Pain* and *Christian Behaviour.*

10. "Reviews." *Blackfriars* 21 (December 1940): 718-720.

Well-written but should have given fuller treatment to retributive and expiatory aspects of suffering.

11. Shuster, George. "Discipline." *New York Herald Tribune Book Review*, 26 December 1943, § 6, p. 6.

"has succeeded in making all these points in terms of orthodox Christianity with unusual effectiveness"; "an intelligent awareness of the great sources from which the English spiritual tradition is derived"

12. Williams, Charles. "Book Reviews." *Theology* 42 (January 1941): 62-63.

"goodness working on goodness, a lucid and sincere intellect at work"

13. Woolley, Paul. "Reviews."

Listed in § VI-A-1; a review of *The Problem of Pain, The Case for Christianity,* and *Christian Behaviour.*

9. *The Screwtape Letters* (1942) and *"The Screwtape Letters" and "Screwtape Proposes a Toast"* (1961).

1. Artifex. "A Number of New Books." *Manchester Guardian,* 24 February 1942, p. 3.

"The book is sparkling yet truly reverent, in fact a perfect joy, and should become a classic."

2. Bacon, Leonard. "Critique of Pure Diabolism." *Saturday Review of Literature* 26 (17 April 1943): 20.

Enthusiastic. Bacon draws a number of parallels between Screwtape's Hell and Hitler's Germany, and in one case, American Schools of Education.

3. Furlong, Monica. "Second Thoughts on Screwtape." *John O'London's* 4 (2 February 1961): 288.

Readable but "curiously unlikeable"; Screwtape in the new letter has become a "rather stupid Tory" betraying in Lewis a loathing for lower classes. Compares Lewis to Swift.

4. Jacks, L. P. *Hibbert Journal* 40 (July 1942): 395.

Dénouement might have been different if Screwtape rather than Wormwood had been the temptor, Screwtape being such an accomplished diabolical psychologist. Only possible literary wobble is putting wise sayings about God in the scoundrel mouth of Screwtape.

5. Joad, C. E. M. "Mr. Lewis's Devil." *New Statesman and Nation* 23 (16 May 1942): 324.

Emphasizes the psychological insights of the book, its tendency to consider all modern beliefs devil-inspired, and the difficulty of responding to its satire without mixed feelings. "Mr. Lewis possesses the rare gift of making righteousness readable"; "Mr. Lewis makes the business of living so extraordinarily difficult. Difficult I know that it is, but is it really as difficult as all that?"

6. Knight, Damon. "Books: Briefly Noted." *Magazine of Fantasy and Science Fiction* 18 (May 1960): 82.

Brief notice of a publication in paperback. "If by any chance you've never read this brilliant brew of Christian apology and supernatural fantasy . . . get it."

7. "Letters from Hell: Truth by Paradox." *Times Literary Supplement*, No. 2091 (28 February 1942): 100.

The reviewer has high praise for the book (which he insists on calling an allegory), showing that the demonic viewpoint allows Lewis to attack errors in the modern world by praising them and to expound theology by attacking the Enemy. "display of much solid Christian doctrine."

8. Mondrone, Domenico. "Berlicche e l'Arte di Dannare gli Uomini."

Listed in § III-E; presumably a review-essay on the Italian translation of *The Screwtape Letters*.

9. O'S, D. *Studies* 31 (September 1942): 400-401.

"shrewd psychology" though a bit vague in disquisitions on being in love.

10. P[urinton], C[arl] E. "Book Notices: Theology." *Journal of Bible and Religion* 12 (February 1944): 65.

The first two paragraphs are a standard notice; the third (and last) paragraph mentions that the reviewer has been using the book in his New Testament course in teaching the Sermon on the Mount—he cites the parallel passages, and concludes, "Indeed, what C. S. Lewis has actually done is to interpret the Sermon . . . in its height and depth in language both searching and winsome."

11. [Skillin, Edward, Jr.] "Short but Neat." *Commonweal* 37 (5 March 1943): 498.

Compares style to the jabbing understated style of Oxbridge debating team. (White's *The Image of Man in C. S. Lewis* identifies the reviewer.)

12. Stopp, F. J. "Lowerarchy." *Month* 26 (September 1961): 184-186.

Minor classic, but the new letter fails as satire and "induces a mental crick in the neck analogous to the author's spiritual cramp."

13. Turner, W. J. "The Devil at Work." *Spectator* 168 (20 February 1942): 186.

"though I am not of his way of thinking. . . . From this Christian standpoint he has written the most vital restatement of religious truths produced in our time . . ."

14. Weeks, Edward. "The Atlantic Bookshelf: The Peripatetic Reviewer." *Atlantic* 172 (September 1943): 123, 125, 127, 128 [128].

     "delightful a series of devilish letters as I have ever had the fun of reading." Not to be confused with Moral Re-Armament.

15. Williams, Charles. *Dublin Review* 211 (October 1942): 170-171.

     Wants to "reinforce the general recommendation"; notes that Lewis's devil is highly intelligent "everywhere except in the centre."

16. ————. "Letters in Hell." *Time and Tide* 23 (21 March 1942): 245-246. Reprints: (1) Anthony Lejeune (ed.), *Time and Tide Anthology* (London: Andre Deutsch, 1956): 255-257; (2) *Mythlore* 2 (Autumn 1970): 22.

     Review in epistolary form to "My Dearest Scorpuscle" from "Snigsozzle"; of the many attempts at imitation, Williams's is one of the few that succeeds.

17. Wormwood. "The Screwtape Letters." *Oxford Magazine* 60 (14 May 1942): 303.

     A review in the form of a letter from the unrepentant Wormwood to his Uncle Screwtape.

10. *A Preface to "Paradise Lost": Being the Ballard Matthews Lectures Delivered at University College, North Wales, 1941, Revised and Enlarged* (1942).

1. Garrod, H. W. "C. S. Lewis on 'Paradise Lost.' " *Oxford Magazine* 61 (19 November 1942): 84-85.

     Garrod suggests the book helps in some intellectual clarification but not in approaching the poetry: "For me, as for

Professor Saurat, the prime hindrance is 'theological rubbish.' "
Lewis does not bring the reader nearer to the aesthetic of Milton.
On the Romantics Lewis takes a free hand with literary history.
Lewis is wrong on Satan; Lewis has a good chapter on Virgil.
Notes misprints.

2. Griffiths, Dom Bede, O. S. P. *Blackfriars* 24 (February
   1943): 77-78.

   "admirably done" defense of Milton's Christian orthodoxy in the
   epic.

3. Knight, Jackson. "Milton the Christian." *Spectator* 169
   (13 November 1942): 460.

   "He makes us take down the poem, and feel it more strongly
   than before, and like it still better." One caveat: thinks Lewis goes
   a bit too far insisting on Milton's "singleness of mind" in the
   importance of his theology.

4. Knights, L. C. "Milton Again." *Scrutiny* 11 (December
   1942): 146-148.

   Lewis's arguments are abstract, irrelevant, and unconvincing.
   Lewis builds a case for Milton's aims "from the outside" rather
   than the center (i. e., physical and moral perceptiveness
   "which nourishes and is nourished by the life of the emotions").
   Lewis provides some useful correctives on Satan but fails to notice
   the superior energy of the first two books. Overall, the book
   is "peripheral."

5. "Milton's Riches: Return to 'Paradise Lost': Epic and
   Modern Taste." *Times Literary Supplement*, No. 2130
   (28 November 1942): 582.

   Special article (full-page review); mainly a summary of content.
   "Here is a strong reinforcement of the case for *Paradise Lost*
   which recent criticism has necessitated"; "Mr. Lewis would have
   us understand and keep to the rubrics." (See "The Stock
   Responses" in *Times Literary Supplement* the next week, p.
   595, for a continuation of the discussion.)

6. Ridler, Anne. "Milton: A Re-Perusal." *Time and Tide* 23 (7 November 1942) : 892.

"needed to restore the critical balance" though lists a few reservations on Lewis's handling of contemporary critics.

7. Saurat, Denis. "Milton's Christianity." *New Statesman and Nation* 24 (14 November 1942) : 325-326.

"brilliant and a pleasure to dispute"; thinks Lewis makes the poem too orthodox in belief and he should have taken *The Treatise of Christian Doctrine* into account in interpreting Milton on the soul and Satan. Saurat writes, "The mysteries of the Christian faith are not susceptible of literary treatment."

8. Smith, Naomi Royde. "Some Recent Books." *Dublin Review* 212 (January 1943) : 90-92.

"rich and crowded book"; Lewis's beliefs implicit throughout; the work a stimulus for any lecturer drawing up a fresh syllabus for any masterpiece in any language.

9. Turner, V. G., S. J. "Books of the Week: What Milton Was Doing." *Tablet* 181 (9 January 1943) : 20.

Excellent critical attempt to "think with" Milton; chapters on epic shed new light on Virgil; chapters on Satan and his followers, the angels, Adam and Eve "superbly done"; Lewis did not adequately consider his own presuppositions of moral theory nor whether a poem can convey something beyond an author's awareness at the time of composition.

11. *Broadcast Talks: Reprinted with Some Alterations from Two Series of Broadcast Talks ("Right and Wrong: A Clue to the Meaning of the Universe" and "What Christians Believe")* Given in 1941 and 1942 (1942). Published in the United States as *The Case for Christianity* (1943).

1. Aubrey, E[dwin] E. "Recent Books." *Journal of Religion* 24 (October 1944): 299.

   A one-paragraph notice: the book "will scarcely convince a really thoughtful atheist, and its virtual acceptance of a personal devil will surely startle intelligent Christians."

2. "Book Notices: Philosophy and Theology." *Journal of Bible and Religion* 12 (November 1944): 266.

   A four-paragraph notice: the last paragraph shows surprise that the four clergymen to whom Lewis showed his material—Anglican, Roman Catholic, Presbyterian, Methodist—could agree theologically.

3. "Books of the Week: Clear Reasoning." *Tablet* 180 (18 July 1942): 32.

   Considers Lewis orthodox, with the gift of making himself understood by the man in the street; stylistically fresh.

4. Dwyer, John F. "Book Reviews." *Thought* 19 (March 1944): 170-171.

   Good apologetic as a popular case against many aspects of anti-Christianity; not specific enough on theology; sidesteps fundamental issues such as Gospel historicity.

5. Holmes, Rev. John Haynes. "Christians of Today." *New York Herald Tribune Weekly Book Review* 20 (14 November 1943): 42.

   Review of *The Case for Christianity* and Nels F. S. Ferre's *Return to Christianity*. Holmes finds the first part of Lewis's book, the discussion of moral law, very good, but the last half incredibly naive—he quotes the passage about this world being "enemy-occupied territory" as an example.

6. J., P. M. "Friar's Bookshelf."

Listed in § VI-A-1; a review of *The Pilgrim's Regress*, *The Case for Christianity*, and *Christian Behaviour*.

7. Jarn, Francis. "Book Reviews." *Franciscan Studies* 25 (June 1944): 195-196.

Nothing new, but clear, interesting style. Question of evil obviously important to author but seems to waver on whether relative or absolute. Presents no "reasonable proof" for existence, intelligence, and will as being in themselves good.

8. O'S., D. "Review: Apologetics."

Listed in § VI-A-1; a review of *Broadcast Talks*, *Christian Behaviour*, and *Beyond Personality*; not identical to the following item in the same periodical.

9. O'S., D. "Reviews: Apologetics." *Studies* 32 (March 1943): 122-124 [123-124].

"strikingly cogent" though feels Catholics will find much that is inadequate.

10. S., G. D. "Book Reviews." *Clergy Review* 22 (December 1942): 561-563.

"unflinching logic" in discussion of natural law but argument from design better than moral law as proof of God. Readers may find line of reasoning difficult to follow in third and fourth talks.

11. [Skillin, Edward, Jr.] "Smart Writing." *Commonweal* 39 (22 October 1943): 17-18.

Stimulating; a bit brittle. Some theological criticism.
(The name of the author is given in White's *The Image of Man in C. S. Lewis*.)

12. Woolley, Paul. "Reviews."

Listed in § VI-A-1; a review of *The Problem of Pain*, *The Case for Christianity*, and *Christian Behaviour*.

13. Yarros, Victor S. "An Invitation to Rough Debunking." *American Freeman* (Girard, Kansas), December 1947.

An editorial attack particularly on the book's traditional images of God—by a rationalist. (Lewis, by the way, is referred to as "C. E. S. Lewis" as well as a "pious paradox-monger and audacious word-juggler.")

12. *Hamlet*: *The Prince or the Poem?* Annual Shakespeare Lecture of the British Academy, 1942; *The Proceedings of the British Academy*, 28 (1942). Eighteen-page pamphlet (1942), later collected in *They Asked For a Paper* (1962) and in *Selected Literary Essays* (1969).

1. Lawrence, William M. *Modern Language Review* 38 (April 1943): 140-142.

"urbane yet provocative argument" though the "subjective and impressionistic approach. . . has been with us for a long time." It "performs a service in putting some fundamental questions squarely before the reader . . ."

2. "The Library." *Notes and Queries* 184 (24 April 1943): 269-270.

Finds Lewis's treatment of critics of the play more odd than necessary; his handling of central theme as worry about what happens after death is well done.

3. "Other New Publications: Literary." *Times Literary Supplement*, No. 2123 (10 October 1942): 503.

A one-paragraph summary; favorable.

13. *Christian Behaviour: A Further Series of Broadcast Talks* (1943).

1. "Book Reviews." *Clergy Review*, n.s. 23 (July 1943): 331.
   Favorable; minor caveat: argument for two sorts of marriage, civil and Christian, ignores that the argument he gives in defense of Christian marriage is deduced from the natural law.

2. *Christian Century* 61 (26 January 1944): 114.
   "sound common sense" with "freshness" though "rather naive faith."

3. Cooke, Alistair, "Mr. Anthony at Oxford."
   Listed in § VI-A-1; a hostile review of both *Christian Behaviour* and *Perelandra*.

4. Forman, Henry James. "Common-Sense Humanist." *New York Times Book Review*, 23 April 1944, § 7, p. 12.
   Compares Lewis's clear-headedness to Benjamin Jowett and Cardinal Newman.

5. "From Hell to Heaven." *Time* 43 (24 January 1944): 94, 96.
   Review in the Religion section, accompanied by a rather inaccurate biography (at least, one assumes Lewis never published a *novel* under the name of Clive Hamilton).

6. J., P. M. "Friar's Bookshelf."
   Listed in § VI-A-1; a review of *The Pilgrim's Regress, The Case for Christianity*, and *Christian Behaviour*.

7. Mozley, J. K. "The Christian Life." *Spectator* 170 (23 April 1943): 392.
   "in general, Mr. Lewis is a quite safe guide."

8. O'S., D. "Reviews—Apologetics."
   Listed in § VI-A-1; review of *Broadcast Talks, Christian Behaviour*, and *Beyond Personality*.

9. "Religion." *Catholic World*.

Listed in § VI-A-1; a review of *The Problem of Pain* and *Christian Behaviour*.

10. Speaight, Robert. "To Mixed Congregations." *Tablet* 181 (26 June 1943): 308.

Considers this a safer guide to Christian ethics than the dualism running through the "acrid brilliance of *Screwtape*."

11. Vann, Gerald, O. P. "Reviews." *Blackfriars* 24 (July 1943): 270-271.

"outstanding" yet "disappoints" because "it does not seem to cohere," failing to give "a whole picture of the unity of the Christian life in its various aspects."

12. Woolley, Paul. "Reviews."

Listed in § VI-A-1; a review of *The Problem of Pain, The Case for Christianity*, and *Christian Behaviour*.

14. *Perelandra* (1943).

1. B., K. *Catholic World* 159 (May 1944): 184.

Generally favorable but finds the fist-fight anticlimactic and sometimes Lewis's "imagination dips over at moments into delirium."

2. Bacon, Leonard. "The Imaginative Power of C. S. Lewis." *Saturday Review of Literature* 27 (8 April 1944): 9.

Enthusiastic and allusive. Regards *Out of the Silent Planet* as a "concoction of the intellect" while its sequel "is the result of the poetic imagination in full blast"; minor bone: "as a crack at science, it won't wash." As an added bonus, there is a woodcut of Lewis on the cover of the issue.

3. Brady, Charles A. *Best Sellers* 4 (15 May 1944): 40-41.

"nothing *contra revelationem* in the grave beauty of these fantasies of free will; . . ." Lewis a "great original."

4. Brunini, John Gilland. "Books of the Week." *Commonweal* 40 (12 May 1944): 90-91.

"whole passages of prose poetry—that inevitably suggest the sweep of Dante and of Milton"; but criticizes some aspects of his speculative theology and plot weakness in loading the dice to favor his Eve. Despite this and the obviousness of Ransom as *deus ex machina*, "writing of the highest order."

5. Clare, Tullis. "Paradise Unlost." *Time and Tide* 24 (1 May 1943): 362-363.

Lewis's "combination of orthodox propaganda and speculative allegory . . . is deeply interesting, and his prophetic vision at the end is remarkable both for its substance and the accidents of its brilliant writing."

6. Cooke, Alistair. "Mr. Anthony at Oxford."

Listed in § VI-A-1; a review of *Christian Behaviour* and *Perelandra.*

7. Derleth, August. "Eden on the Planet of Perelandra." *Chicago Sun Book Week*, 9 April 1944, § 5, p. 2.

"engagingly written, if at times a little tiring" and "no concession whatever to pulp fiction."

8. Donaghy, William A. "Salathiel's Progress: Perelandra." *America* 71 (29 April 1944): 104.

"Metaphysics, mysticism, theology are welded into symphonic harmony by a style as sharp and shining as a sword. . . . not just another Wellsian phantasmagoria nor Jules Verne with a dash of demonology."

9. Farber, Marjorie. "Imperfect Paradise." *New York Times Book Review*, 26 March 1944, § 7, p. 4.

Exciting, but the "bare intellectual bones intrude on fantasy" and Lewis sounds like "a somewhat unconvinced Christian who is trying to reassure himself." Reviewer says with all its faults the novel is delightful; hopes Lewis's "religious conscience will now relax a bit."

10. Godfrey, Clare. "New Fiction." *New York Herald Tribune Weekly Book Review*, 2 April 1944, § 6, p. 8.

   Lewis "brought to its fashioning gifts of imagination and scholarship. However, the theme is frequently lost in the shapes he has created for his imaginings of life on the planet Venus, . . . with its shifting islands, Atlantidean flowers and fruits . . . a place of nightmare horror."

11. H., G. B. "Friars' Bookshelf." *Dominicana* 29 (Summer 1944): 141-142.

   Like symbolism as a mode of literary expression in general, "lacking in clarity and intelligibility"; "neither an entertaining nor enlightening novel," its only distinction is "the peculiar yet beautiful imaginative passages."

12. Hobson, Harold. "A Novel of Adam and Eve on the Planet Venus: A London Letter." *Christian Science Monitor Weekly Magazine Section*, 5 June 1943, p. 11.

   "great narrative and descriptive powers"; can be enjoyed on two levels, narrative and theological. Lewis a dualist, though "in the last resort" he finds at the heart of evil a "profound weakness."

13. Marriott, Charles. "New Novels." *Manchester Guardian*, 30 April 1943, p. 3.

   Lewis not always successful in conveying planetary atmosphere.

14. Miller, P. Schuyler. "From Numenor to Edgestow."

   Listed in § VI-A-1; a review of the Ransom Trilogy.

15. Muir, Edwin. "New Novels." *Listener* 29 (6 March 1943): 546.

   "though it is brilliantly managed, one has frequently the feeling that the fable and the meaning are precariously connected"

16. O'Brien, Kate. "Fiction." *Spectator* 170 (14 May 1943):
458.

"too great a weight of circumstantial detail, and too laboured an insistence on relating the ineffable to the obvious." Subject asks too much of prose; it is fit only for "verse at its most immense."

17. Pryce-Jones, Alan. "New Novels." *Observer*, 25 April 1943, p. 3.

"the myth is clouded in metaphysical vapour, the springs of an original and fascinating story drain away into portentious symbols." "As an interplanetary novelist he should read more Verne and less Aquinas."

18. "Visit to Venus." *Times Literary Supplement*, 1 May 1943, p. 209.

"rare power of inventive imagination, . . . graphic vigor of language." "How far the reader will be able to accept Mr. Lewis's cosmology will depend entirely on his or her own attitude towards first and last things."

15. *The Abolition of Man: or, Reflections on Education With Special Reference to the Teaching of English in the Upper Forms of Schools* (1943).

1. B., A. "Among the New Books." *San Francisco Chronicle*, 10 August 1947, p. 13.

"his deliberate avoidance on this occasion of his usual spiritual and theological concerns tends to turn the Tao into something very like the Code of the Pukka Sahib."

2. Bruehl, Charles. "Book Reviews." *Homiletic and Pastoral Review* 48 (May 1948): 636.

Reviewer finds the book a "sound essay in semantics" and does not seem to grasp more.

3. Hollis, Christopher. "Books of the Week: The Growth of Ignorance." *Tablet* 183 (19 February 1944): 92.

   Reviewer takes the book on face value as a commentary on education and the dangers of metaphysical subjectivism in textbook assumptions.

4. Leon, Philip. "Reviews." *Hibbert Journal* 42 (April 1944): 280-282.

   Leon digresses to discuss the organizers of Nature as suffering from inertia: over all, he agrees with Lewis and wants people to be taught to desire the *tao*.

5. Walsh, Chad. "Whatsoever Things are True: On the Universality, Irrationality and Necessity of Morals." *New York Herald Tribune Book Review*, 13 April 1947, § 7, p. 5.

   "This quiet little book is uniquely calculated to infuriate John Dewey's disciples and all other moralists who want to pick and choose from among the scraps of universal morality . . ." Most vulnerable is impression it gives that the world's moral systems are more in agreement than is so, though Walsh thinks Lewis is aware of the danger.

16. *Beyond Personality: The Christian Idea of God* (1944).

1. Denecke, Charles, S. J. "Lewis, C. S." *Best Sellers* 5 (15 May 1945): 38.

   "an admirably simple explanation of the essential facts of Christian Revelation"

2. Dwyer, John F. *Thought* 20 (September 1945): 572-573.

   "best of the Lewis books" with Protestant point of view but definitely allied against creedless Christianity.

3. E., H. P. "Accuse Not Nature . . ." *Punch* 207 (11 October 1944): 321.

   Finds too much emphasis on killing natural selves: "curiously heterodox tendency to equate 'nature' and 'sin.' " (A paragraph notice.)

4. Eppinga, Jacob Dirk. "Reviews." *Westminster Theological Journal* 8 (May 1946): 225-227.

   Claims Lewis's interpretations of Trinity, Incarnation, Redemption not wholly orthodox; also considers his illustrations and analogies too often inclined to drag transcendence down to immanence.

5. Fox, Thomas A., C. S. P. "Book Reviews." *Homiletic and Pastoral Review* 46 (October 1945): 77.

   Full doctrine of grace, supernatural life and the means of fostering it is not here but "If the crowd is not 'getting' C. S. Lewis, then I'm afraid it is getting none of us."

6. Fremantle, Anne. "Books of the Week." *Commonweal* 42 (14 September 1945): 528-529.

   Shows that Lewis and the author of *The Cloud of Unknowing* say a number of the same things, but finds fault with Lewis's assumption that any church will do.

7. Holmes, John Haynes. "Faith at Work." *New York Herald Tribune Weekly Book Review*, 23 September 1945, § 6, p. 12.

   "His clarity of thought and simplicity of expression have a magic about them which makes plain the most abstruse problems of theological speculation."

8. O'S., D. "Reviews: Apologetics."

   Listed in § VI-A-1; a review of *Broadcast Talks, Christian Behaviour,* and *Beyond Personality.*

9. R., W. B. "Friars' Bookshelf." *Dominicana* 30 (Winter 1945): 299-300.

   Lewis fails to answer how the transformation of men to sons of God can be brought about. Since he avoided the "true answer" (the sacraments) he "was forced to flee from reality."

10. Smith, G. D. "Nature and Spirit, According to a Recent Work." *Clergy Review* 25 (February 1945): 62-69.

An examination of Lewis's "dynamist" concept of worship "in contrast to Catholic teaching" of the nature of man, the Fall, and grace. Smith regards Lewis's view of divine adoption as different from Catholic teaching; also believes in Lewis "the natural is opposed to the spiritual" whereas in scholastic theology the "natural in man includes the spiritual." Considers Lewis should grasp more firmly the "clear-cut distinction between the natural and the supernatural." See Donnelly's "Protest on C. S. Lewis," and Gardner's item of the same title, in § IV-C; both letters discuss this review.

11. "Theology of Discovery: Mr. C. S. Lewis's Talks." *Times Literary Supplement*, 21 October 1944, p. 513.

"Mr. Lewis has a quite unique power of making theology an attractive, exciting and (one might almost say) uproariously fascinating quest."

12. Thomas, Ivo, O. P. *Blackfriars* 26 (January 1945): 34-35.

Favorable; brief; gives several theological objections, including Lewis's "curious reluctance to assert God's timelessness."

13. Van Til, Cornelius. *United Evangelical Action* 5 (15 May 1946): 21.

"not arresting in thought"; "Lewis goes off on a vague, pantheising form of Christianity" setting aside the creator-creature relationship.

14. Williams, Charles. "Critic's Commentary." *Time and Tide* 26 (16 June 1945): 506.

"in the main it drives straight"

17. *That Hideous Strength: A Modern Fairy-Tale for Grown-ups* (1945).

1. Bacon, Leonard. "Confusion Goes to College." *Saturday Review of Literature* 29 (25 May 1946): 13-14.

   "a ghastly but in many places a magnificent nightmare"; Lewis may have gotten himself tangled in the plot and with unsympathetic characters, but tells a good, energetic tale and gives "wild glimpses of truth."

2. Beresford, J. D. "Five Novels." *Manchester Guardian*, 24 August 1945, p. 3.

   Sees moral weakness in the brute force used by Ransom and Merlin to achieve victory; "weak in construction."

3. Clare, Tullus. "New Novels." *Time and Tide* 26 (15 September 1945): 777-778.

   "Mr. Lewis's brilliant imagination is robust as well as ingenious." ". . . full of delightful odds and ends" though the characters tend to be uninspiring.

4. Collins, Leslie. "Tall Tale of Good vs. Evil." *Chicago Sun Book Week*, 26 May 1946, § 5, p. 12.

   "poetic mind, a scholar's regard for the correct word, an incomparably warm, subtle humor, a knack of making plausible the unreal, and an imagination that knows no bounds." "The Lewis versatility is almost without end."

5. E., H. P. "Technocracy Takes Charge." *Punch* 209 (29 August 1945): 191.

   "Mr. Lewis's triumph [is] to have shown, with shattering credibility, how the pitiful little souls of Jane and Mark Studdock became the apocalyptic battlefield of Heaven and Hell."

6. Fremantle, Anne. "Truth, Terrors, Thrills." *New York Herald Tribune Weekly Book Review*, 2 June 1946, § 7, p. 12.

"This whole strange story reads horribly like an illustration for Mr. Huxley's recent monograph 'Science, Liberty and Peace.' . . . the whole fantasy, gigantic as it is, seems hardly heavyweight enough for the implications." Fremantle notices the theme of St. Augustine's two cities (which Charles Moorman developed in his second book on the Inklings); she ends by feeling that Lewis was better at theological fiction (*The Screwtape Letters, The Great Divorce*) than fantastic novels.

7. Greene, Graham. *Evening Standard* [English], 24 August 1945, p. 6.

Sinister institute sections well written; "good" characters unconvincing; allegory "a little too friendly."

8. Hamm, Victor H. *Thought* 21 (September 1946): 545-547.

"in the Chestertonian genre" and an allegory of good and evil making mere human characters and situations seem trivial; narrative not entirely successful but "full of original insights and rarely brilliant writing."

9. McSorley, Joseph. "New Books." *Catholic World* 163 (June 1946): 277-278.

Sharp irony, skillful caricature, but there should have been some pruning; his "flair for the occult has run away with him."

10. Miller, P. Schuyler. "From Numenor to Edgestow."

Listed in § VI-A-1; a review of the Ransom Trilogy.

11. Muir, Edwin. "New Novels." *Listener* 34 (6 September 1945): 274.

"like a conjuring trick, a matter of technique"; Lewis is "artistically lax," unable to fuse the novel's aspect as thriller with the demands of both high art and theology.

12. "Myth Making." *Times Literary Supplement*, No. 2273 (25 August 1945): 401.

Points out the likeness to the novels of Charles Williams and mentions "Taliessin Through Logres"; finds the ideas good but the "creative imagination" weak, and the whole too obviously moralistic.

13. Orwell, George. "The Scientist Takes Over." *Manchester Evening News*, 16 August 1945, p. 2.

Regards it mainly as a crime story, marred by the presence of the supernatural.

14. R., W. B. and P. M. S. "Friar's Bookshelf."

Listed in § VI-A-1; review of *That Hideous Strength* and *The Great Divorce*.

15. Spencer, Theodore. "Symbols of a Good and Bad England." *New York Times Book Review*, 7 July 1946, § 7, p. 10.

Spencer observes that "the titular director [of N.I.C.E.] is a patent caricature of H. G. Wells," but his main point is that the placing of fantasy (particularly involving Merlin) in a realistic, earthly setting makes the fantasy seem silly—unlike the imaginative suspension of disbelief he could give to the first two volumes of the trilogy.

16. "Theological Thriller." *Time* 47 (10 June 1946): 52, 54.

"well-written, fast-paced satirical fantasy"; "loaded with enough spiritual wisdom for a dozen stories." "As in many moral tales, Good is less sharply drawn than Evil; some readers may think good Dr. Ransom's mysterious sources of power more druidical than Christian." "The devil abroad in his 20th Century world is the ultra-rational scientist-technocrat."

18. *The Great Divorce: A Dream* (1945).

1. Auden, W. H. "Red Lizards and White Stallions." *Saturday Review of Literature* 29 (13 April 1946): 22-23.

   "generally entertaining" and "generally instructive." Auden sees the purpose of the book to reconcile the doctrine of man's free will with the doctrine of eternal damnation. He dislikes the use of Scottish dialect, and the combination of desire for recognition and lack of desire to communicate to the public in Lewis's artist; he believes theologically wrong the mention of historic people as damned ("Dante or no Dante") and the change of the red lizard (lust) to a white stallion ("a universe in which all lizards were horses would be a less valuable universe").

2. "Book Notices: Religion in Literature." *Journal of Bible and Religion* 14 (November 1946): 252.

   A six-paragraph notice praising Lewis as the "Master of the Unexpected Shock" in this "jazz version of Dante's *Divine Comedy*." The review concludes, "This is most effective preaching in the form of fiction."

3. Caswell, Wilbur Larremore. "Divorce Between Heaven and Hell: C. S. Lewis's Latest Book." *Churchman* 160 (1 May 1946): 13-14.

   "his most brilliant, original and stimulating work to date," second only to *Christian Behaviour*; only caveat: "the author betrays what will seem to many of us an exaggerated and unjustified intolerance and suspicion of liberalism."

4. Deane, A. C. "A Nightmare." *Spectator* 176 (25 January 1946): 96.

   Satire "jars horribly when the theme is the doom of lost souls." Reviewer finds no feeling of tenderness, infinite love, supernatural redemption in "these glittering yet distasteful pages."

5. Denecke, Charles, S. J. *Best Sellers* 6 (1 April 1946): 1-3.

   "rare ability to throw light on the most abstruse of truths"; a warning for Catholics that Lewis does not recognize "truth must be embodied in a living and divinely instituted and infallible Church" so "there will necessarily be a looseness about his treatment of the nature and necessity of Grace."

6. Dock, E. K. T. "Mr. Lewis's Theology." *Scrutiny* 14 (Summer 1946): 53-59.

Reviewer finds, among other things, "that Mr. Lewis is not sufficiently self-conscious to be a good moralist"—that is, that Lewis confuses his own feelings with Church doctrine, to overstate what is obviously, for Mr. Dock and his sympathizers, a matter of degree and emphasis, to be hedged with appropriate parenthetical reservations.

7. Donnelly, Malachi J., S. J. "Book Reviews." *Theological Studies* 7 (September 1946): 494-495.

"very interesting as an imaginative analysis of attachment and detachment" but warns Catholics Lewis must be read with permission.

8. "Dream of the After-World." *Times Literary Supplement,* 2 February 1946, p. 58.

"will set the thoughtful meditating on the nature of heaven and hell, not on whether the vision of either is first-rate or second-rate." "Those who find themselves in agreement with the arguments put up by the Ghosts for not being saved will be unlikely to finish this book."

9. Dwyer, John F. "Book Reviews." *Thought* 21 (December 1946): 746-747.

Not necessary to assume for the book's thesis that the once-damned may later be saved; fantasy more subtle than *Screwtape*. Influence of Dante noted.

10. H., R. C. *Providence Sunday Journal,* 5 May 1946, § 6, p. 8.

Brief. For the damned, "a great divorce between illusion and reality"; a good sermon but not so good as fiction. "full of straw-men."

11. Hennessy, Augustine P., C. P. *Sign* 25 (April 1946): 56.

Shrewd fantasy makes one truth inescapable, that "the eternal frustration of hell is due not to God's unwillingness to forgive but to the damned soul's inability to change its perverted mind."

12. Keenan, Charles. "Heaven and Hell." *America* 74 (16 March 1946): 618-619.

   Most successful on human motives; "suffers by the inclusion of discussions of topics that cannot be treated in a page or two without leaving an impression of inadequacy, perhaps of heterodoxy."

13. Lloyd, Roger. "Full Heaven and Scarce World." *Time and Tide* 27 (19 January 1946): 60.

   "In Mr. Lewis's cosmos this apposition of motives for social order is the fundamental thing. On earth we cooperate for need . . . . In heaven . . . to enjoy joy." "all very witty . . . But it is desperately earnest and really rather terrible. . . . [but] to be saved by Him may well be a process involving an experience of the terrible."

14. McMahon, Francis E. "Trip by Bus to Paradise," *Chicago Sun Book Week*, 17 March 1946, § 5, p. 2.

   Rare gift of clothing serious material in "almost rollicking fantasy" though *Screwtape* fans may be disappointed. Rigorously affirms Anglican orthodoxy.

15. R., W. B. and P. M. S. "Friar's Bookshelf."

   Listed in § VI-A-1; review of *That Hideous Strength* and *The Great Divorce*.

16. Sugrue, Thomas. "Terrifying Realities of the Soul." *New York Herald Tribune Weekly Book Review*, 3 March 1946, § 7, p. 4.

   "The success he has had . . . shows . . . there are only two things necessary for the production of a good book: a subject with which every one is concerned and a writer with style and wisdom to treat it. That's all."

19. *George Macdonald: An Anthology.* [Edited by Lewis] (1946).

1. Brady, Charles A. "Between Allegory and Myth." *New York Times Book Review*, 27 July 1947, § 7, p. 27.

   Lewis's preface "as luminous a piece of criticism as he has ever written."

2. "Myth and Form." *Times Literary Supplement*, 23 March 1946, p. 139.

   Lewis's prefatory definition and discussion of myth are significant.

20. *Essays Presented to Charles Williams.* [Edited by Lewis] (1947).

1. Haynes, Renée. "Memorial Searchlights." *Time and Tide* 28 (20 December 1947): 1370.

   Memoir conveys a "real sense of the personal impact of Charles Williams" though Lewis's dismissal of Williams's criticism as "least valuable part of his work" is "surprising."

2. "Telling Stories." *Times Literary Supplement*, 19 June 1948, p. 345.

   The leading article (central essay) meditates on the volume's topics. Tolkien (on Fairy Stories), Dorothy Sayers (on Dante's narrative power), and Lewis (on the theory of stories) are mentioned by name. Lewis's essay is a "gallant effort to come to grips" with Story.

3. Van Der Weele, Steven J. *Calvin Theological Journal* 3 (April 1968): 57-64 [57, 63-64].

   Primarily a review of books by and about Charles Williams;

the author also reviews *Essays Presented to Charles Williams.*
He finds the three essays on the art of the narrative "remarkable"
as indicating not only a "serious crisis of the imagination in
contemporary literature" but also "changing definitions of
knowledge and truth."

21. *Miracles: A Preliminary Study* (1947; with a revised third chapter, 1960).

1. "Books of the Week: Mr. Lewis's Apologetic." *Tablet* 189
   (31 May 1947): 267-268.

   "one of the most persuasive and valuable works of Christian
   apologetic written of recent years." Faults Lewis on uniformity
   of nature as "simply a reasonable faith" rather than "evident
   insight of the intellect" and on his remarks that God "*presumably*"
   maintains nature in existence and that God is "*almost*" not in
   time.

2. Carnell, Edward John. *United Evangelical Action* 6
   (1 February 1948): 24.

   Brief; a real contribution to apologetics though "gives evidence of
   theological uncertainity at points" and does not struggle with
   Old Testament miracles or the relation between miracles and the
   canon.

3. Denecke, Charles, S. J. *Best Sellers* 7 (1 October 1947);
   107-108.

   In resumé of argument on the possibility of miracles "Mr.
   Lewis is at his excellent best." Some "serious errors": e.g., that
   reason in man is a supernatural occurrence; the treatment of the
   Incarnation has an inadequate distinction between the human and
   the divine.

4. Eisler, Robert. *Hibbert Journal* 45 (July 1947): 373-377.

Closely reasoned, hostile critique from a logical positivist
perspective. Claims Lewis misunderstands modern scientific method
(as in Karl Popper's *Logic of Scientific Research*) by assuming,
like Hume, that science proceeds through a "logic of inductive
inference" through the "regularity of Nature's course." Science
proceeds by the possibility of falsifying and disproving, and it does
not matter how a thinker comes by his "hunch" since his
proposition can be tested. Reviewer also discusses E. A. Milne's
work in theory of mathematical deduction in relation to Lewis's
arguments.

5. Madgett, A. Patrick, S. J. "Two Borderline Books." *Books on
Trial* 6 (December-January 1947-1948): 159.

Arguments have "clever and sometimes brilliant analogies,"
but the reviewer dislikes Lewis's view of reason as the
"supernatural element in man," and Lewis's view that the
existence of God cannot be rigorously proved by creation; he
considers "definitely Modernist" Lewis's view that Old Testament
miracles may be considered expression of truth in "mythical
form." "One can only regret that Anglican Lewis . . . did not have
the Catholic lay theologian's advantage of sound censorship."

6. "Miracles Rationalized." *Times Literary Supplement*,
14 June 1947, p. 298.

Reviewer gives historical background of attitudes toward
miracles—notes Lewis "casts his net fairly wide" and ignores the
question of "how a miraculous event is to be discerned," as well as
contemporary cases of miracle, but sees it as an "impressive
book." "He has shown that it is irrational to overlook the possiblity
of the miraculous . . ."

7. *Moody Monthly* 48 (January 1948): 375.

Lewis "shows" Hume's false premises and "has a genius for
helping one to see the old truths with a new perspective."

8. Myres, John L. "Miracles." *Nature* 160 (30 August 1947):
275-276.

Primarily a summary. Considers Lewis's lack of historical
training and considerations a drawback; ultimately suggests that

Lewis has established a possibility or even a probability but not absolute proof of miracles [i.e., Lewis has done what he set out to do].

9. Otto, M. C. "Book Reviews." *Crozer Quarterly* 25 (January 1948): 61-64.

Lewis's warning about modern Biblical scholarship is "direct encouragement of obscurantism." Considers Lewis's method [reason pointing beyond reason] "intellectually subversive," and Lewis's definitions of experience, reason, historical inquiry, etc., inadequate. His assertions on the naturalistic conception of morality are "almost willful refusals to understand. . . . flagrant misinterpretation of what a mature naturalist espouses."

10. Ramsey, I. T. "Book Reviews." *Theology* 64 (February 1961): 73-75.

Contrasted with Louis Monden, *Le Miracle, Signe de Salut* (1960).

11. Raven, C. E. "Can Miracles Happen?" *Spectator* 178 (16 May 1947): 566.

Lewis's weakness is that on "his own confession, he has not made up his mind about Nature, and consequently is inconsistent in his thinking." Raven thinks Lewis holds to a "pre-Darwinian concept of Creation as an act, not a process" and "to a doctrine of the Godhead which has room neither for the Logos nor for the Holy Spirit."

12. S., A. *Dominicana* 32 (December 1947): 288-289.

Lucid but "cannot be recommended for Catholics because of the several errors it proposes. . . . [and] too loose terminology": division between naturalism and supernaturalism inadequate; explanation of incarnation, resurrection too natural. "Mr. C. S. Lewis needs someone to hand him a good treatise on Catholic Apologetics."

13. Schell, Joseph D. *Commonweal* 47 (19 December 1947): 259.

Greatest merit in "strikingly original and apt analogies." Some caveats: errs in extending definition of supernatural to include reason in man; logic of saying God's creation of nature less susceptible to rigorous proof than God's existence deserts logic by which he proved God's existence.

14. Sculpholme, A. C. "Book Reviews." *Theology* 50 (October 1947): 395-397.

"Perhaps his broad handling of the New Nature . . . is among Dr. Lewis's most valuable contributions to modern theology." "The rather rare combination of the gifts of poet, philosopher and theologian is quite irresistible."

15. Smith, G. D. "Notes on Recent Work: Dogmatic Theology." *Clergy Review* 29 (February 1948): 110-122 [115-116].

"abounds in good things well said"; Smith sees Lewis's view that man's mind is the "spearhead of the supernatural" as seeming to have some similarity to de Lubac's thesis that "created spirit is of itself and necessarily destined to a supernatural end."

16. Smith, Kevin. "Reviews: Apologetics." *Studies* 36 (December 1947): 485-487.

Excellent "demolition of materialism." Occasionally Lewis may enjoy playing *enfant terrible* inside Christianity, destroying in a moment's skepticism or illogicality truths he has painstakingly built up, such as remark that God as creator is only "over-whelmingly probable." Handling of Hume and other issues, Lewis's mind is Protestant, especially in falling back on faith, ultimately distrusting reason. Lewis is too optimistic about an age when every man can be "his own Pope." Historical should precede philosophical in inquiry on miracles [reverse of Lewis]. Still, Lewis "has done much to lay the foundations for a good and sincere examination" of the Gospel testimonies.

17. Smith, T. V. "Holy Logic." *Saturday Review of Literature* 31 (31 January 1948): 28-29.

"At the ingenuity of the book I stand aghast. But I am not touched by its covert appeal to piety, nor moved to credence by its overt argument." "The 'sweetening' is done with . . . psychological skill" but there is too little evidence, and on the incarnation, wish-fulfillment.

18. Sprott, W. J. H. "Would You Believe It?" *New Statesman and Nation* 36 (31 May 1947): 398-399.

    Sprott does not believe it, and points to some of the points at which he fails to (the argument for human reason being founded on Divine Reason, the Incarnation, for examples).

19. Walsh, Chad. "A Convincing Brief for Miracles." *New York Times Book Review*, 28 September 1947, § 7, pp. 5, 34.

    A good discussion of Lewis's argument and method. "Few readers will put it down unfinished. Many will later wish they had."

22. *Arthurian Torso: Containing the Posthumous Fragment of 'The Figure of Arthur' by Charles Williams and a Commentary on the Arthurian Poems of Charles Williams by C. S. Lewis* (1948).

1. Oakeshott, Walter. *Cambridge Review*, 26 February 1949, p. 420.

    Expresses appreciation of Williams's ideas (and poems) as a reflection of the medieval period. Lewis's contribution "the work not only of a literary critic of the first rank, but also of one who was the poet's intimate friend."

2. Vinaver, Eugene. "An Arthurian Dialogue." *Manchester Guardian*, 6 January 1949, p. 3.

    An enthusiastic three-paragraph review. Lewis's comments are "a work of creative criticism."

23. *Transposition and Other Addresses* (1949). Published in the United States as *The Weight of Glory and Other Addresses*. Five essays.

1. Artifax, "Some Fine Books." *Manchester Guardian*, 28 February 1949, p. 3.

   "To follow one of his arguments is like watching a master chess-player who makes a seemingly trivial and unimportant move which ten moves later turns out to be a stroke of genius."

2. T., E. M. "Among the New Books." *San Francisco Chronicle*: *This World*, 16 October 1949, p. 30.

   Lewis's method of analogy and "sweet reasonableness" effective though "not all of his readers will share the sentiments of Oxford students and not everyone will grant him his whopping generalities about the nature of the human predicament."

3. Walsh, Chad. "C. S. Lewis on the Heavenly Goal." *New York Times Book Review*, 18 September 1949, § 7, p. 3.

   "The Weight of Glory" and "Membership" are the best of the essays—the latter is Lewis's fullest treatment of the nature of the church.

24. *The Lion, the Witch and the Wardrobe*: *A Story for Children* (1950).

1. Davis, Mary Gould. "Books for Young People." *Saturday Review of Literature* 33 (9 December 1950): 42.

   Beautiful word pictures and similar to George Macdonald in the underlying theme of struggle between good and evil.

2. Morgan, Ann V. *Sheffield Telegraph*, 3 November 1950.
   [PF]
   Reviewer, age 10, finds it "a very interesting book."

3. "A Significant Fairy Tale." *Guardian*, 23 February 1951.
   [PF]
   Reviewer considers it an excellent story, though a trifle lacking
   in the gentle melancholy characteristic of H. C. Andersen fairy
   stories; but the story is so good it needs little comment.

4. "Theme and Variations." *Times Literary Supplement*:
   Children's Book Section, 17 November 1950, p. vi.
   Review of Lewis's *The Lion, the Witch and the Wardrobe*, D.
   Barton's *Saints and Heroes for Boys*, E. W. Grierson's *The
   Story of St. Francis*, L. S. Elliott's *Children of Galilee*, and J. G.
   Thomas's *One More Baby*. Lewis's book receives about half of
   this review of religious literature for children; it is praised for
   being more like a myth than an allegory. "admirable at fairy-story
   level; but also at the deep, unformulated level of myth"

5. "Through the Wardrobe." *Times Literary Supplement*, 8
   December 1950. [PF]
   "The connexion with a greater story is plain and gives depth to the
   tale, but it is exciting and well told enough itself to stand in no
   need of allegorical interpretation."

6. Tickell, Thomas More. "Fantasy." *Time and Tide* [Children's
   Christmas Number] 31 (2 December 1950) : iv.
   "It could not be better." [Reviewer is age 7½.]

7. Walsh, Chad. "Earthbound Fairyland." *New York Times
   Book Review*, 12 November 1950, § 7, p. 20.
   Thought the fairytale atmosphere "curiously cut-and-dried"
   (unlike the whimsical or numinous which adults prefer in
   fairy tales) but his daughters, age 6 and 8, would not let him stop
   reading it.

25. *Prince Caspian*: *The Return to Narnia* (1951).

1. Bechtel, Louise S. "Come Hither! Hear the Magic Horn! A Dragon Waits!" *New York Herald Tribune Book Review,* 11 November 1951, p. 5.

   Better than first Narnia story; "easier reading with a simpler plot."

2. Brady, Charles A. "Book Reviews." *Renascence* 4 (Spring 1952): 182-184.

   "the ancient glee of childhood and the still more ancient magic of the pre-human creation run through every page." Suggests "that Byzantium of idea which is to history what high Logres is to Britain."

3. "C. S. Lewis's Children's Classic." *Church Times*, 30 November 1951. [PF]

   A very good parable, but also a "first-rate story" though not so good as *The Lion, the Witch and the Wardrobe*. "It will be a children's classic."

4. Fenner, Phyllis. *Library Journal* 76 (15 December 1951): 2123.

   "Plenty of excitement . . . but I can't believe the average child will like it."

5. "Folklore and Fantasy." *Saturday Review of Literature* 34 (10 November 1951): 70-71.

   "good plot, convincing characters, and the graceful wording that distinguishes this writer."

6. *Junior Bookshelf* 15 (December 1951): 276.

   "It is a picturesque, romantic story, with hints here and there of Dr. Lewis's erudition and deeper facets of his talent."

7. Walsh, Chad. "Fairyland Revisited." *New York Times Book Review*, 11 November 1951, § 7, p. 26.

Lacks the poetic magic and wonder of George Macdonald and the story is a bit complicated, but it shows a deep respect for a child's imagination and is not marred by cuteness or archness.

26. *Mere Christianity: A Revised and Amplified Edition, with a New Introduction, of the Three Books "Broadcast Talks," "Christian Behaviour," and "Beyond Personality"* (1952). The American edition has variants in the subtitle.

1. Miltner, Charles C. "Books." *Ave Maria* 78 (4 July 1953): 25.

"Its aim is to show the reasonableness of Christianity . . . in most respects the author succeeds"

2. O'Grady, Brendan. "Insight into the Christian Faith." *Integrity* 7 (February 1953): 41.

"many memorable insights into human behavior and the Christian faith"

27. *The Voyage of the "Dawn Treader"* (1952).

1. Bechtel, Louise S. "All Ages Will Enjoy Together Fun, Magic Facts in New Books." *New York Herald Tribune Book Review*, 16 November 1952, p. 3.

"It is a complicated, different sort of fairy tale, exciting and beautiful."

2. Hector, Mary Louise. "Books for Young Readers." *Books on Trial* 11 (November 1952): 84.

   Reviewer uncertain whether Lewis's juveniles have "hidden meanings" but considers them great adventure stories and predicts the "juveniles will come in for scrutiny by some unlikely persons, college seniors writing term papers, for instance."

3. Walsh, Chad. "Caspian and Reepicheep." *New York Times Book Review*, 16 November 1952, § 7, p. 37.

   Prince Caspian by comparison a letdown; this has "strong poetic sense" and awareness of mystery.

28. *The Silver Chair* (1953).

1. "Children's Classic." *Church Times*, 18 September 1953. [PF]

   Good for adults, but philosophical points not too highbrow for children, who absorb the meaning to various degrees.

2. Graham, Eleanor. *Junior Bookshelf* 17 (October 1953): 199.

   "strange lack of tenderness"; "It is striking in the descriptions of human character and behaviour, seeming to imply great contempt for the human race." ". . . it offers little inducement to read on through the book, and it is not likely to fire the imagination to the point at which the meaning of the allegory will become plain and sink in."

3. *Times of India*, 27 December 1953. [PF]

   High above its contemporaries as a "work of art." It has "serious purpose" and is "beautifully written."

4. Walsh, Chad. "Mythical Land." *New York Times Book Review*, 27 December 1953, § 7, p. 14.

   Delightful adventure with sardonic wit that should also please an adult.

29. *The Horse and His Boy* (1954).

1. Crouch, Marcus S. "News from England." *Horn Book* 31 (April 1955): 68.

   "has excitement and humor" but "lacks some of the burning spiritual conviction that made his earlier stories so memorable."

2. Crozier, Mary. "Fantasies and Feasts.' *Manchester Guardian*, 8 October 1954, p. 11.

   "one wonders if the spell is not wearing a little thin"; "Aslan, the great Lion, the God figure who presides over the action, is a thought priggish."

3. Lewis, Naomi. "The Young Supernaturalist." *New Statesman and Nation* 48 (2 October 1954): 404.

   A number of children's books considered. Lewis's "fairy tales have had to serve as a platform for so many small irritabilities that one could hardly discover his skill as a story-teller for the noise." This one his "best-mannered" though "least magically wild."

4. Walsh, Chad. "Back to Narnia." *New York Times Book Review*, 17 October 1954, § 7, p. 44.

   Lewis at his least-inspired is better reading than most writers for the young, but this one "relatively uninspired."

30. *English Literature in the Sixteenth Century, excluding Drama (The Oxford History of English Literature, Vol. III)* (1954).

1. B., H. S. *Cambridge Review* 76 (14 May 1955): 531.

   After reading the introductory chapter "few of us will be able to speak of the Renaissance or Humanism or Puritanism . . .

without looking over our shoulders [at] . . . Mr. Lewis."
Account of Drab age "most original and stimulating part of the
book." It will be "for many years the best guide available" for the
subject.

2. Bertram, James. "The English Renaissance." *New Zealand
   Listener*, 14 January 1955. [PF]

   Bertram sees Lewis as "more deeply read than most living men"
   in this period, and the most Johnsonian in method. Ranks it with
   Bush's volume among Oxford history scholarship, and by far
   the most lively. A book no literature student "dare neglect."

3. Bradner, Leicester. *Renaissance News* 8 (Spring 1955):
   19-22.

   "one must reluctantly call it a disappointing performance."
   Reviewer says Lewis's dislike of the period shows and he
   "apparently does not believe in literary history." Dislikes terms
   "Drab" and "Golden," says the book is filled with too many
   minor figures but finds the opening chapter "full of interest,"
   chapter on close of the Middle Ages in Scotland "truly
   magnificent" and treatments of Spenser and Sydney good.

4. Chalker, John. *Studia Neophilologica* 28 (1956): 56-59.

   "Professor Lewis is a historian telling a story, and he tells it with
   consummate skill." Writing has liveliness and pungency;
   background material excellent; reviewer dislikes terms "Drab" and
   "Golden" as division of poetry. Chalker says the book may
   act as a stimulus to the Tudor period, largely ignored except
   for drama.

5. Charlton, M. B. "The Renaissance." *Manchester Guardian*,
   8 February 1955. [PF]

   Critic says Lewis, "one of Oxford's greatest literary scholars,"
   was the obvious choice for this task. Lewis doesn't hide his own
   religious beliefs, which are "disconcerting at first." Considers
   the book outstanding in judgment and style.

6. Cohen, J. M. "Judgments." *Sunday Observer*, 5 December 1954, p. 8.

"He is as forceful a guide to the territory assigned to him as ever he was on his chosen ground." Chapter on Scotland at close of Middle Ages is perhaps book's best.

7. "Contemporaries of Shakespeare." *Church Times*, 3 December 1954. [PF]

It "would be difficult to over-praise it." Lewis's judgments never venomous like Lytton Strachey, or exaggerated as Chesterton often is. Will be the "last word" for a long time on many writers.

8. Davie, Donald. "Entering into the Sixteenth Century." *Essays in Criticism* 5 (April 1955): 159-164.

"far and away the best piece of orthodox literary history that has appeared for many a long year. . . . Mr. Lewis excites us. If he sometimes annoys us, after all that, too, is a kind of excitement." Davie points out how unsympathetic to modern taste almost all the judgments in the book are, how useful the book is as a guide to "enter into" certain works (but not the sonnet sequence), and how certain shifts of tone are due to an uncertainty about audience.

9. Devlin, Christopher. "Sixteenth Century Literature." *Month* 199, n.s. 13 (June 1955): 373-374.

Literary book of "beauty and harmony" but inadequate as history. Scales weighted too heavily in Drab-Golden division of poetry; many important omissions; also Lewis assumes sixteenth century England became Protestant without any sense of violent change.

10. Evans, B. Ifor. "On Books and People." *Truth*, 5 November 1954. [PF]

By "some miracle," Lewis produced a "brilliant" and interesting book on the period, "as great a tour de force in criticism as I have seen in this generation." Judgments are "individual, controversial, but never unjust." Finds Lewis best on Sidney and Spenser.

11. Gardner, Helen. "Learning and Gusto." *New Statesman and Nation* 48 (30 October 1954) : 546.

> "He has written what is and will remain for some time to come a standard book of reference and he has also written a book, a work which is continuously enjoyable, provocative and stimulating, yet satisfying." Caveats: sometimes over-correction makes certain aspects of the book a little off center; objection to "drab" and "golden" division of poetry. But book abounds in breadth of learning, conscientious scholarship, the "strength of his capacity for enjoyment."

12. Harrison, Charles A. "The Renaissance Epitomized." *Sewanee Review* 63 (January-March 1955) : 153-161.

> Review of *The Portable Renaissance Reader*, ed. J. B. Ross and M. M. McLaughlin; *A Renaissance Treasury*, ed. H. Haydn and J. C. Nelson; and *English Literature in the Sixteenth Century, Excluding Drama*, by Lewis. The latter will take its place among "perennially consulted monuments of sustained critical exposition." Some oversimplifications such as the contention that the modern theory of sovereignty, incipient in the sixteenth century, is unequivocally acquiescence in legislative absolutism. Idiosyncracies include Lewis's quarrel with the humanists and use of epithet "drab." Attitude toward humanists inconsistent with satisfaction in Spenser. Lewis throws off "exquisite insights' 'in a "variously enlightening and variously crochety book."

13. L., J. B. *Oxford Magazine*, December 1954. [PF]

> Book is "a wonderful achievement." How did he do it? He is a born writer, a born reader, a good scholar, and a man passionately interested in ideas. The book is a "triumphant refutation" of the idea that Lewis's popular theology writing was a distraction: that knowledge strengthens this work.

14. *Listener* 52 (4 November 1952) : 773.

> Main cavil is some of Lewis's "questionable terminology" (as Drab-Golden). "Perhaps the highest praise that can be given to this volume is to say that it is a fitting complement to *The Allegory of Love*."

15. MacLure, Millar. *Canadian Forum* 35 (July 1955): 94.

Most provocative, opinionated, and best written of Oxford History of English Literature volumes to date, "done with the superb confidence of one who has never been frightened of his own opinions." Reviewer lists some faulty emphases and omissions.

16. Maxwell, J. C. "Reviews." *Durham University Journal*, n.s. 16 (June 1955): 133-137.

A "remarkable work." "This is the work of a man who really wants to tell the truth and to make it available and operative for all who are interested in the subject." Singles out introductory material and chapter on Scotland for special praise, sees Lewis's attitude on humanism the book's most controversial aspect, treatment of Marlowe "one notable failure" and the bibliography as having a "certain capriciousness" detailed in the review.

17. Rowse, A. L. "Skelton to Donne." *Sunday Times*, 16 January 1955. [PF]

Expected Lewis to do a "remarkable" volume but nothing "so magnificent," with "such intellectual vitality, such sweep and imagination, such magnanimity." Considers Lewis at his best on the Scots and thinks Lewis's theological expertise helped him with the period. Criticizes omission of Robert Parsons.

18. Sewell, Elizabeth. "Book Reviews." *Thought* 30 (Autumn 1955): 454-455.

Often readable, sometimes dropping "back into the catalogue vein"; reviewer disappointed Lewis did not attempt to explain the change in English literature from the beginning to the end of his period.

19. Shapiro, I. A. "Tudor Verse and Prose." *Birmingham Post*, 5 October 1954. [PF]

Volume's "readability" may "astonish" those nurtured on literary histories of the past half-century. More important, Lewis writes a coherent story rather than the usual unrelated essays on authors. This book "will never be 'killed' by future research" since it is concerned mainly with the permanent literary value of the works it discusses, less with historical importance. Critic says Lewis is "unjust" to Renaissance humanists and raises several other critical points, then asks, "Can Oxford really afford to let him migrate to Cambridge?"

20. Sharrock, Roger. "Drab and Golden." *Tablet* 204 (16 October 1954): 369.

Lewis's handling of Renaissance and of religious controversy are good (objects to use of word "Papist"); chapter on psychological character of Puritans and the parallel with modern Marxism "brilliantly sustained"; chapters on Spenser and Sidney contain the "finest criticism."

21. Wain, John. "Pleasure, Controversy, Scholarship." *Spectator* 193 (1 October 1954): 403-405.

"Mr. Lewis, now as always, writes as if inviting us to a feast." Lewis's view of the Renaissance: "On the whole it is rather a relief not to have to pretend to admire the humanists as men of letters; one is free to admire them the more, as Mr. Lewis does, for their real achievements, which were *technical*." Regards section on Elizabethan satire the "most balanced and just"; the Shakespearian sonnets, most original; on Spenser, whom Wain thinks Lewis over-rates, the most provocative.

22. Willcock, G. D. "Reviews." *Review of English Studies* 7 (1956): 195-197.

The reviewer considers the Oxford History of English Literature volume a perceptive critical history not easy to read but never losing "awareness of the texture of the work considered." He comments on the necessity to keep Lewis's definitions in mind to understand some of Lewis's judgments—e.g., on humanists. Caveats at end of review: Lewis does not give Lyly the "novelist" his due and in his "entirely laudable determination to cut away from biographical 'sincerity,' " in *Astrophel and Stella,* perhaps "the baby has . . . been thrown out with the bath water."

23. Winters, Yvor. "Reviews." *Hudson Review* 8 (Summer 1955): 281-287.

Winters finds Lewis's book of some value in his discussion of ideas but says "Lewis simply has not discovered what poetry is," seeing the entire period with a Romantic prejudice and liking prettiness too much. Lewis's basic critical defect: he does not find and proceed from the best poems. In short, an energetic attack on Lewis's bias for Golden poetry.

24. Zandvoort, R. W. *English Studies.*

Listed in § VI-A-1; a review of *English Literature in the Sixteenth Century* and *De Descriptione Temporum.*

31. *"De Descriptione Temporum," An Inaugural Lecture by the Professor of Medieval and Renaissance English Literature in the University of Cambridge* (1955). A twenty-two page pamphlet; later collected in *They Asked for a Paper* (1962) and in *Selected Literary Essays* (1969).

1. Every, George, S. C. M. "Book Reviews." *Theology* 58 (July 1955): 270-271.

"As a historian of culture, though not as a theologian, Professor Lewis seems to me to minimize the difference between pagan and Christian, and to exaggerate distinctions in the modern world that are as yet very unsettled."

2. "The Greatest Divide." *Time* 65 (2 May 1955): 94.

A report of Lewis's inaugural lecture with extended quotation. This appears in the "Education" section.

3. Hough, Graham. "Old Western Man." *Twentieth Century* [London] 157 (February 1955): 102-110.

Sees Lewis's "most original" notion that of a world divided by allegiance to two quite different historical-cultural worlds. Hough analyzes the heated reactions to Lewis's lecture and finds them centered, not on the lecture but on Lewis's supernaturalist presuppositions. The old liberal-conservative debate now is "at bottom a theological one" says Hough, a dissociation between external forces (science) and imaginative-emotional ones. Religious and scientific humanists must rebuild a shattered unity.

4. Maud, Ralph. "C. S. Lewis's Inaugural." *Essays in Criticism* 5 (October 1955): 390-393.

Discusses Lewis's pedagogical methods (critical gamesmanship). Article is in part a refutation of Donald Davie's review of Lewis's Oxford history volume in *Essays in Criticism* 5 (April 1955): 159-164, listed in the previous subsection.

5. "Time Disciplined." *Times Literary Supplement,* 25 March 1955, p. 181.

Lewis's essay is stimulating, with many ideas, but he did not deal with those writers and painters who transcend their age.

6. Zandvoort, R. W. *English Studies.*

Listed in § VI-A-1; a review of *English Literature in the Sixteenth Century, Excluding Drama* and *De Descriptione Temporum.*

32. *The Magician's Nephew* (1955).

1. Crozier, Mary. "Chance, Kings and Desperate Men." *Manchester Guardian,* 8 July 1955, p. 8.

"beautifully limpid style and rather donnish humour enliven what might otherwise become a too complicated business"; "Mr.

Lewis may well find that the seven stories have made a minor children's classic."

2. Fuller, Edmund. "For 10–14s: A Fairy Tale, A Fantasy, a Witch." *Chicago Sunday Tribune Magazine of Books* [*Books for Children*], 13 November 1955, part 4, § 2, p. 36.

A review of *The Wicked Enchantment* by Margot Benary-Isbert and *The Magician's Nephew*. Lewis's book receives three paragraphs, the two longer of which summarize the story. The last paragraph consists of one sentence: "As, in awesome tones, Aslan calls all things into being, Lewis has touched perhaps the loveliest, most stirring moment in all his wealth of fancy."

3. Hector, Mary Louise. *Books on Trial* 14 (October 1955): 104.

"surface adventures are lively and eerie." "meanings . . . obscure, tentative, personal" but young readers will get the basic idea of happiness and strength in goodness.

4. *Junior Bookshelf* 19 (July 1955): 147-149.

The review (one very long paragraph) is not just summary and praise: it suggests the Abominable Word corresponds to atomic weapons, and the magician uncle corresponds to the amoral scientist, as interpretive comments. It also points out Lewis's tendency to inflict physical indignities on unpleasant characters (the uncle taken to be a plant); and it regrets the obviousness of the moral lessons and the tendency to toss in any idea which may occur to the writer. "The series . . . cannot be numbered amongst the best of our time."

5. Walsh, Chad. "Return to Narnia." *New York Times Book Review*, 30 October 1955, § 7, p. 40.

One of the best of the Narnia series: "glows with the sort of mythology that C. S. Lewis created at his best, replete with religious and philosophical implications."

6. Williams-Ellis, Amabel. "Traditional Tales." *Spectator* 195 (8 July 1955): 51-52 [52].

"the present reviewer still cannot swallow Aslan, the *deus ex machina* of all his fairy tales." See the letter in reply to this review from Dorothy L. Sayers, listed in § III-G.

33. *Surprised by Joy: The Shape of My Early Life* (1955).

1. Ames, Alfred C. "A Prominent Christian Tells of His Pagan Youth." *Chicago Sunday Tribune Magazine of Books,* 5 February 1956, § 4, p. 3.

    "The record of his pagan years, in large part more entertaining than edifying"; unromantic accounts of school days "provide shocking material." Story of his "accession into Christendom is . . . significant both for others who have been compelled to enter and for those still without."

2. Dwyer, John F. "Book Reviews." *Thought* 31 (Summer 1956): 307.

    Mostly in good Lewis style, though some "monotonous"; disappointing chapters on influences leading to his conversion; too rigid an exclusion of materials not related to his fall and conversion.

3. Fremantle, Anne. "The Universe Rang True When Fairly Tested." *Commonweal* 63 (3 February 1956): 464-465.

    Fremantle retells the story well, with comparisons of Milton's "enormous bliss" to Lewis's Joy, and Bunyan's Delectable Mountains to Lewis's hills of childhood; she also comments that the point of the "Bloodery" in the English public schools was to produce supermen to run the Empire, like the training in Sparta and Nazi Germany—no wonder the thoroughly romantic Lewis did not fit in.

4. Gill, Theodore A. "Not Quite All." *Christian Century* 73 (9 May 1956): 585.

    "totally absorbing" but "a singularly unsatisfactory autobiography." Suggests the chapter on homosexuality in public school is a smokescreen. Considers it an engaging book, with some good theological insights, not quite honest as autobiography, since Lewis did not fully understand himself, yet compelling to read.

5. Hailsham, Lord. "Dr. Lewis's Pilgrimage." *Spectator* 195 (9 December 1955): 805-806.

"Dr. Lewis does not attempt to argue [about the validity of his religious experience]. He simply describes—and his powers of description and acute self-analysis will qualify him to do so." The reviewer compares his experiences in public schools, at Oxford, and as a Christian convert with those of Lewis. Minor caveats: feels Lewis's picture of public school life overdrawn, inaccurate; dislikes remarks against those in public life.

6. Hertzel, Leo. "Questions for Another Book." *Homiletic and Pastoral Review* 56 (April 1956): 615, 617-618.

"The book is vague where it should be most specific; emotional where it should be most logical." Book is delightful in its description of early life, people and places he knew, but unsatisfactory as story of religious quest since it does not end with choice of a church.

7. "Joy and Conversion." *Times Literary Supplement*, 7 October 1955, p. 583.

"God moves, indeed, in a mysterious way, and this book gives a brilliant account of one of the oddest and most decisive end-games He has ever played."

8. K., M. "Friars' Bookshelf." *Dominicana* 41 (September 1956): 267-268.

"Despite its incompleteness [that Lewis did not become Roman Catholic] . . . retains its place as an excellent autobiography."

9. Kilby, Clyde S. "C. S. Lewis and the Long Road He Took to Christianity." *New York Herald Tribune Book Review*, 5 February 1956, p. 5.

"more than a spiritual autobiography"; some of the best parts are on people he knew.

10. Masterman, Margaret. "C. S. Lewis: The Author and the Hero."

Listed in § II; a biographical essay based on *Surprised by Joy*, appearing soon after the volume.

11. Matthew, T. S. "Then Signals from Another World." *New York Times Book Review*, 5 February 1956, § 7, pp. 5, 25.

Story "peters out" as a narrative after Lewis is wounded as a soldier in WW I; his dealing with the subject of his autobiography is hard to follow, "crevassed with gaps"; "impressive" but leaves the reader "cold" in trying to "dissect the most incandescent of human emotions."

12. Sayers, Dorothy. "Christianity Regained." *Time and Tide* 36 (1 October 1955): 1263-1264.

"delightful and humorous candour." "The limpidity of these waters may disguise their depth, so clearly do they reveal the bottom. But any illusions about this can be quickly dispelled by stepping into the river."

13. Scrutten, Mary. "Confused Witness." *New Statesman and Nation* 50 (1 October 1955): 405.

Lewis's reasoning "sheer soapsuds"; he is a gifted scholar and novelist, not equipped for apologetics and *Pilgrim's Regress* is a better account of his conversion than this.

14. Swenson, May. "The Circular Pursuit." *Nation* 182 (2 June 1956): 474-475.

The autobiography is skimpy on sexual details and disappointing as a guide to the non-Christian (*joy* turns out not to be the real goal).

15. Walsh, Chad. "Back to Faith." *Saturday Review* 39 (3 March 1956): 32-33.

Walsh notes the restraint in the book and the "curious air of objectivity."

16. Watkin, E. I. "Prayer of Aspiration." *Pax* 45 (Winter 1955): 137.

"delights by its manner, its literary art"; agrees with Lewis's emphasis on "the primacy of God in Himself over God for and in ourselves" because "it excludes any subjectivist understanding of religious experience."

34. *The Last Battle: A Story for Children* (1956).

1. "The End of a Saga." *Times Literary Supplement: Children's Books Section*, 11 May 1956, p. v.

   "an impressive book"; "Dr. Lewis's philosophy does not always bear analysis: his attitude for instance, to 'civilization' " but "when he writes as a writer and not as a thinker he rises to the nobility and beauty of his theme." The reviewer's comment on Lewis's contradictory attitude toward civilization led to Lewis's explanation quoted in a footnote in R. L. Green's *C. S. Lewis* (listed in § III-A), p. 51. (Green does not give his source: presumably it was a direct communication from Lewis.)

2. Farjeon, Annabel. "Sense and Magic." *New Statesman and Nation* 52 (17 November 1956): 636, 638.

   "the most extraordinary conglomeration of ideas I have ever come across in childish fiction."

3. Walsh, Chad. "War in Narnia." *New York Times Book Review*, 30 September 1956, § 7, p. 46.

   "The Christian symbolism is clear enough, but the book can stand on its own feet as a deeply moving and hauntingly lovely story apart from the doctrinal content."

35. *Till We Have Faces: A Myth Retold* (1956).

1. "Allegory of Love." *Times Literary Supplement*, 21 September 1956, p. 551.

   The reviewer, believing the work to be an allegory, interprets the palace of Psyche as "a vision of joy and reality given to those who are dead to the world and have accepted God as lover of the soul," and discusses the double allegorical role of Ungit, both "a primitive way of approach to the Divine and [as animal instincts leading to selfishness and pride] a prime cause of sin."

2. Blisset, William. *Canadian Forum* 36 (January 1957): 238-239.

Compares Lewis's myth-retelling to Robert Graves's method especially in adopting narrator's point of view. Believes the long first book "is a most remarkable swift narrative and the self-revelation . . . of a complex mind and character" but the brief second book belabors the pagan myth.

3. Boucher, Anthony. "The Best Science-Fantasy Books of 1957." *Magazine of Fantasy and Science Fiction* 14 (March 1958): 110.

Till We Have Faces is listed, with the comment that Lewis's book "is, to be blunt, a masterwork of art in the form of a tale of men and gods."

4. ———. "Recommended Reading." *Magazine of Fantasy and Science Fiction* 12 (June 1957): 109.

"a profoundly moral and spiritual work, but treating directly the relation of man to his gods outside of the diagram of any specific theology, as richly meaningful to Moslem or Mormon as to members of the author's own Church." "his major work to date"; "no writer knows better than the creator of Screwtape the infinite subtlety and complexity of human motives." "As a story, as a fantasy, as a study in human psychology, as a grappling with spiritual dilemmas, above all as a work of art this book is magic."

5. "Briefly Noted: Fiction." *New Yorker* 32 (9 February 1957): 116-117.

Finds the dominant theme is man's destructive impulse in the unloved toward those they appear to love, man's chances of winning God's love and learning the way to love. Considers tone "missionary"—plausible, self-indulgent.

6. Curley, Thomas F. "Myth into Novel." *Commonweal* 65 (8 February 1947): 494-495.

   "The virtue of C. S. Lewis's version is its modernity: dense and intricate, the tale moves to its conclusion weighted with the semi-wilful perversion of a woman who wants to suffer only so long as the suffering is unjust."

7. Davis, Robert Gorham. "Cupid and Psyche." *New York Times Book Review*, 13 January 1957, § 7, p. 5.

   "love is quite literally given wings again." An unusually perceptive review which points out, briefly, for example, the connection between Orual and Lewis, and the summary in this novel of many of Lewis's nonfiction ideas.

8. Derrick, Christopher. "Love Is the Key." *Tablet* 208 (6 October 1956): 278.

   "splendid" story. Underlying idea is that evil in some way is "asymptotic to non-existence" possibly reducing the "mysterium iniquitatis" to the "more manageable problem of our own non-comprehension of time" with Psyche's sister mouthing the delusions in her complaint to the gods. The story "would be great if only because of the majesty and absoluteness of their reply."

9. Eppler, Carl F. "Book Reviews." *Arizona Quarterly* 14 (Spring 1958): 81-84.

   "It is a rope woven so tightly and artfully it can scarcely be separated even for analytical purposes into its various strands"; "quite unlike its predecessors." "The old Lewis dichotomy between good and bad . . . is no longer insisted on." Less like the English novelistic tradition than recent Continental with their "intricate symbolism and musical structure." It is "clearly superior to anything else he has done" and "one of the masterpieces of modern English prose fiction."

10. Gardiner, Harold C. "Five Novels: Three Nuggets Among Them." *America* 96 (2 February 1957): 507, 508 [507].

    Favorable; sees Christian implications on vicarious suffering, sense of "dark horror" at root of pagan religions, and the seminal idea of a "pale enlightenment" dawning into full glory.

11. Kilby, Clyde S. "The Straight Tale of Barbarism." *Eternity* 8 (April 1957): 24.

This book is the "most difficult" but it may be the "most rewarding" of Lewis's writings; the "symbols are the book."

12. Maddocks, Melvin. "C. S. Lewis Reworks a Myth." *Christian Science Monitor*, 10 January 1957, p. 7.

"a good mine of meanings"; suggests since Orual becomes mystically identified with Psyche, Lewis may have in mind two means of salvation: revelation through love and a slower emancipation through suffering and conscience.

13. Meath, Gerard. O. P. "Reviews." *Blackfriars* 38 (December 1957): 536.

Sees Fox as a symbol of using the intellect as escape for love. Suggests a conversion and rebirth interpretation but fears interpretation has "the danger of ruining the story."

14. Parris, Robert. "Psyche's Double-Exposure." *New Republic* 136 (21 January 1957): 19-20.

It is a pagan myth forced into a Christian box unsuccessfully, peculiarly frustrating in "not being able to decide who is who and what is what," a "symbolic novel without a real person in it" and uneven in diction.

15. Redman, Ben Ray. "Love Was the Weapon." *Saturday Review* 40 (12 January 1957): 15.

A sensitive religious allegory "in which rationalism is shown to be blind when it stands on the threshold of revelation." Maia's name called significant but not explained.

16. Rolo, Charles J. "Reader's Choice." *Atlantic* 199 (February 1957): 78-85 [84-85].

The reviewer finds the novel difficult (on a single reading) but well done as a narrative—he emphasizes the psychological aspects. "brilliant," eloquent, vivid, intense, swift-moving with a "string of complex psychological dramas" played out unobtrusively within its framework.

17. Schultz, Susan A. *Asbury Seminarian* 20 (June 1966): 93-94.

"Perhaps Lewis's genius as a writer is partly in the fact that the story can have various meanings, depending on the background of the reader; or it may be enjoyed simply as a 'tale that is told.' "

18. Tucker, Martin. "The Face of Love." *Chicago Review* 2 (Summer 1957): 92-94.

Review of *Till We Have Faces* and Erich Fromm's *The Art of Loving*. Tucker finds Fromm's book the better of the two artistically —of course, he considers "the scene" between Psyche and Orual to be the climax (presumably, from the review, the one in which Orual convinces Psyche to light the lamp) and thus the latter half an anticlimax. (He compares Lewis's style to that in Marguerite Yourcenar's *Hadrian's Memoir* and finds it wanting.)

19. V., J. "Among the New Books." *San Francisco Chronicle: This World*, 10 March 1957, p. 22.

"gives the reader a hard time ferreting out the meaning," but the reviewer sees it is "a direct grappling with the problem of human suffering" and "a restatement of his metaphysical doctrine" in *Surprised by Joy*.

20. Walsh, Chad. "A Haunting and Lovely Ancient Legend Brilliantly Refashioned by C. S. Lewis." *New York Herald Tribune Book Review*, 20 January 1957, p. 3.

Much which reminds one of Charles Williams; theme of human and divine love suggested; this is an "older Lewis with deepening insights into the mysteries of the gods and of men."

21. ———. "Toward Silence." *Renascence* 10 (Winter 1957): 103-104.

"an exploration of depth, . . . less satire, less wit, less humour than Lewis' public has come to expect." "of all Lewis' books, this is the most difficult. . . . Perhaps it is true that all religious insight, as it grows and deepens, moves toward music, liturgy, or silence. . . . *Till We Have Faces* represents a far stride toward a direct perception of the love that moves the sun and the other stars."

22. White, T. H. "Psyche and Psychology." *Time and Tide* 37 (13 October 1956): 1227-1228.

White praises the concrete detail of the book and the comparisons which make "the moral or abstract observations" also concrete, but he feels the final revelation—that Orual was "possessively jealous of Psyche"—does not need a god to reveal it; the Fox could have seen it just as easily as not.

36. *Reflections on The Psalms* (1958).

1. Augustine, Dom James. *Downside Review* 78 (September 1960): 131-134.

"One listens, spell-bound, as he unravels one knotty problem after another," but *Reflections* fights shy of the doctrine of retribution and its obvious implications in the Psalms, as both Old and New Testament are full of it.

2. Bourke, Joseph, O. P. *Blackfriars* 40 (September 1959): 389-391 [390-391].

Lewis has "a number of wise and helpful solutions to difficulties"; he tended to sit too loose on his subject, bringing in irrelevancies; a lack of technical equipment sometimes shows through, as in failure to grasp the Semite world and thought.

3. Hyman, Frieda Clark. *Judaism* 8 (Spring 1959): 187-190.

Reviewer contrasts Jewish and Christian approach on the Psalms and on worship. Regards Judaism as teaching a higher kind of love and faith which Lewis does not understand.

4. Macaulay, J. C. "As One Amateur to Another." *Eternity* 10 (March 1959): 38.

"provocative"; reviewer raises several minor criticisms on theology and style.

5. Martindale, C. C. "Reviews: The Psalms." *Month*, n.s. 21 (January 1959): 53.

Book a stimulus; Lewis deals inadequately with historical Psalms and those passing into triumph. Shows what Lewis means by his view on "second meanings" in Scripture.

6. Sauer, Albert Von Rohr. "Book Review." *Concordia Theological Monthly* 33 (June 1962): 379.

Finds much that is useful; disagrees with Lewis on pagan myth and on his method of allegorizing the end of Psalm 137.

7. "Understanding the Psalms." *Times Literary Supplement*, 12 September 1958, p. 517.

On difficult Psalms Lewis "probes through to the humanity behind the passion." On allegorical method "shows a fine understanding of the wholeness of the Bible." Gives "less attention than one might have expected to the literary quality of the Psalms and none at all to the circumstances in which they were composed."

8. Walsh, Chad. "The Meaning Within." *New York Times Book Review*, 9 November 1958, § 7, p. 16.

The book lacks "concentrated impact" but "is full of illuminating observations."

37. *The Four Loves* (1960).

1. "The Analysis of Love." *Times Literary Supplement* [*Religious Book Section*], 15 April 1960, p. ix.

Partial metamorphosis of Lewis from his concern with the

Devil and the supernatural in the book's common sense and naturalistic, if pre- and anti-Freudian and overly schematic, discussion of love.

2. Bloesch, Donald G. "Love Illuminated." *Christian Century* 77 (14 December 1960): 1470.

Reviewer calls book a "masterpiece"; compares Lewis's view of charity with Anders Nygren's concept of *agape*.

3. Braybrooke, Neville. "Theology and Horses." *Time and Tide* 41 (7 May 1960): 518.

Compares *The Four Loves* with *The Allegory of Love* to show the basic fusion between the professorial and *Screwtape* writer; finds this "fresh."

4. Butrym, Alex J. "Feature Book Review." *Marriage* 46 (August 1964): 28-31.

Not new but fresh insights; Lewis's inexperience in parenthood and marriage a drawback, though his large reading helps to compensate.

5. D'Arcy, Martin. "These Things Called Love." *New York Times Book Review*, 31 July 1960, § 7, p. 4.

Loves not seen "clearly determined by their relation to our human nature as such and our condition as creatures"; but the book should be "a minor classic . . . Lewis combines a novelist's insight into motives with a profound religious understanding of our human nature."

6. Demant, V. A. "Four Loves." *Frontier* 3 (Autumn 1960): 207-209.

"a religious book . . . . But readers who do not want the religion will find many tips for the enhancement of their natural loves." Treatment of *eros* weakest.

7. Derrick, Christopher. "The Invisible Worm." *Tablet* 214 (9 April 1960): 346-347.

"illuminating and sad," "provokes . . . Pelagian rejoinder." "Perhaps the ultimate point of the book is linguistic" and we should apply word "love" to human relationships more cautiously.

8. Fuller, Edmund. "Delving into the Nature and Aspects of Love." *Chicago Sunday Tribune Magazine of Books*, 31 July 1960, § 4, p. 6.

"amazing wealth of aspects and . . . depth of insight"; "extremely good and fresh, often funny, on the troubled issue of Eros."

9. Gerlach, John-Baptist, O. P. *Cross and Crown* 13 (December 1961): 478-479.

"sustained wisdom, insight, and startlingly acute description . . . . his humour is sure proof of a healthy equilibrium."

10. Harris, Sydney J. "Love's Geography." *Saturday Review* 43 (10 September 1960): 24.

The book is valuable for its "candor, common sense, wryness, and deep seriousness" and its deep insights. Note that Harris's comment "Possibly because Lewis is unmarried, there are only slight and shallow references to conjugal love . . ." is corrected by a letter from Lina S. Lippner, Joy Davidman's aunt, in the issue of 12 November 1960, p. 37.

11. Kilby, Clyde S. "Love Silhouetted." *Christianity Today* 5 (10 October 1960): 40.

Favorable but says Lewis most brilliant on controversial topics "which we suppose we have long since settled."

12. MacIntyre, Alasdair. "Love and Mr. Lewis." [Manchester] *Guardian*, 8 April 1960, p. 13.

Lewis the learned critic "has been completely defeated and ousted by Mr. Lewis, the arch and patronizing lay theologian." Worst, "his book does not *help*."

13. McNamara, P. M., O. S. M. *Ave Maria* 92 (15 October 1960): 26-27.

"the perfect antidote to all the silly and confused things that are being spoken and written about love these days."

14. Novak, Michael. "The Way Men Love." *Commonweal* 72 (19 August 1960): 430-431.

Book has good common sense and is especially good in perceiving the West's chronic illness of Manicheanism as seen in the inability to laugh at, or with, eros.

38. *Studies in Words* (1960; Second Edition, with three new chapters, 1967).

1. Badawi, M. M. *Cairo Studies in English*, 1961-1962, pp. 197-205.

"Only a man in whom love of literature is totally inseparable from 'love and knowledge of words' could write such a book." Badawi lists some minor criticisms, especially Lewis's tendency to take I. A. Richards only at his most extreme.

2. Banjo, Ayo. *Ibadan* [University of Ibadan, Nigeria], February 1969. [PF]

The book shows different shades of meaning can be present when a poet writes a word. Ambiguities are thus inevitable but can be resolved. Lewis's erudition leaves reader "breathless."

3. Bean, William B. *Archives of Internal Medicine* 114 (December 1964). [PF]

Reviewer laments the tendency of technical writers to ignore literary style and lucidity; recommends this book as an educational aid.

4. Berry, Francis. "Didling the Vocabulary." *Universities Quarterly*, March 1961. [PF]

Calls tone "magisterial" with some homely touches embarrassing. Intrinsically fascinating, yet more than a little tedious to read, its attitude is "disappointing" and its purpose "obscure."

5. Campbell, Jackson J. "Book Reviews." *Journal of English and Germanic Philology* 61 (January 1962): 144.

> "only a little this side of excellent when taken at the level of its intention" but Lewis "never grapples with the more difficult cases where the newly developed Latin sense . . . comes back to influence the meaning of an English word borrowed from Latin at an earlier stage," a special problem in studying Milton's diction.

6. Cawley, A. C. *Aumla: Journal of the Australasian Universities Language and Literature Association*, 1960. [PF]

> Finds the book full of "ingenium" and "wit." One caveat: Lewis's insistence that "the meaning of a word is insulated by its context" limits multiple associations in poetry.

7. Christophersen, Paul. *English Studies* 45 (June 1964): 256-259.

> "No intelligent reader can fail to find pleasure in the lucidity and pungency of Professor Lewis's writing, and none, even among specialists, can fail to learn a great deal from it."

8. "The Critics," transcript of BBC program aired 18 September 1960, comments by Helen Gardner, Riccardo Aragno, Ivor Brown. [PF]

> Gardner called Lewis "a born teacher" and commended the book as full of ideas about human behavior, showing acutely the underlying motives in corrupting words. Aragno called the book "absorbing" and Brown "extremely instructive." Gardner questioned Lewis's avoidance of legitimate use in changing contexts, but called book "frightfully important" and not a specialized book.

9. D., E. E. "Ancient, Fragile and Immensely Potent . . ." *Die Suid Afrikaanse Bankers Tydskrif* [*The South African Bankers' Journal*], August 1961, pp. 184-187. [PF]

> Scholarship apart, finds the book useful and entertaining. Author thinks some of Lewis's ideas could help raise the level of South African English.

10. "The Dialect of the Tribe." *Times*, 15 September 1960.
    [PF]

    Lewis uses his "rare erudition" in classical language and
    Old English to define words precisely, says critic, and no
    teacher "has left his beneficial imprint more firmly" on the Oxford
    English School than he. Book is lucid and witty.

11. Dobson, E. J. "Reviews." *Review of English Studies*, n.s. 13
    (November 1962): 433-436.

    "excellent book, which deserves to be widely known and
    used"; not much to offer in way of pure fact that is helpful above
    beginner level, but helpful because of its philosophical bent.
    Could have been more accurate in its semantic history; errs in
    discussion of verbal concept of voice and several other details.

12. *English*, Spring 1961. [PF]

    Such investigation called a "slippery business" and even
    Lewis's careful scholarship doesn't avoid jumps from one sense
    to another. But Lewis is never dogmatic, and it is a "fascinating
    book" even for the general reader.

13. Falle, George. *Canadian Forum* 41 (December 1961): 209.

    Full of acute observations, stimulating as set of footnotes to the
    history of ideas, but the movement from study of words to
    speculations on language of poetry "is achieved only by means of a
    devious and questionable logic."

14. Gardner, Helen. "The Listener's Book Chronicle." *Listener*
    64 (22 September 1960): 479.

    "it is a pleasure to agree or disagree with a writer who puts
    his points so clearly, so considerately, and so entertainingly."
    Criticism: Lewis is "inclined to interpret context too narrowly, as
    immediate context."

15. H., E. R. "Two Views of Language." *English Studies*
    [University of South Africa], March 1968. [PF]

    Of interest not only to semanticists but to literary critics since
    it shows the temptation of reading current meanings into older
    texts. "Highly recommended."

16. H., T. *Law Society's Gazette* 58 (March 1961). [PF]

    Describes Lewis's discussion of "nature" as it bears on legal theory.

17. Hammerton, H. J. "Histories of Words." *Yorkshire Post*, 19 September 1960. [PF]

    Favorable summary; critic calls Lewis a "Ben Hur with languages" who "even at his most technical . . . manages to avoid dullness."

18. Jewkes, W. T. *General Linguistics,* November 1968. [PF]

    Two usually suspect attitudes receive justification in the book: the belief that literary language is more valuable to study than spoken language, and that language study can never totally disassociate itself from humane studies in general.

19. M., F. E. "Words." *Law Journal*, 2 November 1967. [PF]

    May give pause to linguistic analysts who insist that language wholly conditions the thinking that takes place within it. Lewis's aim is accurate reading, to overhaul our approach to language, and to throw light on ideas and attitudes. Critic points out Lewis draws attention to the remarkable tendency of adjectives imputing goodness to become terms of disparagement, e.g., "innocent," "pious."

20. "New Books on Words." *Journal of the American Medical Association* 202 (27 November 1967). [PF]

    Book will be appreciated by anyone who likes to look up words in the dictionary. Physicians will be interested particularly in treatment of "nature," "sad," "sense," "conscious" and "life" as well as many of the others.

21. Nissim, Ezekiel. "The Weight of the Word." *Thought* [India], 12 November 1960. [PF]

    Favorable summary of contents. Critic says it would be a "great pity" if only university students read it; recommends it to writers and the final chapter to book reviewers.

22. Partridge, Eric. "Word and Meaning." *Sunday Times*, 11 September 1960. [PF]

Choice of words discussed shows his belief in the human spirit and his "wide-ranging scholarship."

23. Potter, Simeon. *Daily Telegraph*, 30 September 1960. [PF]

Critic finds the book has a friendly professorial mood with the special merit of showing words' backgrounds in great literature with "luminous comments."

24. Potter, Stephen. "? Hoc [Donum] Anno Novo." *Spectator* 205 (14 October 1960): 571.

"The coverage is not wide but the verbal agriculture is intensive." "quickens our perceptions of word sense." Also a review of Eric Partridge's *Charm of Words*.

25. "Professor Lewis on Linguistics." *Times Literary Supplement*, 30 September 1960, p. 627.

Very favorable; chapter on "wit" rebutting William Empson "masterly." Disagrees with certain of Lewis's uses of quotations.

26. *School Librarian*, 4 March 1961. [PF]

Book communicates Lewis's enthusiasm for "responsibility to our language." Though written for university students, not beyond intelligent sixth formers.

27. Strang, Barbara M. H. "Reviews." *Durham University Journal*, n.s. 23 (December 1961): 45-47.

Lewis has "exaggerated notion of the function of the isolated word or expression in the communicative role of language" and "an exaggerated notion of the independence a language has from its users." But "it is the fruit of immense, meticulous, and well-knit reading expounded with a clarity that has its own beauty."

28. Toynbee, Philip. "Guarding the Language." *Observer*, 11 September 1960. [PF]

Lewis's "formidable scholarly apparatus . . . at its best." High interest for those interested in use and history of words. Mild criticism that Lewis gives too little credit to usefulness of words bifurcating into new distinctions.

29. Van de Laar, E. *Levende Talen.* [PF]

A lot of interesting information *about* words, but will not enlighten students' linguistic insight.

30. "Verbal Inquiry." *Times Educational Supplement,* 4 October 1960. [PF]

Reviewer finds it a "warm and entertaining inquiry" showing painlessly the danger in misuse of words. Critic has mild dislike for last chapter which he thinks slips into tone of a lecture.

31. von Lindheim, Begislav. *Anglia* 74 (1961): 62-64.

In German. This collection of lectures is not comprehensive and not learnedly annotated; it *is* moral in its emphasis. Lewis's terminology is generally well done, with the possible exception of "methodological idiom." Occasionally his distinctions in meanings of words are not precise; occasionally Lewis is wilful in his judgments. Five technical corrections. (We wish to thank Fr. Raleigh Denison for help in annotating this item.)

32. Wain, John. "Book Reviews." *Twentieth Century* [London], 169 (January 1961): 86-88.

Says only half a dozen scholars could have carried such a book off as successfully as Lewis, who combines classics, English linguistic history, a concern for what texts are saying, and decades of reading into the background for this book. Regards it as good to keep handy for marginalia.

33. White, John P. "Language and Logic." *Tablet* 214 (26 November 1960): 1092.

More lucid and historically aware than William Empson's *The Structure of Complex Words* and more acute than Logan Pearsall Smith's study. Suggests some of Lewis's statements are more on philosophy than linguistic puzzles.

34. Wimsatt, W. K., Jr. *Philological Quarterly* 40 (July 1961): 355.

   Overlooking theoretical issues in this review, Wimsatt finds the lexicographical chapters clear, graceful, and of merit. There is, however, "not a little about this book that suggests a *Spirit of St. Louis* making its flight in 1960"—that is, Lewis's reliance on his own experience with words leads him to ignore (perhaps through ignorance) the scholarship in the field. Wimsatt lists eight scholars that the student should consult after reading Lewis. (This review is part of the bibliography of English Literature for 1660-1800.)

35. ———"Words." *Oxford Magazine*, 8 June 1961, pp. 404-405. [PF]

   Wimsatt argues against Lewis's ideas on verbal interpretation. He is particularly concerned about Lewis's theoretical insistence on univocal meanings as inclined toward subduing legitimate, receptive, imaginative readings when trying to understand an old author's intention. In Lewis's own less theoretical passages, Wimsatt thinks Lewis himself is sensitively aware of accumulated meanings.

36. "A Word for It." *Leicester Mercury*, 9 September 1960. [PF]

   It is "primarily for students but not as academic as you might think" and much of it is "fascinating."

39. *The World's Last Night and Other Essays* (1960). Seven essays.

1. Clancy, J. "Education and Moral Wisdom." *Catholic World* 191 (May 1960): 126-130 [128-130].

   Favorable except on social education where Lewis "generalizes glibly" but still stings into some truth.

2. Deasy, Philip. "Critic of Our Age." *Commonweal* 71 (4 March 1960): 632.

Style has "Chestertonian flavor" but newest Screwtape piece "pallid stuff"; Lewis at his "astringent best" in "Lilies that Fester."

3. Fuller, Edmund. "Welcome Essays by C. S. Lewis." *Chicago Sunday Tribune Magazine of Books*, 21 February 1960, § 4, p. 2.

"qualified both to please Lewis' expanding following and to win him new readers." Fuller likes especially the new Screwtape letter.

4. Glauber, Robert H. "C. S. Lewis in a Happily Familiar Form." *New York Herald Tribune Book Review,* 21 February 1960, p. 7.

"gentle essays"; "still that rare writer who sees the theological implications of market-place problems"; the book "reveals in Lewis a kind of growing mellowness."

5. Harris, Sydney J. "Shafts from a Christian Marksman." *Saturday Review* 43 (5 March 1960): 21-22.

Harris considers each of the essays, evaluates its usefulness to the reader, and reaches conclusions about Lewis's virtues and failures as a writer—all in all, an excellent model of a critical review. An interesting general passage is an attempt to classify Lewis's theological writings: "he has provid[ed] us with apologetics ('The Great Divorce' and 'Miracles'), theodicy ('The Problem of Pain'), hermeneutics ('Reflections on the Psalms'), and his own sort of irenics ('Beyond Personality')." An example of the treatment of the essays: Harris finds that "too many of Lewis's upper-middle-class Oxonian prejudices gleam through the Devil's mask" in "Screwtape Proposes a Toast"; he refers to the labor leader "stuffed with sedition" as an example. Over all, Lewis is a fine analytical writer but better at "mass-demolition" than at suggesting where to go. He has some areas of Christian weakness (i.e., uneasy with mysticism, unconcern for social relevance, formalism in approaching the Bible).

6. Jeanne, Sister M., O. S. F. "Book Review." *Good Work* 23 (Michaelmas 1960): 130.

The Screwtape piece is a "brilliant exposé of the current cult of mediocrity"; passages on culture-mongers "particularly trenchant."

7. Kilby, Clyde S. "Provocative Essays." *Christianity Today* 4 (25 April 1960): 32-33.

Favorable; Kilby considers the Screwtape letter best, finds essay on prayer "valuable," and suspects the healing described was of Mrs. Lewis.

8. Knight, Damon. "Books: Briefly Noted." *Magazine of Fantasy and Science Fiction* 19 (August 1960): 102.

"the nimble C. S. Lewis again dangles himself like a yo-yo over the pit of free inquiry, turns cartwheels and loops the loop, yet the string never breaks and he never falls in. Like his previous works of Christian apology, this one is full of half-truths, misstatements, evasions, sleight of hand and downright falsehood." Knight cites a passage about new discoveries never reducing Christian faith to knowledge or to "patent absurdities" as an example of the final point, referring to the third-to-last paragraph of "Religion and Rocketry"; also on this essay, he comments, "His speculations about life on other planets . . . are too well-tethered to be valuable."

9. Le Fort, Thomas, O. P. "Plea for Wisdom." *Dominicana* 46 (September 1961): 43-50.

Le Fort defends Lewis's apologetic against science as criticism against a technological concept of life and a plea for "wondering contemplation," and relates this positively to Catholic doctrine.

10. Peel, Robert. "Wit and Orthodoxy." *Christian Science Monitor*, 11 February 1960, p. 11.

Lewis overemphasizes sin to the expense of love and grace; more like a "sardonic court jester" in the halls through which pace the "majestic figures of Barth, Tillich et al." Tonic to a "too easy faith and a too easy skepticism" but misses the "healing vision."

11. Walsh, Chad. "A Toast to Mr. Slubgob with Some Pertinent Remarks." *New York Times Book Review*, 21 February 1960, § 7, p. 14.

A "really packed little book" showing "a sharpening sociological interest" in several essays; the new Screwtape piece "first-rate."

40. *A Grief Observed* (1961, under the pseudonym of N. W. Clerk; 1964, posthumously, under C. S. Lewis).

1. "Argument with Sorrow." *Times Literary Supplement*, 10 November 1961, p. 803.

An "independent and inquiring organism rebels against the established consolations while fighting its own perplexity and pain. The author of this brief journal-record is just such an inquirer, turning a merciless analytic eye on his mental sufferings, as a research chemist borrows his own limbs for experiment." The conclusion is ambiguous, the author making contact either with his dead wife's intelligence or with his own. "the journal has a strange, firm magneticism."

2. Lindskoog, Kathryn. "No Door to God Slammed Shut." *Eternity* 15 (July 1964): 42.

The journal was a "safety valve for his grief"; Lewis abandons his usual reserve on his private life. Hardly a gift book for the bereaved—"too vivid, ruthless, and startling."

41. *An Experiment in Criticism* (1961).

1. Allison, Nicholas. "Learning to Be More Discriminating Readers." *Sheffield Telegraph*, 15 January 1966. [PF]

   Favorable; the reviewer stresses Lewis's point that the quality of a book cannot be evaluated except by considering the kind of reading it invites.

2. Bell, Alan. "Brave Unknown of Air War." *Age* [Melbourne], 6 April 1966. [PF]

   This "shrewdly mischievous" book brought more warm assent from readers and bowled over more pedants' applecarts than most of the century's volumes on literature.

3. Bergonzi, Bernard. "Open to Books." *Spectator* 207 (17 November 1961): 718, 720.

   "This theory has its attractive aspects, but it seems to me logically and practically difficult to establish." ". . . the encounter with a book is necessarily a more active business than Professor Lewis allows for: a dialogue, rather than a surrender." "One would, I think, be foolish to swallow all of this vigorous, unfair, provocative book; but one would be more foolish to ignore it."

4. Brett, R. L. "Reviews." *Review of English Studies*, n.s. 14 (February 1963): 97-98.

   "well-written and skilfully argued"; "The specific value of literature considered as Logos is that it introduces us to experiences other than our own. It is when he comes to relate these that Mr. Lewis is not explicit enough." "But although there may be no *problem* of belief here, Mr. Lewis does not make clear whether his theory of value is ultimately naturalistic or non-naturalistic."

5. Daiches, David. "Just How Should a Critic Approach a Book?" *New York Times Book Review*, 17 December 1961, § 7, p. 6.

    The book is provocative, but Lewis somewhat misunderstands F. R. Leavis and some other critical approaches which are his target.

6. Derrick, Christopher. "The Christian Critic." *Tablet* 215 (16 December 1961): 1208-1209.

    A truculent argument against a "cultural priesthood" which offers something like a surrogate religion. Lewis's distinction between good and bad reading is original and delicately worked.

7. Fraser, John. "Books in Review." *Meanjin* [Australia], 21 (June 1962): 241-243.

    Too much "crude dichotomizing" in Lewis's mind. "The avoidance of any direct engagement with the arguments of first-rate minds was always, of course, a feature of Lewis's popular theological books." Fraser sees an "unfortunate, muddled, English adolescent" target of much of Lewis's work.

8. "The Function of Criticism." *Times Literary Supplement*, 3 November 1961, p. 790.

    "A stimulating trumpet blast," but in remarks on the relation between literature and life and evaluative critics, Lewis merely shows there are some bad critics; in setting up the apparatus of the "experiment," he shows keen analytic ability; the "experiment" itself is rather tame and at bottom not far removed from F. R. Leavis's description of the "common reader."

9. Hope, Francis. "Don't Follow the Leader." *Time and Tide* 42 (23 November 1961): 1980.

    Lewis did not prove the split between aesthetic and moral judgments of literature, and the primacy of the first is unprovable.

10. Kermode, Frank. "Against Vigilants." *New Statesman* 62 (3 November 1961): 658-659.

    An urbane, "vigorous and schematic" essay.

11. Logan, Terence P. "Book Reviews." *Modern Language Journal* 50 (December 1966): 563.

"an interesting compound of brilliance and nonsense." In some digressions Lewis engages in the kind of criticism he sets out to correct. But as a whole "a very sensitive attempt to articulate a professional's attitude to the stuff of his craft; on this level it succeeds eloquently."

12. Lyons, Clifford P. "Books." *South Atlantic Quarterly* 41 (Autumn 1962): 540-541.

"gay and swift dance of illuminating ideas"; "in part strategy for silencing evaluative critics." Lewis shows the "New Critic" really has a moral-spiritual view of nature and the function of art.

13. "Notes on Current Books." *Virginia Quarterly Review*, Autumn 1962, pp. cxx-cxxi.

Lewis's attempt to break away from preconceptions of literary merit as criteria for taste of readers ends by locating value in the objective. Lucid.

14. "Reading Good and Bad." *Times*, 26 October 1961, p. 17d.

"a wealth of valuable distinctions and robust common sense," but "good writing has to do with truth as well as beauty" and the book also is "not helped by an occasional heaviness of touch." However, there is "profound warning against the dangers of teaching and reading English literature as . . . substitute for moral philosophy."

15. Rogers, Timothy. *English* [London], Spring 1962, pp. 26-27.

A "short, lucid book," but it fails to allow that "a certain valuing is implicit" in the surrender to a book. "it is for its apparatus rather than its findings that the experiment is most valuable."

16. Schofield, C. H. "Bond or Bard, Just Enjoy It." *Yorkshire Evening Press*, 4 April 1966. [PF]

The book is a "now classic broadside." Schofield calls Lewis "one of the sanest, healthiest of literary critics" and an "arch-enemy of the Puritan outlook" in literary studies.

17. Wain, John. "C. S. Lewis Throws Down a Challenge." *Observer*, 22 October 1961, p. 31.

"highly personal, very original and, though soberly written, full of a kind of guarded high-spiritedness that makes it very attractive to read"; it "contains a number of sharp challenges to the Cambridge party line" which the reviewer defines and describes.

42. *They Asked for a Paper: Papers and Addresses* (1962). Twelve essays.

1. Bateson, F. W. "The Last Edwardian." *New Statesman* 63 (16 March 1962): 376.

The 1954 inaugural lecture is a magnificent use of justifiable hyperbole; other essays in the collection are a less justifiable use of the method.

2. Caveliero, G. "Book Reviews." *Theology* 65 (August 1962): 348-349 [348].

"as a moralist Dr. Lewis can be brusque and too knowing by half, but his touch never fails when he is describing the goodness of God and the glories of the new creation."

3. Everett, Barbara. "Reviews and Comment." *Critical Quarterly* 4 (Summer 1962): 180-181.

The value is mainly in the "communication of a complete and serious approach to literature, and to theological questions." "Lilies That Fester" is one of the best essays.

4 "In the Margin." *Times Literary Supplement*, 30 March 1962, p. 219.

Critic sees pleasure in how these supplement Lewis's major works and at "seeing him exercise his muscles on themes farther removed from his normal interests." Feels the Oxford school of linguistic philosophy is an influence that cannot be missed throughout the book.

5. MacCurtain, Austin. "Book Reviews." *Studies* 51 (September 1962) : 187-189.

    Lewis is an excellent teacher with his stress on experience as corrective to intellectual extravagance. He is at his best in Kipling essay and on discussion of Freud's theory of literature.

6. Stewart, J. I. M. "Old Western Man." *Listener* 67 (8 March 1962) : 431-432.

    Critic feels Lewis has trouble relating to his juniors of the contemporary world; prefers Lewis the scholar to the author of these essays where he is a moral tutor.

43. *Letters to Malcolm: Chiefly on Prayer* (1964).

1. Cavanaugh, H. "Two By and One About C. S. Lewis."

    Listed in § VI-A-1; review of *Letters to Malcolm, The Discarded Image,* and Kilby's *Christian World of C. S. Lewis.*

2. "Final Achievement." *Times Literary Supplement,* 27 February 1964, p. 173.

    Favorable remarks on his overall Christian writing; "this last book may well be one to be more valued than many of the others."

3. Hart, Jeffrey. "C. S. Lewis: 1898-1963." *National Review* 16 (24 March 1964) : 240, 242-243.

    Listed in § II; largely an obituary.

4. King, Francis. "Hear Us, O Lord." *New Statesman* 67 (21 February 1964) : 302.

    Lewis sometimes "gives the impression of being a mere collector of ready-made beliefs" but the book has "shrewd asides."

314

5. McNaspy, C. J. *America* 110 (15 February 1964): 231, 234-235.

   A "no-bluff centrality"; warm, direct, personal. Also an obituary: description of Lewis in person and as lecturer.

6. Pryce-Jones, Alan. "C. S. Lewis' Last Book." *New York Herald Tribune*, 13 February 1964, § 2, p. 21.

   ". . . for the present day Lewis has an important contribution to make." "Nobody with an inner life, however disheveled and incoherent that life may be, will fail to delight in his cogency. In his modesty, too." "Lewis never loses a most happy incandescence."

7. Scott, Nathan A., Jr. "Dialogue with Deity." *Saturday Review* 47 (7 March 1964): 41.

   Lewis has a "Christian sensibility," grappling with the problem of doubt and prayer in a warmly personal way. He does not resolve the Christian faith into "maxims of moral allegory and ethical abstraction."

8. Walsh, Chad. "The Keynote Is Honesty." *New York Times Book Review*, 1 March 1964, § 7, pp. 12, 14.

   "a down-to-earth book by a man who was a warm human being, the possessor of a clear mind, and whose commitment to Christianity was as steadfast as his refusal to put on spiritual airs."

44. *The Discarded Image: An Introduction to Medieval and Renaissance Literature* (1964).

1. Adkinson, R. V. *Revue des langues vivantes* 33 (1967). [PF]

   "It carries out with admirable economy the task of establishing the nature of the Medieval world as objectively as the evidence allows. No one can ask more of descriptive criticism."

2. Allen, D. C. "Reviews." *English Language Notes* 2
   (December 1964): 133-135.

   Lewis's tracing of the origins of medieval Christian cosmology
   is exciting though occasionally "naive." The remaining survey of
   the majority opinion of the Middle Ages on the nature of the
   universe often plods.

3. Bradbrook, M. C. "Medieval Model." *New Statesman*, n. s.
   68 (7 August 1964): 188.

   Review of *The Discarded Image* and Morris Bishop's *Petrarch
   and his World*. Six paragraphs are spent on Lewis's book, one on
   Bishop's. The author suggests that Lewis constructed the Model
   of the Medieval Universe out of his own reading, rather than
   by the medieval writers being aware of such a universe all the
   time—and backs this up with an anecdote, a comment Lewis
   made to Bradbrook shortly before his death that at least he
   would never have to read *Piers Plowman* and Skelton again, both
   of whom (Bradbrook suggests) did not fit his tidy medieval
   Model. Bradbrook also suggests that the conclusion of *The
   Discarded Image*, which states that all models of the universe are
   false (and which ignores the different methods used in reaching
   the modern, scientific "Model"), is deliberately provocative, in
   order to start the type of debate which Lewis enjoyed.

4. Brewer, D. S. "A Walk Over Fine, Rough Country."
   Birmingham Post, 9 June 1964. [PF]

   The critic says *The Allegory of Love* and the Oxford history
   volume will last longer, but this one is good.

5. *British Book News*, No. 287 (July 1964): 519.

   Very favorable; the reviewer calls Lewis's death a "grievous blow
   to both medieval and theological studies." "Admirers of Lewis's
   books for children will especially enjoy the chapter on the
   Longaevi or Fairies . . . ."

6. Burrow, John. "The Model Universe." *Essays in Criticism*
   15 (April 1965): 207-211.

   "rich and intriguing book"; the reviewer contrasts Lewis with
   Northrup Frye's "model." Both see cosmology and religion as

"essentially uncommitted to each other in the Middle Ages" but differ in their relationship of science and cosmology: for Frye, they are separate; for Lewis, science must always "have its supposals."

7. Carter, A. H. "One About, One By."

Listed in § VI-A-1; review of *The Discarded Image* and C. S. Kilby's *The Christian World of C. S. Lewis.*

8. Cavanaugh, H. "Two By and One About C. S. Lewis."

Listed in § VI-A-1; review of *Letters to Malcolm, The Discarded Image,* and Kilby's *Christian World of C. S. Lewis.*

9. *Choice* 1 (October 1964): 312.

The critic says the book suffers from being a series of notes rather than an ample, coherent exposition, and it lacks commentary on literary texts. "nonetheless a valuable companion."

10. Cutler, Edward. "Literature." *Library Journal* 89 (15 September 1964): 3316.

"Professor Lewis's habit of illustrating his thesis with examples drawn from the whole scope of medieval literature may often make for rough going for the actual beginner."

11. Davies, R. T. *Notes and Queries* 209, n. s. 11 (September 1964): 350.

"most distinguished addition to the growing body of introductory aids for the student of medieval literature. Moreover, when he delivered it as lectures, C. S. Lewis was a great pioneer."

12. del Tufo, Joseph P. "An Introduction to the Medieval Mind." *Philippine Studies,* [PF]

The critic feels book organizes a wealth of material into a "lucid whole" and provides background against which all previous reading of medieval and Renaissance authors becomes more intelligible.

13. Dronke, Peter. *Oxford Magazine,* 26 November 1964. [PF]

The reviewer challenges Lewis's assumption that there was a

unified model characteristic of the medieval mind. He believes this denies the individualism alive in the middle ages and certain historical transitions. Otherwise, "the book is full of sparkling and provocative assertions that range from the seriously challenging to the preposterous," and the reviewer lists several examples of each.

14. Dunn, E. Catherine. "Book Reviews: Renaissance and Reformation." *Catholic Historical Review* 51 (April 1965): 87.

Dunn feels the chapters, except the first and last, have an aridity and ponderous weight which an actual lecture avoids. She rejects Lewis's use of the term "model" to include historiography and educational curriculum in the arts.

15. *Études Anglaises* 18 (1965). [PF]

"Ce petit volume enrichit d'une manière appreciable notre conaissance de la pensée médiévale, qui fut aussi dans une grande mesure la pensée de la Renaissance anglaise."

16. Gardner, Helen. "Book Reviews." *Listener* 72 (16 July 1964): 97.

Largely personal memories of Lewis. "And where else in modern literary scholarship can we find so generous and enthusiastic a temper?"

17. "Grete Clerke of Oxford." *Times Literary Supplement*, 16 July 1964, p. 632.

"it represents Lewis the expositor at his best, and communicates the zest that he brought to the study of literature, philosophy and religion alike."

18. Hardie, Colin. *Medium Aevum* 37 (1968): 95-97. [PF]

A favorable descriptive review. The critic wishes Lewis had included some fuller discussions and further topics, such as numerology; he also lists several minor errors.

19. Haynes, Renée. "A Soothsayer."

Listed in § VI-A-1; a review of *The Discarded Image* and *A Mind Awake*.

20. Holloway, John. "Grand Design." *Spectator* 212 (5 June 1964) : 760.

"its range, its lucid learning, its luminous style . . . perhaps the memorial to the work of a great scholar and teacher, and a wise and noble mind." Caveats: the outline is a bit too neat, and Lewis leaves out something important when he links medieval realism with the cosmic order.

21. Jennings, Elizabeth. "Milton the Visionary." *Daily Telegraph*, 28 January 1965. [PF]

In a review mainly on two books on Milton, the critic says Lewis was "an exciting critic" who made the most abstruse subject scintillating and was "in love with literature."

22. Kirsch, Robert R. "Essays on Criticism Argue for Return to Sense, Sensibility." *Los Angeles Times Calendar*, 3 March 1966. [PF]

"Provides an interesting and useful extension of Miss Sontag's theories . . . it has the kind of 'transparence' she speaks about but frequently lacks."

23. Laski, Marghanita. BBC review broadcast, 6 June 1964. [PF]

Laski finds book "splendid" and "exciting" but not quite the book those who heard the lectures at Oxford had hoped for. Not long or complete enough, it does not include much that was of value in his lectures and Lewis "cheats a little" in leaving out conflicting materials.

24. McAuley, James. "Homesick for the Old Ways." *Australian*, 20 February 1965. [PF]

The reviewer is not much attracted to Lewis as apologist and novelist, but calls him a "great interpreter of literature." He dislikes last chapter; feels Lewis overemphasized the subjective factor in the new model, which is less speculative than the old.

25. "Medieaval Modellers." *Church Times*, 3 April 1964. [PF]

The critic discusses the medieval world view, based on Lewis's book; he says an amateur is "left gasping" that a man who did so much in other fields could possibly know so much about medieval literature.

26. Moore, Harry T. "Between Book Ends." *St. Louis Post-Dispatch*, 28 April 1964. [PF]

   It is fortunate that Lewis took friends' advice and collected these "highly informative . . . attractive" lectures.

27. Newbold, Geoffrey. "Pagan Thought and Christian Faith." *Bolton Evening News*, 15 May 1964. [PF]

   The reviewer considers this book, though not exactly a "literary" introduction, an excellent invitation to suspension of disbelief and entrance into the poetry of the medieval world view.

28. Schleuter, Paul. "Scholar and Wit."

   Listed in § VI-A-1; a review of *The Discarded Image* and Kilby's *Christian World of C. S. Lewis.*

29. Sewell, Gordon. "The Wisdom of C. S. Lewis."

   Listed in § VI-A-1; a review of *The Discarded Image* and *A Mind Awake.*

30. Singleton, Charles S. "The Universe of C. S. Lewis." *New York Review of Books* 2 (30 July 1964): 10-12.

   The reviewer finds the book a successful guide for the beginning student, introducing him to the medieval universe of Dante and Thomas Aquinas; he comments about Lewis's chapter on fairies, ". . . Lewis was probably at his best always when he was dealing with a 'truancy' "; also he points out that Lewis omits all detailed discussion of how Christian salvation was fitted to this model, probably because (for Lewis) that part of the Image had not yet been discarded.

31. Spiers, John. "The Last of C. S. Lewis." *Use of English*, Summer 1967. [PF]

   Lewis goes to "remarkable lengths in detaching ideas from their contexts." His "eccentricities (or perversities) of critical taste and judgment" make his work "entirely unreliable for all its erudition." Is this what the Middle Ages believed, or what Lewis personally believed?

32. Taylor, Jerome. "Book Review: Literature." *Thought*, 1965, pp. 291-292. [PF]

"Neither scholarly nor rigorous" but "a useful distillation." The reviewer disagrees with Lewis's ignoring the historical development and changes in the image, also its variations from writer to writer. As example he analyzes the treatment of "nature." He considers the last chapter "profound."

33. Vidler, Alec. "Unapologetic Apologist."

Listed in § VI-A-1; a review of *The Discarded Image* and C. S. Kilby's *The Christian World of C. S. Lewis.*

34. Walsh, Chad. "The Feel of a Viewpoint." *Living Church*, 11 October 1964. [PF]

Erudite but for general reader it has "Lewis' always engaging style, wit, and sudden flashes of insight, plus the pleasure of entering the sensibility of past centuries."

45. *Poems*. Ed. Walter Hooper (1964).

1. Derrick, C. H. "C. S. Lewis and the Evolutionary Myth." *Good Work* 28 (Winter 1965): 23-26.

In the old elegaic tradition in which the "ancient grief" is "once again faced honestly" in "sharp polarity with a robustly lyrical appetite for life and light and color." Item also discusses Lewis's views on cultural evolution as a modern myth.

2. Derrick, Christopher. "The Lay of the Dinosaur." *Tablet* 218 (26 December 1964): 1464-1465.

Technically interesting though little of the imaginative splendor of his prose. Often elegaic due to strong tragic consciousness of the Fall. Lewis may in retrospect "seem like a lonely Churchill of the nineteen-thirties."

3. Howard, Thomas H. "Plucking Pizzicato." *Christianity Today* 9 (18 June 1964): 30.

> The "glorious best of Lewis. For here, with the gemlike beauty and hardness that poetry alone can achieve, are his ideas about the nature of things that lay behind all of his writings." He was "never afraid of the naive, the moving, or the lyric, but he severely avoids the treacly and bathetic."

4. Kidd, Virginia. "Books." *Magazine of Fantasy and Science Fiction* 29 (October 1965): 98.

> "while this posthumous volume is a continuous delight, the mantle of poet is one that [Lewis] wore, I think, only in odd moments." "the occasional poems of a man so skilled in the arts of language and theology are far better reading than a great deal that passes for poetry nowadays." The few verses on specifically science-fictional topics "will not particularly please the hard-core science-fiction fan—but in all likelihood neither does the great trilogy."

5. Kilby, Clyde S. "Music on the Brittle Side." *New York Times Book Review*, 23 January 1966, § 7, p. 34.

> "long-evident sensitivity to the sound and meaning of words as well as a rich variety of poetic forms," but the "music is often on the brittle side"; primary value is in the content of these "idea poems," but collection has "an important place in the Lewis canon."

6. Lindskoog, Kathryn. "Young King Cole but No Catchy Couplets." *Eternity* 16 (November 1965): 40-41.

> Not for "a casual American reader . . . for those who seriously care about poetry and who like to grapple with ideas or delight in fancy." They are "meticulously worked out, masterpieces of skill, wit, imagination and discipline." Lifelong efforts in difficult verse forms partially account for extraordinary prose skill.

7. Lord, Russell. "Modern Poetry—Free—and Too Easy?" *Christian Science Monitor*, 24 March 1966, p. 12.

> "refreshing and imaginative" though "often shows a literal rather

than a metaphorical approach, too frequently satisfied with hackneyed diction or uncommunicated statements about experience."

8. "The Scholar's Tale." *Times Literary Supplement*, 7 January 1965, pp. 1-2.

A summary of Lewis's ideas (using *Poems* as a reviewer's starting point), which finds Lewis not an Old Western Man but another Chesterton. Lewis made some middle-aged (before he was of middle age) prejudices of the Edwardian, Chestertonian era into eternal verities and never dealt adequately with the problems of his own day. His best work is *The Allegory of Love*, the Oxford history volume, and the "childlike kind of romance" in his fantasies.

46. *"Screwtape Proposes a Toast" and Other Pieces* (1965). Published as an English paperback only; no reviews located. Eight essays, including one not available elsewhere.

47. *Of Other Worlds: Essays and Stories.* Ed. Walter Hooper (1966). Nine essays, three short stories, and one incomplete novel.

1. Barrows, Herbert. "A Christian Off Duty."
Listed in § VI-A-1; a review of *Of Other Worlds* and *Letters of C. S. Lewis*.

2. Bredvold, Louis I. "The Achievement of C. S. Lewis."

Listed in § VI-A-1; review of *Studies in Medieval and Renaissance Literature* and *Of Other Worlds.*

3. Burgess, Anthony. "Matters of Romance." *Spectator* 217 (23 September 1966): 384.

Lewis is interesting and "disconcerting" on stories; in the essay "On Criticism" he is "lucid, urbane," but the collection in substance is "unmemorable."

4. Kitching, Jessie B. "Nonfiction." *Publisher's Weekly* 191 (16 January 1967): 78.

Two of the stories "undeniably poor" and the novel unfinished "because he could not, really, visualize the ignominious ending . . ."

5. Lobdell, J. C. "Books in Brief." *National Review* 19 (13 June 1967): 651-652.

Favorable; the essay on the genesis of Narnia is the most interesting as a classic individual statement of the psychology of literary invention.

6. Merril, Judith. "Books." *Magazine of Fantasy and Science Fiction* 32 (February 1967): 24-26.

The reviewer does not personally enjoy Lewis's fiction. Her favorite essay is "On Stories": "Lewis expresses with unique clarity and comprehension, the essential *virtu* of all of the many kinds of story that make up 's-f.' " On "On Criticism": "it is as cogent a commentary on the purpose and function of literary criticism as I can recall, and should be required reading for authors *and* critics both." Extensive quotation from other essays.

7. "Occasions." *Times Literary Supplement,* 15 September 1966, p. 860.

"worth preserving"; the book helps explain Lewis's taste for science fiction and fairy tale; the reply to J. B. S. Haldane's attack on his science-fiction show him a skilled controversialist.

8. "Two Sides of a Scholar." *Australian.*

Listed in § VI-A-1; a review of *Of Other Worlds* and *Studies in Medieval and Renaissance Literature.*

48. *Studies in Medieval and Renaissance Literature*. Ed. Walter Hooper (1966).

1. Bredvold, Louis I. "The Achievement of C. S. Lewis."

   Listed in § VI-A-1; review of *Studies in Medieval and Renaissance Literature* and *Of Other Worlds*.

2. Burrow, John. "Allegory." *Essays in Criticism* 17 (January 1967): 89-95 [89-90].

   Dual review of Lewis's *Studies in Medieval and Renaissance Literature* and Rosemond Tuve's *Allegorical Imagery: Some Medieval Books and Their Posterity*. No real comparison: one review and then the other. On Lewis's book: "Those who are familiar with Lewis's work will not find much novelty in this book. Yet it contains things which I am glad to have seen. The . . . well-merited strictures on Geoffrey of Monmouth, for example, have about them no air of the bottom of the barrel."

3. Bush, Douglas. "Book Reviews." *College English*, 28 (December 1966): 254-255.

   A general evaluation of Lewis as critic (using Lewis's terms of *golden* and *drab*). In this volume, Lewis is "brilliant" in defining literary values, less adequate "on the period's ideological currents and cross-currents." On Lewis as a whole, at his best "we are stirred by a mind of large stability and wholeness of outlook."

4. Evans, Ifor. "A Word for C. S. Lewis." *Birmingham Post*, 18 June 1966. [PF]

   The reviewer says the "recent silly attack" on Lewis by "puny minds" who hated the fact he was a Christian shows something is wrong with the state of letters, and perhaps the country as a whole. He calls Lewis the greatest English medievalist of our time.

5. Friedman, Lionel J. "Briefer Mention." *Romance Philology* 22 (August 1968): 119-120.

   The reviewer finds the collection "an apology for sanity and historicity," and important for critical position rather than scholarship, especially the first three essays.

6. G., C. "Reviews." *Italian Studies* 22 (1967): 117-119. [PF]

   A review of the three essays on Dante and the one on Tasso; the critic finds the book written "with impressive lucidity and simplicity."

7. "Language and Literature." *Choice* 3 (January 1967): 1011-1012.

   "Though the style is colloquial, often witty, with even 'homely' examples, the scholarship is on the highest level, as is usual with Lewis."

8. Lobdell, Jared. "C. S. Lewis' Renaissance." *National Review* 18 (27 December 1966): 1332-1333.

   Favorable; most interesting is Lewis's writing on self-conscious poetic construction.

9. "Medieval Medley." *Times Literary Supplement*, 14 July 1966, p. 616.

   "show the characteristic qualities of Lewis's mind: the lucidity, the ready and witty illustration of argument, the width of learning, the Johnsonian common sense and the un-Johnsonian courtesy to those who disagree."

10. Mulryan, John. *Cithara* 7 (May 1968): 76-77. [PF]

    In a generally favorable review, Mulryan says Lewis is an "exasperating" critic, as with his anti-renaissance bias, and in his unscholarly, sentimental wish for the Malory he knew in school rather than Vinaver's rake. Mulryan considers "De Audiendis Poetis" the best chapter.

11. Roscelli, William John. *Library Journal* 91 (August 1966):
3730.

    "only the essay on medieval thought and imagination reveals
    Lewis in top form."

12. "Two Sides of a Scholar." *Australian*.

    Listed in § VI-A-1; a review of *Of Other Worlds* and *Studies in
    Medieval and Renaissance Literature*.

13. Williams, Kathleen. "Recent Studies in the English
Renaissance."

    Listed in § VI-A-1; a review of *Studies in Medieval and
    Renaissance Literature, Spenser's Images of Life*, and John Lawlor's
    Patterns of Love and Courtesy.

49. *Letters of C. S. Lewis*. Ed. W. H. Lewis (1966). Includes
"Memoir of C. S. Lewis" by W. H. Lewis, which is
separately listed in § II.

1. Barrows, Herbert. "A Christian Off Duty."

    Listed in § VI-A-1; a review of *Of Other Worlds* and *Letters
    of C. S. Lewis*.

2. Bennett, Joan. "Current Books: Away from the Charabanc."
Listener 75 (19 May 1966): 731.

    A "vivid and faithful portrait" of Lewis. (Memoir of special
    importance, especially on Lewis's relationship to the menage he
    supported.)

3. Douglas, J. D. "Current Religious Thought: Letters from
C. S. Lewis." *Christianity Today* 10 (16 September 1966):
54.

    Lewis shared his joys, sorrows, wisdom and caring with all kind of people "with a unique combination of logic, imagination,—and tact. He was eminently *sensible*." The book "shows a characteristic tongue-in-cheekiness."

4. Greeley, Andrew M. "A Chap in His Place." *Reporter* 36 (12 January 1967): 64.

The letters show a "mildly tragic figure" who managed to enjoy life because he never thought himself unhappy and he had, above all, his faith. The "real Lewis" does not appear in the letters, though the letters "make it quite clear how important that faith was." The reviewer praises in general Lewis's nonepistolary writings.

5. Grigson, Geoffrey. "A Sectary of Backness." *New Statesman* 71 (13 May 1966): 695.

The letters show priggishness, stale vocabulary, and "literary mediocrity" of preachment and exhortation; and they are selfconsciously backward.

6. Hazelton, Roger. "C. S. Lewis: No Further than Gethsemane." *New Republic* 156 (18 February 1967): 25-27.

The letters show wit, insight, and eloquence: "He kept his balance, and helped others to keep theirs"; "The dominant impression of these letters is that C. S. Lewis lived as he taught."

7. Mulvey, C. E. "Books." *Commonweal* 85 (13 January 1967): 405-406.

The letters give insight into Lewis's capacity for friendship and brilliant conversation and, in his closing years, spiritual strength. Also "filled with the scholarly esoterica of scholarly reading." (The memoir "is the best of its kind that I have ever read." It has a candor "that is a higher form of praise than panegyric.")

8. Sire, James W. "The Many Faces of C. S. Lewis." *Prairie Schooner* 40 (Winter 1966-1967): 364-366.

The letters are a fascinating example of Lewis's range: they show his patience and love for common people; they trace the development of his ideas and relations with friends, adding some new insights.

9. Wain, John. "Friends and Strangers." *Observer*, 15 May 1966, p. 26.

The letters show Lewis's "essential goodness and generosity," and many features of his personality. A certain imbalance in that Lewis regularly saw, and did not write to, most of his closest friends. (The memoir is "elegant and informative.")

10. Wills, Garry. "Ghostly Wisdom." *National Review* 19 (4 April 1967): 369-371.

The volume is too carefully edited and has little self-revelation: "it is the hidden Lewis we need." On the other hand, the best romantics insist on order because they "know chasms open around us" and the best rationalists know how little the brain can do; the letters do show *that* Lewis. The review contains some interesting conjectures about the romantic side of Lewis, in connection to *The Screwtape Letters* primarily.

50. *Spenser's Images of Life*. Ed. Alastair Fowler (1967).

1. Adams, Robert M. "Reviving Spenser." *New York Review of Books* 10 (6 June 1968): 32-34 [32, 33].

"he touched nothing that he did not adorn, usually by simplifying it"; too bad this book did not have a chance to flower "into its proper order of complexity." Its argument is lucid but a bit over-schematic and lacking subtle finishing touches it would have had if Lewis had lived to finish it.

2. Cruttwell, Patrick. "How Many Ways of Looking at a Poem?" *Hudson Review* 21 (Spring 1968): 197-207 [198-199, 202-203, 206].

"in the last analysis, I have always found the work of this original

and powerful mind to be radically flawed, not finally
enlightening." Lewis refused to see the Middle Ages and
Renaissance as they were but as "happy contrasts to the modern
age which *he* lived in, and hated."

3. Heninger, S. K., Jr. "Reviews." *Renaissance Quarterly* 23
(Spring 1970) : 89-90.

   Critic wonders how much is Lewis and how much is Fowler,
   especially in the emphasis on iconography. Generally, "the parts
   are admirable, even if a whole cannot be perceived . . . ,"

4. Hough, Graham. "Books: C. S. Lewis, Dr. Fowler and
Edmund Spenser." *Cambridge Review*, November 1967.
[PF]

   Favorable review; the critic says, "The book is best read as a happy
   and unexpected supplement to what is in *The Allegory of Love.*"

5. "Language and Literature: English and American." *Choice* 5
(December 1968) : 1308.

   The book "will not convince many readers that *The Faerie Queen*
   imaginatively embodies all the ideas [that Lewis] finds in it."
   Lewis was "one of the great literary historians of the century,"
   however.

6. Lobdell, J. C. "Books in Brief." *National Review* 20 (8
October 1968) : 1027.

   It is "a rough and rather brief approximation" of what Lewis
   would have written but should set Spenser criticism on "a new and
   profitable track." Since Lewis's approach requires a knowledge
   of and taste for emblems and iconography, it is doubtful whether
   even Lewis's "brilliance" can restore Spenser to popularity.

7. Williams, Kathleen. "Recent Studies in the English
Renaissance."

   Listed in § VI-A-1; a review of *Studies in Medieval and
   Renaissance Literature, Spenser's Images of Life*, and John Lawlor's
   Patterns of Love and Courtesy.

51. *Christian Reflections*. Ed. Walter Hooper (1967). Fourteen essays.

1. Kilby, Clyde S. "But His Arguments are Lingering On." *Chicago Tribune Books Today*, 9 April 1967, § 9, p. 8.

    The book is "of special interest to people whose philosophy runs to futility, determinism, and atheism."

2. "Personal Orthodoxy." *Times Literary Supplement*, 23 March 1967, p. 246.

    The volume makes one wonder why Lewis was so popular in 1940s and 1950s: "in the end is there not a hint of censoriousness, a suggestion that those who do not share his robust orthodoxy are morally suspect, and surely a hostility to science and scientists which is almost ludicrous?" The reviewer is most uneasy in the pieces dealing with society. The final essay on Biblical criticism makes the issue most clear on his conservatism as "uncomfortable."

3. Stauffer, J. Paul. "A Reasoning Christian." *Spectrum: A Quarterly Journal of Adventist Forums* 1 (Spring 1969): 60-64.

    Lewis had a "cultivated and adroit and urbane mind, a mind disciplined to make precise distinctions, a mind skilled in logic and orderly analysis." But the reviewer is slightly disappointed because Lewis's world is "a world that now seems curiously remote from us."

4. Tutcher, John. "On Common Ground." *Books and Bookmen* 12 (April 1967): 31-32.

    Lewis is a "brilliant Christian apologist" who "buried his head in the sand" by deliberate choice on questions of churchmanship, but he "is no modernist."

5. Wirt, Sherwood E. "A Tasty Dish by C. S. Lewis." *Christian and Christianity Today* [London], 14 April 1967, p. 16.

    "a tasty mixed dish"; the essays with a strong appeal to reason and the assault on "higher" criticism are good; the essay on church music reveals "he knows nothing about church music."

52. *Letters to an American Lady*. Ed. Clyde S. Kilby (1967)

1. Anton, Rita. *America* 118 (3 February 1968): 162-163.

   The book shows "the sympathy, comfort, and finally friendship of a great and holy man." The reviewer, an amateur grapho-analyst, analyzes Lewis's handwriting from the sample in the end papers.

2. Ashanin, C. B. "Book Notes." *Encounter* [Butler University College of Religion, Indiana], 29 (Winter 1968): 101.

   "since he is too close to us, perhaps the possessor of these letters, Wheaton College, might have exercised better judgment and delayed their publication."

3. Lindskoog, Kathryn. "Love in Action; Signed, C. S. Lewis." *Eternity* 19 (September 1968): 52-53.

   "To readers unacquainted with Lewis's literary power, most of these letters seem as humble as a laundry list."

4. Lobdell, J. C. "Books in Brief." *National Review* 20 (13 August 1968): 815.

   "What this book triumphantly is, is an *example* of Christian life in action, a welcoming of the duty of counsel, a remarkable demonstration of Lewis's belief in the Way of Exchange."

5. Ostling, Joan K. "Lights and Shadows." *Christianity Today* 12 (16 February 1968): 36.

   The letters give insight into the kind of Christian Lewis was. Poignant references to death.

6. Reist, J. S., Jr. *Foundations* [Baptist], 11 (July-September 1968) 283-284.

   "These letters are warm and very human communications from a deeply moved and deeply moving Christian. As such, they incarnate a theology of hope . . ."

53. *A Mind Awake: An Anthology of C. S. Lewis*. Ed.
Clyde S. Kilby (1968). A collection of short quotations
from Lewis, on Christian themes.

1. Haynes, Rence. "A Soothsayer."

   Listed in § VI-A-1; a review of *The Discarded Image* and *A Mind Awake*.

2. Howard, Thomas. "Old Truths and Modern Myths."

   Listed in § VI-A-1; the review includes *A Mind Awake* and White's *The Image of Man in C. S. Lewis*.

3. Noel, Henry. "Skeptic Turned Apostle." *Catholic World* 211 (May 1970): 92.

   The reviewer thinks the book is a delightful selection for already-confirmed Lewis fans but unlikely to appeal to new readers.

4. Sewell, Gordon. "The Wisdom of C. S. Lewis."

   Listed in § VI-A-1; a review of *The Discarded Image* and *A Mind Awake*.

5. Sheehan, Thomas M. "Book Reviews." *America* 122 (7 February 1970): 134-135.

   "All [the quotations] reflect Lewis' strong belief that life is a metaphor in the minds of men but a reality in the Mind of God."

6. West, Richard. "The Critics, and Tolkien, and C. S. Lewis—Reviews."

   Listed in § VI-A-1; a review of seven books on or by Lewis, including *A Mind Awake, Selected Literary Essays*, and *Narrative Poems*.

7. "With Intent to Persuade." *Times Literary Supplement*, 25 July 1968, p. 786.

   The collection is not as good an introduction to Lewis as any Lewis work, but it is a good reminder for those who are acquainted of the wit, principles and prejudices of him.

54. *Selected Literary Essays*. Ed. Walter Hooper (1969). Twenty-two essays.

1. Brown, Terence. "Spoilt Poet." *Irish Press*, 21 March 1970. [PF]

   The volume includes some first-rate Lewis, though sometimes brilliant analogy feigns truth and heartiness dismisses complexities.

2. F., R. "From Sheakespeare to C. S. Lewis." *Kentish Gazette*, 27 February 1970. [PF]

   "A pleasure to read—he was a stylist. . . . it is almost refreshing now to read a critic who unashamedly assumes that the literature he is discussing is about something, and may be defended."

3. Fletcher, Janet. *Library Journal* 94 (1 October 1969): 3450-3451.

   "Readers who wish to follow the development of Lewis' thought may object to the arrangement of selections roughly by the chronology of the subject matter rather than in order of composition. . . ." A "readable" book though often "dogmatism or romanticism tended to narrow his perceptions."

4. "Hard, polemical, black-or-white, them-or-us."

   Listed in § VI-A-1; review of *Selected Literary Essays* and *Narrative Poems*.

5. Lloyd, M. W. "Reviews." *Review of English Studies*, n.s. 22 (May 1971): 239-241.

   "Lewis as a literary critic requires no personal discipleship, no adherence to an exclusive critical method; though it is often necessary to be able to follow an argument." The critic finds the collection "a good example of Lewis's characteristic way of combining a magisterial exposition with the verve of an undergraduate discovering the inner life of a literary form." Lewis's critical writing "is a memorial to an English school, at every level of operation."

6. *New Republic* 162 (7 February 1970): 38. [PF]

> "Lewis's little cultural tourmobile is well worth boarding though it misses some monuments. A man who makes interesting even an inquiry into alliterative metre is worth knowing."

7. Norman, Sylvia. *Aryan Path* 16 (1970). [PF]

> "Lewis leaves no question as he found it; his corkscrew probing spirals downwards till he reaches antipodean daylight in a landscape we never glimpsed before."

8. *Oxford Magazine*, November 1970?. [PF]

> The essays are lucid; Lewis is in his characteristic role of patient guide. The reviewer is uneasy about the implications of the critical approach in *Experiment in Criticism* occasionally applied in these essays.

9. *Press*, 21 February 1970.

> Listed in § VI-A-1; a review of *Selected Literary Essays* and *Narrative Poems*.

10. Raymond, John. "Books for the Week." *Tablet*, 24 January 1970. [PF]

> The critic finds the collection stimulating, an example of Lewis who was "all of a piece throughout." But Lewis can hearten or exasperate depending on the reader's temperament, as his own ability to respond as an Elizabethan would have was both his strong and weak point. He communicated partly through his tone of sheer enjoyment, but this very Elizabethan or medieval identification sometimes seemed arrogant in its gap of sympathy for modern subjectivity.

11. Taylor, Welford Dunaway. *Modern Language Journal* 54 (November 1970): 546-547.

> "Its selections are in Lewis's finest vein. . . . This collection is impressive because it amply shows that Lewis could retain his independence of approach and originality of thesis on a truly catholic scale." "Editorial quirks . . ."

12. West, Richard. "The Critics, and Tolkien, and C. S. Lewis—Reviews."

Listed in § VI-A-1; a review of seven books on or by Lewis, including *A Mind Awake, Selected Literary Essays,* and *Narrative Poems.*

55. *Narrative Poems.* Ed. Walter Hooper (1969). Four poems, one unfinished.

1. [Christopher, Joe R.] *Choice* 9 (April 1972): 215.

"A photographic reproduction of the 1969 English edition. . . . The poems clearly indicate Lewis's tradition which runs back through George Macdonald's fantasies to the fairytales of German romanticism. Of cultural interest, although not of modern vitality."

2. "Hard, polemical, black-or-white, them-or-us."

Listed in § VI-A-1; review of *Selected Literary Essays* and *Narrative Poems.*

3. *Press,* 21 February 1970.

Listed in § VI-A-1; a review of *Selected Literary Essays* and *Narrative Poems.*

4. West, Richard. "The Critics, and Tolkien, and C. S. Lewis—Reviews."

Listed in § VI-A-1; a review of seven books on or by Lewis, including *A Mind Awake, Selected Liberary Essays,* and *Narrative Poems.*

56. *God in the Dock*: *Essays on Theology and Ethics*. Ed.
Walter Hooper (1970). Published in England as
Undeceptions: *Essays on Theology and Ethics* (1971).
Forty-eight essays and seventeen letters.

1. Bremner, James. *Life and Work*, June 1971. [PF]

   The pieces in such a collection are inevitably unequal, but they
   still retain "freshness and relevance." Though many may disagree,
   Lewis's championing of orthodoxy is not to be dismissed lightly.
   "A remarkable book."

2. Burke, T. Patrick. "Books." *Commonweal* 94 (2 April
   1971): 94.

   "The train-ride of reasoning is thoroughly enjoyable." "The book
   is a splendid defense of the old, of the old which has often
   enough become bizarre because it is old. . . . But one would have
   liked to stay on [the train] till another station turned up."

3. Cattanach, W. D. *Scotsman*, 10 April 1971. [PF]

   Many of the essays are over twenty years old but "very few are
   dated." The reviewer thinks Lewis showed good sense in his
   Christian orthodoxy which has recently had a "very bad press."

4. [Christopher, Joe R.] "Religion." *Choice* 8 (September
   1971): 849.

   The reviewer is probably incorrect in saying that this is the last
   collection Hooper is going to make of Lewis's writings: he
   misread Hooper's statement in his "Preface" (p. 7) that his years
   of searching for Lewisian material in periodicals is over.
   Otherwise typical of the brief notices in *Choice*. Christopher
   recommends the book as a *supplement* to other books by Lewis,
   and says the American edition is preferable to the British because
   of its index.

5. Colbert, James G., Jr. "C. S. Lewis on God." *University
   Bookman*, Winter 1972, pp. 39-42.

   Colbert questions editor Hooper's reasons for collecting essays

on subjects better treated by Lewis in books, although partially
agreeing with one reason. He finds three essays especially timely:
"The Dangers of National Repentance," "Delinquents in the
Snow," and "The Humanitarian Theory of Punishment."
Also see Colbert's comment on his review in *CSL* 3
(May 1972): 9.

6. Derrick, Christopher. "Contemplation and Enjoyment."

   Listed in § VI-A-1; a review of *Undeceptions* and White's
   Image of Man in C. S. Lewis.

7. Hardy, Daniel. "C. S. Lewis Versus the 'Liberals.' "
   Birmingham Post, 10 April 1971. [PF]

   The critic thinks the collection shows Lewis's religious concerns
   better than some of his longer books. Despite Lewis's considerable
   gifts as a theologian and philosopher, most theologians since
   his death would say we can't go back to such strong supernaturalism
   and "his way is not ours."

8. Lockerbie, D. Bruce. "God in the Dock: C. S. Lewis."

   Review of *God in the Dock* and Carolyn Keefe's *C. S. Lewis:
   Speaker and Teacher*; listed in § VI-A-1.

9. McShane, Philip. "Sermons of a Layman." *Hibernia*, 1971.
   [PF]

   Though he disagrees with elements of Lewis's theology, McShane
   says "it is refreshing to meet such conviction in these days
   when the fashion is doubt." Instead of the current "problem of
   God" theology, Lewis writes on the "problem of man."

10. Nauer, Barbara. "Good Summer Fiction and God and
    Gospels on Trial." *America* 124 (12 June 1971): 617-618.

    "The reader's mind gets blown." On Walter Hooper: "intelligent
    editorship is a severely unappreciated communicational art."
    "In C. S. Lewis . . . God had a witness and advocate of exceptional
    power."

11. Roberts, Roger L. "Faith Defended." *Church Times*, 7 May 1971. [PF]

    Lewis is at his brilliant best as a "translator" of fundamental orthodox beliefs into terms intelligible for ordinary people. His defense of supernaturalism makes the book "urgently relevant."

12. S[imcox], C[arroll] E. "Book Reviews." *Living Church* 162 (14 February 1971): 14.

    "One of the brightest gems is a marvelous parody of Herodotus. . . ." "I don't see how you can possibly miss a thoroughly good time with it on every page. If you do miss, write me an angry letter."

13. "This Week." *Christian Century* 87 (30 December 1970): 1566.

    "we are struck less by the possibility of learning something new from the late don than by our renewed enjoyment of the way Lewis stated things."

C. Books about Lewis

Note: § VI-A-3 contains some related reviews.

   1. Richard B. Cunningham: *C. S. Lewis: Defender of the Faith* (1961).

1. Lindskoog, Kathryn. "Would You Believe . . . A Bad Book on C. S. Lewis?" *Eternity* 19 (March 1968): 44-45.
The spelling is good.

2. Ostling, Joan K. "Shotgun Approach on C. S. Lewis." *Christianity Today* 12 (19 January 1968): 29.
Over territory mainly covered by previous writers on Lewis.

3. "Religion." *Choice* 5 (June 1968): 512.
"A keen analysis of the diverse kinds of literature that Lewis uses" in his apologetics. "Among the numerous current books about Lewis's faith, Cunningham's is one of the best."

   2. Jocelyn Gibb (ed.): *Light on C. S. Lewis* (1966).

1. "Face Value." *Times Literary Supplement*, 11 November 1965, p. 996.
"This is a dislikeable book, confused in intention and uneven in execution. It has some good things, but it hovers uncertainly

between obituary tribute and attempts at a more penetrating analysis of character."

2. Griffiths, Dom Bede, O. S. B. *Month* 221, n. s. 35 (June 1966): 337-341.

Griffiths contrasts his own memories of Lewis with authors of these essays. He regards integration of reason with spirit and imagination as the most fundamental problem of Lewis's work. He discusses Lewis's "mere" Christianity in contrast to his own Catholicism, and Lewis's cultural and intellectual conversion as Lewis's fundamental value.

3. Lobdell, J. C. "Books in Brief." *National Review* 18 (23 August 1966): 851-852.

The Owen Barfield, Nevill Coghill, John Lawlor and J. A. W. Bennett essays are good; the others, unexceptional. The Hooper bibliography is excellent. Stella Gibbons emphasizes the wrong things or the right things in the wrong way.

4. Robson, W. W. "C. S. Lewis." *Cambridge Quarterly* 1 (Summer 1966): 252-272. Reprinted as "The Romanticism of C. S. Lewis" in *Critical Essays* (London: Routledge and Kegan Paul; New York: Barnes and Noble, 1967), pp. 56-75.

Using *Light on C. S. Lewis* as a reviewer's base, Robson sums up Lewis's critical accomplishments. While praising Lewis as a man, he finds his criticism thin—as a critic, a Chesterton (in paradoxical style) who was misplaced in the modern period, good at exposition but poor at interpretation. The major theses: (1) Lewis has too much concern with the minutiae of morals in his homiletics; he is best at philosophical and abstract thought, not common morals. (2) As Owen Barfield points out, the early novels have streaks of immaturity in them. (3) Lewis is rightly compared to Chesterton, for Lewis was a *conscious* Edwardian. (4) He argued too much in his criticism (often from a philistine viewpoint)—in *Experiment in Criticism*, for example, he produces propaganda by attacking only straw men. (5) Lewis's emphasis on the triviality of literature (when compared to religious truth) often meant he failed to stress what meaning is there. (6) His criticism and literary history are often partially ruined by having no application to life today. (7) His historical point of view (looking at each work from its own age) is invalid—he does not look at the present age this way. (8) Lewis's "boyish romanticism" leads him to juvenile trash often, but also to enjoyment of Spenser (whom he could never convince the Common Reader to like). (9) To sum up, he combined a propensity to argue with a taste for minor romantic poetry.

5. Strange, Arthur. *America* 114 (23 April 1966): 596, 598.

> The essayists do not always see the man as clearly as one might wish, but "his friends have indeed done well by him" and Hooper's bibliography is useful.

3. Carolyn Keefe (ed.): *C. S. Lewis: Speaker and Writer* (1971).

1. Lockerbie, D. Bruce. "God in the Dock: C. S. Lewis."

> Listed in § VI-A-1; review of *God in the Dock* and Keefe's *C. S. Lewis: Speaker and Teacher*.

4. Clyde S. Kilby: *The Christian World of C. S. Lewis* (1964).

1. Carter, A. H. "One About, One By."

> Listed in § VI-A-1; review of *The Discarded Image* and Kilby's *The Christian World of C. S. Lewis*.

2. Cavanaugh, H. "Two By and One About C. S. Lewis."

   Listed in § VI-A-1; review of *Letters to Malcolm, The Discarded Image*, and Kilby's *Christian World of C. S. Lewis*.

3. Lindskoog, Kathryn. "C. S. Lewis: the Man and His Materials." *Eternity* 15 (October 1964): 42-43.

   The volume is "by far the most complete array of information on Lewis to date." The reviewer questions several minor points of fact.

4. Schleuter, Paul. "Scholar and Wit."

   Listed in § VI-A-1; a review of *The Discarded Image* and Kilby's *Christian World of C. S. Lewis*.

5. Vidler, Alec. "Unapologetic Apologist."

   Listed in § VI-A-1; a review of *The Discarded Image* and Kilby's *The Christian World of C. S. Lewis*.

5. Peter Kreeft: *C. S. Lewis: A Critical Essay* (1969).

1. [Christopher, Joe R.] "Language and Literature: English and American." *Choice* 6 (December 1969): 1396.

   "concerned more with Lewis as a thinker than as a writer." Kreeft adds *objectivity* to the usual discussions of *romanticism* and *rationality* in Lewis. "The bibliography is adequate but misses some important secondary sources."

2. West, Richard. "The Critics, and Tolkien, and C. S. Lewis— Reviews."

   Listed in § VI-A-1; a review of seven books on or by Lewis, including Kreeft's *C. S. Lewis: A Critical Essay*.

6. Chad Walsh: *C. S. Lewis: Apostle to the Skeptics* (1948).

1. Bixler, J. S. *Crozer Quarterly* 26 (October 1949): 370.

   Walsh lacks the style and the color of Lewis, and he does not give the sweep of his logic or why, for all Lewis's emphasis on reason, he is "so consistently unsympathetic to the plight of modernist Christianity." "Lewis is not—as yet—a sufficiently important writer to make a detailed analysis of his ideas and their antecedents seem worth while."

2. Paulding, Gouverneur. "British 'Discovery' of Religion." *New York Herald Tribune Book Review*, 24 July 1949, § 7, p. 6.

   Both Lewis and Walsh neglect the importance and contributions of professional clergy, historical theology, and the sacraments. Lewis is a "peculiarly British phenomenon," not understood as such by Walsh. Lewis misses the wilder Christian mystery of love.

3. Shuster, George N. "Of Prose and Verse: Influential Apologist." *New York Times Book Review*, 17 July 1949, § 7, p. 14.

   A "good-natured, rambling and quite personal book." Authoritativeness of Lewis due to his scholarship but its feel due to his "patient and quizzical observation of human nature" which irritated skeptics. The best pages are on the allegorical romances. This is probably a prelude to future studies on the contemporary "Anglican movement" in literature—Dorothy Sayers, T. S. Eliot, Christopher Isherwood and others [perhaps "Isherwood" is a slip for "Fry"].

4. Titus, Joseph H. "Books of the Day." *Churchman* 163 (1 November 1949): 18.

   The analysis helps one understand Lewis, but Walsh "occasionally overlooks some of his subject's more serious faults."

7. William Luther White: *The Image of Man in C. S. Lewis* (1969).

1. [Christopher, Joe R.] "Language and Literature: English and American." *Choice* 7 (April 1970): 234-235.

   The reviewer compares White's book to Boss's dissertation, "The Theology of C. S. Lewis," and Cunningham's *C. S. Lewis: Defender of the Faith* (both listed in § IV-B). "The bibliography is excellent, the index poor. Over all, satisfactory but not exciting."

2. Derrick, Christopher. "Contemplation and Enjoyment."

   Listed in § VI-A-1; a review of *Undeceptions* and White's *Image of Man in C. S. Lewis*.

3. Howard, Thomas. "Old Truths and Modern Myths."

   Listed in § VI-A-1; the review includes *A Mind Awake* and White's *The Image of Man in C. S. Lewis*.

4. Nelson, Elizabeth R. "Philosophy and Religion." *Library Journal* 94 (1 October 1969): 3453-3454.

   The book will appeal to both Lewis fans and students of dogmatic Christianity.

4. Ortmayer, Roger. "Religion Notes." *Saturday Review* 53 (28 February 1970): 74.

   Brief. "Those of us who, because of our atrophied awareness of images, do not find Lewis completely lucid, need the William Luther Whites to stimulate our sensitivities."

6. West, Richard. "The Critics, and Tolkien, and C. S. Lewis—Reviews."

   Listed in § VI-A-1; a review of seven books on or by Lewis—including White's *The Image of Man in C. S. Lewis*.

VII. Indices

A. Index of Masters' Theses

Aymard, Elaine. "C. S. Lewis's Narnian Chronicles: or, On the Other Side of the Wardrobe Door." Unpublished thesis for the Diplome d'Etudes Superieures d'Anglais [master's degree]: Universite de Toulouse, Faculte des Lettres et des Sciences Humaines, Juin 1967. 179 pp.

Listed in § III-G; see also Aymard's "On C. S. Lewis and the *Narnian Chronicles*" in the same section.

Bailey, J. O. "The Scientific Novels of H. G. Wells." Unpublished M. A. thesis: University of North Carolina, 1927.

See the listing of Bailey's doctoral dissertation in VII-B.

Burleson, Lyman E. "An Analysis of Major Christian Doctrines in C. S. Lewis' Space Trilogy." Unpublished M.A. thesis: East Tennessee State University, 1967. 65 pp.

Listed in § III-D.

Cenit, Gloria Alfoja. " 'The Christian Life—A Warfare:' A Curriculum Unit Based on C. S. Lewis' *The Lion, the Witch, and the Wardrobe*." Unpublished M.A. thesis in Christian Education: Wheaton College, 1968. 94 pp.

Listed in § III-G.

Como, James T. "The Rhetoric of Illusion and Theme: Belief in C. S. Lewis' *Perelandra*." Unpublished M.A. thesis: Queens College, the City University of New York, 1970. 100 pp.

Listed in § V-A.

Crowell, Faye Ann. "The Theme of the Harmful Effects of Science in the Works of C. S. Lewis." Unpublished M.A. thesis: Texas A&M University, 1971. 87 pp.
Listed in § IV-E.

Cunningham, Don Rodger. "D. H. Lawrence and C. S. Lewis: A Study in Contrast." Unpublished M.A. thesis: Indiana University, 1972. 80 pp.
Listed in § V-A.

Daniel, Jerry L. "A Rhetorical Analysis of the Apologetic Works of C. S. Lewis." Unpublished M.A. thesis in Speech: University of Wyoming, 1969. 150 pp.
Listed in § IV-C.

Fitzpatrick, John F. "From Fact to Fantasy: A Study of C. S. Lewis' Use of Myth." Unpublished M.A. thesis: City College of the City University of New York, 1972. 95 pp.
Listed in § III-D.

Foulon, Jacqueline. "The Theology of C. S. Lewis' Children's Books." Unpublished M.A. thesis: Fuller Theological Seminary, 1962. 100 pp.
Listed in § III-G.

Grant, Myrna. "A Radio Adaptation of *The Lion, the Witch and the Wardrobe.*" Unpublished M.A. thesis: Wheaton College (Ill.), 1971. 64 pp. + nine separately numbered scripts of approximately a dozen pages each.
Listed in § III-I.

Hannay, Margaret Patterson. "Mythology in the Novels of C. S. Lewis." M.A. thesis: College of St. Rose (Albany, N.Y.), 1970. 101 pp.
Listed in § III-A; see also the related essays, "C. S. Lewis' Theory of Mythology" (§ III-A), "The Mythology of *Out of the Silent*

Planet" (§ III-D), "The Mythology of *Perelandra"* (§ III-D),
"Arthurian Cosmic Myth in *That Hideous Strength"* (§ III-D),
and "Orual: The Search for Justice" (§ III-H).

Hook, Martha Boren. "Christian Meaning in the Novels of
C. S. Lewis." Unpublished M.A. thesis: Southern Methodist
University, 1959. 95 pp.
Listed in § III-A.

Kawano, Roland Mamoru. "The Creation of Myth in the Novels
of C. S. Lewis." Unpublished M.A. thesis: University of
Utah, 1969. 75 pp.
Listed in § III-A.

Keefe, Carolyn. "A Case Study of C. S. Lewis' Ten Radio Talks
on Love." Unpublished M.A. thesis: Temple University,
1968.
Listed in § II; see also Keefe's essays in her *C. S. Lewis:
Speaker and Teacher* in that section.

Kerns, Joan Elaine [Joan K. Ostling]. "Fighting Western
Anomie: The Social and Ethical Philosophy of C. S. Lewis."
Unpublished M.A. thesis: University of Illinois, 1966.
128 pp.
Listed in § IV-F.

Martell, Clare Lorinne. "C. S. Lewis: Teacher as Apologist."
Unpublished M.A. thesis: Boston College, 1949. 91 pp.
Listed in § IV-C.

Oury, Scott. "The Value of Something Other: A Study of
C. S. Lewis's Attention to 'The Object Itself.' " Unpublished
M.A. thesis: Fairleigh Dickinson University (Madison,
N.J.), n.d. 42 pp.
Listed in § I.

Presley, Horton Edward. "Fantasy, Allegory, and Myth in the
Fiction of C. S. Lewis." Unpublished M.A. thesis:
University of Illinois, 1952.
Listed in § III-D.

Ringer, David K. "C. S. Lewis' Use of the Christian World-
View as Structure in the Science Fiction Trilogy."
Unpublished M.A. thesis: McNeese State College (Lake
Charles, La.), 1968. 81 pp.
Listed in § III-D.

Rogers, Margaret Anne. "C. S. Lewis: A Living Library."
Unpublished M.A. thesis: Fairleigh Dickinson University,
1970. 119 pp.
Listed in § I.

Springer, J. Randall. "Beyond Personality: C. S. Lewis' Concept
of God." Unpublished M.A. thesis: Wheaton College,
Ill., 1969. 119 pp.
Listed in § IV-B.

Stillwell, Kathryn A. [Kay (or Kathryn) Lindskoog]. "The
Lion of Judah in Never-Never Land: The Theology
and Philosophy of C. S. Lewis expressed in His Fantasies
for Children." M.A. thesis: Long Beach
Teachers College, 1957. 113 pp.
Listed in § III-G.

Thomas, Mary Burrows. "The Fairy Stories of C. S. Lewis."
Unpublished M.A. thesis: University of Oklahoma,
1964. 64 pp.
Listed in § III-G.

B. Index of Doctoral Dissertations

Adams, Frank Davis. "The Literary Tradition of the Scientific Romance." Ph.D. dissertation: University of New Mexico, 1951.
Listed in § III-D.

Bailey, J. O. "Scientific Fiction in English, 1817-1914: A Study of Trends and Forms." Ph.D. dissertation: University of North Carolina, 1934. *Note*: This is an expansion of the M.A. thesis on H. G. Wells listed in VII-A.
Listed in III-D in its expanded book form, *Pilgrims Through Space and Time.*

Beattie, Sister Mary Josephine, R.S.M. *The Humane Medievalist: A Study of C. S. Lewis' Criticism of Medieval Literature.* Ph.D. dissertation: University of Pittsburgh, 1967.
Abstract: *Dissertation Abstracts* 27 (1966-1967): 3136A.
Listed in § V-B.

Boss, Edgar. "The Theology of C. S. Lewis." Th.D. dissertation: Northern Baptist Theological Seminary (Chicago), 1948.
Listed in § IV-B.

Carnell, Corbin Scott. *The Dialectic of Desire: C. S. Lewis' Interpretation of "Sehnsucht."* Ph.D. dissertation: University of Florida, 1960. Abstract: *Dissertation Abstracts* 20 (1959-1960): 4653.
Listed in § II.

349

Christopher, Joe Randell. *The Romances of Clive Staples Lewis.* Ph.D. dissertation: University of Oklahoma, 1968. Abstract: *Dissertation Abstracts International* 30 (1969): 3937A-3938A.

Listed in § III-A; see also the essays drawn from it (usually in expanded form): "A Study of C. S. Lewis's *Dymer*" (§ III-B), "Considering *The Great Divorce*" (§ III-F), "An Introduction to Narnia" (§ III-G), and "A Brief Study of Implied Disjunctive Syllogisms" (§ IV-C).

Cunningham, Richard B. *The Christian Apologetic of C. S. Lewis.* Th.D. dissertation: Southern Baptist Theological Seminary (Louisville, Kentucky), 1965(?). Abstract: *Dissertation Abstracts* 27 (1966-1967): 242A.

Listed in § IV-B under its published title, *C. S. Lewis: Defender of the Faith.*

Dowie, William John, S. J. *Religious Literature in a Profane Time: Charles Williams, C. S. Lewis, and J. R. R. Tolkien.* Ph.D. dissertation: Brandeis University, 1970. Abstract: *Dissertation Abstracts International* 31 (1970): 2911A.

Listed in § III-D.

Futch, Ken. *The Syntax of C. S. Lewis's Style: A Statistical Look at Some Syntactic Features.* Ph.D. dissertation: University of Southern California, 1969. Abstract: *Dissertation Abstracts International* 30 (1969): 2002A.

Listed in § I.

Haigh, John D. "The Fiction of C. S. Lewis." Ph.D. dissertation: University of Leeds, 1962.

Listed in § III-A.

Hart, Dabney Adams. *C. S. Lewis's Defense of Poesie.* Ph.D. dissertation: University of Wisconsin, 1959. Abstract: *Dissertation Abstracts* 20 (1959-1960): 3293.

Listed in § V-A.

Higgins, James Edward. *Five Authors of Mystical Fancy for Children: A Critical Study*. Ed.D. dissertation: Columbia University, 1965. Abstract: *Dissertation Abstracts* 26 (1965-1966): 4629-4630.

Listed in § III-C under its published title, *Beyond Words: Mystical Fancy in Children's Literature*.

Hoff, Jacobo E., S.J. "The Idea of God and Spirituality of C. S. Lewis." Dissertation: Pontifica Universitas Gregoriana Facultas Theologica, 1969.

Listed in § IV-B; see also Hoff's book, *The Idea of God and Spirituality of C. S. Lewis*, in the same subsection.

Hooey, Sister Mary Amy, R.S.M. *An Applied Linguistic Analysis of the Prose Style of C. S. Lewis*. Ph.D. dissertation: University of Connecticut, 1966. Abstract: *Dissertation Abstracts* 27 (1967): 3441A.

Listed in § I.

Manlove, Colin N. "The Fairy Tale: And Its English Development, 1850-1960." Unpublished dissertation: Pembroke College (Oxford University), 1967. 139 pp. [*Note*: this is identified as a dissertation (with a query beside the word) on the copy in the Wheaton College (Ill.) C. S. Lewis Collection; the ms. does not so identify itself, and the Collection librarian has not yet checked the matter.]

Listed in § III-A.

Moorman, Charles Wickliffe. "Myth and Modern Literature: A Study of the Arthurian Myth in Charles Williams, C. S. Lewis and T. S. Eliot." Ph.D. dissertation: Tulane University, 1953. Abstract: *Tulane University Bulletin* 54 (1953): 35-39.

Listed in § III-D under its published title of *Arthurian Triptych*; the material on Lewis also appears in an article, "Space Ship and Grail," listed in the same subsection.

Norwood, William Durward, Jr. *The Neo-Medieval Novels of C. S. Lewis*. Ph.D. dissertation: University of Texas at Austin, 1965. Abstract: *Dissertation Abstracts* 21 (1965-1966): 2221.

> Listed in § III-A; see also the essay, "Unifying Themes in C. S. Lewis' Trilogy," listed in § III-D which summarizes the material on the Ransom Trilogy; and the essay, "C. S. Lewis' Portrait of Aphrodite," listed in § III-H, which reprints the chapter on *Till We Have Faces*.

Reilly, Robert J. *Romantic Religion in the Work of Owen Barfield, C. S. Lewis, Charles Williams, and J. R. R. Tolkien*. Ph.D. dissertation: Michigan State University, 1960. Abstract: *Dissertation Abstracts* 21 (1960-1961): 3461-3462.

> Listed in § III-A under its published title, *Romantic Religion: A Study of Barfield, Lewis, Williams, and Tolkien*.

Russell, Mariann Barbara. *The Idea of the City of God*. Ph.D. dissertation: Columbia University, 1965. Abstract: *Dissertation Abstracts* 26 (1965): 3350.

> Listed in § III-D.

Samaan, Angele Botrose. "The Novel of Utopianism and Prophecy: With Special Reference to Its Reception." Ph.D. dissertation: University of London, 1963.

> Listed in § III-D; see the article, "C. S. Lewis, the Utopist, and His Critics," in the same subsection.

Schmerl, Rudolf Benjamin. *Reason's Dream: Anti-Totalitarian Themes and Techniques of Fantasy*. Ph.D. dissertation: University of Michigan, 1960. Abstract: *Dissertation Abstracts* 21 (1960-1961): 2298.

> Listed in § III-D.

Trowbridge, Clinton W. *The Twentieth Century British Supernatural Novel*. Ph.D. dissertation: University of Florida, 1958. Abstract: *Dissertation Abstracts* 18 (1958): 1800.

Listed in § III-A.

Urang, Gunnar. "Shadows of Heaven: The Uses of Fantasy in the Fiction of C. S. Lewis, Charles Williams, and J. R. R. Tolkien." Ph.D. dissertation: University of Chicago, 1969.

Listed in § III-A under its published title, *Shadows of Heaven: Religion and Fantasy in the Writings of C. S. Lewis, Charles Williams, and J. R. R. Tolkien.*

White, William Luther. *The Image of Man in C. S. Lewis*. Ph.D. dissertation: Northwestern University and Garrett Theological Seminary, 1968. Abstract: *Dissertation Abstracts* 29 (1968-1969): 2354A.

Listed in § I as published under the same title.

Wright, Marjorie Evelyn. *The Cosmic Kingdom of Myth: A Study in the Myth-Philosophy of Charles Williams, C. S. Lewis, and J. R. R. Tolkien*. Ph.D. dissertation: University of Illinois, 1960. Abstract: *Dissertation Abstracts* 21 (1960-1961): 3464-3465.

Listed in § III-A; see the chapter reprinted, "The Vision of Cosmic Order in the Oxford Mythmakers," listed in the same subsection.

C. Index of Authors and Editors

Note: anonymous items are not listed.

Augustine, Dom James. VI-B-36-1.
Aymard, Elaine. III-G-3. III-G-4.

B., A. VI-B-15-1.
B., H. S. VI-B-30-1.
B., K. VI-B-14-1.
Babbage, Stuart Barton. II-2. IV-F-1.
Bacon, Leonard. VI-B-9-2. VI-B-14-2. VI-B-17-1.
Badawi, M. M. VI-B-38-1.
Bailey, George. II-3. II-4.
Bailey, J. O. III-D-4.
Balsdon, Dacre. II-5.
Banjo, Ayo. VI-B-38-2.
Barfield, Owen. See also G. A. L. Burgeon. II-6. II-7. II-8. II-9.
    III-I-2. IV-A-3.
Barnhouse, Donald Grey. I-3.
Barrington-Ward, Simon. I-4. IV-C-3.
Barrows, Herbert. VI-A-1-1.
Bateson, F. V-C-1.
Bateson, F. W. II-10. VI-B-7-1. VI-B-42-1.
Bayley, P. C. V-B-3.
Bean, William B. VI-B-38-3.
Beaton, Cecil W. H. II-11.
Beattie, Sister Mary Josephine. V-B-4.
Bechtel, Louise S. VI-B-25-1. VI-B-27-1.
Bechtel, Paul M. II-12.
Bell, Alan. VI-B-41-2.
Bennett, J. A. W. II-13. II-14. V-B-5.
Bennett, Joan. V-C-2. VI-B-49-2.
Beresford, J. D. VI-B-17-2.
Berger, Harry, Jr. V-B-6.
Bergier, Jacques. I-5.
Bergonzi, Bernard. V-D-2. VI-B-41-3.

Knights, L. C. VI-B-6-4. VI-B-10-4.
Knowlton, Edgar C. VI-B-4-11.
Kostič, Veselin. V-C-6.
Kranz, Gisbert. I-31. I-32. I-33. II-63. II-64. II-65. II-66. III-A-32. III-H-6. IV-A-20. IV-F-8.
Kreeft, Peter. I-34. III-G-42.
Kruener, Harry H. II-67.
Kuhl, Rand. II-68.
Kuhn, Daniel K. IV-A-21.
Kuhn, Helmut. I-35.

L., A. VI-B-8-5.
L., J. B. [J. B. Leishman?] VI-B-30-13.
Lambert, Byron C. IV-A-22.
Landers, Joyce. III-E-8. IV-A-23.
Laski, Marghanita. VI-B-44-23.
Lawlor, John. I-36. II-69. V-B-25. V-B-26.
Lawrence, William M. VI-B-12-1.
Lawson, Craig. III-I-18.
Lazare, Christopher. VI-B-2-2.
Leavis, Q. D. IV-F-9.
Lee, Ernest George. IV-C-30.
Le Fort, Thomas. VI-B-39-9.
Leishman, J. B. See J. B. L. for a possible review. VI-B-6-5.
Leon, Philip. VI-B-15-4.
Levey, Michael. III-G-9.
Lewis, Arthur O., Jr. III-D-50.
Lewis, Elaine Lambert. VI-B-5-5.
Lewis, Naomi. VI-B-29-3.
Lewis, W. H. II-70. II-71.
Ley, Willy. VI-A-3-1.
Linden, William. III-G-44.

McSorley, Joseph. VI-B-17-9.
Maddocks, Melvin. VI-B-35-12.
Madgett, A. Patrick. VI-B-21-5.
Malania, Leo. IV-A-26.
Manlove, Colin. III-A-39.
Manzalaoui, Mahmoud. V-B-29.
Marriott, Charles. VI-B-14-13.
Marron, M. A. VI-B-8-6.
Marsh, David. III-I-24.
Martell, Clare Lorinne. I-39. IV-C-32.
Martindale, C. C. VI-B-36-5.
Mascall, E. L. VI-B-5-7.
Masterman, Margaret. II-76.
Matthews, T. S. III-H-7. VI-B-33-11.
Maud, Ralph. VI-B-31-4.
Maxwell, J. C. VI-B-30-16.
Meath, Gerard. VI-B-35-13.
Merchant, Father Robert. IV-A-27.
Merril, Judith. VI-B-47-6.
Miller, P. Schuyler. VI-A-1-13.
Milne, Marjorie. III-B-5.
Miltner, Charles C. VI-B-26-1.
Milward, Peter. V-B-30.
Molnar, Thomas. IV-F-14.
Mondrone, Domenico. III-E-10.
Montgomery, J. W. III-G-47.
Moore, Francis John. VI-B-8-7.
Moore, Harry T. VI-B-44-26.
Moore, John M. VI-B-8-8.
Moorman, Charles. III-A-40. III-D-53. III-D-54. III-G-48.
    V-B-31. V-B-32.
Morgan, Ann V. VI-B-24-2.
Morgan, Kathleen E. V-F-5.
Morley, Christopher. VI-B-5-9.

Viswanatham, K. V-A-39.
von Hendy, Andrew. V-B-46.
von Lindheim, Begislav. VI-B-38-31.
von Puttkamer, Annemarie. III-A-50.

W., C. L. Attributed to Charles Williams. VI-B-4-15.
Wain, John. I-55. II-94. VI-A-3-3. VI-B-30-21. VI-B-38-32.
    VI-B-41-17. VI-B-49-9.
Waldock, A. J. A. V-D-39.
Walker, Jan C. V-B-47.
Wallace, Robert. III-G-65.
Wallis, Ethel. III-D-82.
Walsh, Chad. I-56. I-57. II-95. II-96. III-A-51. III-D-83.
    III-D-84. III-I-25. IV-C-48. VI-B-15-5. VI-B-21-19.
    VI-B-23-3. VI-B-24-7. VI-B-25-7. VI-B-27-3. VI-B-28-4.
    VI-B-29-4. VI-B-32-4. VI-B-33-15. VI-B-34-3. VI-B-35-20.
    VI-B-35-21. VI-B-36-8. VI-B-39-11. VI-B-43-8. VI-B-44-34.
Warburton, Robert W. V-A-41.
Warren, C. H. VI-B-2-5.
Warren, Eugene. III-D-85. III-D-86. III-I-26.
Watkin, E. I. VI-B-33-16.
Watson, George. V-A-42.
Watt, Ian. V-A-43.
Watts, Alan W. IV-C-50.
Weatherby, H. L. IV-D-10.
Weathers, Winston. I-58.
Webb, M. J. IV-C-49.
Weeks, Edward. VI-B-9-14.
West, Richard C. I-43. II-97. II-98. VI-A-1-22.
West, Robert H. V-D-40. V-D-41.
White, John P. VI-B-38-33.
White, T. H. VI-B-35-22.
White, William Luther. I-59.
Whiting, George Wesley. V-D-42.

D. Index of References to Works by Lewis in the Annotations of this Checklist

Note: the danger of the following list of references to Lewis's essays, poems, and books in the annotations of this checklist is that a number of the major surveys simply comment upon too many of Lewis's fifty-some books for each mentioned work to have been listed, and thus they do not appear in this indexing. Books and dissertations particularly, such surveys may be found in Sections I, II, III-A, IV-B, and V-A.

The Abolition of Man. Reviews in VI-B-15. I-7. II-41. III-A-43. III-D-84. IV-A-10. IV-A-18. IV-A-34. IV-E-2. IV-F-4. IV-F-5. IV-F-6. IV-F-8. IV-F-21. V-A-7.

"After Ten Years" (in *Of Other Worlds*). III-A-19. VI-B-47-4.

The Allegory of Love. Reviews in VI-B-4. I-22. I-56. II-15. II-38. II-69. II-78. II-85. IV-A-20. V-B-1. V-B-3. V-B-4. V-B-5. V-B-6. V-B-8. V-B-10. V-B-11. V-B-12. V-B-14. V-B-15. V-B-16. V-B-17. V-B-20. V-B-21. V-B-22. V-B-23. V-B-24. V-B-25. V-B-26. V-B-28. V-B-32. V-B-34. V-B-35. V-B-36. V-B-37. V-B-38. V-B-40. V-B-41. V-B-42. V-B-43. V-B-46. V-B-51. VI-B-30-14. VI-B-37-3. VI-B-44-4. VI-B-45-8. VI-B-50-4.

"The Anthropological Approach" (in *Selected Literary Essays*). V-B-27. V-B-44.

Arthurian Torso. Reviews in VI-B-22. I-18. I-19. I-54. III-G-16. V-A-11. V-F-1. V-F-3. V-F-5. V-F-6. V-F-7.

"Basic Fears" (uncollected letters). IV-A-14.

Beyond Personality. Reviews in VI-B-16. See also the reviews of *Mere Christianity*, VI-B-26. II-58. IV-C-13. IV-C-21. VI-A-1-14. VI-B-39-5.

"Bluspels and Flalansferes: A Semantic Nightmare" (in *Rehabilitations and Other Essays* and in *Selected Literary Essays*). I-59. VI-B-6-5.

"Boxen" (unpublished juvenilia). III-A-27.

Broadcast Talks. Alternate title: *The Case for Christianity*. Reviews in VI-B-11. See also the reviews of *Mere Christianity*, VI-B-26. II-58. IV-C-8. IV-C-9. IV-C-23. VI-A-1-14.

"Capital Punishment" (in *God in the Dock*). IV-F-3.

The Case for Christianity. Alternate title: *Broadcast Talks*. Reviews in VI-B-11. See also the reviews of *Mere Christianity*, VI-B-26. III-I-21. IV-C-24. IV-C-35. IV-C-44. VI-A-1-11. VI-A-1-24.

Christian Behaviour. Reviews in VI-B-13. See also the reviews of *Mere Christianity*, VI-B-26. II-58. III-D-30. IV-C-35. VI-A-1-5. VI-A-1-11. VI-A-1-14. VI-A-1-17. VI-A-1-24. VI-B-18-3.

Christian Reflections. Reviews in VI-B-51. III-E-5. IV-A-15.

"A Christian Reply to Professor Price" (in *God in the Dock* under the title "Religion without Dogma?"). IV-C-38.

"Christianity and Culture" (in *Christian Reflections*). IV-D-8. V-A-19.

"Christianity and Literature" (in *Rehabilitations and Other Essays* and in *Christian Reflections*). V-A-19. VI-B-6-1.

[The Chronicles of Narnia.] See also the individual titles. I-53. II-21. II-35. II-36. II-43. II-60. III-A-10. III-A-13. III-A-15. III-A-17. III-A-26. III-A-32. III-A-44. III-A-48. III-A-54. III-D-62. IV-B-6. V-B-4. V-A-15. V-B-17. V-B-25. VI-B-44-5.

III-A-43. III-A-44. III-A-48. III-A-50. III-A-52. III-A-54.
III-I-21. IV-E-2. IV-F-6. V-B-25. V-D-40. VI-A-1-13.
VI-B-45-4.

[Reaction to Manzalaoui's "Lydgate and English Prosody"
(uncollected).] V-B-29.

Reflections on the Psalms. Reviews in VI-B-36. II-34. III-A-43.
III-A-52. IV-A-22. IV-A-23. VI-B-39-5.

Rehabilitations and Other Essays. Reviews in VI-B-6. IV-F-19.
VI-A-1-8.

"Rejoinder to Dr. Pittenger" (in *God in the Dock*). IV-C-37.
IV-C-46.

"Religion and Rocketry" (in *"The World's Last Night" and
Other Essays*). Alternate titles: "Will We Lose God in
Outer Space?" and "Shall We Lose God in Outer Space?"
VI-B-39-8.

"Religion without Dogma?" (in *God in the Dock*). Alternate
title: "A Christian Reply to Professor Price." IV-C-39.

"Reply" (in *God in the Dock*, appended to "Religion without
Dogma?"). IV-C-39.

"A Reply to Professor Haldane" (in *Of Other Worlds*).
III-D-30. IV-E-2. VI-B-47-7.

The Screwtape Letters. Criticism in III-E; reviews in VI-B-9. I-13.
I-56. II-23. II-29. II-36. II-43. III-A-3. III-A-5. III-A-20.
III-I-1. III-I-5. III-I-6. III-I-8. III-I-11. III-I-13. III-I-15.
III-I-17. III-I-18. III-I-20. III-I-21. III-I-22. IV-A-9. IV-C-9.
IV-C-35. IV-C-50. V-D-40. VI-B-5-2. VI-B-5-4. VI-B-13-10.
VI-B-17-6. VI-B-18-9. VI-B-18-14. VI-B-37-3. VI-B-49-10.

"Screwtape Proposes a Toast." Criticism in III-E; reviews in
VI-B-9, VI-B-39, and VI-B-46. I-1. IV-F-8.

"Screwtape Proposes a Toast" and Other Pieces. Reviews
(none located) in VI-B-46.

Joe Randell Christopher received his Ph.D. in English from the University of Oklahoma in 1969. He is presently Associate Professor of English at Tarleton State University in Stephenville, Texas.

Joan Kerns Ostling received her M.A. in English from the University of Maryland and is now a candidate for the Ph.D. in English at New York University.

THE SERIF SERIES: BIBLIOGRAPHIES AND CHECKLISTS

GENERAL EDITOR: William White, Wayne State University

---

1 *Wilfred Owen (1893-1918): A Bibliography* by William White, with a prefacing note by Harold Owen
   SBN: 87338-017-7/ 41pp

2 *Raymond Chandler: A Checklist* by Matthew J. Bruccoli
   SBN: 87338-015-0/ ix, 35pp

3 *Emily Dickinson, A Bibliography: 1850-1966* by Sheila T. Clendenning
   SBN: 87338-016-9/ xxx, 145pp

4 *John Updike: A Bibliography* by C. Clarke Taylor
   SBN: 87338-018-5/ vii, 82pp

5 *Walt Whitman: A Supplementary Bibliography (1961-1967)* by James T. F. Tanner
   SBN: 87338-019-3/ vi, 59pp

6 *Erle Stanley Gardner: A Checklist* by E. H. Mundell
   SBN: 87338-034-7/ ix, 91pp

7 *Bernard Malamud: An Annotated Checklist* by Rita Nathalie Kosofsky
   SBN: 87338-037-1/ xii, 63pp

8 *Samuel Beckett: A Checklist* by J. T. F. Tanner and J. Don Vann
   SBN: 87338-051-1/ vi, 85pp

9 *Robert G. Ingersoll: A Checklist* by Gordon Stein
   SBN. 87338-047-9/ xxx, 128pp

10 *Jean-Paul Sartre in English: A Bibliographical Guide* by Allen J. Belkind
    SBN: 87338-049-5/ xx, 234pp

11 *Tolkien Criticism: An Annotated Checklist* by Richard C. West
    SBN: 87338-052-5/ xvi, 73pp

12 *Thomas Wolfe: A Checklist* by Elmer D. Johnson
    SBN: 87338-050-9/ xiv, 278pp

13 *A List of the Original Appearances of Dashiell Hammett's Magazine Work* by E. H. Mundell
    SBN: 87338-033-9/ viii, 52pp